SÁTIRE
from AESOP to BUCHWALD

SATIRE

from AESOP to BUCHWALD

Edited by

FREDERICK KILEY

and

J. M. SHUTTLEWORTH

Macmillan Publishing Company
New York

Collier Macmillan Publishers
London

Macmillan Publishing Company
866 Third Avenue
New York, N.Y. 10022
Seventeenth Printing—1990
Library of Congress Catalog Card No. 70-134892
ISBN: 0-02-363590-8

Caricature facing title page by James Gillray (1757-1815)

ACKNOWLEDGMENTS

Esther Root Adams. For "To a Rich Man" and "Pilgrim Dads Land on Mass. Coast Town." From *Nods and Becks* by Franklin P. Adams. Reprinted by permission.

The Bodley Head Ltd. For selection from *Penguin Island* by Anatole France. Reprinted by permission of The Bodley Head Ltd.

Art Buchwald. For "A Late, Late Briefing" by Art Buchwald. Copyright © 1957 by The New York Herald-Tribune, Inc. Reprinted by permission of the author.

———. For "A Test for GOP Speechwriters" by Art Buchwald. Copyright © 1968 by Art Buchwald. Reprinted by permission of the author.

Jonathan Cape Ltd. For "The Bear," "Forgive O Lord," and "Departmental" by Robert Frost. From *The Poetry of Robert Frost* edited by Edward Connery Lathem. Reprinted by permission of Jonathan Cape Ltd., on behalf of the Estate of Robert Frost.

———. For "Naming of Parts" by Henry Reed. From *A Map of Verona and Other Poems* by Henry Reed. Reprinted by permission of Jonathan Cape Ltd.

———. For selections from *Babbitt* by Sinclair Lewis. Reprinted by permission of Jonathan Cape Ltd.

The Clarendon Press. For "Epigrams" by John Donne, from *Donne's Poetical Works*, Vol. I, Herbert J. C. Grierson, ed. Reprinted by permission of the Clarendon Press, Oxford.

———. For selection from *Hudibras* by Samuel Butler, edited by John Wilders, Reprinted by permission of the Clarendon Press, Oxford.

Datamation. For "Postal System Input Buffer Device" by J. Robertson and G. Osborne. Copyright © 1960 by F. D. Thompson Publications, Inc. Reprinted by permission of the publisher.

Dodd, Mead & Company. For selection from *Penquin Island* by Anatole France. Copyright 1909 by Dodd, Mead & Company. Copyright renewed by A. W. Evans, 1937. Reprinted by permission of Dodd, Mead & Company, Inc.

Doubleday & Co., Inc. For "The Landing of the Pilgrim Fathers" by Franklin P. Adams. Copyright 1928 by Doubleday Doran, from *Column Book of F.P.A.* by Franklin P. Adams. Reprinted by permission of Doubleday & Co., Inc.

———. For "Men Are Not Descended Off of Monkeys" from *The Old Soak's History of the World* by Don Marquis. From "Men Are Not Descended Off of Monkeys," copyright 1923 by New York Tribune, Inc., from *The Old Soak's History of the World* by Don Marquis. Reprinted by permission of Doubleday and Company, Inc.

———. For "The Valiant Woman" by J. F. Powers, copyright 1947 by J. F. Powers, from *The Prince of Darkness and Other Stories* by J. F. Powers. Reprinted by permission of Doubleday & Co., Inc.

Faber and Faber Ltd. For "The Love Song of J. Alfred Prufrock" and "The Hippopotamus" by T. S. Eliot. From *Collected Poems 1909-1962* by T. S. Eliot. Reprinted by permission of Faber and Faber Ltd.

———. For "The Unknown Citizen" by W. H. Auden. From *Collected Shorter Poems 1927-1957* by W. H. Auden. Reprinted by permission of Faber and Faber Ltd.

Jules Feiffer. For cartoon from *The Village Voice Reader*. Copyright © 1960 by Jules Feiffer. Reprinted by permission of Jules Feiffer.

Thomas Hornsby Ferril. "Freud on Football" by Thomas Hornsby Ferril. Copyright © 1957 by Thomas Hornsby Ferril. Reprinted by permission of the author.

Granada Publishing Ltd. For "i sing of Olaf," "the Cambridge Ladies," and "my sweet old etcetera" by E. E. Cummings. From *Complete Poems 1936-1962* by E. E. Cummings. Reprinted by permission of the publisher, Granada Publishing Ltd.

Hamish Hamilton Ltd. For "The Kings" from *Poems* by A. D. Hope. Copyright © by A. D. Hope. Reprinted by permission of Hamish Hamilton Ltd.

Harcourt Brace Jovanovich, Inc. For "i sing of Olaf" by E. E. Cummings. Copyright, 1931, 1959 by E. E. Cummings. Reprinted from his volume, *Poems 1923-1954* by permission of Harcourt Brace Jovanovich, Inc.

ACKNOWLEDGMENTS

———. For "the Cambridge ladies" by E. E. Cummings. Copyright, 1923, 1951, by E. E. Cummings. Reprinted from his volume, *Poems 1923–1954* by permission of Harcourt Brace Jovanovich, Inc.

———. For "my sweet old etcetera" by E. E. Cummings. Copyright, 1926, by Horace Liveright; renewed, 1954, by E. E. Cummings. Reprinted from *Poems 1923–1954* by E. E. Cummings by permission of Harcourt Brace Jovanovich, Inc.

———. For selection from *Babbitt* by Sinclair Lewis, copyright, 1922, by Harcourt Brace Jovanovich, Inc., renewed, 1950, by Sinclair Lewis. Reprinted by permission of the publisher.

———. For "The Love Song of J. Alfred Prufrock" and "The Hippopotamus" by T. S. Eliot. From *Collected Poems 1909–1962* by T. S. Eliot, copyright, 1936, by Harcourt Brace Jovanovich, Inc.; copyright © 1963, 1964, by T. S. Eliot. Reprinted by permission of the publisher.

———. For "Naming of Parts" by Henry Reed. From *A Map of Verona and Other Poems,* copyright, 1947, by Henry Reed. Reprinted by permission of Harcourt Brace Jovanovich, Inc.

Harper & Row, Publishers, Inc. For "The War Prayer" from *Europe and Elsewhere* by Samuel L. Clemens. Copyright, 1923, 1951, by The Mark Twain Company. Reprinted by permission of Harper & Row, Publishers, Inc.

———. For "Die Meister-Genossenschaft" from *The Benchley Roundup* by Nathaniel Benchley, ed. Copyright, 1922, by Harper & Row, Publishers, Inc. Reprinted by permission of Harper & Row, Publishers, Inc.

Harvard Lampoon, Inc. For "Prologue—Concerning Boggies" from *Bored of the Rings* by Henry N. Beard and Douglas C. Kenney. "Prologue" copyright © 1969 by the *Harvard Lampoon*. Reprinted by permission of the *Harvard Lampoon.*

Harvard University Press. For "Abraham to Kill Him" and "God Is Indeed a Jealous God" by Emily Dickinson. Reprinted by permission of the publishers and the Trustees of Amherst College from Thomas H. Johnson, Editor, *The Poems of Emily Dickinson,* Cambridge, Mass.: The Belknap Press of Harvard University Press, Copyright, 1951, 1955, by The President and Fellows of Harvard College.

A. M. Heath & Company Ltd. For "The Valiant Woman" from *The Prince of Darkness and Other Stories* by J. F. Powers. Reprinted by permission of the publisher.

Holt, Rinehart and Winston, Inc. For selections from *Generation of Vipers* by Philip Wylie. Copyright 1942, © 1955, 1970 by Philip Wylie. Reprinted by permission of Holt, Rinehart and Winston, Inc.

———. For "The Bear," and "Forgive O Lord" by Robert Frost. From *The Poetry of Robert Frost,* edited by Edward Connery Lathem. Copyright 1928, © 1969 by Holt, Rinehart and Winston, Inc. Copyright © 1956, 1962 by Robert Frost. Reprinted by permission of Holt, Rinehart and Winston, Inc.

———. For "Departmental" by Robert Frost. From *The Poetry of Robert Frost,* edited by Edward Connery Lathem. Copyright 1936 by Robert Frost. Copyright © 1964 by Lesley Frost Ballantine. Copyright © 1969 by Holt, Rinehart and Winston, Inc. Reprinted by permission of Holt, Rinehart and Winston, Inc.

Arthur Hoppe. For "Jubilation at A-CBM" by Arthur Hoppe. Copyright © 1969 by the *San Francisco Chronicle.* Reprinted by permission of the author.

———. For "Man's Black Magic" by Arthur Hoppe. Copyright © 1969 by the *San Francisco Chronicle.* Reprinted by permission of the author.

Indiana University Press. For "Dirge" from *New and Selected Poems* by Kenneth Fearing. Copyright, 1956, by Indiana University Press. Reprinted by permission of the publisher.

Alfred A. Knopf, Inc. For "Do Not Weep, Maiden, For War Is Kind," "A Newspaper Is a Collection of Half-Injustices," "A Man Said to the Universe," "I Saw a Man Pursuing the Horizon," "God Fashioned the Ship of the World," "If There Is a Witness," and "A God Is Wrath" from *The Collected Poems of Stephen Crane,* by Stephen Crane.

———. For "The Hills of Zion" by H. L. Mencken. Copyright 1926 by Alfred A. Knopf, Inc., and renewed 1954 by H. L. Mencken. Reprinted from *A Mencken Chrestomathy* by permission of the publisher.

Robert Lantz–Candida Donadio Literary Agency, Inc. For "Early Morning of a Motion-Picture Executive" from *YMA, AVA; YMA, ABBA; YMA, OONA; YMA, IDA; YMA, AGA and Others* by T. Meehan. Copyright © 1959–1967, by Thomas Meehan. This material originally appeared in *The New Yorker.* Reprinted by permission of Robert Lantz–Candida Donadio Literary Agency, Inc.

Little, Brown and Company. For "After Great Pain, a Formal Feeling Comes" by Emily Dickinson. Copyright 1929, © 1957 by Mary L. Hampson. From *The Complete Poems of Emily Dickinson,* edited by Thomas H. Johnson. Reprinted by permission of Little, Brown and Co.

———. For "Apparently With No Surprise" and "Much Madness Is Divinest Sense" by Emily Dickinson. From *The Complete Poems of Emily Dickinson,* edited by Thomas H. John-

son, by permission of Little, Brown and Co.
Macmillan and Co. Ltd. For "Ah, Are You Digging on My Grave?" "New Year's Eve," "Channel Firing," and "In Church" from *Collected Poems* by Thomas Hardy, by permission of the Hardy Estate; Macmillan & Co. Ltd., London, and The Macmillan Company of Canada Ltd.

The Macmillan Company. For "Ah, Are You Digging on My Grave?" "New Year's Eve," "Channel Firing," and "In Church" from *Collected Poems* by Thomas Hardy. Copyright 1914, 1925, by The Macmillan Company. Reprinted by permission of the publisher.

The Macmillan Company of Canada Limited. For "Ah, Are You Digging on My Grave?" "New Year's Eve," "Channel Firing," and "In Church" from *Collected Poems* by Thomas Hardy, by permission of the Hardy Estate; Macmillan & Co. Ltd., London, and The Macmillan Company of Canada Limited.

John Murray Ltd. For "In Westminster Abbey" by John Betjeman. From *Collected Poems* by John Betjeman. Reprinted by permission of John Murray Ltd.

The National Observer. For "If the Spirit of Rebellion Runs Its Course" by Edwin A. Roberts, Jr. Copyright © 1968 by *The National Observer*. Reprinted by permission of *The National Observer*.

The New Yorker. For "The Cliché Expert Testifies on the Atom" by Frank Sullivan. Reprinted by permission; Copr. © 1945 The New Yorker Magazine, Inc.

——. For "Inflexible Logic" by Russell Maloney. Reprinted by permission; Copr. © 1940, 1968 The New Yorker Magazine, Inc.

Random House, Inc. For Introduction to *Feiffer's Album*. Copyright © 1963 by the Curtis Publishing Company. Reprinted from *Feiffer's Album*, by Jules Feiffer, by permission of Random House, Inc. and the author.

——. For "Portrait of a Minister" from *The Triumph of Infidelity* by Timothy Dwight, published in Carlisle: *American Satire in Prose and Verse*.

——. For "The Sale of the Hessians" by Benjamin Franklin, published in Carlisle: *American Satire in Prose and Verse*.

——. For selection from *Home as Found* by

James Fenimore Cooper, published in Carlisle: *American Satire in Prose and Verse*.

——. For "The Unknown Citizen" by W. H. Auden. Copyright 1940 and renewed 1968 by W. H. Auden. Reprinted from *Collected Shorter Poems 1927–1957*, by W. H. Auden, by permission of Random House, Inc.

Satire Newsletter. For "After Great Drink" by Nils Peterson. Copyright © 1968 by *Satire Newsletter*. Reprinted by permission of the publisher.

——. For "A Modest Proposal . . ." by John M. Stuart. Copyright © 1968, by *Satire Newsletter*. Reprinted by permission of the publisher.

Simon & Schuster, Inc. For "Early Morning of a Motion-Picture Executive" from *YMA, AVA; YMA, ABBA; YMA, OONA; YMA, IDA; YMA, AGA and Others* by T. Meehan. Copyright © 1959–1967, by Thomas Meehan. This material originally appeared in *The New Yorker*. Reprinted by permission of Simon & Schuster, Inc.

——. For "The Pardoner's Prologue and Tale" by Geoffrey Chaucer, from Chaucer: *Canterbury Tales*, Robert Lumiansky, translator. Copyright © 1948 by Simon and Schuster, Inc. Reprinted by permission of the publisher.

——. For quotations from *Mr. Clemens and Mr. Twain* by Justin Kaplan. Copyright © 1966 by Simon & Schuster, Inc. Reprinted by permission of the publisher.

The Viking Press, Inc. For "The Kings" by A. D. Hope. From *Collected Poems 1930–1965* by A. D. Hope. Copyright © 1960 by A. D. Hope. Reprinted by permission of The Viking Press, Inc.

——. For "Unfortunate Coincidence," "Résumé," and "Indian Summer" by Dorothy Parker. From *The Portable Dorothy Parker*. Copyright 1926, renewed 1954 by Dorothy Parker. Reprinted by permission of The Viking Press, Inc.

Ira Wallach. For "The Keeper of the Gelded Unicorn" by Ira Wallach. From *Hopalong Freud and Other Modern Literary Characters*. Copyright © 1951 by Ira Wallach. Reprinted by permission.

Ann Wolfe. "For "The Grey Squirrel" from *Kensington Gardens* by Humbert Wolfe, published by Ernest Benn Ltd. Reprinted by permission of Miss Ann Wolfe.

CONTENTS

vii

CONTENTS

CONTENTS

CONTENTS

CONTENTS

SÁTIRE
from ÁESOP to BUCHWÁLD

INTRODUCTION

Satire is one of the oldest forms of literature and certainly one of the most durable. Until we reach perfection in some faraway Nirvana, it will as certainly continue to endure. Despite the cries of those who feel its sting, satire is a constructive art. It seeks not merely to destroy but to rebuild. It is critical of human institutions, human vices and follies, and often of individual humans themselves; many times it is written in anger and frustration, but its aim is to inspire reform. Thus satire, though it may not seem so on the surface, is actually conservative. It values what man has achieved through centuries of bloodshed, disaster, and discouragement. It cherishes a sound society, good traditions, and wise, viable institutions. It venerates moderation. It values the general welfare and the public good. It is the enemy of folly, corruption, idiosyncrasy, ignorance, and probably most often of pride and hypocrisy, because these failures of the human spirit threaten to destroy the few things of value man has, most painfully, nourished through the ages.

Thus it is that an Art Buchwald column can attack the pomposities of bureaucracy and an Al Capp comic strip can attack the often irresponsible protest groups which are also attacking the pomposities of bureaucracy, yet both writers can be writing traditional satire. Both are attacking extremes which threaten the general welfare of society. Thus it is also that a Japanese film like *Yojimbo* and an American film like *Cat Ballou* can attack the excesses of violence and the sentimental clichés of the American Western, one from the outside and at a distance, the other from the inside and close-up.

Satire is not a gentle art. It must often use shock and exaggeration to make its point—shock to snap us awake and exaggeration to dramatize. Satire must break through the crust of familiarity which obscures our judgment of matters we are too closely involved in to judge objectively. Ridicule is the chief weapon of satire, but not the chief aim. Having ridiculed is in itself no real achievement unless the ridicule inspires at least a fresh sense of awareness among the audience. Ideally, satire should lead to reform. Ironically, it does so rarely. The world being what it is, reform comes most slowly.

THE SATIRIST'S NATURE

The typical satirist is a blend of idealist and realist. He is an idealist in that he wants to improve the world. He is keenly conscious of the great discrepancy between what the world could be and what it actually is. He is a realist in that he recognizes he must go beyond the customary avenues of appeal in order to influence. Thus he turns to art, to satire.

The satirist must have a tough skin. He is not likely to be popular, except among the few who recognize and value what he is doing. The life of the satirist is almost certain to be controversial and often risky. Many people, especially those most likely to be targets of satire, do not respond well to ridicule. There simply are not any "beloved" satirists. Despite the absurd romanticizing we have given his existence, even Samuel Clemens lived a tortured, uncertain, misunderstood life. His *Huckleberry Finn*, like Jonathan Swift's *Gulliver's Travels*, is now ironically a children's classic. Yet both books are satires attacking man's hypocrisy, brutality, pride, and inhumanity. So it is often the lot of the satirist to be misunderstood. To many readers, despite his true intent, the satirist seems to be posing as someone who claims to know what is right because (the reasoning goes) he is attacking what is wrong. Thus the satirist is often a man slightly suspect and seldom fully trusted.

THE AUDIENCE

The audience to which the satirist addresses himself reveals something of the truly conservative nature of satire. It is an audience of the reasonably intelligent, educated, and rational. There is no point in appealing to extremes, to fools and knaves. Satire is wasted on fools, who are too ignorant or self-engrossed to recognize the ridicule. It is also lost on knaves, who, though they well may recognize the ridicule, are too arrogant or deceitful to do anything but ignore it.

THE SATIRIST'S DEVICES

Satire as a literary art employs such technical devices as parody, irony, mock-epic, travesty, burlesque, lampoon, caricature, epigram, fable,

2

and, in special ways, the heroic couplet. There are variations of these, such as high and low burlesque, so called by the manner of treatment. In high burlesque, a low or frivolous subject is treated in a mockingly dignified way. In low burlesque, a lofty or serious subject is treated in derisive fashion. *The Beggar's Opera* is a famous example of high burlesque. In this Reader, "Postal System Input Buffer Device" is an excellent example of low burlesque. Comedian Pat Paulsen's "non-candidacy" in the 1968 Presidential race and much material on television shows like Rowan and Martin's "Laugh-In" are also low burlesque.

Satire often uses a special kind of narrator called a "mask" or *persona*. This is the character through whom the action is observed or related. It is not normally to be construed as the author's voice. In *A Modest Proposal*, for example, Swift uses the mask of an aging, well intentioned, seemingly logical governmental representative to voice in utter sincerity the unspeakably horrible suggestion that the panacea to Ireland's economic woes is the slaughter and processing of one-year-old children as foodstuff for export. To interpret that voice as Swift's is to seriously misread the satire. Similarly, satire often has a character who serves as a standard or norm against which to measure the other characters. In *Gulliver's Travels*, it is the Portuguese sea captain who rescues Gulliver in the final book, or the King of the Giants in Book II; in Sir Thomas More's *Utopia*, it is Raphael Hythloday.

So satire is a deliberately controlled kind of literature. When it fails, it fails because it loses control. The writer who is all direct attack, all abuse, with no aesthetic distance between himself and his subject, may write invective or diatribe but probably not satire. Such criticism has been made of Philip Wylie's *Generation of Vipers*. If a writer is highly personal, splenetic, bitter, and offensive, he may write sarcasm but not satire. If he triggers a blunderbuss to puncture tissue paper, he has overdone things—one common excess of the fledgling satirist. If he uses a chisel to demolish the Eiffel Tower, he has been too gentle—a second shortcoming of the novice. The seasoned satirist faces other problems, the chief one of which is simply long-windedness. One finds this flaw in both Horace and Juvenal, in Rabelais, in Cervantes, in Swift, in Clemens, in Sinclair Lewis. Had Lewis in *Babbitt*, for example, stuck with his original scheme of giving us one twenty-four-hour day in the life of George Babbitt, he may not have written as successful a novel, but

3

he almost certainly would have written a better satire. The final third of *Babbitt* finds Lewis striking out at targets he has already devastatingly demolished. With satire as with sermonizing, enough is enough.

THE DEVELOPMENT OF SATIRE

Satire in the West began with the Athenians of the fifth, fourth, and third centuries B.C., but it flourished under the Romans. This is not surprising because at its height Roman culture characteristically valued those same virtues satire traditionally seeks to restore—balance, harmony, proportion, moderation, decorum, taste, good sense. Nor is it surprising that the modern "Golden Age" of satire in English occurred during the eighteenth century, the so-called "Neo-Classical" period in English literature, when many writers were consciously striving to imitate and revive the styles of the great Romans. Dryden and Pope, for example, wrote a number of imitations, often clearly stating the Roman source in the title itself. Such imitations are not literal copies or updated versions with modern names and places. Rather they imitate the spirit of the original. Samuel Johnson wrote a famous description of life in London, imitating Juvenal's *Third Satire,* on life in Rome. Johnson's is quite different from Juvenal's on the surface, but closely resembles it in spirit.

Satire in general is of two types distinguished by tone. "Horatian" satire is urbane, warm, witty, gentle, chiding, aiming to correct through broad laughter. "Juvenalian" satire is harsher, more biting, angry, contemptuous, indignant, aiming to reform through mocking ridicule. (It is sometimes called "Menippean" after its inventor, whose works are lost but whose style was followed by Juvenal and Lucian.) Addison is Horatian, Swift Juvenalian; Art Buchwald is Horatian, Al Capp Juvenalian.

ORGANIZATION OF THIS READER

In this Reader, we have tried to collect samples of the best short satires ever written. We have tried to avoid including excerpts from the great long satires. There is no chapter from *Gulliver's Travels* or *Don Quixote* or *Gargantua and Pantagruel* or *A Connecticut Yankee* or *Catch-22,*

4

nor any excerpt from *Candide, Rasselas, Lysistrata, The Frogs,* or *The Beggar's Opera.* We feel such works are best read complete and that most teachers who use this Reader in their classes prefer things that way. In choosing translations, we have sought those which are not only lively and clear but which also appeal to audiences of the 1970's. In those few instances when such translations were not available, we have offered our own. The satires are arranged chronologically (with a few obvious exceptions) to illustrate the historical development of satire in Greece, Rome, Western Europe, England, and America. All the devices and techniques of satire are illustrated.

One last word—satirists are notorious for setting traps for readers; the reader must always be alert, objective, and alive to the satire, lest he himself become an unwitting victim. Unlike the romantic or sentimental novelist who wants the reader to "throw himself into the story" and become emotionally involved with the characters and events, the satirist wants his reader to remain detached enough to grasp the entire range of the satire, to keep his balance, to see clearly once again what he may have lost sight of temporarily. The reader who accepts Lemuel Gulliver as a standard or ideal by which to judge humanity (thus "identifying with" Gulliver) may feel smug enough in Book I as Gulliver towers, a giant morally and physically, above the small and petty Lilliputians. However, in Book II when Gulliver finishes proudly describing the political, national, ethical, and moral life of contemporaneous Europe to the King of the Giants in Brobdingnag (who *does* represent a kind of rational standard), and the King picks Gulliver up to tell him "My little friend Grildrig, . . . I cannot but conclude the bulk of your natives to be the most pernicious race of little odious vermin that Nature ever suffered to crawl upon the surface of the earth," then such a gullible reader may indeed squirm, for he has been trapped, and he sits—a fool. At this point, he can remain a fool, or he can strike childishly back at the satirist, or he can chuckle at his own foolishness and then, his balance and perspective restored, get on with his business.

Aesop and Babrius
TWO FABLES

Aesop
THE FOX AND THE GRAPES

Aesop, who is probably more legendary than historical, is supposed to have lived from about 620 to 560 B.C. He apparently invented the fable in which animals, personifying humans, afforded him a medium to satirize man's faults indirectly. Translation by J. M. S.

A fox, just at the time of the vintage, stole into a vineyard where the ripe sunny grapes were trellised up on high in most tempting show. He made many a spring and a jump after the luscious prize; but, failing in all his attempts, he muttered as he retreated, "Oh, well! What does it matter! The grapes are sour anyway!"

Babrius
THE OXEN AND THE BUTCHERS

Babrius, evidently an Etruscan who knew Greek, lived sometime in the second century A.D. He is credited with collecting or writing a large number of fables and was evidently responsible for keeping the Aesopic fables alive. Translation by F. K.

One day all the oxen gathered together and decided to kill all the butchers. So they sharpened up their horns and got ready, but before they could set out, one of the oldest oxen spoke: "Do not forget that butchers are masters of their trade. They kill us, but they do it quickly. If we slaughter them, there are still hordes of other men to kill us, but none of them as skillful as the butchers."

Martial
EPIGRAMS

Marcus Valerius Martialis (c. 40–104 A.D.) was the most productive of the Latin epigrammatists. His 1,561 satires ridicule and scorn timeless Roman fakes, sycophants, spongers, snobs, and many other ridiculous characters who make up human life anywhere. Translation by J. M. S.

I, xxvii

To think that Acerra smells
Of day-old wine is wrong; Acerra always
Drinks till dawn.

III, ix

Rumor has it that Cinna writes verses against me.
Couldn't be.
He whose poems no man reads writes nothing.

III, xviii

In your opening remarks, Maximus, you moaned about a cold in the
throat.
Once you've already excused yourself, why do you continue to babble?

Lucian
DIÁLOGUES

Lucian, a Greek satirist of the second century A.D., *was one of the first to develop the satiric potential of the dialogue. He uses fantasy freely, letting us overhear private conversations between gods, between gods and mortals, and among the dead. Religious dogma and philosophical inanities seem to be his most common targets. Lucian also established the imaginary "true history" form of satire such as we find in More's* Utopia, *Swift's* Gulliver's Travels, *and Voltaire's* Candide. *An excellent recent collection of his works is* Lucian: Satirical Sketches, *translated by Paul Turner in a Penguin Books edition. The order of the following dialogues is that suggested by H. W. and F. G. Fowler in their anthology,* The Works of Lucian (*Oxford: 1905*). *The translation, following a suggestion by Gilbert Highet in* The Anatomy of Satire *that Lucian reads "with the same subtlety as a freshman preaching atheism," is by F. K.*

from DIALOGUES OF THE DEAD
HERMES AND CHARON

Here "modern" times are belittled by contrast with "ancient" times when men were men; even Hermes and Charon are reduced to petty bourgeois bargaining.

HERMES   All right, let's settle up what you owe me now so we won't have any squabbles afterwards.

CHARON   Fair enough—that way there's no trouble.

HERMES   That anchor you wanted was five drachmas.

CHARON   Hey, that's pretty steep.

9

HERMES   Dammit, that's what it cost me. And the oarstrap was two obols more.

CHARON   Well, put down five drachmas and two obols then.

HERMES   And it was five obols more for the sail-mending needle.

CHARON   Okay, okay, put that down too.

HERMES   And another two drachmas for the wax to plug up your leaks, the nails you wanted, and the rope for bracing.

CHARON   Well, you practically *stole* those, didn't you?

HERMES   Unless I missed something, that was all you ordered. Now what about payment?

CHARON   Actually, I'm a little short right now. But as soon as there's a good plague or war, I can up my prices and then I'll have plenty of capital.

HERMES   So I'm supposed to sit around and pray for disasters?

CHARON   Sorry about that. There's nothing I can do, what with no war and all.

HERMES   Yeah—well, I suppose it *is* better to have peace even if I have to wait for my money. Ah, but in the old days, Charon, when men were really men! Do you remember how they used to come in down here, covered by blood and all full of wounds? But today, what do you get? A few sorry creatures poisoned by their wives or their own children, or killed by easy living, a fat, pasty, soft, sorry lot. It's sure not like it used to be. You know, it's money that sends most of them here; they fight each other all the time over it.

CHARON   True, that does seem to dog most of them through life.

HERMES   Well, then, you shouldn't mind if I hound you for my money, eh?

PHILIP AND ALEXANDER

In this, Lucian's version of the "generation gap," Alexander endures the ridicule of Philip, his father and a great king and conqueror himself. Philip's conquests were largely in Greece whereas Alexander's were in Africa and the Near East.

PHILIP   Ah, ha! *Now* try to deny I'm your father and you're a mortal like the rest of us.

ALEXANDER Oh, I knew I was your son. I just thought that "godlike bit" was useful in politics; so I used the oracles a little.

PHILIP What! You ought to have known better than to trust those damn lying oracles.

ALEXANDER No, no. I mean I *used* the oracles. I used them to make my enemies think I was a god. That way, they were easier to beat.

PHILIP Come on. You didn't need a backwoods trick like that to beat those bush leaguers you were fighting, with their bitty little bows and flimsy wicker shields. Now beating *Greeks* was a man's job. I mean going up against the Boiotians and Phocians and Athenians, and that infantry from Arkadia and those horsemen from Thessalonia and those javelin throwers from Eleon and those quick, light-shielded warriors from Mantineia, and Throcians and Illyrians and Paionians—now *there* was a man's war! But those Medes and Persians and Chaldaeans—nothing but flower children, with their dainty little golden decorations. Don't you know that a paltry ten thousand Greeks whipped all of them before you were even born? Why, that whole cowardly bunch took off and ran before our troops even got close enough to shoot the first arrow!

ALEXANDER Maybe so, but the Scythians and those Indians up on their elephants were pretty terrifying, and I whipped them. What's more, I did it without having to plant spies or buy off traitors or break my oath or lie in public like you. And after I took Thebes, the rest of Greece didn't cost me another single man.

PHILIP So I've heard from Clitus—remember him? You ran him through at supper one night when he had guts enough to say I was a better general than you. And what's all this I hear about you wearing Persian clothes over there in front of Macedonian citizens? You'd think you *lost* the war. And what about murdering that poor little schoolteacher Callisthenes in a lion's den, and marrying all those foreign princesses, and that nonsense with your adjutant—what was his name?—Hephaestion? I know you were trying to copy Achilleus and his thing with Patroklos and make like a god, you and your big ego. What do you suppose the troops said about that one? Bah! Ridiculous! At least you kept your paws off Darius' wife when you took his kingdom, and you did look after his mother and children. At least there you acted like a king.

ALEXANDER   You seem to forget how I was always out in front of the men. Didn't you admire that? I was the first man—*the first*—to jump inside the walls at Oxydracae. You know I got hurt pretty badly there.

PHILIP   Stupid. Oh, I think it's fine for a king to get out front occasionally and get wounded a little now and then, but for you it was really dumb! Remember, you were supposed to be a god. They really must have laughed at you every time they saw you carried off bleeding and screaming. And they must have laughed at your oracle too. Since when would you need a medic if you were Zeus' son? Now that you're dead, your rotting, swollen body must be really getting the horselaugh up there on earth. And another thing—you claim that pretending to be a god made it easier for you to win. Well, what about this, oh Immortal One; didn't your godliness reduce the glory of your victories? Huh? Gods are always supposed to win. Some mind you've got.

ALEXANDER   But all men admired me. They compare me to Hercules and Dionysus. Neither one of those could take that rock fortress Aornos in Afghanistan that I took!

PHILIP   There you go playing that god stuff again. You ought to be ashamed. This is me—old Dad. Come off your high horse. "Know thyself." You're dead now, Alexander; admit it.

MENIPPUS AND TIRESIAS

Menippus is talking in Hades with Tiresias, the blind prophet who appears in many Greek legends, notably in the plays Oedipus Rex *and* Antigone *by Sophocles. Tiresias, like prophets all the way from those of the Old Testament to Al Capp's Old Man Mose, frequently speaks indirectly, which irritates his listeners, then truthfully, which alienates them. Menippus was a Greek philosopher who wrote satire about 250 B.C. His works are lost, but his biting, sarcastic tone has come down to us through Varro, Lucian, and Juvenal. In fact, "Juvenalian" or harsh, stinging satire is sometimes called "Menippean" and contrasted with the gentler "Horatian" satire popularized by Horace.*

MENIPPUS I'll tell you, Tiresias, it's really hard to see if you *are* blind or not. It doesn't matter much since none of us has anything but empty sockets left in these skeleton heads of ours. . . . I understand you're supposed to be the only person who has been both male and female. Tell me, which one has the better life?

TIRESIAS The woman by far, Menippus. She has much less to do. She can boss men around. She never has to go to war or man the battlements when the city is attacked. She doesn't have to get mixed up in politics or work for the government. She doesn't have to serve in court.

MENIPPUS True, but in that terrifying play *Medea* of Euripides, Medea mourns for women, for the terrible time they have in childbirth. Say—when you were a woman, did *you* ever have a baby?

TIRESIAS Why do you want to know?

MENIPPUS Oh, no reason really. But tell me if you don't mind.

TIRESIAS Well, I wasn't barren. But then I didn't actually have a baby either.

MENIPPUS I see. But you could have? I mean, you had the right organs and all?

TIRESIAS Of course.

MENIPPUS And did your female organs gradually develop into male ones or was it all at once?

TIRESIAS I don't see why you keep asking. I don't think you'd believe anything I said anyway.

MENIPPUS Now, now, you couldn't expect me to accept such a story literally, without evidence, could you?

TIRESIAS I suppose you don't believe all those stories of women being changed into birds and trees and animals by the gods.

MENIPPUS If I run into any of them, I'll ask them to see what they say. But tell me, were you a prophet when you were a woman too, or did that gift come when you changed into a man.

TIRESIAS You really are badly informed, aren't you? Have you never heard of how I settled an argument among the gods, then Hera, in a rage, blinded me—and Zeus, to make up for it a little, gave me the ability to see the future and speak prophetically?

MENIPPUS Oh, come on, Tiresias. Are you still sticking to that old tale? You so-called seers are all alike. You never utter the plain truth.

LUCIAN

from DIALOGUES OF THE GODS

In his dialogues among the deities, Lucian uses low bur-
lesque—that is, he treats serious subjects in a low manner,
thus making them victims of ridicule.

EROS AND ZEUS

Here Zeus' predilection for mating with mortals is satirized.
A key element in the satire is the revelation that all-power-
ful Zeus is sometimes a victim of Eros, the young boy-god
of love.

EROS   All right, all right! But even if I did something wrong, Zeus,
you should forgive and forget because I'm only a child, remember.
I don't know any better.

ZEUS   Only a child! You're as old as the hills! Just because you don't
shave and your hair's not white, you can't get away with this *"kid"*
stuff, you little rat!

EROS   But what have I ever done to make you want to punish me?

ZEUS   Damn you! What have you ever done? You've made a fool of
me once too often. You've made me a satyr! You've made me a bull!
And a shower of gold, and a swan, and an eagle! You have never
let one woman fall for me just for myself. Always there is some gim-
mick. Oh, they respond to the bull or the swan all right, but if they
see the real me, they're scared to death.

EROS   Well, naturally. No mortal can withstand the sight of your face.

ZEUS   How is it that fragile mortals like Branchus and Hyacinth do
not faint at the sight of their beloved Apollo?

EROS   Don't forget how Daphne fled in terror from him despite his
beauty. If you want to score with the women, you've got to quit
rattling that huge shield and toting all those thunderbolts around.
You must get your hair curled or wear ribbons like Bacchus and put
on a lovely purple robe and gold sandals and bring music and dancing with you. Then they'll all come running to you.

ZEUS   Get out of here! If I have to do all that, I'll get along without
them.

14

EROS   Good. But if you want to avoid all that, forget about all your catting around too.

ZEUS   Oh no! I don't plan to quit *that*. But I'm tired of all this rigmarole. You! You figure me out a way around it, and then I'll leave you alone.

POSEIDON AND HERMES

Here Lucian continues his burlesque of classical Greek myth. This time Zeus is "lying-in," having just given birth to Dionysus under uncommon circumstances. The satire is reinforced by the tone of the conversation itself. Ganymede, mentioned leeringly by Poseidon, is a Trojan shepherd boy with whom Zeus sometimes consoles himself. Athena (Wisdom), mentioned later on, was born from Zeus' forehead after he swallowed Metis (Thought). Semele is another of the earthly maidens who attracted Zeus. Cadmus, her father, founded many of the ancient Greek cities, Thebes being chief among them.

POSEIDON   Hermes, I'd like a word with Zeus.

HERMES   Sorry, but it's out of the question.

POSEIDON   Oh, come now. Just let him know I'm here.

HERMES   You can't bother him right now, Poseidon. It's just a bad time, that's all.

POSEIDON   Oh, I get it. You mean he and Hera—they're, uh . . . .

HERMES   Oh no, not *that*. In fact, quite the opposite.

POSEIDON   Ah, ha. He's in there with Ganymede, eh?

HERMES   No, no, not that either. He's, well, he's not feeling too good.

POSEIDON   Oh? Well that sounds serious. What's the trouble?

HERMES   It's so embarrassing, I'm ashamed to tell you.

POSEIDON   Come, now, Hermes; you can tell your old uncle Poseidon.

HERMES   Well, uncle, he's—he's—he's just had a baby.

POSEIDON   What! Impossible! How? Who is the father—I mean, don't tell me old Zeus has been a woman too all this time without our knowing it. But he didn't have any signs—I mean, his stomach never. . . .

HERMES   That's right—because the baby wasn't in his stomach.

15

POSEIDON I see. He popped it out of his head again, just like with Athena. He's got a fertile mind, that Zeus.

HERMES No, you're wrong again. Semele's child came out of Zeus' thigh.

POSEIDON Great! Now there's a god for you—gets pregnant from head to foot. Who did you say? Semele? Who's Semele?

HERMES She is Cadmus' daughter, from Thebes. Zeus, uh, got her, uh—you know.

POSEIDON And then *he* had the child?

HERMES That's right. I know it looks odd. But it was *Hera's* fault. Hera is awfully jealous. She went to Semele in disguise after Zeus had, uh, been there. She got Semele to make Zeus appear in all his power and glory—you know, the lightning and thunder and clouds, the whole thing. Anyway, one of the thunderbolts set the place on fire, and Semele was burned to a crisp. So Zeus had me go cut the half-grown child out of her womb and make a slit in his thigh and put it in there. Now he's given it birth, and he's, uh, indisposed from his motherhood.

POSEIDON Wild! Say, where's the baby?

HERMES I delivered him to some nymphs down in Nysa; they'll raise him. His name is Dionysus, by the way.

POSEIDON Is my kingly brother both father and mother of this Dionysus, then?

HERMES I guess so. I don't know; this is a confusing job. Look, I really have to get back to him—you know, with lots of boiling water and clean sheets and all that.

ZEUS QUESTIONED

In this dialogue, Cyniscus, a voice from earth probably representing the Cynic philosophers, questions Zeus on free will and predestination.

CYNISCUS Hear me, Zeus, I won't bother you with a normal prayer. I won't ask for riches or a kingdom. Those prayers must be hard for you—you never seem to answer them anyway. But I would ask one little gift.

ZEUS   And what would that be? I will grant your gift, especially since you claim it is such a small one.

CYNISCUS   Please give me an answer to one little question.

ZEUS   That ought to be easy. Ask what you like.

CYNISCUS   Zeus, I know you have read what Homer and Hesiod say about Destiny and the Fates. Is it true what they say—that Destiny and the Fates predetermine every man's life?

ZEUS   Quite true. The Fates control all. Everything is spun in their webs. No variations are allowed.

CYNISCUS   So when Homer mentions things like "dying before your appointed time" he is off his rocker?

ZEUS   Of course. There are simply no exceptions to what the Fates decree; there are no flaws in their design. When poets are properly inspired by the Muses, they speak truly; however, when they speak on their own, they are subject to error. One cannot be too harsh toward them for this—they are merely mortal, after all.

CYNISCUS   All right. But answer another question: How many Fates are there—three?

ZEUS   Certainly.

CYNISCUS   Then what is this I hear about Destiny and Fortune? What kinds of powers are they? People are claiming *they* really control everything.

ZEUS   Do not expect to be given all the answers. Tell me why you are inquiring anyway.

CYNISCUS   First answer another question. Are you under the power of the Fates also? Are you tangled in their web?

ZEUS   Of course. What is strange about that?

CYNISCUS   Oh, I was just remembering that speech of yours in Homer where you threaten to haul the whole world up on your golden chain, and you challenge all the other gods to get down on the chain and pull and you will haul them up too, along with the earth and sea and everything else. That speech always impresses me with your colossal power. Now you tell me that you and your golden chain and all your might are hanging by one trivial thread. It appears the Fates are the mighty ones—they have you dangling like a fish.

ZEUS   What is your point with all these questions?

CYNISCUS   Just this, and for the gods' sake—oops, for the Fates' sake

17

—do not lose your temper: If the Fates control everything, why are we always pouring out libations and offering sacrifices to you? It seems silly if our piety cannot affect anything.

ZEUS Now I know who has been corrupting your mind. It is all those so-called philosophers who constantly criticize us gods. They always try to pollute the people's thinking and interfere with traditional religious services. They keep saying we carry no sway over mortal matters, but *they* are going to get *theirs*.

CYNISCUS Sever my thread if they have influenced me! I simply inferred that conclusion from what you were telling me. May I go back to my questioning?

ZEUS Oh, ˄ll right, if you have nothing better to do.

CYNISCUS The Fates, then, control all that happens?

ZEUS Right.

CYNISCUS Can you influence their design or re-direct their threads?

ZEUS Of course not.

CYNISCUS Shall I then make the obvious point about the pointlessness of piety?

ZEUS Your point is clear, thank you. Remember, however, that sacrifices are a gesture of respect for deity, not merely payment for favors.

CYNISCUS All right; you have agreed that piety is profitless, that we just offer it as acknowledgment of your immortality. A philosopher could well ask what your vaunted immortality amounts to. It could appear that you and I have something in common—namely, that the Fates control us both. In fact, you are trapped worse than I because I am released at death but you must struggle in the Fates' web forever, till the end of your endless thread.

ZEUS You forget what great pleasure the immortal life is.

CYNISCUS Nonsense. It may be for you because you are king and you can haul the whole world up on a chain if you want to. But take Hephaestus. He is just a crippled smithy, a poor worker. And take Prometheus. He endured horrible torture for ages. Then there is your own father, who is still suffering. You deities suffer love and receive wounds and even have to work for mortals sometimes. That does not sound like great pleasure to me. The truth, it would appear, is that some of you are lucky and others not. Some of you have your temples robbed, which no doubt reduces your dignity. Some of you are even melted down on earth for your gold and silver—but undoubtedly the Fates ordain that.

ZEUS   Now you have gone too far. You will regret having said *that.*

CYNISCUS   I stand in something less than terror, Zeus. You know you cannot harm me unless it is already part of the Fates' design. In fact, you are powerless to punish those who fleece your temples; most of them escape. Evidently the Fates plan for them to.

ZEUS   I knew it! You *are* one of those damnable philosophers out to undermine the whole system.

CYNISCUS   Touchy about that, aren't you? How come? Well, I have another question, and you are certainly the highest authority around. What exactly is this system of yours? Is there a power which controls even the Fates?

ZEUS   As I have said, there are certain things you are not fated to understand. And why all these questions? I gave you permission for just *one* request originally. You are just trying to degrade deity.

CYNISCUS   Nonsense. You just said the Fates controlled all. Are you changing your mind? Do you claim more power for yourself?

ZEUS   Certainly not. We gods are agents for the Fates.

CYNISCUS   You mean you are just employees in the service of the Fates? Sort of civil servants in the heavenly government?

ZEUS   I cannot follow you.

CYNISCUS   I will explain. A carpenter has certain tools which, though they are very functional, cannot replace the carpenter. Similarly, the carpenter alone cannot construct a boat without the tools. Destiny really runs the system; you gods are merely the tools he uses. I suppose we really ought to pray directly to Destiny. But then, maybe even the Fates cannot change things once they are in the design. In fact, each Fate no doubt jealously guards her work against tampering by the other two.

ZEUS   Now you blaspheme even the Fates! You are an anarchist pure and simple. Will you not admit that we gods should be honored at least for leaking to you through our press secretaries (the prophets and oracles) predictions about the Fates' designs?

CYNISCUS   Now, Zeus, of what value is foreknowledge if we are powerless to alter events? If we could lock ourselves in our bedrooms on those days the oracles predict we will find steel spears in our chests on the battlefield, then we would be getting somewhere. But such is not our lot. The Fates might lure me to hunt, for example, and then arrange for a spear to miss the wild boar and stick me. Why did the oracle warn Laius about his cursed son Oedipus when Oedipus was fated to slaughter his father anyway? And another thing —your blasted oracles are always ambiguous, like the one who caused Croesus to cross the Halys by not explaining that the kingdom thus fated to fall might be his *own* rather than that of Cyrus the Persian king.

ZEUS You forget that Croesus angered Apollo.

CYNISCUS Deities should be more even tempered. Anyway, if Croesus was fated to fall, he was fated to receive bad information; therefore, even your oracles are Destiny's agents.

ZEUS That's it; pile on the scorn. We gods are useless, purposeless, without influence—just a lot of carpenter's tools. I must say, though, I can understand some of your scorn, what with my letting you chatter away so long although I am able to cut you down with a thunderbolt at any instant.

CYNISCUS So fire away! That is, fire away if the Fates have so decreed it. Then I would forgive you because you could not help yourself; you would be no more accountable than that other agent, the thunderbolt. That reminds me of another question I want to ask of both you and Destiny. Perhaps you can handle it alone. Why is it you allow so many crimes, including sacrilege, yet fire off your thunderbolts at helpless trees and mountains and ships' masts and even at harmless travellers on the open road? How about an answer to that one? Or am I not fated to understand this either?

ZEUS You are not. You go too far with these questions. I do not see the point of all this anyway.

CYNISCUS Neither am I fated to understand certain other matters of Fortune, I suppose—like why good men die in poverty, yet criminals, lechers, and perverts pass their lives in wealth; or why Socrates was murdered and his murderers not punished; or why many more similar injustices I could name are allowed.

ZEUS You evidently do not understand how the sinful are punished in Hades and the good rewarded there.

CYNISCUS I cannot know anything about that until I die and actually get to Hades, now can I? In the meanwhile, I would prefer to live in comfort and health. If it is my fate to have vultures tear out my liver after I am dead, why that's fine; but I will certainly forego the privilege of suffering like Tantalus and doing without a drink of water during my lifetime.

ZEUS   Don't you believe in our system of justice at all?

CYNISCUS   I have heard that Minos, a Cretan, has such a system down here. Tell me about him; I hear he is one of your countless sons.

ZEUS   And what do you wish to know about him?

CYNISCUS   Whom does he punish?

ZEUS   Evil-doers, naturally, like murderers and temple robbers.

CYNISCUS   And whom does he reward with a happy hereafter?

ZEUS   The good, the virtuous, and the pious.

CYNISCUS   Why, Zeus?

ZEUS   Why? Because the evil deserve punishment and the good have earned a reward.

CYNISCUS   Suppose a man committed a crime he could not help. Would Minos punish him?

ZEUS   Of course not.

CYNISCUS   Then, logically, Minos would not reward a man for a virtuous act he could not help.

ZEUS   Correct.

CYNISCUS   It seems to me, Zeus, that Minos has no right at all to punish or reward in any situation.

ZEUS   What! Why not?

CYNISCUS   Because we have no power as men to do anything by choice. As you have said, the Fates control all. So if a man murders, it is really the Fates who are murderers; if a man robs a temple, it is really the Fates who are temple robbers. Out of fairness, Minos would have to punish Destiny, not Sisyphus, and the Fates, not Tantalus, because neither man was acting out of free will.

ZEUS   I will not tolerate another of your impudent questions. You are nothing but an impious philosopher. I will listen no further. I am leaving.

CYNISCUS   What! Wait! I have one more question. Where do the Fates live? How do they plot out all those millions of details since there are three of them? What a job! I would hate to be fated to be

21

a Fate. Fortune certainly has not smiled happily on *them*. I would rather continue poor as I am than have to sit through all eternity at their task with all that responsibility. If these last questions are too much for you, Zeus, I will get along on the information I have. What you already told me gives me some understanding of Destiny and the overall scheme of things. And anyway, as you are so fond of saying, perhaps that is all I am *fated* to know.

Zeus is no longer listening for he is sinking to raptness as of yore, to go on working evermore in his unweeting way

Horace
BOOK I, SATIRE IV

*Horace (65–8 B.C.) is the founder of that gentle, urbane
style of satire which bears his name. In the satire printed
here, he points out the foolishness and excesses of many of
the poets of his time, and he justifies his own satiric approach. Much of this is tongue-in-cheek, especially as Horace looks at himself in the closing sections. Horatian satire
preaches moderation and speaks with unquestioned ra-
tionality. Horace tries to enlist rather than shock his reader.
He tries to persuade rather than upset. He wants us to
agree with him, to see things his way. An Horatian satirist
believes people are more likely to reform when they feel a
little ashamed or embarrassed than when they are harshly
ridiculed or wickedly attacked. One of the most conservative of satirists, Horace never loses sight of his goal, never
indulges his spleen, is never trapped by his own machinery.
He is always in command, the voice of sweet reason itself.
In this satire, the many names he mentions are not important in themselves; they are politicians of the period or
characters in popular plays no longer extant. They simply
add to the conversational, everyday tone of the satire. This
translation is by J. M. S.*

Those good old poets Eupolis, Cratinus, and Aristophanes—true poets
—never hesitated to name names. They didn't pull their punches. If
someone was a rascal, a thief, a lecher, a cut-throat, that's what they
called him. Lucilius, my predecessor, depends entirely upon those poets
as his models; he follows them in everything but meter and rhythm.
Lucilius is caustic, you know, with a sharp nose for news, but his verse
is rugged and rough. His fault is he wrote too much. Just to show off,
he'd rattle out two hundred lines an hour standing on one foot. The

words just flowed in a stream, but the stream was always a bit murky, always something there you wanted to filter out. And he's wordy, repetitive, garrulous, verbose, windy—too lazy to write well—correctly, I mean. As for the amount, who can count it?

Now, here's Crispinus with money to burn, giving me good odds: "You take your tablet," he says, "and I'll take mine. We'll set a place and time and pick some judges and we'll see who can write the most, Horace, you or me."

Thank the gods for making me slow-witted, gentle, and hesitant to speak. But you go ahead, Crispinus, huff and puff like the air in a goatskin bellows; blow and puff until the fire softens the iron.

That blitheful fellow Fannius passes out his books and cases and his picture; he gets *his* readers that way. But no one reads my stuff, and I do hate to recite it in public; after all, satire offends—at least half the world. Just pick anyone, anyone you want, from a crowd; he's either mad with greed or driven by ambition. Over here is one mad for love of somebody else's wife; there's another in love with boys. This man is quick after silver; Albius is wrapped up in bronzes; another is an entrepreneur—in the market sun-up to sundown. You know the kind, offices east and west and points between and rushing among them, blown from crisis to crisis like a column of dust in a whirlwind, afraid that he'll have a capital loss or at best that he won't make a profit.

All these people dread verses and hate a satiric poet. "Stay away from *him*," they say, "he carries a sharp knife." His friends, himself— makes no difference if he can just get a laugh. And if he once gets it dribbled down on paper, he delights to have it spread among the vulgar, like old women and slave-boys as they come home from the bakery or the public fountain.

But, just a minute. Let me give a quick answer to that. First, I'll remove my name from the list of true poets. After all, it takes more than meter to make a poem, and you really can't count anyone a poet who just records conversations, as I do. Now, if one is inspired, if he's born a genius, if he has a gifted tongue, then call him a poet. There are those—critics mostly—who ask whether or not this new comedy is really poetry since it's hardly fiery, inspired neither in diction nor subject, and, except for a more-or-less regular meter, little more than prose. "But, there's fire here," you argue. "The angry father storms at his dissolute son, who's madly passionate for his prostitute mistress. Even worse, he rejects the well-dowried wife the old man chose, and goes reeling out, led by torch bearers in daylight, dead drunk."

Yes, yes, it's realistic. Wouldn't Pomponius get the same sort of lecture if his father were still around? Yet it's clear that it's not enough to write out a line of simple words that your ordinary father—like the one in the play—would use. Take these words of mine or those that Lucilius used to write, break up the rhythm, the meter, change their order, shuffling them all about; it wouldn't be like breaking up Ennius' lines:

> When loathsome Discord's din
> Had War's bronze posts, her iron-clad gates, broken in.

In these lines, even when dismembered, you'll find the limbs of a poet.

Ah, well; enough of this. We'll decide whether or not this satiric stuff is poetic some other time. The only question that concerns us now is whether satire really deserves your suspicion. You've seen those minions of the law, Sulcius the tracker and Caprius. They stalk about with writs in hand—just after the facts—hoarse with hate, the terrors of a robber's life. But if a man is honest and lives with clean hands, he can scorn them both. Even though you may be like those highwaymen Caelius and Birrius, that doesn't mean I'm a common informer like Sulcius or Caprius. So why should you fear me? No shop or book-stall displays my works for the mob or for Hermogenes Tigellius (that *swell* musician) to thumb through. I recite only to my friends, privately, and then only when they insist, never in public and not before just anybody. There are some who read their books in the middle of the Forum, even in the baths—the echoing vault gives them voice, you know. It's that sort of thing that soothes their empty-headed vanity; they never even consider whether what they do is out of taste or season.

A critic says to me, "You satirists delight in hurting people, and you do it with such relish!" Really now, where could anyone possibly find such stuff in my writings? Can this accusation come from one of my friends? I'll tell you this: the man who backbites an absent friend, who won't defend him when someone else attacks, who is a wit at his friend's expense, I tell you, the man who can make up what he couldn't have seen, who can't keep a secret, that man is a black-hearted rascal. Beware of him, good Romans, beware. You've seen the kind. You've been at those big dinner parties where they sit four to a couch that was designed for three. There's always one there who loves to mud-splatter everyone present (or absent), except the host who provides the bath, and he later gets him as well, when the wine and the god of truth reveal what's deep in his heart. And *you* think he's witty and genial and terribly frank—you who hate such black-hearted rascals. If, on occasion, I have laughed because "frilly Rufillius reeks of perfume or Gargonius stinks like a goat," does that make me a spiteful dog? Suppose, for the moment, the talk turned to the thefts of Petillius Capitolinus. You would certainly defend him in *your* own quaint way: "Now, he's been a friend, a close friend, since we were boys and he's done a lot for me whenever I asked. I'm delighted he's safe here in town, but I must admit I am a bit curious about how he managed to escape conviction." Why, that's as black as the squid's ink; it drips with venom. That sort of malice will always be far from me; if it's not in my heart, it won't be in my pages.

Should my words be a bit free, a little too light, I hope you'll make allowances. The best of fathers taught me the habit of avoiding mistakes by pointing them out to me wherever he saw them. He'd encourage me to live thriftily, frugally, content with what he had saved for me. "Don't you see," he would say, "how miserable young Albius is and how broke Baius is? Now there's a lesson not to squander what I've given you." To keep me from a grubby affair, he'd tell me, "Don't be like Scetanus." If I were tempted by another's wife when I might enjoy a proper liaison, he'd say, "You know the story of Trebonius; he was caught in the act, and now look at his reputation. My boy, I'll leave it to the philosophers to give you reasons for what to seek and what to avoid, if only I can uphold the tradition handed down from our forefathers, and if, as long as you need me, I can protect your life and name. In the course of time, Horace, you'll grow strong in mind and body; then you'll be able to swim without support." With words like these he shaped and trained me. If he were advising me to do something, he'd say, "There's your example," and point to a man of character. Or, again, if he were telling me what to avoid, he'd say, "Can you really doubt that this is completely wrong and dishonorable when you see so-and-so is in such disgrace?" In just the way a neighbor's funeral terrifies a sick glutton and makes him take care of himself for fear of death, so the young mind is turned from mistakes by the disgrace of others.

Thanks to his training I am free of those disastrous vices and at fault only in those *little* things which you can easily forgive. Perhaps even these faults will go with the years, and with honest friends and self-criticism. For, you know, when I retire to my couch or go for a walk in the courtyard, I never forget myself: "This is better . . . if I do that I'll be happier . . . my friends will like me for this . . . he didn't behave well there; I wonder if I'll ever act like that—by mistake." Thus, tight-lipped, I counsel myself.

Then, when I find the time, I jot down my thoughts—one of those minor vices I mentioned. If you can't take it, my friend, be careful, for there's a large band of poets to come to my rescue—for we're more than half the world, you know—and like the Jews, we'll make you a convert.

Juvenal
SATIRE VI

ON WIVES

*Juvenal (c. 60–c. 140 A.D.) made famous the biting, sting-
ing satiric tone called "Juvenalian." In his sixteen satires, all
apparently written in his middle age, he excoriates most of
the vices of Rome. Juvenal never lets up; he constantly attacks. For a man of wit and sensitivity who has suffered and
been forced to watch others suffer, Juvenal says, "it is difficult not to write satire." This same spirit inflames Rabelais, Swift, and Clemens, for example. Juvenal, like them,
exaggerates and overstates. He carries realism to an extreme
in order to shock his audience and thereby awaken them to
indignation. His third, sixth, and tenth satires, on city life,
women, and human vanity are his best. The third has been
imitated—by Boileau, Oldham, Dryden, and Johnson, for
example—and parts of it adapted to longer works—by
Gay in* Trivia *and Pope in* The Dunciad. *The tenth satire is
most famous in its imitation by Johnson,* The Vanity of Human Wishes. *In the sixth satire, Juvenal ranges from sca-
brous invective through witty burlesque to melodramatic
absurdity, perhaps even to overtones of tragedy, as he re-
counts how Roman wives deceive, domineer, despise, and
maybe even do in their husbands. The translation is by F. K.*

I believe Chastity still lurked upon the earth in the primeval days of
Saturn, days when hoary mankind endured the dank of caverns at a
common hearth with herd and household idols, days when wives made
a litter of leaves, hay, and hides flayed from beasts slain on the hillside
—wives not like you, the Cynthia of Propertius, nor you, the Lesbia of
Catullus, whom a sparrow's fall could force to tears, but wives whose

nipples nursed heroic babes, whose hair flew freer than their lusty mates' brute belching. In those dawn days beneath newborn skies, men, sprung from the split-limbed oak or leapt from the loamy dust, lived not like us and knew not parents as we know now. Still under young Jove, Chastity lingered, but not after his golden beard grew, after Greeks swore oaths by others' heads, after men grew fearful for the fruits of their fields, and gardens grew walls against thieves. Then Astraea, the last innocent mortal, took wings with Chastity to the dim constellations.

To shudder in lust in your neighbor's bed, my friend Postumus, and to blaspheme the marriage gods is now an ancient, acknowledged abuse. All other vices and dishonor came late, flourished first in the Iron Age, but adultery sprung from the Silver. Even so, now you approach a betrothal; you visit the barber to prepare your appearance; perhaps you have proffered a band for her finger.

What! You, Postumus, you, a man of good sense—are *you* taking a wife? What madness has driven you to that last extremity? Will you submit to such slavery when there's no shortage of rope for hanging nor ledges to leap from, when you can always plunge off the Aemilian Bridge? Or if you lack such desperation could you not take a boy to your bed, one who would bend to your will, never grow quarrelsome, never cajole you for gifts as the price paid for favors, nor chide your indifference if you felt not like loving?

Even you, Ursidius, seem bent to follow the Julian Law encouraging marriage. You now want to sire a sweet little heir, though it cost you the delicacies you presently savor. What is not possible if Ursidius should wed—if you, long renowned as a prince among rakes, who has hid in the closets of innumerable wives, should docilely die on the gallows of matrimony? Even *you* are now seeking a virtuous wife. O doctors, let bleed some hot blood from his veins. . . .

Do our public places reveal even one worthy woman? Can all Rome's theaters tender a single one you may love without mistrust? As Bathyllus dances the Swan-Jove's possession of Leda, Tuccia can barely control her emotions; the Apulian maiden shivers and sighs as though transported by a lover's clasp; Thymele stares all rapt, for here the country girl studies the ways of the world. . . .

When Eppia, the wife of a Senator, flew off in the arms of a burly gladiator to Pharos and along the Nile to the notorius city of Alexandria, Heaven itself thundered disgust at the wanton ways of our Rome. Scorning her home, husband, sister, and country, she deserted the tear-ridden babes of her womb. Though born to good fortune, warm hearth, and soft bed, she ridiculed the imperial pelagic realm even as she flouted her good Roman name—a practice grown common among our spoiled high-born wives. With brass forged in adultery, she endured howling tempests as she crossed many seas. For the bravery of the female bent on bold wicked ways is a marvel of perverseness, though it fail in the face of danger met honorably, when she will chill, tremble, and faint.

If her husband takes her aboard ship, she screams "Cruelty!" The smell of sea water sickens her stomach; her head swirls with the ship's sway in the waves and she vomits in her husband's arms. But escaping with her lover, she never knows an unsteady moment. She sloughs down her meals with the crew, prowls the deck like an old mariner, and even takes a hand at hawser and lanyard. . . .

You think Eppia's tale untypical? Listen then to what Claudius, descendant of the deities, suffered at the hands of his wife. Many a night when her spouse and Emperor had fallen asleep, this royal strumpet deserted her august wedding bed for a public whore pillow. Hiding her head in a hood, she stole out with only one maid. Concealing her black hair with a blonde wig, she went to her work in a stench-ridden brothel. There in her personal stall she posed as Lycisca, offering her nude painted nipples and baring the royal gate of thy birth, O nobly fathered Britannicus! Here in nymphomaniacal passion she served legions of common Romans, each putting down his filthy fee. Here she sweated her lusts long after the other nocturnal trulls had left fully spent. Still unquenched, she carried home to her husband's bed her reeking, grimy loins, collapsed, and slept exhausted through half the next day.

Should I waste my time going on to warn of hideous aphrodisiacs and insane incantations, or venomous powders served by envious step-mothers to unbegotten sons, or the even more monstrous crimes their base natures drive women to unleash? Their venereal vices, after all, are the least of their flaws.

"But why," you may ask, "does Censennia's spouse call her the ideal wife?" It is because she gained him a million sesterces; that is the price of his blindness to her license. He was never pierced by Venus' shaft nor seared by her flame. The dowry alone spurred his desires. Now his wife beckons whatever lover she will, writes whatever letters of lust she wishes, and all before her husband's eyes. A wealthy woman wedding a money-loving man marries not at all.

"But surely," you say, "cannot one ideal woman be found among all these mobs?" Suppose you find one, a beauty, a charmer, wealthy, and fertile, with ancestors' statues dignifying her dwelling, with chastity more radiant than the Sabine women—admittedly a specimen rare as a black swan. But who could endure this paragon of virtue? . . .

"Have mercy, Apollo; and Thou, Diana, spare thy wrath! My babes have offended no one, spring thy shafts at her, their mother." So in vain did Amphion cry, but immortal Apollo loosed his bowstring, and thus did Niobe commit to Hades all her sons and daughters and their father too because in her vanity she called herself more noble than royal Apollo's mother.

And what use is great beauty, great talent in a wife when she constantly catalogs those attributes for you? They lose their rightful esteem when her pride parades them constantly before you. And what man's love was ever so great he could not yearn to escape the wife he must always praise to heaven? Nor who fail to hate such a wife seven hours in every twelve? . . .

If you cannot expect love from the woman you marry, what then is the point of your betrothal? Why waste your money on the wedding celebrations, the parties, and the wedding night's gift of glittering gold? If you really are passion's slave, bound to a single woman, then get your neck ready for the yoke. You will never find a woman, despite her cries of love, who can resist tormenting a devoted husband. The greater his love, the greater his loyalty and consideration, the less her reciprocation. You will never send a gift to friends over her objection; you will never sell a stool if she demurs; nor will you buy a toga without her nod. She will rearrange your friendships and lock the door on your oldest friends who have visited with you from youth. Panders, animal trainers, gladiators—all can draw up a will to suit themselves, but you will be cozened to name even your own rivals in yours.

"Crucify that slave!" screams your wife.

31

"But what capital offense has he done?" you ask. "Who reported the crime? Who are the witnesses? Can the wretched man not have a hearing at least when his life may be at forfeit?"

And she: "You brainless speck! How can you call this slave a man? How can you doubt his guilt? It is my word that condemns him. Let *my* will be done!"

Thus does she rule the home. But soon enough she will desert her monarchy for another, then another. She accumulates a new kingdom before the wedding decorations are removed from the old. Five autumns will see eight husbands, and this sorry log will be etched upon her tomb.

Abandon all hope of peace so long as your mother-in-law still breathes. She is the instructress of your wife's wanton ways. She advises how to gain control of the coffers, how to encourage a lover's long letters, how to bribe the household servants, how to employ a fashionable physician when all he will cure are pretended ills, and how to secrete a twitching seducer. Surely you cannot expect a mother to teach her daughter virtues she never possessed. No, turpitude breeds only turpitude. . . .

The marriage bed is no place for the weary husband to seek sleep, for there he will find only bickering. In that sacred place the shameless wife rails her spouse like a tigress bereft of her cubs. To conceal her own secret amours, she invents indiscretions of his and is quick to cry crocodile tears bemoaning a mythical mistress. These tears are always ready to well and the cuckolded husband to kiss them away, thinking them tears of true grief. Ah, the poor worm. If he rifled her desk, he would find letters to make a centurion blush. Should he surprise her in the arms of a slave or a soldier, he would tremble in terror before her tempestuous wrath, for no creature's impudence rivals hers, caught *in flagrante delicto*.

But you ask how these horrors can happen. The truth—the irony—is we have too long suffered peace. Soft luxury has set upon us, worse enemy than dozens Rome has earlier conquered. Once poverty was driven from Rome, no crime, no degeneracy was beneath our wilful indulgence. Ill-gotten gold ushered in foul foreign habits. Boredom from leisure and indulgence from corruption grew. Can Venus be modest when she staggers in drunkenness, gorges herself with odd foods at midnight, and guzzles all liquor she can discover—when the chamber swirls about her head, the furniture dances, and every object is twin? . . .

Even now I hear my old cronies suggest, "Lock the wench in!" But who can keep herd on the servants? The wife will simply begin with them. The barefoot tart treading the stones is no worse than her borne regally by eight thewy Syrians.

In order to visit the games, Ogulnia will hire all she could recklessly want—a costume, servants, a chair, cushions, female companions, a nurse, and a pretty messenger girl. Even after that, she, profligate still, hands out what is left of the household wealth to whichever callow athlete has pleased her. Many of these Ogulnias are hardly well off, but they ignore the restraints their poverty should dictate. Men often have sense for their dwindling riches; Aesop's ant has perhaps taught them to fear winter's cold and starvation. But not your Ogulnia. She never wastes a thought on what extravagance costs. . . .

Even though a wife who is musical can be a nuisance, what with her foolish frills and emotional indulgences, she is better for you than the social fly-about who lives from party to party and gossip to gossip. She will insinuate man's gatherings, daring even to thrust her firm face and unwomanly breast before uniformed generals—and with you embarrassed standing by. She will talk about anything—what the Chinese and Thracians are doing, what goes on between stepmother and stepson, who is lover to whom, which rake the Roman wives most lust after, who got which widow pregnant and when, how every wife acts with her lovers—why she can even write the words which pass between them! She takes note of the comet which threatens Armenian and Parthian kings; she transmits the latest rumors and even invents her own, such as news that the River Niphates has burst over its banks and rushes rampant across entire distant districts, toppling towns and innundating lands—this she broadcasts at every corner.

Just as insufferable is the virago who accosts her long-suffering neighbors and lashes them cruelly with her sharp whip despite innocent pleas for mercy. Should a dog's bark disturb her daily slumbers, she springs at her servants and barks her commands: "Quick with the whip; first to the mistress and then to the beast."

She is terrifying to the eyes, a harpy, a vulture. She waits until nightfall to visit the baths and stew in the steam and the oils and the sweat.

Exhausted from straining at the heavy weights, she bares her wet flanks to the massager's hands and revels under his intimate strokes until he announces the close of the session with a resounding slap on the top of her thigh. Her houseguests meantime, tired and hungry, tremblingly await her return. Finally she comes, face flushed from her labors, bringing thirst enough to drain dry with her dinner the three-gallon flask which is set before her, and from which at once she quaffs two pints to stir her evening's appetite. A moment more and she spews it all up again, drenching the floor with the bilge from her stomach. The rivulet races across marble flooring, and the golden basin reeks with wasted Falernian for she vomits like a viper trapped in a vat. The nauseated husband turns aside his eyes to keep his bile within.

But worse yet is the wife who, at the first mouthful of food, lauds the great Virgil, pardons dying Dido, and sets the poets one against the other, Virgil on the one scale and Homer counterbalanced. The grammarians, the rhetoricians, the whole multitude have become but audience. Neither lawyer nor auctioneer nor even another woman dares interject a remark. Her wordfall grows to such a racket one would swear all the pots and bells were being clanged together. Let no one anymore parade with cymbals and trumpets to free the eclipsed moon from a witch's spell—just loose one woman's torrential tongue.

She defines and moralizes like a tendentious philosopher. Desiring to be thought wise and eloquent, she would do better to wear a short tunic like a man, offer a slain pig to Sylvanus like a man, and plunge into the public penny bath with all the other men.

Never let your wife study history. Let her often encounter in her reading things she does not comprehend. That woman too is hateful who forever scans the grammar of Palaemon, who precisely observes all the foolish rules of language, who cites like a pedant lines you have never heard, who quickly corrects her barbaric female companions at the least slip from grammatic propriety such as no man would ever notice: let husbands be allowed at least a slip in grammar.

Whatever little modesty remains in modern woman evaporates when she clasps green emeralds about her neck and dangles heavy pearls from her long earlobes: nothing is more shameless than a wealthy wife. She puffs out her face with dough and offers a cheek reeking with unctuous oils to her husband's kiss. Her lover will caress fair soft skin, but never will her husband be so honored. All her sweet perfumes she will squander in sin, never in the marital embrace. Husband gone, she reveals her face in moist doughy degrees; layer after layer of pastry she peels stickily away, and then she bathes the residue in the precious milk of asses, a whole herd of which she would trundle with her had she to travel to the very Hyperborean pole. Husband home, she lays on such layers and salves and lumps one cannot tell if she makes up a face or medicates an ulceration.

It is instructive to know how these wives carry on during the day. If the husband has turned his back in sleep at night, woe to the woolmaid come morning. The dressing maids will have their gowns rudely ripped away. The Liburnian chair-man will be set upon for tardiness though he be on time, and will suffer for the husband's sleepiness. One servant will have a rod shattered on his back. Another will flow blood from the leather strap. A third will grow stripes from the cruel cat.

Some of these wives hire executioners a year at a time. As the lashes whistle, the wives will powder cheeks or chat with friends or examine the tailoring of gold embroidered gowns. As the whips fall and fall, the wives will slowly read the journals. Finally the floggers will slump exhausted. Only then will such women sharply order them away and the ordeal quitted.

The household of such a wench is governed as severely as the court of Phalaris the Sicilian tyrant. If she wishes to appear especially alluring for an early adultery in the garden or near the shrine of wanton Isis, the unfortunate maid who combs her hair will have her own tresses torn and tunic rent from back and bosom.

"Why does this curl stand up?" her mistress demands, and down flies the oxhide thong stinging innocent flesh because of one unruly ringlet. How is poor Psecas to blame? Would it be her fault too if the virulent wife liked not the slope of her own nose?

The regimen is so rigid that a maid is assigned to each side of her head. One maid who formerly served her mistress' mother, and spent many years as seamstress and wool-maid, oversees the preparations. To her is delegated the honor of voicing first opinions; then the other maids, each according to rank, utter an appropriate remark. You would think a grave matter of state, life, or honor were before the court, so serious is this passion for primping. . . .

And then there are the soothsayers. After observing the lungs of a fresh killed dove, an Armenian or Commagenian seer will promise a Roman woman a virile young lover or a large gift from a childless rich man. Such seers seek into the breast of a chicken or run slimy fingers through a puppy's intestines—or, sometimes it is said, even those of a boy. Every utterance of the astrologer is sacred to Roman women. All the better if he has been in exile or in a far off prison with heavy chains holding his arms. His prophecies are most believed if he has been condemned and the sentence all but executed.

Your esteemed wife now seeks to know when her own sickly mother's death will at last come, having already inquired as to yours. She asks when she may attend her sister's funeral, and her uncle's, and whether her lover will outlive herself. Of course, she does not understand how to read the heavens, how to know when gloomy Saturn threatens, nor under what conjunction Venus will smile favorably, nor how to discern the months of loss from the months of gain. Count your blessings if your wife does not profess knowledge of the Zodiac. Beware her whose hands clutch a well-thumbed calendar as if it were a ball of warm, sweet-scented amber, her who never consults but is always consulted, her who will not go to greet her long travelling husband home from the seas should the numbers of Thrasyllus the astrologer fall not propitious. She will first consult her charts to determine the correct hour if she wants to drive to the first mile-stone. If she finds an itch upon her eyelid, she will not salve it without reading her horoscope. If she is ill abed, she will eat at no hour unsuited to the forecasts of Petosiris, the seer of ancient Egypt. . . .

Your poor wife, however, does risk the perils of childbirth and all the woes of nursing to which her womanly lot condemns her. Yet how often does the gilded bed contain a woman lying in? The skill and drugs of the abortionist, murderer of life within the womb, are so great there never need be birth. Cheer up, my poor fellow; give her the killing drink yourself because, should her womb grow gravid, you might find yourself father to an Ethiopian. Then hence a time a Moorish heir whom you would never deign to meet by day shall write his name to every blank upon your will. . . .

If one charlatan supplies astrological lore to unbalance your life, a worse sells spells and Thessalian potions by which your wife may ruin your reason and lather your loins. Thence follows forgetfulness and all sense of what, yesterday, occupied your hours. Perhaps even that can be endured if you do not fall raving like Caligula, into whose wine Caesonia dropped an excrescence from the head of a newborn foal. What ordinary modern Roman wife could resist following where a very Empress leads. Caligula's potion set torch to the world and brought it tumbling to ruin no less than if Juno herself had made royal Jove insane. Why, less guilty then was Agrippina's deadly mushroom which released the palsied, slavering old Claudius from mortal weariness. . . .

So I warn you friends, all, you who have grown a good rich estate, beware for your lives. Trust not even one single dish. Warm breads are often dark with a mother's poison. That which is offered you by her mother, give first taste of to someone else. And always allow your frightened tutor first sip from every cup.

I wonder if you think this all a fancy fraud? Do you think Satire is strapping on the high boots of Tragedy? Do you think I have shunned propriety and chanted in Sophoclean grandeur tales unknown to the Rutulian hills and the skies of Latium? How I myself wish that I were so guilty! But listen to Pontia crying out her crimes: "I did it, I confess, I gave my own children poisonous aconite. The act is known, with my own hands I did it all!" "What!" she is asked, "did you, most vicious of vipers, slay two—two—at one unspeakable meal?"

"Yes," she screams back, "and seven, had there been seven to slay!"

We must believe what Tragedy tells of savage Medea, who fed Jason his own pitiable progeny; and of Procne whose hands served the flesh of Itys, their son, to Tereus, her woebegone husband. It cannot be denied; these women were wicked monsters of evil. The most cause that can be made for them is that they slew not for money. We are horror-struck less at terrible crimes when it is passion, lust, and anger that drives the woman to the deed, that plunges her headlong like a great stone down the mountain side when ground beneath and slopes around all give way. But when a woman commits a heinous crime, calculated in cold sobriety, the horror is intolerable.

Our Roman women may see enacted faithful Alcestis accepting her husband's dire fate. Yet, if they were granted the same chance, not one

37

of them would take it; instead, they would gladly swap a husband's life for a lapdog's. On every corner in Rome, you will meet a Belus, an Eriphyle, or a Clytemnestra—husband-slayers all. The only difference from those ancient monsters is this: Clytemnestra swung a brutal two-edged axe with her own arms, but today a cowardly, cunning bit of toad's lung serves the crime as well. Still beware, my friends. For even if you, Agamemnons all, secure yourselves like Mithridates by eating often of counter-toxins, then quite likely you shall know immortally the sharp knife's hot piercing steely farewell.

Geoffrey Chaucer
from
THE CANTERBURY TALES

The greatest writer of medieval England, Chaucer has con-structed in The Canterbury Tales *one of the most monu-mental satires in the history of western literature. It oper-ates on several levels, attacks a large number of targets, and employs numerous satiric techniques. There is first of all the symbolic journey from London, the city of man, to Canterbury, the city of God. The travellers are pilgrims, both laity and ecclesiastics. One of them is the pilgrim Chaucer, along to report the goings-on for Chaucer the poet. This device makes two levels of irony possible. The pilgrims have agreed at a London inn to tell stories to help pass time as they travel to and from Canterbury. They make a contest of it, the innkeeper agreeing to go along as host and judge of the storytelling. The innkeeper's judgments and management of the storytelling form another part of the satire. For example, he properly invites the Knight to speak first, but then allows the drunken, foul-mouthed Miller to insinuate himself into the second storytelling po-sition to tell a dirty story. This interruption brings in an-other satiric pattern. The Miller's story is about a carpenter; so the Reeve (formerly a carpenter) follows with an even dirtier story about a miller. Each tale, furthermore, betrays the character of its teller. This becomes a basic structural pattern throughout the rest of the tales. The Friar tells a satanic tale about a summoner, who in turn tells a revolting tale about a friar. The Wife of Bath tells a story intimating that a wise man always allows his wife the upper hand in marriage. Her Prologue revealed that she victimized five husbands, the last being a clerk. The Clerk aptly tells a tale completely reversing the Wife's position. In almost every*

*tale, the teller unwittingly reveals his own inner nature. Un-
fortunately the trip to Canterbury is never completed. The
party pauses on the outskirts of that city late in the afternoon of the third day of the pilgrimage to hear a very long,
pious sermon by the Parson. Not everyone has told a tale,
let alone the two tales going and two more returning which
had been agreed upon at the inn; so* The Canterbury Tales,
*lengthy as it is, remains a fragment. The modern reader may
find* The Canterbury Tales *a more enjoyable reading experience if he approaches it at first through a vital colloquial
prose translation like that of Robert M. Lumiansky, from
which we borrow here.*

THE PARDONER'S PROLOGUE AND TALE

*Perhaps the most despicable pilgrim on the journey is the
Pardoner, who sells his pardons in flagrant violation of
Church law and his position of trust. Worse yet, the Pardoner has massive intellectual vanity. He announces to the
gathering his precise* modus operandi; *then he proceeds to
try to get away with it. His tale itself is a moral* exemplum
*on the text "The love of money is the root of all evil." But
the moral tale is put to a perverted use. Ironically, the
Pardoner's foul game blows up in his face when he tries to
get the innkeeper-host, Harry Bailly, to buy his phony
relics. Bailly not only refuses, but threatens the Pardoner
physically. The Pardoner has singled out a relatively gullible, relatively unintelligent victim, only to be rebuffed and
publicly humiliated. Poetic justice. But Bailly's rebuff may
have been motivated for the wrong reasons—an even more
ironic twist for the highly intelligent, widely experienced,
unscrupulous Pardoner. The opening words of the Host are
his emotional reaction to the Physician's Tale in which a
young girl and her father, an unthinking, literal-minded
man, are horribly exploited. Notice when the Host asks the
Pardoner to tell the next tale what the immediate reaction
of the other pilgrims is.*

40

The words of the Host to the Physician and the Pardoner: Our Host started swearing as if he were crazy. "Help! By Christ's nails and blood," he said, "that was a false fellow and a false judge. May such judges and their witnesses find deaths as shameful as the heart can imagine! All the same, this poor virgin was killed, alas! She paid too dearly for her beauty! Therefore, I always say that you can see that gifts of Fortune and of Nature are the cause of death for many a creature. Her beauty was the death of her, I dare say. Alas, she was slain so piteously! From both these gifts I spoke of just now, people very often get more harm than profit.

"But truly, my own dear master, that was a sad tale to hear—nevertheless, let it pass, it doesn't matter. I pray God to save your noble body, and also your urinals and chamber-pots, your syrups and medicines, and also every box full of your remedies; God and our Lady St. Mary bless them! As I hope to prosper, you are a proper man, and like a prelate, by St. Ronyan! Didn't I say that well? I can't say the medical terms, but I do know that your story has so pierced my heart that I have almost caught a bad pain. By God's bones, unless I have some medicine or a draught of moist and malty ale, or else hear a merry story at once, my heart will break with pity for this poor maiden. You fine friend, you Pardoner," said he, "tell us some gay stories or jokes immediately."

"It shall be done," said the Pardoner, "by St. Ronyan! But first," he said, "I must have a drink and eat a cake here at this alehouse."

But at once the gentlefolk objected. "No, don't let him tell us any ribaldry! Tell us some moral thing so that we can be instructed, and then we shall be glad to listen."

"I agree, certainly," said the Pardoner. "But I must think up some honest piece while I drink."

Here follows the Prologue of the Pardoner's Tale: *Radix malorum est cupiditas*. "Ladies and gentlemen," he said, "when I preach in churches, I strive to have a haughty speech and ring out the words as round as a bell; for I know all that I say by heart. My text is always the same, and ever has been—Greed is the root of all evil.

"In the beginning I announce where I come from, and then I show my papal bulls, one and all. First I show our bishop's seal on my license to protect myself, so that no one, priest or cleric, will be so bold as to interrupt me as I do Christ's holy work. And after that I tell my tales. I show bulls of popes, cardinals, patriarchs, and bishops, and I speak a few words in Latin to flavor my preaching and to stir the congregation to devotion. Then I show my long glass cases, crammed full of rags and bones—they are relics, everybody thinks. Then I have a shoulder bone from a holy Jew's sheep set in metal. 'Good men,' I say, 'pay attention to my words: if this bone is dipped into any well, and if a cow, or calf, or sheep, or ox is swollen from eating a worm or from being stung by an insect, take some water from that well and wash his tongue; he will at once be cured. Furthermore, any sheep which takes a drink from that well will be cured of pox and scabs and of every other sore. Take heed of what I say: if the farmer who owns the livestock will take a drink from this well every week, after fasting, before the cock crows, just as this holy Jew taught our ancestors, his livestock and his goods will multiply. And, sirs, it also cures jealousy; for even if a man is in a jealous rage, let him make his soup with this water and he shall nevermore distrust his wife, though he knows it to be true that she has been so unfaithful as to have had two or three priests.

" 'Here is a mitten which you can also look at. The man who puts his hand into this mitten will see his grain multiply, after he has sown it, no matter whether it is oats or wheat, if he contributes pennies or else groats.

" 'Good men and women, I warn you about one thing: if there is any man now in this church who has done a horrible sin and who is afraid and ashamed to be shriven of it, or any woman old or young who has made her husband a cuckold—such folk shall have no power or grace to make an offering to my relics in this church. But if whoever finds himself free from such fault will come up and make an offering in the name of God, I shall absolve him by the authority which was granted to me by papal bull.'

"By this trick I have gained a hundred marks year after year since I became a pardoner. I stand in my pulpit like a cleric and, when the ignorant people have taken their seats, I preach as you have just heard and tell a hundred other false tales. Then I take pains to stretch my neck out and nod east and west over the congregation, like a dove sitting on a barn. My hands and tongue go so fast that it is a joy to see me at work. All my preaching is about avarice and similar sins, in order to make the people generous in contributing their pennies, especially to me. For my purpose is nothing but profit, and not at all the correction of sin. I don't care if their souls go wandering when they are buried! Certainly, many a sermon grows out of an evil purpose: sometimes to please and flatter folk, to get advancement by hypocrisy, and sometimes for vanity and sometimes for hatred. For when I am afraid to quarrel in other ways, then I sting a fellow so sharply with my tongue in preaching that he can't escape being falsely defamed, if he has been rude to my brethren or to me. Even though I don't call him by name, everyone knows by signs and other circumstances who it is I mean. Thus I get even with folk who mistreat us; in this fashion I spit out my venom in the guise of holiness, to appear holy and true.

"But I shall explain my purpose briefly. I preach for nothing but avarice; therefore, my theme is now and always was: *Radix malorum est cupiditas.* In this way I am able to preach against the same vice which I practice: avarice. Yet, though I am guilty of that sin myself, I can still make other folk turn away from it and bitterly repent. But that's not my main purpose; I preach only for avarice. That ought to be enough about this subject.

"Then I tell them many samples of old stories about ancient times. For ignorant people love old stories; they can easily remember and repeat such things. Why, do you think that I would willingly live in poverty as long as I can preach and win gold and silver by my teaching? No, no, I never really considered that! For I will preach and beg in various countries, but I will do no labor with my hands, or live by making baskets to keep from being an idle beggar. I will not copy any one of the apostles. I will have money, wool, cheese, and wheat, even though it's given to me by the poorest page or widow in a village, whose children will consequently starve. No, I'll drink liquor from the vine and have a jolly wench in every town. But listen, ladies and gentlemen, in conclusion; your desire is that I tell a story. Now that I have drunk a draught of malty ale, I hope, by God, that I can tell you something which you will like reasonably well. For, though I am a very vicious man myself, I can tell you a moral tale which I am accustomed to preach when I am working. Now hold your peace! I shall begin my tale."

Here begins the Pardoner's Tale: Once upon a time in Flanders there was a group of young people much given to dissipation, such as riotous living, gambling, and frequenting brothels and taverns, where they danced and played dice both night and day, to the music of harps, lutes, and guitars, and also ate and drank beyond their capacities. In this way they wickedly performed the devil's work within these devil's temples through abominable excesses. Their oaths were so great and so damnable that it was terrifying to hear them swear. They tore apart the body of our blessed Lord—it seemed to them that the Jews had not tortured him enough—and each of them laughed at the others' sins. And then small and shapely dancing girls would enter, and young girls selling fruit, singers with harps, bawds, and cake-sellers—all the confirmed agents of the devil—to kindle and blow the fire of lust that goes hand in hand with gluttony.

I take Holy Writ as my witness that licentiousness results from wine and drunkenness. Look how drunken Lot, against the laws of nature, slept with his two daughters without knowing it; he was so drunk that he did not know what he was doing. Herod, as anyone who reads the stories knows, when he was full of wine at his own feast, gave the order right at his own table for innocent John the Baptist to be slain. Seneca was without doubt correct when he said that he could see no difference between a man who is out of his mind and a man who is drunk, except that insanity, when it occurs in an ill-tempered man, lasts longer than drunkenness.

Oh, gluttony, filled with wickedness! Oh, first cause of our ruin! Oh, origin of our damnation, until Christ redeemed us with His blood! To come to the point, see how dearly this cursed wickedness was paid for! All this world was corrupted by gluttony. Our father Adam and also his wife were driven from Paradise to labor and suffer because of that sin. There is no doubt about that, for as long as Adam fasted he was in Paradise, so I read, but when he ate of the forbidden fruit on the tree, he was at once cast out into trouble and pain. Oh, gluttony, well should we complain of you! Oh, if a man only knew how many illnesses follow excess and gluttony, he would be more moderate in his diet at the table. Alas, the short throat and the tender mouth; they cause men—east, west, south and north—to labor hard in earth, air, and water to provide a glutton with his rare food and drink! Oh, Paul, you treated this subject well: "Meat for the belly and the belly for meat; God shall destroy both." So says Paul. Alas, it is an ugly thing, by my faith, to say these words but uglier is the deed, when a man so drinks of the white and red wines that he makes a privy of his throat through such wicked excess.

The Apostle, weeping, says movingly: "There are many of those people about whom I told you—I say it now weeping, with a piteous voice: they are enemies of the cross of Christ; their end is death; the belly is their God!" Oh, stomach! Oh, belly! Oh, stinking gut, filled with dung and corruption! From either end of you, foul noises come forth. How great is the labor and cost to feed you! How these cooks stamp and strain and grind to turn substance into accident in order to satisfy your gluttonous appetite! They knock the marrow out of the hard bones, for they throw away nothing which will slide softly and sweetly down the gullet. The glutton's sauce is made tasty by spices of leaves, bark, and roots, to give him still a keener appetite. But, truly, the man who makes a habit of such delicacies is dead even while he lives in those vices.

Wine is a lecherous thing, and drunkenness is full of strife and wretchedness. Oh, drunken man, your face is distorted, your breath is sour, you are a foul thing to embrace, and a sound seems to come from your drunken nose as if you kept repeating "Samson, Samson!" And yet, God knows, Samson never drank wine. You fall down like a stuck pig; your tongue is lost, and all your self-respect. For drunkenness is the true tomb of a man's wit and discretion. That man who is dominated by drink cannot keep a secret; that is sure. Therefore, hold yourself aloof from the white and the red, and especially from the white wine of Lepe, which is sold in Fish Street or in Cheapside. This Spanish wine is secretly blended with other wines in stock, and from it rise fumes so powerful that a man who takes three drinks, though he believes himself at home in Cheapside, finds he is in Spain at the town of Lepe—not at La Rochelle or Bordeaux. And then he will say, "Samson, Samson!"

But listen to one word, ladies and gentlemen, I beg you. All the great deeds and victories in the Old Testament, I swear, were accomplished through the true and omnipotent God by abstinence and prayer. Read the Bible, and you will learn this. Look at Attila, the great conqueror; he died shamefully and dishonorably in his sleep, bleeding steadily from the nose because of drunkenness. A military leader should live soberly. And more important still, consider very carefully what God commanded Lemuel—I mean Lemuel, not Samuel; read the Bible and see what is expressly stated about giving wine to those charged with the dispensation of justice. No more of this matter for that much should suffice.

Now that I have spoken of gluttony, I shall next forbid your gambling. Gambling is the true mother of lies, deceit, cursed perjury, blasphemy of Christ, and manslaughter, and also a waste of time and money. Furthermore, it is a reproof and a dishonor to be considered a common gambler. And, always, the higher the rank of the gambler, the more despicable is he considered. If a prince gambles, his governing and policy are held in low repute by general opinion. Stilbon, who was a wise ambassador, was sent from Sparta to Corinth, in great pomp, to make an alliance. And when he arrived, it happened by chance that he found all the highest officials of that land gambling. Therefore, as soon as possible, he stole home to his country, and said, "I will not lose my reputation there and so lay myself open to defamation as to ally you with gamblers. Send other wise ambassadors, for I swear that I had rather die than make an alliance for you with gamblers. For you who are so glorious in honor shall not be allied with gamblers by my efforts or treaties." So said this wise philosopher.

Observe also that the King of Parthia, as the book tells us, scornfully sent a pair of golden dice to King Demetrius because he was so accustomed to gamble; his glory or renown was utterly without value for him. Lords can find other kinds of games honest enough to pass the time.

I shall now speak a word or two in the manner of the old books about great and small oaths. Violent swearing is an abominable thing, and false swearing is even more to be reproved. The high God forbade all swearing—witness Matthew; but holy Jeremiah says this particularly about swearing: "You shall swear true oaths and not lie; swear discreetly and also righteously." But idle swearing is a sin. Observe that in the first table of the high God's illustrious commandments, the second of His commandments is: "Take not my name amiss or in vain." You see, He forbade such swearing ahead of homicide or many other cursed sins; I say it stands in that order. Be sure of this fact if you understand His commandments; that is the second commandment. Later I shall show you clearly that vengeance shall not leave the house of the man who is too outrageous in his swearing. "By God's precious heart," and "by His nails," and "by the blood of Christ that is at Hailes, seven is my number and yours is five and three!" "By God's arms, if you cheat, I will run this dagger through your heart!"—such is the fruit which comes from the two bitchy bones: swearing, anger, falsehood, homicide. Now, for the love of Christ who died for us, give up your oaths, both large and small. But now, sirs, I shall tell my tale.

These three rioters of whom I tell were seated in a tavern drinking, long before any bell rang for nine o'clock. And as they drank, they heard a bell toll before a corpse which was being carried to its grave. One of them called to his servant: "Boy, hurry and ask at once whose corpse it was that just passed by. And see that you get his name straight."

"Sir," replied the boy, "that's not at all necessary. I was told that two hours before you arrived. He was, by God, an old crony of yours, and last night he was suddenly killed as he sat straight up on his bench completely drunk. A stealthy thief, whom men call Death, who kills all the people in this country, came and cut his heart in two with a spear, and went away without a word. During this plague, he has slain a thousand. And, master, before you go into his presence, it seems to me that it will be necessary for you to be wary of such an opponent. Always be ready to meet him; my mother taught me that. I'll say no more."

"By St. Mary," said the tavern keeper, "the boy speaks true, for this year Death has slain the men, women, children, laborers and servants in a large village over a mile from here. I think he must live there. It would make great sense to be warned before he did you any harm."

"Yes, by God's arms!" said this rioter. "Is it so dangerous to meet him? I shall seek him out by roads and paths, I swear by God's worthy bones! Listen, friends, we three are of one mind; let's each of us give his hand to the other two, and each of us will become the other's brother. Then we shall slay this false traitor Death. He who has slain so many shall himself be slain, by God's worthiness, before night!"

These three pledged their faith together, each to live and die for the other two, as though they had been born brothers. And they jumped up in a drunken rage and went out towards the village which the tavern-keeper had told them about. And they swore many a horrible oath, completely tearing Christ's blessed body apart—Death shall be slain, if they can catch him!

When they had gone not quite half a mile, just as they were about to cross a fence, they met a poor old man. This old man greeted them very humbly and said, "Now, lords, God save you!"

The proudest of these three rioters replied, "Hey, bad luck to you, fellow! Why are you all covered up except for your face? Why have you lived so long and grown so old?"

The old man stared into his face and said: "Because I cannot find a man in any city or any village, though I walked to India, who wishes to change his youth for my age. And, therefore, I must continue to have my age for as long a time as it is God's will. Alas, not even Death will take my life. And so I walk about like a restless prisoner and knock both early and late with my stick upon the earth, which is my mother's door, saying, 'Dear mother, let me in; look how I shrink, flesh, skin, and blood! Alas, when shall my bones find rest? Mother, I will trade my strongbox, which for so long has been in my bedroom, for a hairshirt to wrap myself in!' Yet she will not do me that favor, and my face is therefore pale and wrinkled.

"But, sirs, it is discourteous of you to speak rudely to an old man, unless he does or says something wrong. You can read for yourselves in Holy Writ: 'You should rise before an old white-haired man.' Therefore, I shall give you some advice: do no harm now to an old man, any more than you would like people to do to you when you are old, if you live that long. And may God be with you, wherever you walk or ride! I must go where I have to go."

"No, old one, by God, you shall not go," the second gambler said at once. "You won't get off so lightly, by St. John! Just now you spoke of that same traitor Death, who kills all our friends in this country. Take my word, you are his spy; so tell where he is or you shall regret it, by God and by the holy sacrament! For, truly, you are in his plot to slay us young folk, you false thief!"

"Now, sirs," the old man answered, "if you are so eager to find Death, turn up this crooked path; for I left him in that wood, by my faith, under a tree. He will stay there; he won't conceal himself because of your boasting. You see that oak? You shall find him right there. May God, who redeemed mankind, save you and amend you!"

The old man spoke thus, and all the rioters ran until they reached the oak tree. And there they found what seemed to them almost eight bushels of fine round florins of coined gold. Then they looked for Death no longer. Each of them was so happy at the sight of the bright, shining florins that they sat down by this precious hoard. The worst of them spoke the first word.

"Brothers," he said; "listen to what I say. I have a great deal of sense, even though I joke and scoff. Fortune has given us this treasure so that we can live our lives in mirth and gaiety, and we shall spend it as easily as it came. Aye, God's precious worth! Who would have thought we should have such luck today? If we could only carry this gold from here home to my house or to yours—you realize, of course, that all this gold is ours—then we would have the highest happiness. Yet we really cannot do it by daylight. People would say that we were obviously highwaymen and would have us hanged because of our own treasure. This money must be transported by night, as carefully and quietly as possible. Therefore, I suggest that we draw straws among us and see where the cut falls. The one who draws the cut must willingly run into town as quickly as possible, and secretly bring bread and wine for us. Meanwhile, two of us will guard the treasure diligently, and, if he doesn't take too long, we shall be able at nightfall to carry the money wherever we agree is best."

He held the straws in his fist, and told the others to draw to see where the cut would fall. It fell to the youngest of the three, and he at once set out for town. But, as soon as he had left, one of the other two spoke to the second: "You know very well that you are my sworn brother; I shall now tell you something to your advantage. You see that our companion is gone, and this great heap of gold, which is to be divided among the three of us, is still here. But if I could so arrange matters that the gold would be divided between us two alone, would I not have done you a friendly turn?"

The second answered: "I don't see how that can be; he knows very well that the gold was left with the two of us. What shall we do? What shall we say to him?"

49

"Shall it be a secret?" asked the first scoundrel. "If so, I'll tell you in a few words what we can do to accomplish this."

"I agree not to betray you," said the second, "upon my word."

"Now," said the first, "you know that we are two, and the two of us are stronger than one. When he returns and sits down, you get up at once as if to tussle with him, and I will run him through the sides while you scuffle with him as if in sport, and you be sure to stab him with your dagger also. Then, all this gold, my dear friend, can be divided between you and me. Both of us will be able to fulfill all our desires and to play dice whenever we like." Thus these two scoundrels agreed to murder the third, as you have heard me say.

The youngest, who went into town, kept turning over in his mind the beauty of the bright new florins. "Oh, Lord!" he said, "if it only were possible for me to have all this treasure for myself alone, no man living under God's throne would live so merrily as I!"

And at last the devil, our enemy, put into his mind the idea of buying poison with which he could kill his two companions. For the fiend found his way of life such that he wished to bring him into trouble. The fellow's clear purpose was to kill both the others and never to repent. He went on into town, without any more loitering, to the shop of an apothecary, whom he begged to sell him some poison to kill his rats; there was a polecat in his yard, also, he said, which had killed his capons, and he was eager to get revenge, if possible, upon vermin which harassed him at night.

The apothecary answered, "You shall have such a mixture, God save my soul, that no creature in all this world who eats or drinks of it, even the equivalent of a grain of wheat, shall fail to die at once. Yes, he shall die in less time than it takes you to walk a mile, this poison is so strong and violent."

This wicked man grabbed up the box of poison and ran quickly to a man in the next street from whom he borrowed three large bottles. He poured his poison into two; the third he kept clean for his own drink; for he planned to work hard all night transporting the gold from its place. When this rioter—bad luck to him!—had filled his three large bottles with wine, he returned to his companions.

What need is there to make a longer sermon of this? They quickly killed him just as they had already planned, and, when that was done,

one said, "Now let's sit and drink and make merry. Afterwards we'll bury his body." It happened that with these words he took up a bottle in which there was poison, and drank, giving his friend a drink from the same bottle. As a result, both immediately died.

Truly, I doubt that Avicenna ever wrote a treatise or chapter in which there were more amazing symptoms of poisoning than these two wretches evidenced before they died. That was the end of these two murderers, as well as of the false poisoner.

Oh, cursed sin of all evil! Oh, treacherous murder, oh, wickedness! Oh, gluttony, luxury, and gambling! You blasphemer of Christ with vulgarity and large oaths, born of habit and pride! Alas, mankind, how can it be that you are so false and so unkind to your Creator, who made you and redeemed you with His precious heart's blood?

Now, good men, may God forgive you your trespasses and keep you from the sin of avarice! My holy pardon can cure you all, so long as you offer nobles, or silver pennies, or else silver brooches, spoons, or rings. Bow your head before this holy document! Come on up, you wives, offer some of your wool! I will at once enter your names here on my roll, and you shall go into the bliss of heaven. I absolve you by my great power—you who will offer—as clean and as white as you were born.—And there, ladies and gentlemen, that's the way I preach. And may Jesus Christ, who is our soul's physician, grant that you receive His pardon, for that is the best; I will not deceive you.

But, sirs, I forgot one word in my tale: I have relics and pardons in my bag, as fine as any man's in England, which were given to me by the Pope's own hand. If any of you wish, out of piety, to make an offering and to receive my absolution, come up at once, kneel down here, and humbly receive my pardon. Or else you can accept pardon as you travel, fresh and new at the end of every mile, just so you make another offering each time of nobles or pennies which are good and genuine. It is an honor to everyone here that you have available a pardoner with sufficient power to absolve you as you ride through the country, in case of accidents which might happen. Perhaps one or two of you will fall off your horses and break your necks. See what security it is to all of you that I happen to be in your group and can absolve you, both high and low, when the soul passes from the body. I suggest that our Host, here, shall be first; for he is most enveloped in sin. Come on, Sir Host, make the first offering right now, and you can kiss each one of the relics. Yes, for just a groat! Unbuckle your purse at once.

"No, no!" said the Host. "Then I would be under Christ's curse! Stop this, it won't do, as I hope to prosper! You would make me kiss your old breeches, and swear they were the relic of a saint, though they were foully stained by your bottom! But, by the cross that St. Helen found, I wish I had your testicles in my hand instead of relics or holy objects. Cut them off; I'll help you carry them. They shall be enshrined in hog's dung!"

The Pardoner answered not a word; he was so angry he would not say anything.

"Now," said our Host, "I will joke no longer with you or with any other angry man."

But at once the worthy Knight, when he saw everybody laughing, said, "No more of this; that's enough! Sir Pardoner, cheer up and be merry; and you, Sir Host, who are so dear to me, I beg you to kiss the Pardoner. And Pardoner, I pray you, come near. Let's laugh and play as we did before."

At once they kissed and rode ahead on their way. Here ends the Pardoner's Tale.

Erasmus
from
COLLOQUIES

Erasmus (1467?–1536) was a Dutch-born scholar and Christian reformer who, in his own day, was a center of controversy because of his religious views and his highly effective methods of attracting popular as well as scholarly attention. A monk at seventeen, he rebelled against the rigidities and constraints of the contemplative life and the unfit company he found in the monastery. Eventually he became ordained in the active priesthood in 1492. Later he studied in Paris, made the acquaintance of several prominent Englishmen, and journeyed to England three times. His famous Juvenalian satire, The Praise of Folly, *attacks abuses within the church and, in particular, the monastic life of the time. It was written while Erasmus was the guest of Sir Thomas More, Lord-Chancellor of England under Henry VIII. An archetype of the conservative satirist, he continually called for reform within the Church at the same time he opposed Luther's movement because it threatened church unity, which he felt too important to be destroyed. Erasmus not only edited many of the writings of the Church Fathers and did modern paraphrases of the New Testament, but he also made a famous translation of the New Testament from Greek into classical Latin. In his* Colloquia Familiaria, *he attacks war, social pretensions, excessive worldliness, church corruption, and, in general, the narrow-minded foolishness of mankind.*

MILITARY AFFAIRS

In this dialogue, Erasmus uses his characters to reveal the hollowness of military glory. Hanno was the name of a Carthagenian commander. Thrasymachus means "bold warrior" and is used, as you will see, ironically. This modernized version is by F. K.

HANNO   What are you doing back here looking like Vulcan when you left looking like Mercury?

THRASYMACHUS   Vulcan? Mercury? What are you talking about?

HANNO   You left with winged feet; now you return with a limp.

THRAS   That's the normal way to return from war.

HANNO   War? What's this about war? *You* at war? Why you're about as brave as a deer.

THRAS   I went for the money.

HANNO   You've come back rich?

THRAS   With an empty purse.

HANNO   At least you weren't burdened down for the trip home then.

THRAS   But I return burdened by sins.

HANNO   Well, *that* is a heavy burden if sins are lead as the prophet claims.

THRAS   In the short time I was gone, I sinned more and saw more evil than in my whole life before.

HANNO   What did you enjoy in the soldier's life?

THRAS   Nothing at all. It was terrible.

HANNO   Why do so many men seem to enjoy it then? I see them head off to war as happy as if they were on their way to a celebration.

THRAS   They are possessed, that's why. Satan is driving them to early damnation.

HANNO   That must be true because these men are not for hire for honest work. But tell me all about the battle.

THRAS   I can't. There was screaming and shouting, and trumpet calls, and people running, and horses galloping all over, and everything

54

was confusing. I don't know what happened. I don't even know where I was.

HANNO   Then why do most of these war veterans around town tell such fine tales? They describe everything exactly, even to what every person said. They seem more like observers than fighters, they know so well everything that went on.

THRAS   They're liars. I can tell you about the action inside my tent. That's the only action I could ever understand. As for the battle, who knows what happened?

HANNO   Do you remember how your leg got hurt?

THRAS   Well, not for sure. Maybe by a stone. Maybe by a horse's hoof.

HANNO   Bet I know.

THRAS   How? Someone tell you?

HANNO   No—just a guess.

THRAS   Guess then.

HANNO   You were so scared you panicked. Then you tripped running away and fell against a rock.

THRAS   Damn! That's right. That's just what happened.

HANNO   Oh—go on home and brag to your wife about your exploits.

THRAS   She'll kill me for coming back empty-handed.

HANNO   But what happened to the plunder? You must have gotten some.

THRAS   It's gone—all of it—long since.

HANNO   How? Who got it?

THRAS   Oh, whores, wine sellers, guys I gambled with.

HANNO   That's the old Army spirit! At least it went the same way it came. I hope you managed to stay away from sacrilege while you were off fighting.

THRAS   Wish I could say yes. But nothing is sacred in war; everything is plundered and destroyed.

HANNO   Now how will you ever make up for *that?*

THRAS   They told us everything was okay in war. They said in a war there was no sacrilege.

HANNO   The old "law of war," eh?

THRAS   Right.

HANNO   But you did not go to the war out of patriotism, but for money. How can that "law" apply to you?

55

THRAS   A good question. Still everyone I knew was there for the same reason.

HANNO   Are you proud of being insane like the rest of that multitude?

THRAS   A chaplain told us in church that it was a just war.

HANNO   Well, the church is seldom wrong. But maybe it was a just war for the prince yet *not* for you.

THRAS   The philosophers said each man has a right to follow his occupation.

HANNO   A lordly occupation—arson, sacrilege, rape, robbery, murder!

THRAS   It's okay for butchers to slaughter animals. What's wrong with soldiers killing men?

HANNO   Had you no fear that your soul could have been lost forever if you died out there?

THRAS   Nope. I prayed to St. Barbara, and she protected me.

HANNO   How did you know she would protect you?

THRAS   Well, she moved her head.

HANNO   When did this happen—in the clear air of morning?

THRAS   Well, no, at night, after supper.

HANNO   By that time I imagine everything was moving at least a little.

THRAS   You're uncanny! Really, I trusted St. Christopher. I studied his picture every day.

HANNO   In your tent? Where did you get a picture of St. Christopher?

THRAS   Well, we sketched one on the tent flap with charcoal.

HANNO   That charcoal Christopher must have been a great comfort. But seriously, I don't see how you can get absolution unless you make a pilgrimage to Rome.

THRAS   I know a way.

HANNO   What way?

THRAS   I'll visit the Dominicans and make a deal with one of the friars.

HANNO   For sacrileges?

THRAS   They can forgive you for robbing Christ himself. Why if I'd cut off Christ's head, they could even grant an indulgence for *that*. They really have authority.

HANNO   Go to it then. I just hope God accepts their absolutions.

THRAS   I expect more of a problem from Satan. God is pretty forgiving.

HANNO   How do you know which priest to approach?

THRAS   Oh, I'll pick the freest wheeler-dealer around.

HANNO   Well, it takes one to know one. If he gives you absolution, I suppose you'll head directly to Holy Communion?

THRAS   Naturally. All my sins will have flown off into his hood. Then I'll really be unburdened. Once he gives me absolution, the sins are his problem.

HANNO   How will you know if you are absolved?

THRAS   Oh, I'll know all right.

HANNO   But how?

THRAS   When he puts his hand on my head and mutters something, I'm absolved.

HANNO   Suppose when he puts his hand on your head, he mutters the wrong thing? He could give you back all your confessed sins. Suppose he says "I absolve you of all your *good* deeds, which I could not find anyway, and I restore to you your soul just as you presented it to me"?

THRAS   That's *his* problem. If I *think* I'm absolved, I'm absolved.

HANNO   That is a dangerous belief. You may not have God's absolution, which is what really counts.

THRAS   Why am I standing here talking with you? You confuse my conscience.

HANNO   A good thing for you if a friend tries to warn you.

THRAS   I'm not so sure. I don't like it. You confuse me.

THE IGNOBLE KNIGHT

Erasmus here exposes Harpalus (whose name means "grasping" or "greedy") for the rascal he is, or rather wants to be. In doing so, he ridicules all who pretend to be more than they honestly are in this world. This modern version is by F. K.

HARPALUS   I need your advice. I won't forget it if you help me.

NESTOR   All right, I'll try to help you get ahead.

HARP   If only we could be born nobles.

NEST   That's idle talk. We can always try to live well enough to be given noble rank, which can be passed on to our children.

HARP   But that would take forever!

NEST   Well, you can always *buy* a title, you know. Princes are always looking for money.

HARP   But titles like that are always ridiculed.

NEST   Then why are you so anxious to gain the title of knight?

HARP   I'll tell you why in private if only you'll show me how to act like a knight in public.

NEST   You want to be an imposter?

HARP   When you can't have the real thing, you try to maintain a certain image. But let's go, Nestor, I need your help. When you know my reasons, you'll see why I'm in such a hurry.

NEST   Well, since you feel so strongly, I'll do my best. Now first of all, get away from here; go where you're not known.

HARP   I'm listening.

NEST   Find some young swingers who are real noblemen, who have real titles. Get accepted into their company.

HARP   I'm still listening.

NEST   Once you do that, people will associate you with your noble friends.

HARP   Yes, yes, I see.

NEST   Don't give yourself away; don't look cheap.

HARP   What?

NEST   Watch how you dress. No wool clothes. Wear silk if you can. If that's too expensive, wear good heavy cotton or linen. Never patch your clothes, even if it means wearing rough canvas.

HARP   I've got it.

NEST   Always have a cavalier tear in your garments—a hole in the cap, a rip in the doublet, a slash in the trousers, a nick in the boots— you know. Keep your conversation elegant and elevated. If a Spaniard joins the group, ask him how things are with the Emperor and the Pope, how your cousin Count Nassau is, and what your other royal friends (make them up) are doing.

HARP   Good, good.

NEST   Wear a small, tasteful ring, preferably a signet.

58

HARP   If I can afford one.
NEST   Oh, fake one. Get a brass ring and pay to have it gilded, then put in some colored glass that looks like a real gem. And be sure to have a shield, complete with your coat-of-arms.
HARP   What shall I use?
NEST   For you—two milk pails and a beer stein.
HARP   Cut it out. Be serious.
NEST   Have you ever been to war?
HARP   Never even seen a battle.
NEST   At least you've cut the throats of a few geese and chickens?
HARP   Oh yes, and like a professional.
NEST   Then use a silver knife and three gold geese.
HARP   On what color field?
NEST   Gules, of course, for all the blood you've spilled.
HARP   Well it was just as red as real blood. Keep talking.
NEST   Every time you stop at an inn, be sure the shield is hung outside.
HARP   What about a helmet?
NEST   Glad you remembered. Have it made with a slit across the mouth.
HARP   Why?
NEST   Well for one thing—to breathe. It will also go well with the slits in your clothing. Do you know what should go on top of your helmet, to complete things?
HARP   Tell me, tell me.
NEST   A dog's head—with long ears.
HARP   I've seen *several* like that.
NEST   Then add horns. You haven't seen several like *that*.
HARP   Good. What about animals for the shield though?
NEST   Better not use stags or hunting hounds, or dragons or griffins— they're the property of the real nobility. Why don't you try two *harp*ies on your shield?
HARP   Great! *Harp*ies!
NEST   Now about your name. That must be carefully chosen. "Harpalus Comensis is too vulgar; it sounds like a begging friar. But "Harpalus von Como"—now *there's* a name fit for nobility.
HARP   I'll remember.

NEST Do you own anything at all?

HARP Not even a pig-sty.

NEST Are you from a good-sized city?

HARP A little hamlet. I can't lie to you; you're my advisor.

NEST True. Tell me, is there a mountain near your hamlet?

HARP Yes.

NEST Has it a big rock anywhere?

HARP Yes, a big steep one.

NEST There it is! You are now "Harpalus, Knight of the Golden Rock."

HARP One more thing. Knights need a motto don't they? Maximilian used "Follow the Golden Mean," and Philip used "He Who Wills," and Charles used "Further Still." What do you think?

NEST I think you could appropriately use "Play Every Card."

HARP Terrific!

NEST Now to other strategems. To help convince the townspeople, you must forge letters or pretend you've received news from persons of high estate. Let the letters be addressed "Most Illustrious Sir" or something like that. Let them mention important events, fiefdoms, great castles, wealth, positions, a profitable marriage. Be sure the letters reach you indirectly so people will know of them. Better still, "lose" them or leave them behind as you move around so they will be discovered "by chance." Gossip will do the rest.

HARP That's easy enough. I can write well, and I can copy anybody else's writing.

NEST Try leaving the letters in your clothes or purse when you go to a tailor shop for mending. The tailors will quickly spread the news. Of course, then you pretend to be offended, as if a confidence had been broken.

HARP That's easy too. I'm a great faker.

NEST Be sure you don't give away the trick. Don't overdo it. If the story spreads naturally through gossip, everyone will believe it.

HARP Okay, I'll do it that way.

NEST The next thing you need is someone to act like your servant. In fact, hire a servant if you can. You'll find there are plenty of boys around willing to do this sort of thing. Right here you can find lots of young, would-be authors who will do your writing for you. And there are plenty of starving printers too. One of them will agree to do a news pamphlet announcing you as a great nobleman, probably in capitals. Pamphlets get around, so this source of advertising may be even better than word of mouth or servant's gossip.

HARP   Good idea. But how do I pay a servant?

NEST   Make *him* turn up profitable enterprises for *you*. Get several candidates, in fact, for the honor of serving you. Send them out to prove their worth. If they lose their hands in the process, then they're useless as servants. If they don't, you profit as well.

HARP   I get it.

NEST   And you'll need certain—skills.

HARP   Better tell me about them.

NEST   You'll need to be good with dice, sharp at cards, a known skirt-chaser, a big drinker, a wild spender, a prodigal, one step out of debtor's prison, and marked by venereal pox if you expect to pass for a knight.

HARP   I, I qualify! But I still don't know how I'm going to get along with no bankroll.

NEST   I'm getting to that. Have you any kind of inheritance?

HARP   Not enough to even buy a horse with.

NEST   Well, then concentrate on selling your image. Once people believe you're a knight, they'll begin to trust you. In fact, some of them will be afraid *not* to give you credit. Dodging your creditors later on may prove simpler than you think.

HARP   Oh, I've dodged a few creditors in my day. But what I fear is when they find out I *really* have no money.

NEST   Now think a minute. One of the best ways to rise in society is to owe money to almost everybody.

HARP   What?

NEST   A creditor, first of all, treats you courteously, almost fawningly. He has an investment in you and wants no harm to come to it. Just give him a payment now and then, and he'll be as happy as if you gave him a birthday present.

HARP   Say, I've noticed that too.

NEST   But stay away from poor men or little merchants. They make a big to-do over nothing. The wealthier cause fewer problems. They are ashamed to press you; they always hope to get their money from you; they fear your anger, for after all everyone knows what a terrifying enemy an angry knight makes. Finally, when you are so far in debt there is no way out, then just pick up and move to another city. Keep moving like that whenever you have to. At each new place, you can work the same tricks again. There are no men in the world so deeply in debt as dukes and princes. If anyone presses you too hard, simply pretend you are insulted and shun the fellow. Pay something to *another* debtor and praise him for not being insultful to one of your rank. Just never pay anyone in full, and never pay something to all your debtors at once. Keep up appearances all the while; never let anyone suspect you have no money.

HARP How do I keep up appearances when I have no money?

NEST Well, if someone has left something for you to look after, pretend it is yours. Borrow money now and then, and repay it quickly and with ceremony. Pay out of a fat purse stuffed with brass coins. Keep a gold coin or two on top. Surely you can invent other such tricks?

HARP Probably. But eventually I've got to be ruined.

NEST Oh, I don't think so—not the way we pamper knights these days.

HARP That's right. They get away with murder.

NEST Never keep a lazy or cowardly servant. And never keep one who is a relative. Those kind always need to be supported; they never pay their own way. Alert your servants to watch for merchants who can be held up and traders who can be robbed. Keep them on the watch for goods lying around in inns and homes, on wagons and ships. Let them know why man is equipped with fingers.

HARP But I don't want them getting caught.

NEST You are *not* thinking like a knight. If they are well dressed and carrying letters—forged of course—to ranking nobility, no one is seriously going to accuse them of stealing for fear of bringing down your wrath. Now if they take anything by force, you can laugh it off by saying they are just training for battle.

HARP You're great! What advice!

NEST There is one fundamental principle of knighthood which you must now understand and master. For a knight to unburden a traveler of his funds is an almost sacred duty. It rebalances the chain of being. It is clearly wrong, you see, for a knight to be insufficiently funded while a mere trader or merchant is unduly fortified in that area. A knight must have his funds to gamble and gambol, if you follow me. And again, remember to insinuate yourself among the noble and wealthy wherever you go. Good places in each town are the finest inns and the reputable baths.

HARP I've thought of going to those places.

NEST But remember your business—you may often find a favorable business condition in such places.

HARP How is that?

NEST Now and then someone forgets his purse there or leaves his keys behind him—do I have to say more?

HARP Now wait—

NEST Will you ever get over your peasant cowardices? Who is going to question a man of your stature, of your speech, conduct, and bearing, you, the Knight of the Golden Rock? Even if there is anyone with the bad taste to question you, who will ever make the concrete accusation? The first suspicion will always fall upon someone innocent, like a guest at the inn who left the day before or that morning. You can always have your servants create a disturbance in the baths or start to fight with the innkeeper. You, of course, remain the soul of dignity, even magnanimously stepping in to calm your righteously indignant, loyal minions. If a shy, decent man has been your victim, he will not raise much fuss. He probably does not want to appear foolish for having left his valuables unguarded, so he will accept his loss.

HARP You're a genius! Have you heard of the Count of the White Vulture?

NEST Naturally.

HARP Well, I heard a good story about him, about how he had a Spanish "nobleman" as guest, and how this Spaniard stole 600 florins, and how the Count never said a word because the Spaniard was supposed to be so noble.

NEST Exactly! Now another useful scheme is to send one of your servants off to war areas now and then, with instructions to loot whatever churches and monasteries he finds along the way.

HARP That seems safe enough.

NEST   There is another way to obtain money that I could tell you.

HARP   Tell me! Tell me!

NEST   Find some excuse to quarrel with those who have money. Monks and friars are especially good targets right now; everyone is jealous of them. Say that one of them ridiculed your coat of arms or even spat on it. Say that one of them insulted your person. Say that one of them wrote ill of you in a letter. Don't confront them directly, but through an emissary broadcast your grievance. Let threats fly all about the countryside. Rant about war, destruction, even executions. Sooner or later, they will beg for a settlement. Then you ask, again indirectly and with high dudgeon, for an astronomical figure as the price of your dignity. If you hint that you will settle for 3000 guilders, they will be ashamed and afraid to offer less than 200.

HARP   Good, good. After that I will threaten to sue others in the courts, eh? What do you think about that?

NEST   Well, really, that is beneath your station—to use the established legal system. But wait, Harpalus, with all this other talk, I have almost forgotten to advise you of perhaps the most basic step an aspirant to the knighthood must take. You must seek out and woo a girl with a substantial dowry. On the surface, you have certain attractions. You are young, free, not bad looking, and you have a, shall we say, relatively uncomplicated mind and character. Let the word go around that you have actually been received at the Emperor's Court. With those qualities, you will be irresistible to the right kind of women.

HARP   Yes, I know one or two who have married like you say. But what if something goes wrong? What if the creditors gang up on me? Worse yet, what if some knights find out I'm not really a knight? That's a worse crime than looting a church—at least the knights think it is.

NEST   Will you never have any boldness? Without arrogance you will never rise in the world. Just look around. If you are not totally blind, you can see that sheer haughtiness and rank gall are everywhere taken for noble character and true wisdom. If ever a question comes up, you simply must have a story ready. Half the people will believe you right away, especially the socially conscious ones, because they exist by perpetual self-delusion. Many of the real nobility will be too "proper" to admit your story is a hoax. And if things really look dark, you simply invent a war to which you have suddenly been called away. Wars forgive everything. But that is only a last resort. Stay alert. Don't go to small towns where your every fart echoes throughout all the best circles. In the great cities you have room to operate. Always keep your ears open to what people are gossiping about you. When they begin to wonder why you have been around so long, why you seem to be staying away from your own country, why you are neglecting your great estates, and when they begin to look into your noble lineage and the source of your wealth—*then* you had better think about moving on. But of course you must move on with great clamor and ado like the lion you are. Announce that the Emperor himself has sent for you, that you must be off soon with the army on a vital campaign. No one will dare bother you under such circumstances especially not merely to collect a little money you may owe them. I suppose your real enemies could be the local poets; they often let their pens speak for them, as many a ruined man has learned. So keep them happy.

HARP You know, you give the best damned advice there is! Now I'll show you've had a good student and a grateful one. You know what I'm going to do? The first good horse I find grazing I'll send back to you for you to keep.

NEST How noble. But you made me a promise at the start which I have not forgotten, and I would like to collect while you are still here. Tell me, what is it that so attracts you to the knighthood?

HARP Well, mainly that they do what they damn well feel like and get away with it! Now doesn't that seem worth it to you?

NEST Ah, I see. Well, in the end I suppose the worst is simply that you owe the world one death. Even the monks in the great Carthusian Monastery must pay *that* debt. And those men executed upon the wheel really have an easier death than more honest men who die in agony—"naturally" as they say—from any of a thousand different accidents and diseases. For the true knight today, nothing survives a man except his corpse, and that only for a little while.

HARP There you are—exactly. That's it! That's life. Right?

Thomas Watson
PASSION

During the Renaissance a gentleman with literary abilities or pretensions was almost obliged to write a sonnet sequence, perhaps a hundred or more poems, which autobiographically narrated his forlorn love for a cold, distant, and unbelievably beautiful mistress. The lady, according to convention, could be described best in metaphor; the more ingenious, the higher the compliment. Thomas Watson published such a series, Passionate Century of Love *(1582), from which the example here is the seventh with the same title. Shakespeare was too great a poet, too much his own man, to accept the traditional comparisons. In his sonnet he ridicules outrageous language, reveals the depth of his love which sees his lady as she is, and pays her the highest compliment of honest admiration. Thus, his satire restores the balance.*

Hark you that list [1] to hear what saint I serve:
Her yellow locks exceed the beaten gold;
Her sparkling eyes in heav'n a place deserve;
Her forehead high and fair of comely mold;
    Her words are music all of silver sound;
    Her wit so sharp as like can scarce be found:
Each eyebrow hangs like *Iris* [2] in the skies;
Her *Eagle's* nose is straight of stately frame;
On either cheek a *Rose* and *Lily* lies;
Her breath is sweet perfume, or holy flame;
    Her lips more red than any *Coral* stone;

[1] Wish.
[2] Goddess of the rainbow.

66

Her neck more white, than aged *Swans* that moan;
Her breast transparent is, like *Crystal* rock;
Her fingers long, fit for *Apollo's* [3] Lute;
Her slipper such as *Momus* [4] dare not mock;
Her virtues all so great as make me mute:
What other parts she hath I need not say,
Whose face alone is cause of my decay.

[3] The God of music and poetry.
[4] The God of criticism and mockery.

William Shakespeare
SONNET 130

My mistress' eyes are nothing like the sun,
Coral is far more red than her lips red,
If snow be white, why then her breasts are dun:
If hairs be wires,[1] black wires grow on her head:
I have seen roses damasked,[2] red and white,
But no such roses see I in her cheeks,
And in some perfumes is there more delight,
Than in the breath that from my mistress reeks.[3]
I love to hear her speak, yet well I know,
That music hath a far more pleasing sound:
I grant I never saw a goddess go,[4]
My mistress when she walks treads on the ground.
    And yet by heaven I think my love as rare,
    As any she [5] belied with false compare.[6]

[1] One sonnet convention was to compare the lady's hair to fine wire drawn from precious metal.
[2] Richly colored; patterned.
[3] Is exhaled; without the modern connotation of odor.
[4] Walk; move.
[5] Woman.
[6] Misrepresented or deceived by false comparison.

Christopher Marlowe
A PASSIONATE SHEPHERD
TO HIS LOVE

Christopher Marlowe (1564–1593) is important primarily for the drama; his Tragical History of Dr. Faustus *was one of the most popular of Elizabethan plays. But this poem, too, was extremely popular, for it had exquisite music, and in its romantic pastoralism it speaks of a happy, peaceful world that never was. The replies of Sir Walter Ralegh (1552?–1618) and John Donne (1572–1631) show what happens to the pastoral theme in the hands of a realist or of a uniquely individual poet. Ralegh ridicules the concept; Donne transforms it.*

Come live with me and be my Love,
And we will all the pleasures prove [1]
That hills and valleys, dales and fields,
Or woods or steepy mountain yields.

And we will sit upon the rocks
And see the shepherds feed their flocks
By shallow rivers, to whose falls
Melodious birds sing madrigals.

And I will make thee beds of roses
And a thousand fragrant posies;
A cap of flowers, and a kirtle [2]
Embroidered all with leaves of myrtle; [3]

[1] Test; try.
[2] Skirt; gown.
[3] An evergreen shrub sacred to Venus and thus a symbol of love.

A gown made of the finest wool
Which from our pretty lambs we pull;
Fair-linéd slippers for the cold,
With buckles of the purest gold;

A belt of straw and ivy buds
With coral clasps and amber studs—
And if these pleasures may thee move,
Come live with me and be my Love.

The shepherd swains shall dance and sing
For thy delight each May morning—
If these delights thy mind may move,
Then live with me and be my Love.

Sir Walter Ralegh
THE NYMPH'S REPLY TO
THE SHEPHERD

If all the world and love were young,
And truth in every shepherd's tongue,
These pretty pleasures might me move,
To live with thee and be thy love.

But time drives flocks from field to fold,
When rivers rage, and rocks grow cold;
And Philomel [1] becometh dumb;
The rest complains of cares to come.

The flowers do fade, and wanton fields
To wayward Winter reckoning yields;
A honey tongue, a heart of gall,
Is fancy's spring, but sorrow's fall.

Thy gowns, thy shoes, thy beds of roses,
Thy cap, thy kirtle, and thy posies,
Soon break, soon wither, soon forgotten,
In folly ripe, in reason rotten.

Thy belt of straw and ivy buds,
Thy coral clasps and amber studs,
All these in me no means can move,
To come to thee and be thy love.

But could youth last, and love still breed,
Had joys no date, nor age no need,
Then these delights my mind might move,
To live with thee and be thy love.

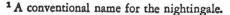

[1] A conventional name for the nightingale.

71

John Donne
THE BAIT

Come live with me, and be my love,
And we will some new pleasures prove,
Of golden sands, and crystal brooks,
With silken lines, and silver hooks.

There will the river whispering run,
Warmed by thy eyes more than the sun,
And there the enamored fish will stay,
Begging themselves they may betray.

When thou wilt swim in that live bath,
Each fish, which every channel hath,
Will amorously to thee swim,
Gladder to catch thee, than thou him.

If thou, to be so seen, beest loth,
By sun or moon, thou darkenest both;
And if myself have leave to see,
I need not their light, having thee.

Let others freeze with angling reeds,
And cut their legs with shells and weeds,
Or treacherously poor fish beset
With strangling snare, or windowy net.

Let coarse bold hands from slimy nest
The bedded fish in banks out-wrest,
Or curious traitors, sleave-silk [1] flies,
Bewitch poor fishes' wand'ring eyes.

[1] Silk filament.

For thee, thou need'st no such deceit,
For thou thyself art thine own bait;
The fish that is not catched thereby,
Alas, is wiser far than I.

John Donne
EPIGRAMS and THE WILL

*John Donne (1572–1631), son of a wealthy London iron-
monger, was educated at Oxford and Cambridge, but did
not take a degree, probably because of his family's Catholi-
cism. Although appointed secretary to Sir Thomas Egerton,
Lord Keeper of the Great Seal, he offended his superior by
marrying Lady Egerton's niece. Following his marriage, his
poetry changed from one of gaiety, cynicism, and scorn of
woman's constancy to one of deeply felt, fully realized love.
In 1615 he took orders in the Anglican church and by 1621
was made Dean of St. Paul's, where his preaching became
famous for its eloquence. His metaphysical poetry with its
colloquial language and witty conceits has long interested
readers. In the past forty years, modern readers have been
attracted by its dramatic intensity and its powerful, sometimes desperate, individuality.*

*Donne's satiric epigrams, like those of most Renaissance
writers, derive from Martial in their tone and breadth of
subject. "The Will" can be viewed in one light as a unified
series of epigrams, for it satirizes by paradox a wide variety
of people and practices. But in its overall conception there
seems to us a more deadly seriousness.*

EPIGRAMS

A LAME BEGGAR

I am unable, yonder beggar cries,
To stand, or move; if he say true, hee lies.

A SELF ACCUSER

Your mistriss, that you follow whores, still takes you:
'Tis strange that she should thus confess it, though it be true.

A LICENTIOUS PERSON

Thy sinnes and haires may no man equall call,
For, as thy sinnes increase, thy haires do fall.

ANTIQUARY

If in his Study he has so much care
To hang all old strange things, let his wife beware.

KLOCKIUS

Klockius so deeply has sworn, ne'er more to come
In bawdie house, that he dares not go home.

THE WILL

Before I sigh my last gasp, let me breathe,
Great love, some Legacies; Here I bequeath
Mine eyes to *Argus*,[1] if mine eyes can see,
If they be blind, then Love, I give them thee;
My tongue to Fame; to 'Ambassadors mine ears;
　　To women or the sea, my tears.
Thou, Love, hast taught me heretofore
By making me serve her who 'had twenty more,
That I should give to none, but such, as had too much before.

My constancy I to the planets give;
My truth to them, who at the Court do live;

[1] *Argus:* called "the all seeing" because he had a hundred eyes.

75

Mine ingenuity and openness,
To Jesuits; to Buffoons my pensiveness;
My silence to 'any, who abroad hath been;
    My money to a Capuchin.[2]
Thou Love taught'st me, by appointing me
To love there, where no love receiv'd can be,
Only to give to such as have an incapacity.

My faith I give to Roman Catholics;
All my good works unto the Schismatics
Of Amsterdam; my best civility
And Courtship, to an University;
My modesty I give to soldiers bare;
    My patience let gamesters share.
Thou Love taughtst mee, by making mee
Love her that holds my love disparity,
Only to give to those that count my gifts indignity.

I give my reputation to those
Which were my friends; Mine industry to foes;
To Schoolmen [3] I bequeath my doubtfulness;
My sickness to Physicians, or excess;
To Nature, all that I in Ryme have writ;
    And to my company my wit.
Thou Love, by making me adore
Her, who begot this love in mee before,
Taughtst me to make, as though I gave, when I did but restore.

To him for whom the passing bell next tolls,
I give my physic [4] books; my written rolls
Of Moral counsels, I to Bedlam [5] give;
My brazen medals, unto them which live

---

[2] *Capuchin:* who takes vows of poverty.
[3] *Schoolmen:* educated theologians who argue with unquestioning certainty.
[4] *physic:* medicine.
[5] *Bedlam:* Bethlehem, a hospital for the insane in southeast London.

In want of bread; To them which passe among
All foreigners, mine English tongue.
Thou, Love, by making me love one
Who thinks her friendship a fit portion
For younger lovers, dost my gifts thus disproportion.

Therefore I'll give no more; But I'll undo
The world by dying; because love dies too.
Then all your beauties will be no more worth
Than gold in Mines, where none doth draw it forth;
And all your graces no more use shall have
Than a Sun dial in a grave.
Thou Love taughtst me, by making me
Love her, who doth neglect both me and thee,
To 'invent, and practise this one way, to 'annihilate all three.

Sir Thomas Overbury and John Earle
CHARACTERS

The Athenian Theophrastus of the third century B.C. *is generally credited with writing the first "characters," short prose sketches of personages who exemplify some particular quality. Like caricatures in drawing, characters exaggerate one feature. The result is a generalized sketch of a "character type" or of a particular virtue or vice, like the meddlesome gossip, the storytelling old soldier, the loyal Tory, the effusive freshman coed, or the bumbling bureaucrat. Character writing grew in England and France, largely in the seventeenth century, following the translation in 1592 of the sketches of Theophrastus. Bishop Joseph Hall's* Characters of Virtues and Vices *(1608) is the first large-scale English character-book. Overbury's characters were collected and published in 1614, a year after his mysterious death in the Tower of London in a still unexplained scandal involving many of the English nobility. Earle's are more subtle and more satiric, revealing a deeper perception of human motivation. They were published in 1628 in a work called* Microcosmographie. *Later La Bruyère in France and Addison, Steele, and Pope in England refined the character, which today is normally found in the serious essay. See Pope's portrait of Atticus, Dwight's sketch of a "modern" minister, Mencken's "The Hills of Zion," Chapter XIV of Babbitt, and Meehan's sketch of a modern motion picture executive for other examples of the character in this Reader.*

Sir Thomas Overbury
A PURITAN

Is a diseased piece of Apocrypha; bind him to the Bible, and he corrupts the whole text; ignorance and fat feed are his founders; his

78

nurses, railing, rabies, and round breeches; his life is but a borrowed blast of wind; for between two religions, as between two doors, he is ever whistling. Truly whose child he is is yet unknown; for willingly his faith allows no father; only thus far his pedigree is found, Bragget [1] and he flourished about a time first; his fiery zeal keeps him continually costive, which withers him into his own translation, and till he eat a Schoolman,[2] he is hide-bound; [3] he ever prays against non-residents, but is himself the greatest discontinuer,[4] for he never keeps near his text; anything that the law allows, but marriage and March beer,[5] he murmurs at; what it disallows and holds dangerous, makes him a discipline; [6] where the gate stands open, he is ever seeking a stile; and where his learning ought to climb, he creeps through; give him advice, you run into traditions, and urge a modest course, he cries out councils. His greatest care is to condemn obedience, his last care to serve God handsomely and cleanly. He is now become so cross a kind of teaching that should the church enjoin clean shirts, he were lousy; more sense than single prayers is not his; nor more in those than still the same petitions; from which he either fears a learned faith, or doubts God understands not at first hearing. Show him a ring,[7] he runs back like a bear; and hates square dealing as allied to caps; a pair of organs blow him out o' th' parish, and are the only clyster-pipes [8] to cool him. Where the meat is best there he confutes most, for his arguing is but the efficacy of his eating; good bits he holds breed good positions, and the Pope he best concludes against in plum-broth.[9] He is often drunk, but not as we are, temporally, nor can his sleep then cure him, for the fumes of his ambition make his

[1] *Bragget:* malt liquor.

[2] *Schoolman:* a preacher educated at Oxford or Cambridge.

[3] *hide-bound:* intractable.

[4] *discontinuer:* absentee; the reference is to priests who fill two or more pulpits to the neglect of one.

[5] *March beer:* strong beer, brewed in March; Puritans were often caricatured as drunkards.

[6] *discipline:* his own belief rather than church doctrines.

[7] *ring:* marriage ring; one of the earthly vanities condemned by Puritans.

[8] *clyster-pipes:* pipes by which a cooling enema was administered.

[9] *plum-broth:* a favorite Christmas dish, although the Puritans rejected the celebration of the holiday.

very soul reel, and that small beer that should allay [10] him keeps him more surfeited, and makes his heat break out in private houses; women and lawyers are his best disciples; the one, next fruit, longs for forbidden doctrine; the other, to maintain forbidden titles; both which he sows amongst them. Honest he dare not be, for that loves order; yet if he can be brought to ceremony, and made but master of it, he is converted.

John Earle
A YOUNG GENTLEMAN OF THE UNIVERSITY

Is one that comes there to wear a gown and to say hereafter he has been at the university. His father sent him thither because he heard there were the best fencing and dancing schools; from these he has his education, from his tutor the oversight. The first element of his knowledge is to be shewn the colleges and initiated in a tavern by the way, which hereafter he will learn of himself. The two marks of his seniority is the bare velvet of his gown and his proficiency at tennis, where, when he can once play a set, he is a freshman no more. His study has commonly handsome shelves, his books neat silk strings,[1] which he shews to his father's man, and is loath to untie or take down for fear of misplacing. Upon foul days, for recreation he retires thither, and looks over the pretty book his tutor reads to him, which is commonly some short history or a piece of *Euphormio*,[2] for which his tutor gives him money to spend next day. His main loitering is at the library, where he studies arms and books of honor, and turns a gentleman-critic in pedigrees. Of all things, he endures not to be mistaken for a scholar, and hates a black suit, though it be of satin. His companion is ordinarily some stale fellow that has been notorious for an ingle [3] to gold hatbands,[4] whom he admires at first,

[10] *allay:* silence.
[1] *strings:* to hold a book cover together.
[2] *Euphormio: Euphormionis Satyricon,* a Latin satire by John Barclay (1582–1621).
[3] *ingle:* sycophant.
[4] *gold hatbands:* worn by noblemen at the universities.

afterward scorns. If he have spirit or wit, he may light of better company, and may learn some flashes of wit, which may do him knight's service in the country hereafter. But he is now gone to the inns of court,[5] where he studies to forget what he learned before, his acquaintance and the fashion.

John Earle
A POT POET

Is the dregs of wit; yet mingled with good drink may have some relish. His inspirations are more real than others, for they do but feign a God, but he has his by him. His verses run like the tap and his invention as the barrel, ebbs and flows at the mercy of the spiggot. In thin drink he aspires not above a ballad, but a cup of sack[1] inflames him and he sets his Muse and nose afire together. The press is his mint and stamps him now and then a sixpence or two in reward of the baser coin his pamphlet. His *Works* would scarce sell for three half-pence, though they are given oft for three shillings, but for the pretty title that allures the country gentleman, and for which the printer maintains him in ale a fortnight. His verses are like his clothes, miserable Centoes[2] and patches, yet their pace not altogether so hobbling as an Almanac's. The death of a great man or the firing of a house furnish him with an argument, and the nine Muses are out straight in mourning gowns, and Melpomine[3] cries "Fire, Fire." He is a man now much employed in commendations of our Navy and a bitter inveigher against the Spaniard. His frequentest works go out in single sheets and are chanted from market to market, to a vile tune and a worse throat, whilst the poor country wench melts like her butter to hear them. And these are the stories of some men of Tyburn,[4] or a strange monster out of Germany, or sitting in a bawdyhouse he

---

[5] *inns of court:* law schools.
[1] *sack:* a dry, strong Spanish wine.
[2] *Centoes:* (1) rags, patches; (2) a poem made up of fragments from other authors.
[3] *Melpomine:* the Muse of Tragedy.
[4] *Tyburn:* where the condemned were executed.

writes God's judgments. He ends at last in some obscure painted cloth, to which himself made the verses, and his life like a can too full, spills upon the bench. He leaves twenty shillings on the score,[5] which my hostess loses.

John Earle
A PRETENDER TO LEARNING

Is one that would make all others more fools than himself, for though he know nothing, he would not have the world know so much. He conceits nothing in learning but the opinion, which he seeks to purchase without it, though he might with less labor cure his ignorance than hide it. He is indeed a kind of scholar-mountebank, and his art our delusion. He is tricked out in all the accoutrements of learning, and at the first encounter none passes better. He is oftener in his study than at his book, and you cannot pleasure him better than to deprehend him: yet he hears you not till the third knock, and then comes out very angry, as interrupted. You find him in his slippers and a pen in his ear, in which formality he was asleep. His table is spread wide with some classic folio, which is as constant to it as the carpet, and hath laid open in the same page this half year. His candle is always a longer sitter-up than himself, and the boast of his window at midnight. He walks much alone in the posture of meditation, and has a book still before his face in the fields. His pocket is seldom without a Greek Testament or Hebrew Bible, which he opens only in the church, and that when some stander-by looks over. He has sentences for company, some scatterings of Seneca and Tacitus, which are good upon all occasions. If he read anything in the morning, it comes up all at dinner; and as long as that lasts, the discourse is his. He is a great plagiary of tavern wit, and comes to sermons only that he may talk of Austin.[1] His parcels are the mere scrapings from company, yet he complains at parting what time he has lost. He is wondrously capricious to seem a judgment, and listens with a sour attention to

[5] *score:* his bill.
[1] *Austin:* St. Augustine.

what he understands not. He talks much of Scaliger,[2] and Casaubon,[3] and the Jesuits, and prefers some unheard of Dutch names before them all. He has verses to bring in upon these and these hints, and it shall go hard but he will wind in his opportunity. He is critical in a language he cannot construe, and speaks seldom under Arminius[4] in divinity. His business and retirement and caller-away is his study, and he protests no delight to it comparable. He is a great nomenclator[5] of authors, which he has read in general in the catalogue, and in particular in the title, and goes seldom so far as the dedication. He never talks of anything but learning, and learns all from talking. Three encounters with the same men pump him, and then he only puts in or gravely says nothing. He has taken pains to be an ass, though not to be a scholar, and is at length discovered and laughed at.

[2] *Scaliger:* Julius Caesar Scaliger (1484–1558) Italian Latin poet or his son Joseph (1540–1609), a famous scholar.

[3] *Casaubon:* Isaac Casaubon (1559–1614), French scholar and translator of Theophrastus' characters.

[4] *Arminius:* Jacobus Arminius (1560–1609), Dutch opponent of Calvinism.

[5] *nomenclator:* speaker of names.

William Shakespeare, King James I, and William Prynne
FOUR INVECTIVES

No satire collection should omit examples of invective, for they are negatively instructive in the principles of satire. Invective is simply pure attack. It is probably not satire at all, at least when it shows no evidence of wit. There is no aesthetic distance, no artistic control, no irony, no art in pure invective. The four examples which follow range from Prince Hal's attack upon Falstaff in Henry IV, Part I, *which is on the borderline between invective and satire, through King James I's attack upon tobacco, which is at least stylistically well done, to the pair of Puritanical attacks by Prynne, which have clearly gone beyond the range of art altogether.*

PRINCE HAL TO FALSTAFF
from *Henry IV, Part I*
Act II, Scene iv

There is a devil haunts thee in the likeness of an old fat man; a tun of man is thy companion. Why dost thou converse with that trunk of humours, that bolting-hutch of beastliness, that swollen parcel of dropsies, that huge bombard of sack, that stuffed cloakbag of guts, that roasted Manningtree ox with the pudding in his belly, that reverend vice, that grey iniquity, that father ruffian, that vanity in years? Wherein is he good but to taste sack and to drink it? Wherein neat and cleanly but to carve a capon and eat it? Wherein cunning but in craft? Wherein crafty but in villainy? Wherein villainous but in all things? Wherein worthy but in nothing?

84

from A COUNTERBLASTE TO TOBACCO

Tobacco was brought to Europe by the Spaniards, but popularized by the British. At the beginning of the seventeenth century, it was a problem of enough concern that the King himself wrote the famous attack from which we have printed excerpts here.

And now good countrymen let us I pray you consider what honor or policy can move us to imitate the barbarous and beastly manners of the wild, godless, and slavish Indians, especially in so vile and stinking a custom. Shall we who disdain to imitate the manners of our neighbor France . . . and that cannot endure the spirit of the Spaniards, . . . shall we, I say, who have been so long civil and wealthy in peace, famous and invincible in war, fortunate in both, we that have been ever able to aid any of our neighbors (but never deafened any of their ears with any of our supplications for assistance), shall we, I say, without blushing, abuse ourselves so far as to imitate these beastly Indians, slaves to the Spaniards, refuse to the world, and as yet aliens from the holy covenant of God? Why do we not as well imitate them in walking naked as they do? In preferring glasses, feathers, and such toys to gold and precious stones, as they do? Yea, why do we not deny God and adore the devil as they do?

• • •

And for the vanities committed in this filthy custom, is it not both great vanity and uncleanliness that at the table, a place of respect, of cleanliness, of modesty, men should not be ashamed to sit tossing pipes and puffing the smoke of tobacco one to another, making the filthy smoke and stink thereof to exhale athwart the dishes and infect the air when very often men that abhor it are at their repast? Surely smoke becomes a kitchen far better than a dining room, and yet it makes a kitchen also often times in the inward parts of men, soiling and infecting them, with an unctuous and oily kind of soot, as has been found in some great tobacco takers that after their death were opened. . . . Now it is become in place of a cure, a point of good fellowship, and he that will refuse to take a pipe of tobacco among his fellows (though of his own election he would rather feel the savor of a sink) is accounted peevish and no good company. . . . Yea, the mistress cannot in a more mannerly way entertain her servant than by giving him out of her fair hand a pipe of tobacco. Herein is not only a great vanity but a great contempt of God's good gifts, that the sweetness of men's breath, being a good gift of God, should be wilfully corrupted by this stinking smoke, wherein I must confess it has too strong a virtue: and so that which is an ornament of nature and can neither by any artifice be at the first acquired, nor once lost be recovered again, shall be filthily corrupted with an incurable stink. . . .

Moreover, which is a great iniquity and against all humanity, the husband shall not be ashamed to reduce thereby his delicate, wholesome, and clean-complexioned wife to that extremity that either she must also corrupt her sweet breath therewith or else resolve to live in a perpetual stinking torment.

Have you not reason then to be ashamed and to forbear this filthy novelty, . . . a custom loathsome to the eye, hateful to the nose, harmful to the brain, dangerous to the lungs, and in the black, stinking fume thereof nearest resembling the horrible Stygian smoke of the pit that is bottomless?

from HISTRIO-MASTIX

Prynne, a Puritan pamphleteer and religious writer who lived 1600–1669, wrote over two hundred works, many of them characteristic Puritan attacks on the numerous vices or suspected vices of the day. Histrio-Mastix (1632) is an attack upon the stage, printed about ten years before the Puritans gained enough control of the government to actually close down most of the theaters. Unfortunately, Prynne's diatribe was badly timed for at the time of its appearance, the Queen herself appeared in a play; so Prynne was imprisoned, fined, and even suffered the loss of his ears. Printed below is the title page and then Prynne's attack on the distressing problem of the women who were cutting their hair short.

HISTRIO-MASTIX
THE PLAYER'S SCOURGE
OR
ACTOR'S TRAGEDIE
DIVIDED INTO TWO PARTS

Wherein it is largely evidenced—by divers arguments, by the concurring authorities and resolutions of sundry texts of scripture; of the whole primitive church, both under the law and the gospel; of 55 synods and councils; of 71 fathers and Christian writers before the year of our lord 1200; of above 150 foreign and domestic Protestants and Popish authors since; of 40 heathen philosophers, historians, poets; of many heathen, many Christian nations, republics, emperors, princes, magistrates; of sundry apostolic, canonical, imperial constitutions; and of our own English statutes, magistrates, universities, writers, preachers—that popular stage plays (the very pomps of the Devil which we renounce in Baptism, if we believe the fathers) are sinful, heathenish, lewd, ungodly spectacles and most pernicious corruptions; condemned in all ages as intolerable mischiefs to churches, to republics, to the manners, minds, and souls of men. And that the profession of play-poets, of stage-players; together with the penning, acting, and frequenting of stage-plays, are unlawful, infamous, and misbeseeming Christians. All pretences to the contrary are here likewise fully answered; and the unlawfulness of acting, of beholding academic interludes, briefly discussed; besides sundry other particulars concerning dancing, dicing, health-drinking, etc.: of which the Table will inform you.

ON WOMEN CUTTING THEIR HAIR SHORT

This practice was called "shingling" in the seventeenth century and was often criticized by moralistic and religious writers.

And as the verdict of human nature condemns men degenerating into women, so from the very selfsame grounds it deeply censures the

87

aspiring of women above the limits of their female sex and their metamorphosis into the shapes of men either in hair or apparel. . . . Even nature herself abhors to see a woman shorn or polled; a woman with cut hair is a filthy spectacle and much like a monster, and all repute it a very great absurdity for a woman to walk abroad with shorn hair, for this is all one as if she should take upon her the form or person of a man, to whom short cut hair is proper, it being natural and comely to women to nourish their hair which even God and nature have given them for a covering, a token of subjection, and a natural badge to distinguish them from men. Yet not withstanding our English gentlewomen (as if they all intended to turn men outright and wear the breeches or to become Popish nuns) are now grown so far past shame, past modesty, grace, and nature, as to clip their hair like men with locks and foretops, and to make this whorish cut the very guise and fashion of the times, to the eternal infamy of their sex, their nation, and the great scandal of religion.

Samuel Butler
from
HUDIBRAS

Hudibras, *a burlesque modeled on* Don Quixote, *is the most important political satire before Dryden and Pope. Here Samuel Butler (1612–1680) attempts to free truth and reason from error and hypocrisy by satirizing the Puritans he thought were especially culpable. The force of its lively comic invention, the curiously effective octosyllabic doggerel, and its mixed subject matter all combined to make it immediately successful (1663) among the newly restored royalists who deeply resented the twenty years of Puritan domination. In this excerpt from Canto One of the First Part (there are three), Butler establishes the character of his Presbyterian hero, Sir Hudibras. Later Hudibras is physically described and we are introduced to his sectarian squire, Ralpho, an ignorant and presumptuous tailor. In the words of John Wilders in his Introduction to the 1967* Oxford edition of Hudibras, *the two enable Butler "to show that scholarship was often no more than futile pedantry, that religion was commonly a pretext for the acquisition of power or wealth, that romantic love was generally a cover for self-interest, and that military honour was the reward for barbarism."*

THE ARGUMENT

Sir Hudibras *his passing worth,*
The manner how he sally'd forth:
His Arms and Equipage are shown;
His Horse's Vertues, and his own.
Th' Adventure of the Bear *and* Fiddle
Is sung, but breaks off in the middle.

89

When *civil* Fury first grew high,
And men fell out they knew not why;
When hard words, *Jealousies* and *Fears*,
Set Folks together by the ears,
And made them fight, like mad or drunk,
For Dame *Religion* as for Punk,[1]
Whose honesty they all durst swear for,
Though not a man of them knew wherefore:
When *Gospel-trumpeter*,[2] surrounded
With long-ear'd rout, to Battel sounded,
And Pulpit, Drum Ecclesiastick,
Was beat with fist, instead of a stick:
Then did Sir *Knight* abandon dwelling,
And out he rode a Colonelling.

A wight he was, whose very sight wou'd
Entitle him *Mirrour of Knighthood;*
That never bent his stubborn knee[3]
To any thing but Chivalry,
Nor put up[4] blow, but that which laid
Right Worshipfull on shoulder-blade:[5]
Chief of Domestick Knights and Errant,
Either for Chartel[6] or for Warrant:
Great on the Bench, Great in the Saddle,
That could as well bind o're,[7] as swaddle:[8]
Mighty he was at both of these,
And styl'd of *War* as well as *Peace.*
(So some Rats of amphibious nature,

[1] Prostitute.
[2] Non-conforming preacher.
[3] An allusion to the Presbyterian refusal to kneel at the Sacrament of the Lord's Supper.
[4] Endured.
[5] Dubbed him knight.
[6] Written challenge to duel.
[7] To the court for trial.
[8] (1) to beat soundly; (2) to wrap in swaddling clothes.

Are either for the Land or Water.)
But here our Authors make a doubt,
Whether he were more wise, or stout.
Some hold the one, and some the other:
But howsoe're they make a pother,
The difference was so small, his Brain
Outweigh'd his Rage but half a grain:
Which made some take him for a tool
That Knaves do work with, call'd a Fool.
And offer to lay wagers, that
As *Mountaigne,* playing with his Cat,
Complaines she thought him but an Ass,[9]
Much more she would Sir *Hudibras.*
(For that's the Name our valiant Knight
To all his Challenges did write.)
But they'r mistaken very much,
'Tis plain enough he was no such.
We grant, although he had much wit,
H' was very shie of using it,
As being loath to wear it out,
And therefore bore it not about,
Unless on Holy-dayes, or so,
As men their best Apparel do.
Beside 'tis known he could speak *Greek,*
As naturally as Pigs squeek:
That *Latin* was no more difficile,
Then to a Blackbird 'tis to whistle.
Being rich in both he never scanted
His Bounty unto such as wanted;
But much of either would afford
To many that had not one word.
For *Hebrew* Roots, although th' are found
To flourish most in barren ground,[10]

[9] In essay II, 12, Montaigne supposes his cat thought him a fool for wasting his time playing with her.
[10] It was generally believed that Hebrew was the natural tongue of man, that a child growing up away from society would naturally speak Hebrew.

He had such plenty, as suffic'd
To make some think him circumcis'd:
And truly so perhaps, he was
'Tis many a Pious Christians case.

He was in *Logick* a great Critick,
Profoundly skill'd in Analytick.
He could distinguish, and divide
A hair 'twixt South and South-west side:
On either which he would dispute,
Confute, change hands, and still confute.
He'd undertake to prove by force
Of Argument, a Man's no Horse.[11]
He'd prove a Buzzard is no Fowl,
And that a *Lord* may be an Owl;
A Calf an *Alderman,* a Goose a *Justice,*
And Rooks *Committee-men* and *Trustees.*[12]
He'd run in Debt by Disputation,
And pay with Ratiocination.
All this by Syllogism, true
In mood and figure,[13] he would doe.

For *Rhetorick,* he could not ope
His mouth, but out there flew a Trope:
And when he hapned to break off
I'th' middle of his speech, or cough,
H' had hard words ready, to shew why,
And tell what Rules he did it by.
Else when with greatest Art he spoke,
You'd think he talk'd like other foke.
For all a Rhetoricians Rules

---

[11] Aristotle uses this proposition. The following lines satirize the kinds of disputation topics then common in the universites. *Buzzard, owl, calf,* and *goose* are all slang for a stupid or doltish person.

[12] Men appointed by Parliament to dispose of church lands.

[13] In proper logical form.

Teach nothing but to name his Tools.
His ordinary Rate of Speech [14]
In loftiness of sound was rich,
A *Babylonish* dialect,
Which learned Pedants much affect.
It was a particolour'd dress
Of patch'd and pyball'd Languages:
'Twas *English* cut on *Greek* and *Latin*,
Like Fustian heretofore on Sattin. [15]
It had an odde promiscuous Tone,
As if h' had talk'd three parts in one.
Which made some think, when he did gabble,
Th' had heard three Labourers of *Babel;*
Or *Cerberus* [16] himself pronounce
A Leash of Languages at once.
This he as volubly would vent,
As if his stock would ne're be spent.
And truly to support that charge
He had supplies as vast and large.
For he could coyn or counterfeit
New words, with little or no wit:
Words so debas'd and hard, no stone
Was hard enough to touch them on.
And when with hasty noise he spoke 'em,
The Ignorant for currant took 'em.
That had the Orator [17] who once,
Did fill his Mouth with Pebble stones
When he harangu'd; but known his Phrase
He would have us'd no other ways.

[14] In the following lines Butler satirizes both the Anglican scholastic style of preaching and the Puritan style of less academic jargon.
[15] The fashion of cutting holes in the coarse fustian so that the satin could show through had disappeared by the time Butler was writing.
[16] Cerberus, the three headed dog guarding the gates of Hades, would naturally speak a leash [set of three] of languages.
[17] Demosthenes.

In *Mathematicks* he was greater
Then *Tycho Brahe* [18] or *Erra Pater:* [19]
For he by *Geometrick* scale
Could take the size of *Pots of Ale;*
Resolve by Sines and Tangents straight,
If *Bread* or *Butter* wanted weight;
And wisely tell what hour o'th' day
The Clock does strike, by *Algebra.*

Beside he was a shrewd *Philosopher,*
And had read every Text and gloss over:
What e're the crabbed'st Author hath
He understood b'implicit Faith,[20]
What ever *Sceptick* could inquere for;
For every *why* he had a *wherefore:*
Knew more then forty of them do,
As far as words and termes could goe.
All which he understood by Rote,
And as occasion serv'd, would quote;
No matter whether right or wrong:
They might be either said or sung.
His Notions fitted things so well,
That which was which he could not tell;
But oftentimes mistook the one
For th'other, as Great Clerks have done.
He could reduce all things to Acts [21]
And knew their Natures by Abstracts,
Where Entity [22] and Quiddity,[23]
The Ghosts of defunct Bodies, flie;
Where Truth in Person does appear,

[18] Danish astronomer who discovered a new star in Cassiopeia.
[19] Probably a reference to William Lyly (1602–1681), English astrologer.
[20] Acceptance of doctrine on another's authority. Butler is here and in the following lines satirizing the overly subtle metaphysical distinctions of scholastic philosophy.
[21] Essences.
[22] Being.
[23] Reasons for being.

Like words congeal'd in Northern Air.
He knew *what's what,* and that's as high
As *Metaphysick* wit can flie.
In *School-Divinity* as able
As he that hight [24] *Irrefragable;* [25]
Profound in all the Nominal
And real ways beyond them all,
And with as delicate a Hand
Could twist as tough a Rope of Sand.
And weave fine Cobwebs, fit for skull
That's empty when the Moon is full;
Such as take lodgings in a Head
That's to be let unfurnished.
He could raise Scruples dark and nice,
And after solve 'em in a trice:
As if Divinity had catch'd [26]
The Itch, of purpose to be scratch'd;
Or, like a Mountebank, did wound
And stab her self with doubts profound,
Onely to shew with how small pain
The sores of faith are cur'd again;
Although by woful proof we find,
They alwayes leave a Scar behind.
He knew the seat of Paradise,
Could tell in what degree it lies:
And, as he was dispos'd, could prove it,
Below the Moon, or else above it:
What *Adam* dreamt of when his Bride
Came from her Closet in his side:
Whether the Devil tempted her
By a *high Dutch* Interpreter: [27]
If either of them had a Navel;

[24] Called.
[25] Alexander of Hales, 13th century English schoolman.
[26] Caught.
[27] Goropius Becanus (1519–1572) argued that High Dutch was the language of Eden.

Who first made Musick malleable: [28]
Whether the Serpent at the Fall
Had cloven Feet, or none at all.
All this, without a Gloss or Comment,
He would unriddle in a moment
In proper terms, such as men smatter
When they throw out and miss the matter.

For his *Religion* it was fit
To match his Learning and his Wit:
'Twas *Presbyterian* true blew,[29]
For he was of that stubborn Crew
Of Errant [30] Saints, whom all men grant
To be the true Church *Militant:*
Such as do build their Faith upon
The holy Text of *Pike* and *Gun;*
Decide all Controversies by
Infallible *Artillery;*
And prove their Doctrine Orthodox
By Apostolick *Blows* and *Knocks;*
Call Fire and Sword and Desolation,
A *godly-thorough-Reformation,*
Which always must be carry'd on,
And still be doing, never done:
As if Religion were intended
For nothing else but to be mended.
A Sect, whose chief Devotion lies
In odde perverse Antipathies;
In falling out with that or this,
And finding somewhat still amiss:
More peevish, cross, and spleenatick,
Then Dog distract, or Monky sick:
That with more care keep holy-day

[28] Pythagoras heard the variations in sound made by a blacksmith's hammer [Lat. *Malleus*].
[29] Probably an allusion to the Presbyterian blue as opposed to Royalist red.
[30] (1) arrant, thoroughgoing; (2) wandering.

96

The wrong, then others the right way: [31]
Compound for Sins, they are inclin'd to,
By damning those they have no mind to;
Still so perverse and opposite,
As if they worshipp'd God for spight.
The self-same thing they will abhor
One way, and long another for.
Free-will they one way disavow,[32]
Another, nothing else allow.
All Piety consists therein
In them, in other men all Sin.
Rather then faile, they will defie
That which they love most tenderly,
Quarrel with *minc'd Pies,* and disparage
Their best and dearest friend, *Plum-porredge;*
Fat *Pig* and *Goose* it self oppose,
And blaspheme *Custard* through the *nose.*[33]
Th'Apostles of this fierce Religion,
Like *Mahomet*'s, were Ass and Widgeon,[34]
To whom our Knight by fast instinct
Of wit and temper was so linkt,
As if Hypocrisie and non-sense
Had got th'Advouson [35] of his Conscience.

[31] The Puritans opposed the celebration of Christmas and insisted on a religious observance of the Sabbath without the popular recreations of bowling, dancing, or tippling.

[32] The Puritans denied man's free will but were often headstrong in insisting on their own rightness.

[33] A reference to the Puritan preachers' habit of speaking in a characteristic nasal tone.

[34] Mohammed was said to have been taken to heaven on a milk-white ass, an alborak. A pigeon had been trained to eat seeds out of the prophet's ear to appear that it was whispering inspired words. Both *ass* and *widgeon* were colloquialisms for *fool.*

[35] The right of appointing a minister.

Rochester
TWO SATIRES

John Wilmot, Earl of Rochester (1647–1680), was a favorite of Charles II for his gaiety and wit. He served briefly in the navy (1665–66) and then married Elizabeth Malet whom he had earlier tried to kidnap. His life in London was one of bawdy riot and dissipation. He was several times banished from the court for his behavior, including an obscene lampoon of the king. His little epitaph on the king indicates his kind of wit:

> *Here lies a Great and Mighty King*
> *Whose Promise none relies on.*
> *He never said a Foolish Thing*
> *Nor ever did a Wise One.*

Rochester was, as he himself said, "for five years together . . . continuously drunk." His death came at age thirty-three when the force of his dissolute life had led him to embrace Christianity.

THE MAIMED DÉBAUCHÉE

Probably a parody of Sir William D'Avenant's romantic epic Gondibert, *this poem reveals much of Rochester's life and of his sense of the pomposity of wise old men.*

As some brave admiral, in former war,
Deprived of force, but pressed with courage still,
Two rival fleets, appearing from afar,
Crawls to the top of an adjacent hill,

From whence (with thoughts full of concern) he views
The wise and daring conduct of the fight,

And each bold action to his mind renews
His present glory, and his past delight:

From his fierce eyes, flashes of rage he throws,
As from black clouds, when lightning breaks away;
Transported, thinks himself amidst his foes,
And absent, yet enjoys the bloody day:

So when my days of impotence approach,
And I'm by pox,[1] and wine's unlucky chance,
Driv'n from the pleasing billows of debauch,
On the dull shore of lazy temperance,

My pains at last some respite shall afford,
Whilst I behold the battles you maintain,
When fleets of glasses sail about the board,
From whose broad-sides volleys of wit shall rain.

Nor shall the sight of honourable scars,
Which my too forward valour did procure,
Frighten new listed soldiers from the wars,
Past joys have more than paid what I endure.

Should some brave youth (worth being drunk) prove nice,[2]
And from his fair inviters meanly shrink,
'Twould please the ghost of my departed vice,
If at my counsel, he repent and drink.

Or should some cold-complexioned sot forbid,
With his dull morals, our night's brisk alarms,
I'll fire his blood by telling what I did,
When I was strong, and able to bear arms.

I'll tell of whores attacked, their lords at home,
Bawds' quarters beaten up, and fortress won,

[1] Syphilis.
[2] Too sensitive; delicate.

Widows demolished, watches overcome,
And handsome ills, by my contrivance done.

Nor shall our love-fits, Cloris,[3] be forgot,
When each the well-locked link-boy, strove t' enjoy
And the best kiss was the deciding lot,
Whether the boy used you, or I the boy.

With tales like these, I will such heat inspire,
As to important mischief shall incline.
I'll make them long some ancient church to fire,
And fear no lewdness they're called to by wine.

Thus statesman-like, I'll saucily impose
And safe from danger valiantly advise,
Sheltered in impotence, urge you to blows,
And being good for nothing else, be wise.

SATIRE AGAINST MANKIND

*This most celebrated of Rochester's poems is in manuscript
entitled ambiguously "A Satyr Against Mankind." For the
ideas he expresses here, Rochester has drawn on Montaigne
and La Rochefoucauld, and the philosophy of Thomas
Hobbes. He indicates the kind of despair to which his ethical nihilism, adopted from Hobbes, has brought him. It ulti-
mately led to his conversion to Christianity.*

Were I, who to my cost already am
One of those strange prodigious creatures *Man,*
A spirit, free to choose for my own share
What sort of flesh and blood I pleased to wear,
I'd be a dog, a monkey, or a bear,
Or anything, but that vain animal
Who is so proud of being rational.
The senses are too gross; and he'll contrive

[3] Rochester's name for an imagined mistress.

A sixth,[1] to contradict the other five:
And, before certain instinct, will prefer
Reason, which fifty times for one does err—
Reason, an *ignis fatuus* [2] of the mind,
Which leaves the light of nature, sense,[3] behind.
Pathless and dangerous wand'ring ways it takes,
Through error's fenny bogs and thorny brakes,
Whilst the misguided follower climbs with pain
Mountains of whimsies heaped in his own brain—
Stumbling from thought to thought, falls headlong down
Into doubt's boundless sea, where, like to drown,
Books bear him up a while and make him try
To swim with bladders of philosophy,
In hopes still to o'ertake the skipping light.
The vapor dances in his dazzled sight,
Till, spent, it leaves him to eternal night.
Then old age and experience, hand in hand,
Lead him to death, and make him understand,
After a search so painful and so long,
That all his life he has been in the wrong.
Huddled in dirt, reas'ning Engine [4] lies,
Who was so proud, so witty,[5] and so wise.
Pride drew him in, as cheats their bubbles [6] catch,
And made him venture to be made a wretch.
His wisdom did his happiness destroy,
Aiming to *know* the world he should *enjoy*.
And wit was his vain, frivolous pretense
Of pleasing others at his own expense.
For wits are treated just like common whores:
First they're enjoyed, and then kicked out of doors.
The pleasure past, a threat'ning doubt remains,

[1] A superior one, to synthesize the reports of the five senses.
[2] A false light; a deluding guide.
[3] Senses are the light of nature because they report the facts to the mind.
[4] Man as a reasoning machine.
[5] Ingenious.
[6] Victims; dupes.

That frights th' enjoyer with succeeding pains.
Women, and men of wit, are dang'rous tools,
And ever fatal to admiring fools.
Pleasure allures; and when the fops escape,
'Tis not that they're beloved, but fortunate;
And therefore what they fear, at heart they hate.

But now, methinks, some formal band and beard[7]
Takes me to task. Come on, sir, I'm prepared!
"Then, by your favor, anything that's writ
Against this gibing, jingling knack called wit
Likes[8] me abundantly; but you'll take care
Upon this point not to be too severe.
Perhaps *my* Muse were fitter for this part;
For I profess I can be very smart
On wit, which I abhor with all my heart.
I long to lash it in some sharp essáy;
But your grand indiscretion bids me stay,
And turns my tide of ink another way.
What rage ferments in your degen'rate mind,
To make you rail at reason and mankind?
Blest, glorious Man! to whom alone kind heav'n
An everlasting soul hath freely giv'n;
Whom his great Maker took such care to make
That from himself he did the image take,
And this fair frame in shining reason dressed,
To dignify his nature above beast—
Reason! by whose aspiring influence
We take a flight beyond material sense,
Dive into mysteries, then soaring pierce
The flaming limits of the universe,
Search heav'n and hell, find out what's acted there,
And give the world true grounds of hope and fear!"
"Hold, mighty man!" I cry; "all this we know

[7] Dignified gentleman; *bands* were collars on the robes of the clergy, lawyers, professors.
[8] Pleases.

From the pathetic pen of Ingelo,[9]
From Patrick's *Pilgrim*,[10] Sibb's *Soliloquies;*[11]
And 'tis this very 'reason' I despise,
This supernat'ral gift, that makes a mite
Think he's the image of the Infinite,
Comparing his short life, void of all rest,
To the eternal and the ever blest—
This busy, puzzling stirrer up of doubt,
That frames deep mysteries, then finds 'em out,
Filling, with frantic crowds of thinking fools,
The reverend bedlams: colleges and schools—
Borne on whose wings, each heavy sot[12] can pierce
The limits of the boundless universe:
So charming[13] ointments make an old witch fly
And bear a crippled carcass through the sky.
'Tis this exalted pow'r whose business lies
In nonsense and impossibilities.
This made a whimsical philosopher[14]
Before the spacious world his tub prefer;
And we have many modern coxcombs[15] who
Retire to think, 'cause they have nought to do.
But thoughts were giv'n for action's government;
Where action ceases, thought's impertinent.
Our sphere of action is life's happiness;
And he that thinks beyond thinks like an ass.
Thus, whilst against false reas'ning I inveigh.
I own right reason,[16] which I would obey:
That reason which distinguishes by sense,
That gives us rules of good and ill from thence;

[9] Nathaniel Ingelo, a contemporary theologian.
[10] Simon Patrick, Bishop of Ely (d. 1707).
[11] Probably a general reference to the prolific and popular writings of the Puritan Richard Sibbes (d. 1635).
[12] Fool.
[13] Magical.
[14] Diogenes (d. 323 B.C.).
[15] Proud fools.
[16] Recognize true reason, common sense.

That bounds desires with a reforming will,
To keep them more in vigor, not to kill.
Your reason hinders; mine helps to enjoy,
Renewing appetites yours would destroy.
My reason is my friend; yours is a cheat:
Hunger calls out, my reason bids me eat;
Perversely, yours your appetite doth mock.
This asks for food; that answers, 'What's o'clock?'

"This plain distinction, sir, your doubt secures;
'Tis not true reason I despise, but yours.
Thus, I think reason righted. But for [17] Man,
I'll ne'er recant. Defend him if you can.
For all his pride and his philosophy,
'Tis evident beasts are, in their degree,
As wise, at least, and better far than he.
Those creatures are the wisest who attain
By surest means the ends at which they aim.
If, therefore, Jowler [18] finds and kills his hare
Better than Meres [19] supplies committee chair,
Though one's a statesman, th'other but a hound,
Jowler in justice will be wiser found.
You see how far Man's wisdom here extends;
Look next if human nature makes amends:
Whose principles are more generous and just,
And to whose morals you would sooner trust.
Be judge yourself; I'll bring it to the test:
Which is the basest creature, man or beast?
Birds feed on birds, beasts on each other prey;
But savage man alone does man betray.
Pressed by necessity, *they* kill for food;
Man undoes man, to do himself no good,
With teeth and claws by nature armed, *they* hunt
Nature's allowance, to supply their want;

[17] But as for.
[18] A hunting dog.
[19] Sir Thomas Meres, a member of the opposition in the House of Commons

But Man, with smiles, embraces, friendships, praise,
Inhumanly his fellow's life betrays,
With voluntary pains works his distress,
Not through necessity but wantonness.
For hunger or for love *they* bite or tear,
Whilst wretched Man is still in arms for fear:
For fear he arms, and is of arms afraid;
From fear to fear successively betrayed—
Base fear! the source whence his best passions came,
His boasted honor, and his dear-bought fame,
The lust of pow'r, to which he's such a slave
And for the which alone he dares be brave—
To which his various projects are designed,
Which makes him gen'rous, affable, and kind,
For which he takes such pains to be thought wise,
And screws his actions in a forced disguise,
Leads a most tedious life in misery
Under laborious, mean hypocrisy.
Look to the bottom of his vast design,
Wherein Man's wisdom, pow'r, and glory join:
The good he acts, the ill he does endure,
'Tis all from fear, to make himself secure.
Merely for safety, after fame they thirst;
For all men would be cowards, if they durst.
And honesty's against all common sense:
Men must be knaves; 'tis in their own defense
Mankind's dishonest: if they think it fair
Amongst known cheats to play upon the square,
You'll be undone—
Nor can weak truth your reputation save:
The knaves will all agree to call you knave."

La Rouchefoucauld
from
MAXIMS

The Duke de la Rouchefoucauld (1613–1680) compressed into a series of maxims entitled Réflexions, Sentences, et Maximes Morales, *published in 1665, a view of man in which self-interest and vanity are the chief motivations. Translation by F. K.*

6. Passion often makes clever men idiots and idiots clever.
19. We all have power enough to endure the misfortunes of others.
38. We promise as far as we hope and keep our promises as far as we fear.
73. One can find women who never have had an affair, but it is rare to find one who has had just one.
76. Real love is like seeing ghosts: all of us talk about it but few have ever seen one.
89. Everyone complains of his memory and no one of his judgment.
93. Old men love to give good advice to console themselves for being unable to set bad examples.
122. If we resist our passions, it is more through their weakness than our strength.
142. As it is the sign of fine minds to express much in few words, so is it the skill of small minds to express little in many.
149. The refusal to accept praise is a desire to be praised twice.
168. Hope, complete trickster that she is, at least leads us to the end of life by an agreeable path.
192. When our vices leave us, we flatter ourselves in the belief that it is we who leave them.

303. No matter how well one is spoken of by others, one learns nothing new.
304. We often pardon those who bore us, but we cannot pardon those whom we bore.
367. There are few honest women who do not grow tired of their role.
583. In the misfortune of our best friends, we always find something not altogether displeasing.[1]

---

[1] This is the maxim which inspired Swift's ironic poem, "Verses on the Death of Dr. Swift."

Andrew Marvell
TWO POEMS

Andrew Marvell (1621–1678) combines the best of the metaphysical ingenuity and the Jonsonian smoothness in his lyric poetry and typifies the later seventeenth century in the viciousness of his satires, all written after 1660. He was abroad during much of the civil war but served as tutor (1650–53) to the daughter of Lord Fairfax, a Parliamentary general, and to a ward of Oliver Cromwell. In 1657, at Milton's request, he was made assistant Latin Secretary to the Council of State. Following the Restoration, he served in Parliament and was noted for his outspoken support of religious toleration.

TO HIS COY MISTRESS

In this short love poem Marvell uses a clear logical syllogism, normally confined to pompous scholastic debates, to argue the necessity of love.

Had we but world enough, and time,
This coyness,[1] Lady, were no crime.
We would sit down, and think which way
To walk, and pass our long love's day.
Thou by the Indian Ganges' side
Shouldst rubies find; I by the tide
Of Humber [2] would complain. I would

---

[1] Modesty; reserve.
[2] The river in the north of England. Hull, Marvell's home, is situated on its banks.

Love you ten years before the Flood,
And you should, if you please, refuse
Till the conversion of the Jews.
My vegetable [3] love should grow
Vaster than empires and more slow;
An hundred years should go to praise
Thine eyes, and on thy forehead gaze;
Two hundred to adore each breast,
But thirty thousand to the rest;
An age at least to every part,
And the last age should show your heart.
For, Lady, you deserve this state, [4]
Nor would I love at lower rate.

But at my back I always hear
Time's wingèd chariot hurrying near;
And yonder all before us lie
Deserts of vast eternity.
Thy beauty shall no more be found,
Nor, in thy marble vault, shall sound
My echoing song; then worms shall try
That long-preserved virginity,
And your quaint [5] honor turn to dust,
And into ashes all my lust:
The grave's a fine and private place,
But none, I think, do there embrace.

Now therefore, while the youthful hue
Sits on thy skin like morning lew, [6]
And while thy willing soul transpires [7]
At every pore with instant [8] fires,
Now let us sport us while we may,

[3] Earthly; in the manner of plants.
[4] Dignified treatment.
[5] Dainty; fastidious; perhaps a suggestion of old-fashioned.
[6] The MS is unclear here but it probably means *warmth* or it may refer to morning *dew*.
[7] Comes forth.
[8] Urgent; eager.

And now, like amorous birds of prey,
Rather at once our time devour
Than languish in his slow-chapped [9] power.
Let us roll all our strength and all
Our sweetness up into one ball,
And tear our pleasures with rough strife
Thorough the iron gates of life;
Thus, though we cannot make our sun
Stand still, yet we will make him run.

FLECKNOE, AN ENGLISH PRIEST AT ROME

Richard Flecknoe was an Irish priest who traveled extensively on the continent. He wrote a few poems, plays, and characters which are not quite so bad as Marvell or Dryden later would have us believe. For both poets, Flecknoe became a vehicle for satiric ideas.

Obliged by frequent visits of this man,
Whom as priest, poet, and musician,
I for some branch of Melchizedek [1] took
(Though he derives himself from my Lord Brooke),
I sought his lodging, which is at the sign
Of the sad Pelican; subject divine
For poetry: [2] there three staircases high,
Which signifies his triple property,
I found at last a chamber, as 'twas said,
But seemed a coffin set on the stairs' head.
Not higher than seven, nor larger than three feet;
Only there was no seeling, nor a sheet, [3]

[9] Slow-jawed; *i.e.,* slow to devour.
[1] See Gen. 14:18.
[2] The Pelican is often used as a symbol for the Church or the sacrificial Christ. It is usually depicted as feeding its young from the blood of its own breast.
[3] Marvell is punning here. *Seeling* can be "funeral wall-hangings" or "wainscoting"; *sheet* can be "bed sheet" or "winding sheet."

Save that th' ingenious door did as you come
Turn in, and show to wainscot half the room.
Yet of his state no man could have complained,
There being no bed where he entertained:
And though within one cell so narrow pent,
He'd stanzas [4] for a whole appartement.

Straight without further information,
In hideous verse, he, and dismal tone,
Begins to exercise,[5] as if I were
Possessed; and sure the Devil brought me there.
But I, who now imagined myself brought
To my last trial, in a serious thought
Calmed the disorders of my youthful breast,
And to my martyrdom prepared rest.
Only this frail ambition did remain,
The last distemper of the sober brain,
That there had been some present to assure
The future ages how I did endure:
And how I, silent, turned my burning ear
Towards the verse; and when that could not hear,
Held him the other; and unchanged yet,
Asked still for more, and prayed him to repeat:
Till the tyrant, weary to persecute,
Left off, and tried t' allure me with his lute.

Now as two instruments, to the same key
Being tuned by art, if the one touched be
The other opposite as soon replies,
Moved by the air and hidden sympathies,
So while he with his gouty fingers crawls
Over the lute, his murmuring belly calls,
Whose hungry guts to the same straightness twined
In echo to the trembling strings repined.

[4] Marvell puns again: *stanzas* in Italian means "room" and, of course, refers to a poetic unit.
[5] May also mean "exorcise."

I, that perceived now what his music meant,
Asked civilly if he had eat [6] this Lent.
He answered yes; with such and such an one.
For he has this of gen'rous, that alone
He never feeds, save only when he tries
With gristly tongue to dart the passing flies.
I asked if he eat flesh. And he, that was
So hungry that though ready to say mass
Would break his fast before, said he was sick,
And th' ordinance [7] was only politic.
Nor was I longer to invite him scant:
Happy at once to make him Protestant,
And silent. Nothing now dinner stayed
But till he had himself a body made.
I mean till he were dressed: for else so thin
He stands, as if he only fed had been
With consecrated wafers: and the Host
Hath sure more flesh and blood than he can boast.
This *basso relievo* [8] of a man,
Who as a camel tall, yet easily can
The needle's eye thread without any stitch [9]
(His only impossible is to be rich),
Lest his too subtle body, growing rare,
Should leave his soul to wander in the air,
He therefore circumscribes himself in rhymes;
And swaddled in's own papers seven times,
Wears a close jacket of poetic buff,
With which he doth his third dimension stuff.
Thus armed underneath, he over all
Does make a primitive sotana [10] fall;
And above that yet casts an antique cloak,
Worn at the first Council of Antioch;

[6] The old form of the past participle; pronounced *et.*
[7] The rule of his order.
[8] Low relief.
[9] The stitch in sewing and the stitch of sharp pain.
[10] Cassock.

Which by the Jews long hid, and disesteemed,
He heard of by Tradition, and redeemed.
But were he not in this black habit decked,
This half transparent man would soon reflect
Each colour that he passed by; and be seen,
As the chameleon, yellow, blue, or green.

He dressed, and ready to disfurnish now
His chamber, whose compactness did allow
No empty place for complementing doubt,
But who came last is forced first to go out;
I meet one on the stairs who made me stand,
Stopping the passage, and did him demand:
I answered, "He is here, sir; but you see
You cannot pass to him but through me."
He thought himself affronted, and replied,
"I whom the Palace never has denied
Will make the way here"; I said, "Sir, you'll do
Me a great favour, for I seek to go."
He gath'ring fury still made sign to draw; [11]
But himself there closed in a scabbard saw
As narrow as his sword's; and I, that was
Delightful, said there can no body pass
Except by penetration [12] hither, where
Two make a crowd, nor can three persons here
Consist but in one substance. Then, to fit
Our peace, the priest said I too had some wit:
To prov't, I said, "The place doth us invite
By its own narrowness, sir, to unite."
He asked me pardon; and to make me way
Went down, as I him followed to obey.
But the propitiatory priest had straight
Obliged us, when below, to celebrate

[11] His sword.
[12] A technical word signifying the occupation of the same space simultaneously by two bodies.

Together our atonement: so increased
Betwixt us two the dinner to a feast.

Let it suffice that we could eat in peace,
And that both poems did and quarrels cease
During the table; though my new made friend
Did, as he threatened, ere 'twere long intend
To be both witty and valiant: I loth,
Said 'twas too late, he was already both.

But now, alas, my first tormentor came,
Who, satisfied with eating, but not tame,
Turns to recite; though judges most severe
After th' assizes' [13] dinner mild appear,
And on full stomach do condemn but few,
Yet he more strict my sentence doth renew;
And draws out of the black box [14] of his breast
Ten quire of paper in which he was dressed.
Yet that which was a greater cruelty
Then Nero's Poem [15] he calls charity:
And so the Pelican at his door hung
Picks out the tender bosom to its young.

Of all his poems there he stands ungirt
Save only two foul copies for his shirt:
Yet these he promises as soon as clean.
But how I loathed to see my neighbor [16] glean
Those papers, which he pealed from within
Like white fleaks rising from a leper's skin!
More odious than those rags which the French youth
At ordinaries after dinner show'th,
When they compare their chancres and poulains.
Yet he first kissed them, and after takes pains

[13] The sessions of civil and criminal court.
[14] Refers to his black garb; also slang for "coffin."
[15] See Seutonius, *Nero*, XXIII.
[16] *I.e.,* the young Italian dining with them.

To read; and then, because he understood
Not one word, thought and swore that they were good.
But all his praises could not now appease
The provok't Author, whom it did displease
To hear his Verses, by so just a curse
That were ill made condemn'd to be read worse:
And how (impossible) he made yet more
Absurdityes in them then were before.
For he his untun'd voice did fall or raise
As a deaf Man upon a Viol playes,
Making the half points and the periods run
Confus'der then the atomes in the Sun.
Thereat the Poet swell'd, with anger full,
And roar'd out, like *Perillus* [17] in's own *Bull:*
"Sir, you read false. That any one but you
Should know the contrary." [18] Whereat, I, now
Made Mediator, in my room, said, "Why?
To say that you read false, Sir, is no Lye." [19]
Thereat the waxen Youth relented straight;
But saw with sad dispair that 'twas too late.
For the disdainful Poet was retir'd
Home, his most furious Satyr to have fir'd
Against the Rebel; who, at this struck dead,
Wept bitterly as disinherited.
Who should commend his Mistress now? Or who
Praise him? Both difficult indeed to do
With truth. I counsell'd him to go in time,
Ere the fierce Poets anger turn'd to rime.
  He hasted; and I, finding my self free,
As one scap't strangely from Captivity,
Have made the Chance be painted; and go now
To hang it in *Saint Peter's* for a Vow.

[17] According to legend Perillus made a brazen bull which destroyed him.
[18] Spoken by the man who had been reading.
[19] Is not untrue; is no occasion for a challenge.

John Dryden
MacFLECKNOE

Poet, dramatist, critic, translator, and satirist, John Dryden is the most versatile man of his age. In each capacity he produced works which alone would cause him to be remembered today. He wrote more than thirty plays, almost a third of them comedies, but his best play is All for Love, *a version of the* Antony and Cleopatra *story. Throughout his career Dryden published long essays in justification or explanation of his work; collectively they form an important body of literary criticism. However, it is in his argumentative poems, his political and personal satires, that we get Dryden at his acerbic best.* MacFlecknoe *is Dryden's response to an attack by another poet. In 1682 Dryden published* The Medal, *a satire on the Earl of Shaftesbury. Two months later it was anonymously answered by a scurrilous attack on Dryden in* The Medal for John Bayes, *a name by which he had been ridiculed ten years earlier in* The Rehersal, *a dramatic satire by the Duke of Buckingham. The* Medal for John Bayes *was presumed to be the work of Thomas Shadwell, who later became poet laureate. So Dryden replied in kind in* MacFlecknoe. *By using the patronymic* Mac (son of) *Dryden depicts Shadwell as the chosen successor to the prince of dullness, Richard Flecknoe.*

All human things are subject to decay,
And, when fate summons, monarchs must obey.
This Flecknoe found, who, like Augustus,[1] young
Was called to empire and had governed long:
In prose and verse was owned, without dispute,
Through all the realms of Nonsense, absolute.

---

[1] Caesar Augustus, the first Roman emperor (31 B.C.–14 A.D.).

This agèd prince, now flourishing in peace,
And blest with issue of a large increase,
Worn out with business, did at length debate
To settle the succession of the state;
And, pond'ring which of all his sons was fit
To reign, and wage immortal war with wit,[2]
Cried, " 'Tis resolved; for nature pleads that he
Should only rule who most resembles me:
Sh——[3] alone my perfect image bears,
Mature in dullness from his tender years;
Sh—— alone of all my sons is he
Who stands confirmed in full stupidity.
The rest to some faint meaning make pretense,
But Sh—— never deviates into sense.
Some beams of wit on other souls may fall,
Strike through, and make a lucid interval;
But Sh——'s genuine night admits no ray,
His rising fogs prevail upon the day:
Besides, his goodly fabric fills the eye,[4]
And seems designed for thoughtless majesty:
Thoughtless as monarch oaks that shade the plain
And, spread in solemn state, supinely reign.
Heywood and Shirley [5] were but types of thee,
Thou last great prophet of tautology:
Even I, a dunce of more renown than they,
Was sent before but to prepare thy way,
And, coarsely clad in Norwich drugget,[6] came
To teach the nations in thy greater name.
My warbling lute, the lute I whilom [7] strung,

[2] Sense; intelligence.
[3] A common practice among the neo-classical satirists to add a suggestiveness, not necessarily to conceal.
[4] Shadwell's obesity was well known.
[5] Thomas Heywood and James Shirley were prolific Elizabethan dramatists whose reputations at the moment were very low.
[6] A coarse wool; the allusion is to John the Baptist.
[7] Formerly.

When to King John of Portugal I sung,[8]
Was but the prelude to that glorious day
When thou on silver Thames didst cut thy way,
With well-timed oars before the royal barge,
Swelled with the pride of thy celestial charge;
And big with hymn, commander of an host,
The like was ne'er in Epsom [9] blankets tossed.
Methinks I see the new Arion [10] sail,
The lute still trembling underneath thy nail.
At thy well-sharpened thumb from shore to shore
The treble squeaks for fear, the basses roar;
Echoes from Pissing Alley [11] Sh—— call,
And Sh—— they resound from Aston Hall.
About thy boat the little fishes throng,
As at the morning toast [12] that floats along.
Sometimes, as prince of thy harmonious band,
Thou wield'st thy papers in thy threshing hand.
St. André's [13] feet ne'er kept more equal time,
Not ev'n the feet of thy own *Psyche's* [14] rime;
Though they in number as in sense excel,
So just, so like tautology, they fell
That, pale with envy, Singleton [15] forswore
The lute and sword which he in triumph bore,
And vowed he ne'er would act Villerius more."
Here stopped the good old sire, and wept for joy,

[8] Flecknoe had visited the court of John IV whose patronage he claimed to have enjoyed.

[9] A reference to Shadwell's plays *Epsom Wells* and *The Virtuoso,* in the latter of which a blanket-tossing scene occurs.

[10] A Greek musician of the 7th century B.C. who, according to Herodotus, was saved from drowning by a dolphin. Shadwell was proud of his musical ability; he had made an operatic version of Dryden's *The Tempest* in 1674.

[11] Off the Strand near the Thames. Aston Hall has not been identified.

[12] Excrement floating on the river after having been collected and dumped there in the morning.

[13] A French dancing master.

[14] A poor opera for which Shadwell wrote the libretto.

[15] A popular opera singer; he played Villerius in D'Avenant's *The Siege of Rhodes* (1656).

In silent raptures of the hopeful boy.
All arguments, but most his plays, persuade
That for anointed dullness he was made.
    Close to the walls which fair Augusta [16] bind
(The fair Augusta much to fears inclined),
An ancient fabric raised t' inform the sight
There stood of yore, and Barbican it hight: [17]
A watchtower once; but now, so fate ordains,
Of all the pile an empty name remains.
From its old ruins brothel houses rise,
Scenes of lewd loves and of polluted joys,
Where their vast courts the mother-strumpets keep,
And, undisturbed by watch, in silence sleep.
Near these a Nursery [18] erects its head,
Where queens are formed and future heroes bred,
Where unfledged actors learn to laugh and cry,
Where infant punks [19] their tender voices try,
And little Maximins [20] the gods defy.
Great Fletcher [21] never treads in buskins [22] here,
Nor greater Jonson dares in socks appear;
But gentle Simkin [23] just reception finds
Amidst this monument of vanished minds:
Pure clinches [24] the suburbian Muse affords,
And Panton [25] waging harmless war with words.

[16] London, which feared a plot to put a Catholic on the throne.

[17] Was called. Archaic words are a convention of the mock-heroic style. *Barbican* was a watch tower in Aldersgate.

[18] A training school for young actors.

[19] Prostitutes. Several Restoration actresses were mistresses to Charles II and his courtiers.

[20] The bombastic Roman emperor Maximinus in Dryden's early play *Tyrannic Love* (1669).

[21] John Fletcher, an Elizabethan playwright whom Dryden praised highly.

[22] *Buskins* were high boots worn by tragic actors in ancient Greece; *socks* (low shoes) were symbols of comedy.

[23] The clown in *The Humors of Simpkin*, a contemporary farce.

[24] Puns.

[25] Thomas Panton, a notorious punster.

Here Flecknoe, as a place to fame well known,
Ambitiously designed his Sh——'s throne.
For ancient Dekker [26] prophesied long since
That in this pile should reign a mighty prince,
Born for a scourge of wit and flail of sense,
To whom true dullness should some *Psyches* owe,
But worlds of *Misers* [27] from his pen should flow;
Humorists and hypocrites it should produce,
Whole Raymond families, and tribes of Bruce.
    Now Empress Fame had published the renown
Of Sh——'s coronation through the town.
Roused by report of Fame, the nations meet,
From near Bunhill, and distant Watling Street.[28]
No Persian carpets spread th' imperial way,
But scattered limbs of mangled poets lay;
From dusty shops neglected authors come,
Martyrs of pies and relics of the bum.[29]
Much Heywood, Shirley, Ogleby [30] there lay,
But loads of Sh—— almost choked the way.
Bilked stationers for yeomen stood prepared,[31]
And H—— [32] was captain of the guard.
The hoary prince in majesty appeared,
High on a throne of his own labors reared.
At his right hand our young Ascanius [33] sate,
Rome's other hope, and pillar of the state.
His brows thick fogs, instead of glories, grace,

[26] Thomas Dekker, an Elizabethan dramatist.
[27] *The Miser* and *The Humorists* were plays by Shadwell. Raymond and Bruce are characters in *The Humorists* and *The Virtuoso* respectively.
[28] A mock-heroic touch, since these streets are fairly close.
[29] Pages from their unsold books had been used under pie crusts or as toilet paper.
[30] John Ogleby (1600–76), a dull translator and poet.
[31] Publishers, cheated by unsalable books, served as guards.
[32] Henry Herringman, London's leading publisher, included both Dryden and Shadwell among his authors.
[33] *I.e.*, the prince, Shadwell. Ascanius was the son of Aeneas, whom Virgil calls "the other hope of great Rome."

And lambent dullness played around his face.
As Hannibal [34] did to the altars come,
Sworn by his sire a mortal foe to Rome,
So Sh—— swore, nor should his vow be vain,
That he till death true dullness would maintain,
And, in his father's right, and realm's defense,
Ne'er to have peace with wit nor truce with sense.
The King himself the sacred unction made,
As king by office and as priest by trade.
In his sinister hand, instead of ball,[35]
He placed a mighty mug of potent ale;
Love's Kingdom [36] to his right he did convey,
At once his scepter and his rule of sway;
Whose righteous lore the prince had practiced young
And from whose loins recorded [37] *Psyche* sprung,
His temples, last, with poppies [38] were o'erspread,
That nodding seemed to consecrate his head.
Just at that point of time, if fame not lie,
On his left hand twelve reverend owls did fly
So Romulus,[39] 'tis sung, by Tiber's brook,
Presage of sway from twice six vultures took.
Th' admiring throng loud acclamations make,
And omens of his future empire take.
The sire then shook the honors of his head,
And from his brows damps of oblivion shed
Full on the filial dullness: long he stood,
Repelling from his breast the raging god; [40]
At length burst out in this prophetic mood:
    "Heavens bless my son; from Ireland let him reign
To far Barbadoes on the western main;

[34] Carthaginian general sworn from the age of nine to hate Rome.
[35] An orb, symbol of power; *sinister*, left.
[36] A pastoral play by Flecknoe.
[37] Remembered.
[38] Because of their narcotic property.
[39] According to legend, twelve vultures flying past him confirmed Romulus' choice of a site for Rome.
[40] Inspiration.

Of his dominion may no end be known,
And greater than his father's be his throne;
Beyond *Love's Kingdom* let him stretch his pen!"
He paused, and all the people cried, "Amen."
Then thus continued he: "My son, advance
Still in new impudence, new ignorance.
Success let others teach; learn thou from me
Pangs without birth, and fruitless industry.
Let *Virtuosos* in five years be writ,
Yet not one thought accuse thy toil of wit.
Let gentle George [41] in triumph tread the stage,
Make Dorimant betray and Loveit rage;
Let Cully, Cockwood, Fopling, charm the pit,[42]
And in their folly show the writer's wit.
Yet still thy fools shall stand in thy defense,
And justify their author's want of sense.
Let 'em be all by thy own model made
Of dullness, and desire no foreign aid;
That they to future ages may be known,
Not copies drawn, but issue of thy own
Nay, let thy men of wit too be the same,
All full of thee, and differing but in name.
But let no alien S—dl—y [43] interpose,
To lard with wit thy hungry *Epsom* prose.
And when false flowers of rhetoric thou wouldst cull,
Trust nature, do not labor to be dull;
But write thy best, and top; and, in each line,
Sir Formal's [44] oratory will be thine.
Sir Formal, though unsought, attends thy quill,
And does thy northern dedications [45] fill.

[41] Sir George Etherege, author of three comedies, the best of which is *The Man of Mode;* the five characters come from his plays.
[42] The people who occupied the floor of the theater around the stage.
[43] Sir Charles Sedley, poet and rake, wrote a prologue for *Epsom Wells.* Dryden suggests that Sedley helped Shadwell with the play.
[44] Sir Formal Trifle, a bombastic character in *The Virtuoso.*
[45] Shadwell dedicated a number of plays to the Duke of Newcastle (in the north of England).

Nor let false friends seduce thy mind to fame
By arrogating Jonson's [46] hostile name.
Let father Flecknoe fire thy mind with praise,
And uncle Ogleby thy envy raise.
Thou art my blood, where Jonson has no part:
What share have we in nature or in art?
Where did his wit on learning fix a brand,
And rail at arts he did not understand?
Where made he love in Prince Nicander's [47] vein,
Or swept the dust in *Psyche's* humble strain?
Where sold he bargains,[48] 'Whip-stitch,[49] kiss my arse,'
Promised a play and dwindled to a farce?
When did his Muse from Fletcher scenes purloin,
As thou whole Eth'rege dost transfuse to thine?
But so transfused as oils on water flow:
His always floats above, thine sinks below.
This is thy province, this thy wondrous way,
New humors to invent for each new play: [50]
This is that boasted bias of thy mind,
By which one way, to dullness, 'tis inclined;
Which makes thy writings lean on one side still,
And in all changes that way bends thy will.
Nor let thy mountain belly make pretense
Of likeness; thine's a tympany [51] of sense.
A tun of man in thy large bulk is writ,
But sure thou 'rt but a kilderkin [52] of wit.
Like mine, thy gentle numbers feebly creep;

[46] Shadwell believed (incorrectly, in Dryden's view) that he was carrying on in the classical tradition of Ben Jonson's comedies.

[47] A character in Shadwell's *Psyche*.

[48] Gave coarse answers to innocent questions, as does Sir Samuel Hearty in *The Virtuoso*.

[49] *Whip-stitch:* quick, presto.

[50] Shadwell had boasted of inventing new humors in each play. The next lines are a play on a passage from the epilogue to *The Humorists* which begins "A humor is the bias of the mind."

[51] Unhealthy swelling.

[52] Small cask.

Thy tragic Muse gives smiles, thy comic sleep.
With whate'er gall thou sett'st thyself to write,
Thy inoffensive satires never bite.
In thy felonious heart though venom lies,
It does but touch thy Irish pen, and dies.[53]
Thy genius calls thee not to purchase fame
In keen iambics [54] but mild anagram.
Leave writing plays, and choose for thy command
Some peaceful province in acrostic land.
There thou may'st wings display and altars raise,[55]
And torture one poor word ten thousand ways;
Or, if thou would'st thy diff'rent talents suit,
Set thy own songs, and sing them to thy lute."
　　He said; but his last words were scarcely heard,
For Bruce and Longvil [56] had a trap prepared,
And down they sent the yet declaiming bard.
Sinking he left his drugget robe behind,
Borne upwards by a subterranean wind.
The mantle fell to the young prophet's part,
With double portion of his father's art.[57]

[53] An allusion to there being no snakes in Ireland where Shadwell had spent some months as a young man.

[54] The classical meter for satire.

[55] In the seventeenth century poems were sometimes written so that they would have recognizable shapes when printed. See George Herbert's "The Altar" or "Easter-Wings."

[56] Characters in *The Virtuoso*. Two ladies in the play spring a trap door under Sir Formal Trifle.

[57] See 1 Kings 19:19 and 2 Kings 2:9–15 where Elisha received the mantle and double portion of the spirit of Elijah.

Joseph Addison
from
THE TATLER and
THE SPECTATOR

The modern literary essay came into its own in 1709 when Joseph Addison and Richard Steele began publication of The Tatler *which ran for twenty-one months, publishing essays on a variety of subjects and an occasional bit of news. It was shortly replaced by* The Spectator, *published daily for nearly two more years. Addison (1672–1719) was Secretary of State and held many other political offices in the early eighteenth century. He nevertheless found time to write prolifically and diversely, revealing throughout a classical polish and gentle kindliness.*

NED SOFTLY THE POET
from *The Tatler*, no. 163.

This celebration of the poetic virtues of Ned Softly is as appropriate today as when Addison wrote it. Only the names have changed. The epigraph from Catullus can be translated "At the same time he is never quite so happy as when he is writing a poem; he delights in and admires himself so much. But true it is, we are all under the same delusion, and there is not one whom you may not see to be a Suffenus in one thing or another." Suffenus is an earlier Ned Softly.

Monday, April 25, 1710.

Idem Inficeto est inficetior Rure
Simul Poemata attigit; neque idem unquam
Æque est beatus, ac Poema cum scribit:

125

Tam gaudet in se, tamque se ipse miratur.
Nimirum idem omnes fallimur; neque est quisquam
Quem non in aliqua re videre Suffenum
Possis.—Catul. *de Suffeno.*

Will's Coffee-house,[1] *April 24.*

I Yesterday came hither about Two Hours before the Company generally make their Appearance, with a Design to read over all the News-
Papers; but upon my sitting down, I was accosted by *Ned Softly,* who
saw me from a Corner in the other End of the Room, where I found he
had been writing something. Mr. *Bickerstaff,* says he, I observe by a late
Paper of yours, that you and I are just of a Humour; for you must
know, of all Impertinencies, there is nothing which I so much hate as
News. I never read a *Gazette* in my Life; and never trouble my Head
about our Armies, whether they win or lose, or in what Part of the
World they lie encamped. Without giving me Time to reply, he drew a
Paper of Verses out of his Pocket, telling me, That he had something
which would entertain me more agreeably, and that he would desire my
Judgment upon every Line, for that we had Time enough before us till
the Company came in.

Ned Softly is a very pretty Poet, and a great Admirer of easie Lines.
Waller is his Favourite: And as that admirable Writer has the best and
worst Verses of any among our great *English Poets, Ned Softly* has got
all the bad Ones without Book, which he repeats upon Occasion, to
show his Reading, and garnish his Conversation. *Ned* is indeed a true
English Reader, incapable of relishing the great and masterly Strokes of
this Art; but wonderfully pleased with the little *Gothick*[2] Ornaments
of Epigrammatical Conceits, Turns, Points, and Quibbles, which are so
frequent in the most admired of our *English* Poets, and practiced by
those who want Genius and Strength to represent, after the Manner of
the Ancients, Simplicity in its natural Beauty and Perfection.

Finding my self unavoidably engaged in such a Conversation, I was
resolved to turn my Pain into a Pleasure, and to divert my self as well

---

[1] Will's Coffee-house was patronized especially by poets and dramatists at a
time when coffee houses were the central meeting places of leisured gentlemen.

[2] *Gothick:* highly elaborate; out of date.

as I could with so very odd a Fellow. You must understand, says *Ned,* that the Sonnet I am going to read to you was written upon a Lady, who showed me some Verses of her own making, and is perhaps the best Poet of our Age. But you shall hear it. Upon which he begun to read as follows:

To Mira, on her incomparable Poems.

I.

When dress'd in Lawrel Wreaths you shine,
   And tune your soft melodious Notes,
You seem a Sister of the Nine,
   Or Phœbus *self in Petticoats.*

2.

I fancy, when your Song you sing,
   (Your Song you sing with so much Art)
Your Pen was pluck'd from Cupid's *Wing;*
   For ah! it wounds me like his Dart.

Why, says I, this is a little Nosegay of Conceits, a very Lump of Salt: Every Verse hath something in it that piques; and then the Dart in the last Line is certainly as pretty a Sting in the Tail of an Epigram (for so I think your Criticks call it) as ever entered into the Thought of a Poet. Dear Mr. *Bickerstaff,*[3] says he, shaking me by the Hand, every Body knows you to be a Judge of these Things; and to tell you truly, I read over *Roscommon's* Translation of *Horace's Art of Poetry* Three several Times, before I sat down to write the Sonnet which I have shown you. But you shall hear it again, and pray observe every Line of it, but not one of them shall pass without your Approbation.

When dress'd in Lawrel Wreaths you shine.

That is, says he, when you have your Garland on; when you are writing Verses. To which I replied, I know your Meaning: A Metaphor! The same, said he, and went on:

And tune your soft melodious Notes.

[3] *Bickerstaff:* Swift had first used the pen name Isaac Bickerstaff in his satiric pamphlets. Addison and Steele adopted it for *The Tatler.*

Pray observe the Gliding of that Verse; there is scarce a Consonant in it: I took Care to make it run upon Liquids.⁴ Give me your Opinion of it. Truly, said I, I think it as good as the former. I am very glad to hear you say so, says he; but mind the next:

You seem a Sister of the Nine.

That is, says he, you seem a Sister of the Muses; for if you look into ancient Authors, you will find it was their Opinion, that there were Nine of them. I remember it very well, said I; but pray proceed.

Or Phœbus *self in Petticoats.*

Phœbus, says he, was the God of Poetry. These little instances, Mr. *Bickerstaff,* show a Gentleman's Reading. Then to take off from the Air of Learning, which *Phœbus* and the Muses have given to this first Stanza, you may observe, how it falls all of a sudden into the Familiar; *in Petticoats!*

Or Phœbus *self in Petticoats.*

Let us now, say I, enter upon the Second Stanza. I find the First Line is still a Continuation of the Metaphor.

I fancy, when your Song you sing.

It is very right, says he; but pray observe the Turn of Words in those Two Lines. I was a whole Hour in adjusting of them, and have still a Doubt upon me, Whether in the Second Line it should be, *Your Song you sing;* or, *You sing your Song?* You shall hear them both:

I fancy, when your Song you sing,
(Your Song you sing with so much Art.)

OR

I fancy, when your Song you sing,
(You sing your Song with so much Art.)

Truly, said I, the Turn is so natural either Way, that you have made me almost giddy with it. Dear Sir, said he, grasping me by the Hand, you have a great deal of Patience; but pray what do you think of the next Verse?

⁴ *run upon Liquids:* move smoothly with liquid sounds.

128

Your Pen was pluck'd from Cupid's *Wing.*

Think! says I; I think you have made *Cupid* look like a little Goose. That was my Meaning, says he; I think the Ridicule is well enough hit off. But we now come to the last, which sums up the whole Matter:

For Ah! it wounds me like his Dart.

Pray how do you like that *Ah!* Doth it not make a pretty Figure in that Place? *Ah!* It looks as if I felt the Dart, and cried out at being pricked with it.

For Ah! it wounds me like his Dart.

My Friend *Dick Easy,* continued he, assured me, he would rather have written that *Ah!* than to have been the Author of the *Æneid.* He indeed objected, that I made *Mira's* Pen like a Quill in one of the Lines, and like a Dart in the other. But as to that—Oh! as to that, says I, it is but supposing *Cupid* to be like a Porcupine, and his Quills and Darts will be the same Thing. He was going to embrace me for the Hint; but half a Dozen Criticks coming into the Room, whose Faces he did not like, he conveyed the Sonnet into his Pocket, and whispered me in the Ear, he would show it me again as soon as his Man had written it over fair.

ON ITALIAN OPERA
from *The Spectator,* no. 18.

Here as elsewhere in The Spectator *the epigraph has some relevance to or makes some comment on the essay. These lines from Horace,* Epistles, II, i, 187, *are translated:*

Now our knights, too, are foolish and vain,
Ignore the sense, but love the painted scene.

Wednesday, March 21, 1710/11.

—Equitis quoque jam migravit ab aure voluptas
Omnis ad incertos oculos et gaudia vana.
                                        —Horace.

It is my design in this paper to deliver down to posterity a faithful account of the Italian opera, and of the gradual progress which it has made upon the English stage: for there is no question but our great-grandchildren will be very curious to know the reason why their forefathers used to sit together like an audience of foreigners in their own country, and to hear whole plays acted before them in a tongue which they did not understand.

Arsinoe [1] was the first opera that gave us a taste of Italian music. The great success this opera met with produced some attempts of forming pieces upon Italian plans, which should give a more natural and reasonable entertainment than what can be met with in the elaborate trifles of that nation. This alarmed the poetasters and fiddlers of the town, who were used to deal in a more ordinary kind of ware; and therefore laid down an established rule, which is received as such to this day, *that nothing is capable of being well set to music, that is not nonsense.*

This maxim was no sooner received but we immediately fell to translating the Italian operas; and as there was no great danger of hurting the sense of those extraordinary pieces, our authors would often make words of their own which were entirely foreign to the meaning of the passages they pretended to translate; their chief care being to make the numbers of the English verse answer to those of the Italian, that both of them might go to the same tune. Thus the famous song in *Camilla,* [2]

> Barbara si t' intendo, &c.
> Barbarous woman, yes, I know your meaning,

which expresses the resentments of an angry lover, was translated into that English lamentation,

> Frail are a lover's hopes, &c.

And it was pleasant enough to see the most refined persons of the British nation dying away and languishing to notes that were filled with a spirit of rage and indignation. It happened also very frequently, where

---

[1] *Arsinoe:* produced at Drury Lane on January 16, 1705, from the Italian with a score by Thomas Clayton.

[2] *Camilla:* in this opera by Bononcine the hero sang in Italian; the heroine in English.

the sense was rightly translated, the necessary transposition of words, which were drawn out of the phrase of one tongue into that of another, made the music appear very absurd in one tongue that was very natural in the other. I remember an Italian verse that ran thus word for word,

And turn'd my rage into pity:

which the English for rhyme sake translated,

And into pity turn'd my rage.

By this means the soft notes that were adapted to *pity* in the Italian fell upon the word *rage* in the English, and the angry sounds that were turned to *rage* in the original were made to express *pity* in the translation. It oftentimes happened likewise that the finest notes in the air fell upon the most insignificant words in the sentence. I have known the word *and* pursued through the whole gamut, have been entertained with many a melodious *the,* and have heard the most beautiful graces, quavers, and divisions bestowed upon *then, for,* and *from;* to the eternal honor of our English particles.

The next step to our refinement was the introducing of Italian actors into our opera; who sung their parts in their own language, at the same time that our countrymen performed theirs in our native tongue. The king or hero of the play generally spoke in Italian, and his slaves answered him in English: the lover frequently made his court, and gained the heart of his princess, in a language which she did not understand. One would have thought it very difficult to have carried on dialogues after this manner without an interpreter between the persons that conversed together; but this was the state of the English stage for about three years.

At length the audience grew tired of understanding half the opera and therefore, to ease themselves entirely of the fatigue of thinking, have so ordered it at present that the whole opera is performed in an unknown tongue. We no longer understand the language of our own stage; insomuch that I have often been afraid, when I have seen our Italian performers chattering in the vehemence of action, that they have been calling us names, and abusing us among themselves; but I hope since we do put such an entire confidence in them, they will not talk against us before our faces, though they may do it with the same safety as if it were behind our backs. In the meantime, I cannot forbear think-ing how naturally an historian who writes two or three hundred years hence, and does not know the taste of his wise forefathers, will make the following reflection: *In the beginning of the eighteenth century the Italian tongue was so well understood in* England *that operas were acted on the public stage in that language.*

One scarce knows how to be serious in the confutation of an absurdity that shows itself at the first sight. It does not want any great measure of sense to see the ridicule of this monstrous practice; but what makes it the more astonishing, it is not the taste of the rabble, but of persons of the greatest politeness, which has established it.

If the Italians have a genius for music above the English, the English have a genius for other performances of a much higher nature, and capable of giving the mind a much nobler entertainment. Would one think it was possible (at a time when an author lived that was able to write the *Phaedra and Hippolytus* [3]) for a people to be so stupidly fond of the Italian opera as scarce to give a third day's hearing to that ad-mirable tragedy? Music is certainly a very agreeable entertainment, but if it would take the entire possession of our ears, if it would make us incapable of hearing sense, if it would exclude arts that have a much greater tendency to the refinement of human nature, I must confess I would allow it no better quarter than Plato has done, who banishes it out of his commonwealth.

At present, our notions of music are so very uncertain that we do not know what it is we like; only, in general, we are transported with any-thing that is not English. So if it be of a foreign growth, let it be Italian, French, or High Dutch, it is the same thing. In short, our English music is quote rooted out and nothing yet planted in its stead.

When a royal palace is burnt to the ground, every man is at liberty to present his plan for a new one; and though it be but indifferently put together, it may furnish several hints that may be of use to a good architect. I shall take the same liberty in a following paper, of giving my opinion upon the subject of music; which I shall lay down only in a problematical manner, to be considered by those who are masters in the art.

[3] *Phaedra and Hippolytus:* Addison wrote the prologue for this play by Edmund Smith (1707).

SATIRE
from *The Spectator*, no. 34.

Here Addison illustrates how the subjects of satire squirm and turn, feeling themselves unfairly treated. The quotation from Juvenal is appropriate: "Every wild beast spares its own kind."

April 9, 1711.

*Parcit
Cognatis maculis similis fera*——
—Juvenal

The club of which I am a member, is very luckily composed of such persons as are engaged in different ways of life, and deputed as it were out of the most conspicuous classes of mankind. By this means I am furnished with the greatest variety of hints and materials, and know everything that passes in the different quarters and divisions, not only of this great city, but of the whole kingdom. My readers too have the satisfaction to find that there is no rank or degree among them who have not their representative in this club, and that there is always somebody present who will take care of their respective interests, that nothing may be written or published to the prejudice or infringement of their just rights and privileges.

I last night sat very late in company with this select body of friends, who entertained me with several remarks which they and others had made upon these my speculations, as also with the various success which they had met with among their several ranks and degrees of readers. Will Honeycomb told me, in the softest manner he could, that there were some ladies (but for your comfort, says Will, they are not those of the most wit) that were offended at the liberties I had taken with the opera and the puppet-show; that some of them were likewise very much surprised, that I should think such serious points as the dress and equipage of persons of quality, proper subjects for raillery.

He was going on, when Sir Andrew Freeport took him up short, and told him that the papers he hinted at, had done great good in the city, and that all their wives and daughters were the better for them; and further added, that the whole city thought themselves very much obliged to me for declaring my generous intentions to scourge vice and folly as they appear in a multitude, without condescending to be a publisher of particular intrigues and cuckoldoms. "In short," says Sir Andrew, "if you avoid that foolish beaten road of falling upon aldermen and citizens, and employ your pen upon the vanity and luxury of courts, your paper must needs be of general use."

Upon this my friend the Templar[1] told Sir Andrew, that he wondered to hear a man of his sense talk after that manner; that the city had always been the province for satire; and that the wits of King Charles's time jested upon nothing else during his whole reign. He then showed, by the examples of Horace, Juvenal, Boileau,[2] and the best writers of every age, that the follies of the stage and court had never been accounted too sacred for ridicule, how great soever the persons might be that patronized them. "But after all," says he, "I think your raillery has made too great an excursion, in attacking several persons of the Inns of Court; and I do not believe you can show me any precedent for your behavior in that particular."

My good friend Sir Roger de Coverley, who had said nothing all this while, began his speech with a Pish! and told us that he wondered to see so many men of sense so very serious upon fooleries. "Let our good friend," says he, "attack every one that deserves it; I would only advise you, Mr. Spectator," applying himself to me, "to take care how you meddle with country squires. They are the ornaments of the English nation; men of good heads and sound bodies! and, let me tell you, some of them take it ill of you, that you mention fox-hunters with so little respect."

Captain Sentry spoke very sparingly on this occasion. What he said was only to commend my prudence in not touching upon the army, and advised me to continue to act discreetly in that point.

By this time I found every subject of my speculations was taken away from me, by one or other of the club: and began to think myself in the condition of the good man that had one wife who took a dislike

[1] *Templar:* a lawyer with chambers in the Temple, London.
[2] *Boileau:* Nicholas Boileau-Despreaux (1636–1711), French poet and satirist.

to his gray hairs, and another to his black, till by their picking out what each of them had an aversion to, they left his head altogether bald and naked.

While I was thus musing with myself, my worthy friend the clergyman, who, very luckily for me, was at the club that night, undertook my cause. He told us, that he wondered any order of persons should think themselves too considerable to be advised; that it was not quality, but innocence, which exempted men from reproof; that vice and folly ought to be attacked wherever they could be met with, and especially when they were placed in high and conspicuous stations of life. He further added, that my paper would only serve to aggravate the pains of poverty, if it chiefly exposed those who are already depressed, and in some measure turned into ridicule, by the meanness of their conditions and circumstances. He afterward proceeded to take notice of the great use this paper might be of to the public, by reprehending those vices which are too trivial for the chastisement of the law, and too fantastical for the cognizance of the pulpit. He then advised me to prosecute my undertaking with cheerfulness, and assured me, that whoever might be displeased with me, I should be approved by all those whose praises do honor to the persons on whom they are bestowed.

The whole club pays a particular deference to the discourse of this gentleman, and are drawn into what he says, as much by the candid ingenuous manner with which he delivers himself, as by the strength of argument and force of reason which he makes use of. Will Honeycomb immediately agreed that what he had said was right; and that, for his part, he would not insist upon the quarter which he had demanded for the ladies. Sir Andrew gave up the city with the same frankness. The Templar would not stand out, and was followed by Sir Roger and the Captain; who all agreed that I should be at liberty to carry the war into what quarter I pleased; provided I continued to combat with criminals in a body, and to assault the vice without hurting the person.

This debate, which was held for the good of mankind, put me in mind of that which the Roman triumvirate were formerly engaged in for their destruction. Every man at first stood hard for his friend, till they found that by this means they should spoil their proscription; and at length, making a sacrifice of all their acquaintance and relations, furnished out a very decent execution.

Having thus taken my resolutions to march on boldly in the cause of virtue and good sense, and to annoy their adversaries in whatever degree or rank of men they may be found; I shall be deaf for the future to all the remonstrances that shall be made to me on this account. If Punch grows extravagant, I shall reprimand him very freely: if the stage becomes a nursery of folly and impertinence, I shall not be afraid to animadvert upon it. In short, if I meet with anything in city, court, or country, that shocks modesty or good manners, I shall use my utmost endeavors to make an example of it. I must, however, entreat every particular person who does me the honor to be a reader of this paper never to think himself, or any one of his friends, or enemies, aimed at in what is said: for I promise him, never to draw a faulty character which does not fit at least a thousand people; or to publish a single paper, that is not written in the spirit of benevolence, and with a love to mankind.

TRUE AND FALSE WIT
from *The Spectator,* no. 62.

The meaning of wit *has changed throughout its several centuries of use; its meaning was different to John Donne in the early seventeenth century than to Byron in the early nineteenth. Addison's definition in the early eighteenth century is the clearest statement of what wit meant to his age. The epigraph is translated as "The source and fount of all good writing is wisdom." The quotation from John Locke comes from his* Essay Concerning Human Understanding, *Chapter XI. Dryden's definition of wit comes from his "Apology for Heroic Poetry" which prefaces* The State of Innocence (1677). *Dominique Bouhours wrote* La Manière de bien Penser (1687).

Friday, May 11, 1711.

Scribendi recte sapere est et principium et fons.
—Horace.

Mr. Locke has an admirable reflection upon the difference of wit and judgment, whereby he endeavors to show the reason why they are not always the talents of the same person. His words are as follow: "And hence, perhaps, may be given some reason of that common observation, that men who have a great deal of wit and prompt memories have not always the clearest judgment or deepest reason. For wit lying most in the assemblage of ideas, and putting those together with quickness and variety wherein can be found any resemblance or congruity, thereby to make up pleasant pictures and agreeable visions in the fancy; judgment, on the contrary, lies quite on the other side, in separating carefully one from another ideas wherein can be found the least difference, thereby to avoid being misled by similitude, and by affinity to take one thing for another. This is a way of proceeding quite contrary to metaphor and allusion; wherein, for the most part, lies that entertainment and pleasantry of wit which strikes so lively on the fancy, and is therefore so acceptable to all people."

That is, I think, the best and most philosophical account that I have ever met with of wit, which generally, though not always, consists in such a resemblance and congruity of ideas as this author mentions. I shall only add to it, by way of explanation, that every resemblance of ideas is not that which we call wit unless it be such a one that gives delight and surprise to the reader. These two properties seem essential to wit, more particularly the last of them. In order, therefore, that the resemblance in the ideas be wit, it is necessary that the ideas should not lie too near one another in the nature of things; for where the likeness is obvious, it gives no surprise. To compare one man's singing to that of another, or to represent the whiteness of any object by that of milk and snow, or the variety of its colors by those of the rainbow, cannot be called wit, unless, besides this obvious resemblance, there be some further congruity discovered in the two ideas that is capable of giving the reader some surprise. Thus when a poet tells us the bosom of his mistress is as white as snow, there is no wit in the comparison; but when he adds, with a sigh, that it is as cold too, it then grows into wit. Every reader's memory may supply him with innumerable instances of the same nature. For this reason the similitudes in heroic poets, who endeavor rather to fill the mind with great conceptions than to divert it with such as are new and surprising, have seldom anything in them that can be called wit. Mr. Locke's account of wit, with this short explanation, comprehends most of the species of wit, as metaphors, similitudes, allegories, enigmas, mottoes, parables, fables, dreams, visions, dramatic writings, burlesque, and all the methods of allusion: as there are many other pieces of wit (how remote soever they may appear at first sight from the foregoing description) which upon examination will be found to agree with it.

As *true wit* generally consists in this resemblance and congruity of ideas, *false wit* chiefly consists in the resemblance and congruity sometimes of single letters, as in anagrams, chronograms, lipograms, and acrostics; sometimes of syllables, as in echoes and doggerel rhymes; sometimes of words, as in puns and quibbles; and sometimes of whole sentences or poems, cast into the figures of eggs, axes, or altars. Nay, some carry the notion of wit so far as to ascribe it even to external mimicry, and to look upon a man as an ingenious person, that can resemble the tone, posture, or face of another.

As true wit consists in the resemblance of ideas, and false wit in the resemblance of words, according to the foregoing instances, there is another kind of wit which consists partly in the resemblance of ideas and partly in the resemblance of words; which for distinction sake I shall call mixed wit. This kind of wit is that which abounds in Cowley more than in any other author that ever wrote. Mr. Waller has likewise a great deal of it. Mr. Dryden is very sparing in it. Milton had a genius much above it. Spenser is in the same class with Milton. The Italians, even in their epic poetry, are full of it. Monsieur Boileau, who formed himself upon the ancient poets, has everywhere rejected it with scorn. If we look after mixed wit among the Greek writers, we shall find it nowhere but in the epigrammatists. There are indeed some strokes of it in the little poem ascribed to Musaeus, which by that, as well as many other marks, betrays itself to be a modern composition. If we look into the Latin writers, we find none of this mixed wit in Vergil, Lucretius, or Catullus; very little in Horace, but a great deal of it in Ovid, and scarce anything else in Martial.

Out of the innumerable branches of mixed wit, I shall choose one instance which may be met with in all the writers of this class. The passion of love in its nature has been thought to resemble fire; for which reason the words *fire* and *flame* are made use of to signify love. The witty poets therefore have taken an advantage from the double meaning of the word fire to make an infinite number of witticisms.

Cowley, observing the cold regard of his mistress's eyes, and at the same time their power of producing love in him, considers them as burning glasses made of ice; and, finding himself able to live in the greatest extremities of love, concludes the torrid zone to be habitable. When his mistress has read his letter written in juice of lemon by holding it to the fire, he desires her to read it over a second time by love's flames. When she weeps, he wishes it were inward heat that distilled those drops from the limbec. When she is absent, he is beyond eighty, that is, thirty degrees nearer the pole than when she is with him. His ambitious love is a fire that naturally mounts upwards; his happy love is the beams of Heaven, and his unhappy love flames of Hell. When it does not let him sleep, it is a flame that sends up no smoke; when it is opposed by counsel and advice, it is a fire that rages the more by the wind's blowing upon it. Upon the dying of a tree in which he had cut his loves, he observes that his written flames had burnt up and withered the tree. When he resolves to give over his passion, he tells us that one burnt like him forever dreads the fire. His heart is an Aetna, that instead of Vulcan's shop encloses Cupid's forge in it. His endeavoring to drown his love in wine is throwing oil upon the fire. He would insinuate to his mistress that the fire of love, like that of the sun (which produces so many living creatures), should not only warm but beget. Love in another place cooks pleasure at his fire. Sometimes the poet's heart is frozen in every breast, and sometimes scorched in every eye. Sometimes he is drowned in tears and burnt in love, like a ship set on fire in the middle of the sea.

The reader may observe in every one of these instances that the poet mixes the qualities of fire with those of love; and in the same sentence speaking of it both as a passion and as real fire, surprises the reader with those seeming resemblances or contradictions that make up all the wit in this kind of writing. Mixed wit therefore is a composition of pun and true wit, and is more or less perfect as the resemblance lies in the ideas or in the words. Its foundations are laid partly in falsehood and partly in truth: reason puts in her claim for one half of it, and extravagance for the other. The only province therefore for this kind of wit is epigram, or those little occasional poems that in their own nature are nothing else but a tissue of epigrams. I cannot conclude this head of mixed wit without owning that the admirable poet out of whom I have taken the examples of it had as much true wit as any author that ever writ and indeed all other talents of an extraordinary genius.

It may be expected, since I am upon this subject, that I should take notice of Mr. Dryden's definition of wit; which, with all the deference that is due to the judgment of so great a man, is not so properly a definition of wit as of good writing in general. Wit, as he defines it, is "a propriety of words and thoughts adapted to the subject." If this be a true definition of wit, I am apt to think that Euclid was the greatest wit that ever set pen to paper. It is certain that never was a greater propriety of words and thoughts adapted to the subject than what that author has made use of in his *Elements*. I shall only appeal to my reader if this definition agrees with any notion he has of wit. If it be a true one, I am sure Mr. Dryden was not only a better poet, but a greater wit, than Mr. Cowley, and Vergil a much more facetious man than either Ovid or Martial.

Bouhours, whom I look upon to be the most penetrating of all the French critics, has taken pains to show that it is impossible for any thought to be beautiful which is not just, and has not its foundation in the nature of things; that the basis of all wit is truth; and that no thought can be valuable of which good sense is not the groundwork. Boileau has endeavored to inculcate the same notion in several parts of his writings, both in prose and verse. This is that natural way of writing, that beautiful simplicity, which we so much admire in the compositions of the ancients, and which nobody deviates from but those who want strength of genius to make a thought shine in its own natural beauties. Poets who want this strength of genius to give that majestic simplicity to nature which we so much admire in the works of the ancients are forced to hunt after foreign ornaments, and not to let any piece of wit of what kind soever escape them. I look upon these writers as Goths in poetry, who, like those in architecture, not being able to come up to the beautiful simplicity of the old Greeks and Romans, have endeavored to supply its place with all the extravagances of an irregular fancy.

DISSECTING OF A BEAU'S HEAD
from *The Spectator*, no. 275.

The beau—a fop or dandy who is excessively attentive to his clothes, his mien, and his ladies—is still with us, whether in Brooks Brothers suits or the exotic garb of the latest sub-cult. The epigraph means "A head no hellebore can cure."

January 15, 1712.

Tribus Anticyris caput insanabile.
—Horace, *Ars Poetica* 300.

I was yesterday engaged in an assembly of virtuosos, where one of them produced many curious observations which he had lately made in the anatomy of an human body. Another of the company communicated to us several wonderful discoveries which he had also made on the same subject by the help of very fine glasses. This gave birth to a great variety of uncommon remarks, and furnished discourse for the remaining part of the day.

The different opinions which were started on this occasion, presented to my imagination so many new ideas, that, by mixing with those which were already there, they employed my fancy all the last night, and composed a very wild extravagant dream.

I was invited methought to the dissection of a beau's head and of a coquette's heart, which were both of them laid on a table before us. An imaginary operator opened the first with a great deal of nicety, which, upon a cursory and superficial view, appeared like the head of another man; but upon applying our glasses to it, we made a very odd discovery, namely, that what we looked upon as brains, were not such in reality, but an heap of strange materials wound up in that shape and texture, and packed together with wonderful art in the several cavities of the skull. For, as Homer tells us that the blood of the gods is not real blood, but only something like it; so we found that the brain of a beau is not a real brain, but only something like it.

141

The pineal gland, which many of our modern philosophers suppose to be the seat of the soul, smelt very strong of essence and orange-flower water, and was encompassed with a kind of horny substance, cut into a thousand little faces or mirrors which were imperceptible to the naked eye, insomuch that the soul, if there had been any here, must have been always taken up in contemplating her own beauties.

We observed a large antrum or cavity in the sinciput,[1] that was filled with ribands, lace and embroidery, wrought together in a most curious piece of net-work, the parts of which were likewise imperceptible to the naked eye. Another of these antrums or cavities was stuffed with invisible billetdoux, loveletters, pricked dances, and other trumpery of the same nature. In another we found a kind of powder,[2] which set the whole company a sneezing, and by the scent discovered itself to be right Spanish. The several other cells were stored with commodities of the same kind, of which it would be tedious to give the reader an exact inventory.

There was a large cavity on each side the head, which I must not omit. That on the right side was filled with fictions, flatteries, and falsehoods, vows, promises, and protestations; that on the left, with oaths and imprecations. There issued out a duct from each of these cells, which ran into the root of the tongue, where both joined together, and passed forward in one common duct to the tip of it. We discovered several little roads or canals running from the ear into the brain, and took particular care to trace them out through their several passages. One of them extended itself to a bundle of sonnets and little musical instruments. Others ended in several bladders which were filled either with wind or froth. But the large canal entered into a great cavity of the skull, from whence there went another canal into the tongue. This great cavity was filled with a kind of spongy substance, which the French anatomists call galimatias, and the English, nonsense. The skins of the forehead were extremely tough and thick, and what very much surprised us, had not in them any single blood-vessel that we were able to discover, either with or without our glasses; from whence we concluded, that the party when alive must have been entirely deprived of the faculty of blushing.

[1] *sinciput:* upper part of the skull.
[2] *kind of powder:* snuff.

The os cribriforme[3] was exceedingly stuffed, and in some places damaged with snuff. We could not but take notice in particular of that small muscle which is not often discovered in dissections, and draws the nose upwards, when it expresses the contempt which the owner of it has, upon seeing anything he does not like, or hearing anything he does not understand. I need not tell my learned reader, this is that muscle which performs the motion so often mentioned by the Latin poets, when they talk of a man's cocking his nose, or playing the rhinoceros.

We did not find anything very remarkable in the eye, saving only that the musculi amatorii, or, as we may translate it into English, the ogling muscles, were very much worn and decayed with use; whereas, on the contrary, the elevator, or the muscle which turns the eye towards heaven, did not appear to have been used at all.

I have only mentioned in this dissection such new discoveries as we were able to make, and have not taken any notice of those parts which are to be met with in common heads. As for the skull, the face, and indeed the whole outward shape and figure of the head, we could not discover any difference from what we observe in the heads of other men. We were informed that the person to whom this head belonged, had passed for a man above five and thirty years; during which time he ate and drank like other people, dressed well, talked loud, laughed frequently, and on particular occasions had acquitted himself tolerably at a ball or an assembly; to which one of the company added, that a certain knot of ladies took him for a wit. He was cut off in the flower of his age by the blow of a paring shovel,[4] having been surprised by an eminent citizen, as he was tendering some civilities to his wife.

[3] *os cribriforme:* sieve-like mouth.
[4] *paring shovel:* a plow pushed by the chest; used for paring turf.

Alexander Pope
THE RAPE OF THE LOCK
and TWO SHORT SATIRES

*Probably the greatest purely literary satirist of all time, Pope
was, in his youth, a member of Addison's circle, but he
gradually drifted away to form a club with Swift, Gay, and
others. His satires reflect this development. In his youth he
is Horatian, but as he ages he tends more toward the Juvenalian. Yet he remains characteristically himself. One
can see the changes in his basic tone by reading first* The
Rape of the Lock (*1714*), *then* The Art of Sinking in
Poetry (*1727*), *the* Epistle to Dr. Arbuthnot (*1735*), *and
finally the completed* Dunciad (*1743*).

THE RAPE OF THE LOCK

*This poem is the finest example of mock-epic or mock-
heroic satire. The incident it relates is completely trivial—
a Lord Petre snipped a lock of hair from a Miss Arabella
Fermor at a social event. (This really happened.) Tempers
flared and a family feud followed. Pope, out to mend the
rift like a good conservative satirist, wrote a two-canto
satire in 1712, which thrust the incident into proper perspective. But Pope saw more to the matter, and two years
later he published the five-canto version we have here. In
this larger work, he expands his satire to make a general
criticism of the inconsequential way in which the leisure
classes waste their time. One must understand something
of the epic to understand* The Rape of the Lock *because
Pope mocks and parodies many of the epic conventions.*
The Iliad, The Aeneid, *and* Paradise Lost *are the chief epic
poems he alludes to. For example, there is an appeal to the*

144

Muse at the beginning. There are supernatural beings at work in mortal affairs. There are epic battles, and catalogs of dress and weaponry, and heroic diction, and epithets, and mock sacrifices. There is even a final apotheosis as the lock itself becomes a heavenly constellation. The reader approaching this impishly witty poem must have patience enough to use the notes faithfully, not because the poem is learned and obscure but because it is allusive and subtle. Remember that the scale here is epically minute; the great battle in Canto III is merely an idle afternoon's card game. Pope's verse is iambic pentameter couplets, introduced into English by Chaucer, and very popular in the eighteenth century as the verse for heroic poems. In fact, since then it has been commonly called "heroic couplets." Its basic nature is that each couplet contains a complete thought. There is usually a pause at the end of the first line and a stronger pause at the end of the second. This framework actually makes the verse sound heroic, and it lends itself to parallel constructions which can seem logical and convincing even when they are not. And Pope invents all sorts of syntactic-poetic tricks within this tight heroic couplet framework. The poetics itself is not of prime importance, but Pope's satire is. The world he ridicules is the world ridiculed by Cummings in The Cambridge Ladies *and Eliot in* The Love Song of J. Alfred Prufrock. *It is the world of social triviality, indifferent to the struggles and injustices around it. And Pope's epic view of it renders it epically trivial.*

CANTO I

What dire offence from amorous causes springs,
What mighty contests rise from trivial things,
I sing—This verse to CARYLL,[1] Muse! is due:
This, even Belinda may vouchsafe to view;
Slight is the subject, but not so the praise,
If she inspire, and he approve my lays.
  Say what strange motive, goddess! could compel

[1] John Caryll, a friend of Pope, urged him to write the poem.

145

A well-bred lord to assault a gentle belle?
O say what stranger cause, yet unexplored,
Could make a gentle belle reject a lord?
In tasks so bold, can little men engage,
And in soft bosoms dwells such mighty rage?
    Sol through white curtains shot a tim'rous ray,
And oped those eyes that must eclipse the day:
Now lap-dogs gave themselves the rousing shake,
And sleepless lovers, just at twelve awake:
Thrice rung the bell,[2] the slipper knock'd the ground,
And the press'd watch [3] return'd a silver sound.
Belinda still her downy pillow press'd,
Her guardian sylph [4] prolong'd the balmy rest:
'Twas he had summon'd to her silent bed
The morning-dream that hover'd o'er her head;
A youth more glittering than a birth-night beau,[5]
(That ev'n in slumber caused her cheek to glow)
Seem'd to her ear his winning lips to lay,
And thus in whispers said, or seem'd to say:
    "Fairest of mortals, thou distinguish'd care
Of thousand bright inhabitants of air!
If e'er one vision touch thy infant thought,
Of all the nurse and all the priest have taught;
Of airy elves by moonlight shadows seen,
The silver token,[6] and the circled green,[7]
Or virgins visited by angel powers,
With golden crowns and wreaths of heavenly flowers;
Hear and believe! thy own importance know,
Nor bound thy narrow views to things below.
Some secret truths, from learned pride conceal'd,

[2] To call for the maid.
[3] A special watch which rang out the latest hour when a certain lever was pressed.
[4] A supernatural being protecting Belinda.
[5] An escort to a royal ball.
[6] A token left by fairies at night in the shoes of hard working maids.
[7] The green showed marks of dancing fairies.

To maids alone and children are reveal'd:
What, though no credit doubting wits may give?
The fair and innocent shall still believe.
Know, then, unnumbered spirits round thee fly,
The light militia of the lower sky:
These, though unseen, are ever on the wing,
Hang o'er the box, and hover round the ring.[8]
Think what an equipage thou hast in air,
And view with scorn two pages and a chair.
As now your own, our beings [9] were of old,
And once inclosed in woman's beauteous mould;
Thence, by a soft transition, we repair
From earthly vehicles to these of air.
Think not, when woman's transient breath is fled,
That all her vanities at once are dead;
Succeeding vanities she still regards,
And though she plays no more, o'erlooks the cards.
Her joy in gilden chariots, when alive,
And love of ombre,[10] after death survive.
For when the fair in all their pride expire,
To their first elements their souls retire:
The sprites of fiery termagants in flame
Mount up, and take a Salamander's name.
Soft yielding minds to water glide away,
And sip, with nymphs, their elemental tea.
The graver prude sinks downward to a gnome,
In search of mischief still on earth to roam.
The light coquettes in sylphs aloft repair,
And sport and flutter in the fields of air.
    "Know further yet; whoever fair and chaste
Rejects mankind, is by some sylph embraced:
For spirits, freed from mortal laws, with ease
Assume what sexes and what shapes they please.

[8] The theater box and Hyde Park ring—fashionable places.
[9] Alluding to the platonic idea that those passions not purified by philosophy
in this life remain with the soul in another.
[10] The "in" card game of the day; see Canto III, l. 27.

147

What guards the purity of melting maids,
In courtly balls, and midnight masquerades,
Safe from the treach'rous friend, the daring spark,
The glance by day, the whisper in the dark,
When kind occasion prompts their warm desires,
When music softens, and when dancing fires?
'Tis but their sylph, the wise celestials know,
Though honour is the word with men below.
  "Some nymphs there are, too conscious of their face,
For life predestined to the gnome's embrace.
These swell their prospects and exalt their pride,
When offers are disdain'd and love denied:
Then gay ideas crowd the vacant brain,
While peers, and dukes, and all their sweeping train,
And garters,[11] stars, and coronets appear,
And in soft sounds, 'Your Grace' salutes their ear.
'Tis these that early taint the female soul,
Instruct the eyes of young coquettes to roll,
Teach infant cheeks a bidden blush to know,
And little hearts to flutter at a beau.
  "Oft when the world imagine women stray,
The sylphs through mystic mazes guide their way,
Through all the giddy circle they pursue,
And old impertinence [12] expel by new.
What tender maid but must a victim fall
To one man's treat, but for another's ball?
When Florio [13] speaks, what virgin could withstand,
If gentle Damon did not squeeze her hand?
With varying vanities, from ev'ry part,
They shift the moving toy-shop of their heart;
Where wigs with wigs, with sword-knots sword-knots [14] strive,
Beaux banish beaux, and coaches coaches drive.
This erring mortals levity may call,

[11] Worn by members of the Order of the Garter (see Canto II, l. 39).
[12] Triviality.
[13] Florio and Damon are names for stereotyped amorous heroes.
[14] Tassels on sword hilts.

Oh, blind to truth! the sylphs contrive it all.
   "Of these am I, who thy protection claim,
A watchful sprite, and Ariel is my name.
Late, as I ranged the crystal wilds of air,
In the clear mirror of thy ruling star
I saw, alas! some dread event impend,
Ere to the main this morning sun descend;
But heaven reveals not what, or how, or where:
Warn'd by the sylph, oh, pious maid, beware!
This to disclose is all thy guardian can:
Beware of all, but most beware of man!"
   He said; when Shock,[15] who thought she slept too long,
Leap'd up, and waked his mistress with his tongue.
'Twas then, Belinda, if report say true,
Thy eyes first open'd on a billet-doux;
Wounds, charms, and ardours, were no sooner read,
But all the vision vanish'd from thy head.
   And now, unveil'd, the toilet stands display'd,
Each silver vase in mystic order laid.
First, robed in white, the nymph intent adores,
With head uncover'd, the cosmetic powers.
A heav'nly image in the glass appears,
To that she bends, to that her eyes she rears;
Th' inferior priestess,[16] at her altar's side,
Trembling, begins the sacred rites of pride.
Unnumber'd treasures ope at once, and here
The various offerings of the world appear;
From each she nicely culls with curious toil,
And decks the goddess with the glitt'ring spoil.
This casket India's glowing gems unlocks,
And all Arabia[17] breathes from yonder box.
The tortoise here and elephant unite,
Transform'd to combs, the speckled and the white.
Here files of pins extend their shining rows,

[15] A lapdog.
[16] Belinda's maid Betty.
[17] Perfumes.

Puffs, powders, patches, Bibles, billet-doux.
Now awful beauty puts on all its arms;
The fair each moment rises in her charms,
Repairs her smiles, awakens every grace,
And calls forth all the wonders of her face:
Sees by degrees a purer blush arise,
And keener lightnings quicken in her eyes.
The busy sylphs surround their darling care,
These set the head, and those divide the hair,
Some fold the sleeve, while others plait the gown;
And Betty's praised for labours not her own.

CANTO II

Not with more glories, in th' ethereal plain,
The sun first rises o'er the purpled main,
Than, issuing forth, the rival of his beams
Launch'd on the bosom of the silver Thames.
Fair nymphs and well-dress'd youths around her shone,
But every eye was fix'd on her alone.
On her white breast a sparkling cross she wore,
Which Jews might kiss, and infidels adore.
Her lively looks a sprightly mind disclose,
Quick as her eyes, and as unfix'd as those:
Favours to none, to all she smiles extends;
Oft she rejects, but never once offends.
Bright as the sun, her eyes the gazers strike,
And, like the sun, they shine on all alike. —
Yet graceful ease, and sweetness void of pride,
Might hide her faults, if belles had faults to hide:
If to her share some female errors fall,
Look on her face, and you'll forget them all.
    This nymph, to the destruction of mankind,
Nourish'd two locks, which graceful hung behind
In equal curls, and well conspired to deck
With shining ringlets the smooth ivory neck.
Love in these labyrinths his slaves detains,

And mighty hearts are held in slender chains.
With hairy springes [18] we the birds betray,
Slight lines of hair surprise the finny prey,
Fair tresses man's imperial race [19] insnare,
And beauty draws us with a single hair.
    Th' adventurous baron the bright locks admired;
He saw, he wish'd, and to the prize aspired.
Resolved to win, he meditates the way,
By force to ravish, or by fraud betray;
For when success a lover's toils attends,
Few ask, if fraud or force attain'd his ends.
    For this, ere Phœbus rose, he had implored
Propitious Heaven, and every power adored:
But chiefly Love—to Love an altar built,
Of twelve vast French romances, neatly gilt.
There lay three garters,[20] half a pair of gloves;
And all the trophies of his former loves:
With tender billet-doux he lights the pyre,
And breathes three amorous sighs to raise the fire.
Then prostrate falls, and begs with ardent eyes
Soon to obtain, and long possess the prize:
The powers gave ear, and granted half his prayer,
The rest, the winds dispersed in empty air.
    But now secure the painted vessel glides,
The sun-beams trembling on the floating tides;
While melting music steals upon the sky,
And soften'd sounds along the waters die;
Smooth flow the waves, the zephyrs gently play,
Belinda smiled, and all the world was gay.
All but the sylph—with careful thoughts oppress'd,
Th' impending woe sat heavy on his breast.
He summons straight his denizens of air;
The lucid squadrons round the sails repair:
Soft o'er the shrouds aërial whispers breathe,

[18] Snares.
[19] Phrase of Virgil.
[20] By ironic contrast to the royal garters in Canto I.

That seem'd but zephyrs to the twain beneath.
Some to the sun their insect-wings unfold,
Waft on the breeze, or sink in clouds of gold;
Transparent forms, too fine for mortal sight,
Their fluid bodies half dissolved in light.
Loose to the wind their airy garments flew,
Thin glittering textures of the filmy dew,
Dipp'd in the richest tincture of the skies,
Where light disports in ever-mingling dyes;
While ev'ry beam new transient colours flings,
Colours that change whene'er they wave their wings.
Amid the circle on the gilded mast,
Superior by the head, was Ariel placed;
His purple pinions op'ning to the sun,
He raised his azure wand, and thus begun:
    "Ye sylphs and sylphids, to your chief give ear; [21]
Fays, fairies, genii, elves, and dæmons, hear:
Ye know the spheres, and various tasks assign'd
By laws eternal to the aërial kind.
Some in the fields of purest ether play,
And bask and whiten in the blaze of day.
Some guide the course of wand'ring orbs on high,
Or roll the planets through the boundless sky.
Some less refined beneath the moon's pale light
Pursue the stars that shoot athwart the night,
Or suck the mists in grosser air below,
Or dip their pinions in the painted bow,
Or brew fierce tempests on the wintry main,
Or o'er the glebe distil the kindly rain.
Others on earth o'er human race preside,
Watch all their ways, and all their actions guide:
Of these the chief the care of nations own,
And guard with arms divine the British throne.
    "Our humbler province is to tend the fair,
Not a less pleasing, though less glorious care;

[21] An echo of Satan addressing his minions in *Paradise Lost*.

To save the powder from too rude a gale,
Nor let the imprison'd essences exhale;
To draw fresh colours from the vernal flowers;
To steal from rainbows, ere they drop in showers,
A brighter wash; to curl their waving hairs,
Assist their blushes and inspire their airs;
Nay, oft, in dreams, invention we bestow,
To change a flounce, or add a furbelow.[22]

   "This day, black omens threat the brightest fair
That e'er deserved a watchful spirit's care;
Some dire disaster, or by force, or flight;
But what, or where, the Fates have wrapp'd in night.
Whether the nymph shall break Diana's law,[23]
Or some frail china-jar receive a flaw;
Or stain her honour or her new brocade;
Forget her prayers, or miss a masquerade;
Or lose her heart, or necklace, at a ball;
Or whether Heaven has doom'd that Shock [24] must fall.
Haste, then, ye spirits! to your charge repair:
The flutt'ring fan be Zephyretta's care;
The drops to thee, Brillante, we consign;
And, Momentilla, let the watch be thine;
Do thou, Crispissa, tend her fav'rite lock;
Ariel himself shall be the guard of Shock.

   "To fifty chosen sylphs, of special note,
We trust th' important charge, the petticoat:
Oft have we known that seven-fold fence to fail,
Though stiff with hoops, and arm'd with ribs of whale;
Form a strong line about the silver bound,
And guard the wide circumference around.

   "Whatever spirit, careless of his charge,
His post neglects, or leaves the fair at large,
Shall feel sharp vengeance soon o'ertake his sins,
Be stopp'd in vials, or transfix'd with pins;

[22] Decorative additions to dresses.
[23] Of chastity.
[24] The lapdog again.

Or plunged in lakes of bitter washes lie,
Or wedged whole ages in a bodkin's eye:
Gums and pomatums [25] shall his flight restrain,
While clogg'd he beats his silken wings in vain:
Or alum styptics with contracting power
Shrink his thin essence like a shrivell'd flower:
Or, as Ixion [26] fix'd, the wretch shall feel
The giddy motion of the whirling mill,[27]
In fumes of burning chocolate shall glow,
And tremble at the sea that froths below!"

He spoke; the spirits from the sails descend;
Some, orb in orb, around the nymph extend;
Some thrid [28] the mazy ringlets of her hair;
Some hang upon the pendants of her ear:
With beating hearts the dire event they wait,
Anxious and trembling for the birth of Fate.

CANTO III

Close by those meads, for ever crown'd with flowers,
Where Thames with pride surveys his rising towers,[29]
There stands a structure of majestic frame,[30]
Which from the neighb'ring Hampton takes its name.
Here Britain's statesmen oft the fall foredoom
Of foreign tyrants, and of nymphs at home;
Here thou, great ANNA! [31] whom three realms obey,
Dost sometimes counsel take—and sometimes tea.

Hither the heroes and the nymphs resort,
To taste a while the pleasures of a court;
In various talk th' instructive hours they pass'd,

[25] Ointments and salves.
[26] In Greek myth, fated to be bound forever to a moving wheel.
[27] A household grinder.
[28] Threaded.
[29] An echo of Dryden's *MacFlecknoe*.
[30] Hampton Court Palace.
[31] Queen Anne.

Who gave the ball, or paid the visit last;
One speaks the glory of the British Queen,
And one describes a charming Indian screen;
A third interprets motions, looks, and eyes;
At every word a reputation dies.
Snuff, or the fan, supply each pause of chat,
With singing, laughing, ogling, *and all that.*
   Meanwhile, declining from the noon of day,[32]
The sun obliquely shoots his burning ray;
The hungry judges soon the sentence sign,
And wretches hang that jurymen may dine;
The merchant from th' exchange returns in peace,
And the long labours of the toilet cease.
Belinda now, whom thirst of fame invites,
Burns to encounter two adventurous knights,
At ombre [33] singly to decide their doom;
And swells her breast with conquests yet to come.
Straight the three bands prepare in arms to join,
Each band the number of the sacred nine.
Soon as she spreads her hand, th' aërial guard
Descend, and sit on each important card:
First Ariel perch'd upon a Matadore,
Then each according to the rank he bore;
For sylphs, yet mindful of their ancient race,
Are, as when women, wondrous fond of place.
   Behold, four Kings in majesty revered,
With hoary whiskers and a forky beard;
And four fair Queens, whose hands sustain a flower,
Th' expressive emblem of their softer power;

[32] An echo of Pope's translation of *The Odyssey,* Book XVII, l. 687 ff.

[33] The mock-epic description of the ombre game demands special knowledge. The game is commonly three-handed, with each player being dealt nine cards (the "sacred nine" refers to the nine Muses). A Matadore is a trump card. Red Kings outranked all other red cards except in a red trump suit. Knaves are jacks. Belinda declares spades trumps, then plays the Ace of Spades, the two of Spades, and the Ace of Clubs, winning five trump cards and one other card. Then she plays the King of Spades and wins the Jack of Clubs, which is the highest card in another game called Loo but simply a lost trump here.

Four knaves in garbs succinct, a trusty band;
Caps on their heads, and halberts in their hand;
And party-colour'd troops, a shining train,
Drawn forth to combat on the velvet plain.
   The skilful nymph reviews her force with care:
"Let Spades be trumps!" she said, and trumps they
     were.
   Now move to war her sable Matadores,
In show like leaders of the swarthy Moors.
Spadillio first, unconquerable lord!
Led off two captive trumps, and swept the board.
As many more Manillio forced to yield,
And march'd a victor from the verdant field.
Him Basto follow'd; but his fate more hard
Gain'd but one trump, and one plebeian card.
With his broad sabre next, a chief in years,
The hoary Majesty of Spades appears,
Puts forth one manly leg, to sight reveal'd,
The rest, his many-colour'd robe conceal'd.
The rebel Knave, who dares his prince engage,
Proves the just victim of his royal rage.
Ev'n mighty Pam, that kings and queens o'erthrew,
And mow'd down armies in the fights of Loo,
Sad chance of war! now destitute of aid,
Falls undistinguish'd by the victor Spade!
   Thus far both armies to Belinda yield;
Now to the baron fate inclines the field.[34]
His warlike Amazon her host invades,
Th' imperial consort of the crown of Spades.

[34] Belinda has four tricks now; she must have a fifth to win for certain because one of her two opponents could still get five tricks. She leads the King of
Clubs but loses to the Baron's Queen of Spades, with which he can trump her,
evidently because he has no more Clubs. With the lead, the Baron plays his
three highest diamonds, all of which must win, and the score is 4–4. The "level
green" is the card table. "Codille" means that an opponent rather than the first
lead wins. The Baron leads his last card, the Ace of Hearts, but loses to Belinda's King because it is a red suit which is not trumps and the King is high.
Belinda wins 5–4, the third party scoring no points.

The Club's black tyrant first her victim dyed,
Spite of his haughty mien, and barb'rous pride:
What boots the regal circle on his head,
His giant limbs, in state unwieldy spread;
That long behind he trails his pompous robe,
And, of all monarchs, only grasps the globe?
 The baron now his Diamonds pours apace;
Th' embroider'd King who shows but half his face,
And his refulgent Queen, with powers combined
Of broken troops an easy conquest find.
Clubs, Diamonds, Hearts, in wild disorder seen,
With throngs promiscuous strow the level green.
Thus when dispersed a routed army runs,
Of Asia's troops, and Afric's sable sons,
With like confusion different nations fly,
Of various habit, and of various dye,
The pierced battalions disunited fall,
In heaps on heaps; one fate o'erwhelms them all.
 The Knave of Diamonds tries his wily arts,
And wins (oh shameful chance!) the Queen of Hearts.
At this, the blood the virgin's cheek forsook,
A livid paleness spreads o'er all her look;
She sees, and trembles at th' approaching ill,
Just in the jaws of ruin, and Codille.
And now (as oft in some distemper'd state)
On one nice trick depends the gen'ral fate,
An Ace of Hearts steps forth: the King unseen
Lurk'd in her hand, and mourn'd his captive Queen:
He springs to vengeance with an eager pace,
And falls like thunder on the prostrate Ace.
The nymph exulting fills with shouts the sky;
The walls, the woods, and long canals reply.
 O thoughtless mortals! ever blind to fate,
Too soon dejected, and too soon elate.
Sudden, these honours shall be snatch'd away,
And cursed for ever this victorious day.
 For lo! the board with cups and spoons is crown'd,

157

The berries crackle, and the mill turns round:
On shining altars of Japan [35] they raise
The silver lamp; the fiery spirits blaze:
From silver spouts the grateful liquors glide,
While China's earth [36] receives the smoking tide:
At once they gratify their scent and taste,
And frequent cups prolong the rich repast.
Straight hover round the fair her airy band;
Some, as she sipp'd, the fuming liquor fann'd,
Some o'er her lap their careful plumes display'd,
Trembling, and conscious of the rich brocade.
Coffee (which makes the politician wise,
And see through all things with his half-shut eyes)
Sent up in vapours to the baron's brain
New stratagems, the radiant lock to gain.
Ah cease, rash youth! desist ere 'tis too late,
Fear the just gods, and think of Scylla's fate!
Changed to a bird, and sent to flit in air,
She dearly pays for Nisus' injured hair! [37]
But when to mischief mortals bend their will,
How soon they find fit instruments of ill!
Just then, Clarissa [38] drew with tempting grace
A two-edged weapon from her shining case:
So ladies, in romance, assist their knight,
Present the spear, and arm him for the fight.
He takes the gift with reverence and extends
The little engine on his fingers' ends;
This just behind Belinda's neck he spread,
As o'er the fragrant steams she bends her head.
Swift to the lock a thousand sprites repair,

[35] Oriental tables.
[36] China cups.
[37] Scylla (no relation to the famous Scylla of Homer's *Odyssey*) cut a lock of her father's hair and gave it to his enemy Minos, for which she was made a bird.
[38] Clarissa, perhaps the third player in the game, provides the scissors for the Baron.

A thousand wings, by turns, blow back the hair;
And thrice they twitch'd the diamond in her ear;
Thrice she look'd back, and thrice the foe drew near.
Just in that instant, anxious Ariel sought
The close recesses of the virgin's thought:
As on the nosegay in her breast reclin'd,
He watch'd th' ideas rising in her mind,
Sudden he view'd, in spite of all her art,
An earthly lover lurking at her heart.
Amazed, confused, he found his power expired,
Resign'd to fate, and with a sigh retired.
The peer now spreads the glitt'ring forfex [39] wide,
T' inclose the lock; now joins it, to divide.
Ev'n then, before the fatal engine closed,
A wretched sylph too fondly interposed;
Fate urged the shears, and cut the sylph in twain,
(But airy substance soon unites again) [40]
The meeting points the sacred hair dissever
From the fair head, for ever, and for ever! [41]
    Then flash'd the living lightning from her eyes,
And screams of horror rend th' affrighted skies.
Not louder shrieks to pitying Heaven are cast,
When husbands or when lap-dogs breathe their last;
Or when rich China vessels, fall'n from high,
In glitt'ring dust and painted fragments lie!
    "Let wreaths of triumph now my temples twine,
(The victor cried) the glorious prize is mine!
While fish in streams, or birds delight in air,
Or in a coach and six the British fair,
As long as *Atalantis* [42] shall be read,
Or the small pillow grace a lady's bed,

[39] The scissors.
[40] Another echo of the battle in *Paradise Lost.*
[41] This couplet at the climax of the poem is the only feminine rhyme in the entire poem.
[42] A popular book of the time, written by a woman, full of gossip, scandal, and silly sentiment.

While visits shall be paid on solemn days,
When numerous wax-lights in bright order blaze,
While nymphs take treats, or assignations give,
So long my honour, name, and praise shall live!"
What Time would spare, from steel receives its date,
And monuments, like men, submit to fate!
Steel could the labour of the gods destroy,
And strike to dust th' imperial towers of Troy;
Steel could the works of mortal pride confound,
And hew triumphal arches to the ground.
What wonder then, fair nymph! thy hairs should feel
The conquering force of unresisted steel?

CANTO IV

But anxious cares the pensive nymph oppress'd,
And secret passions labour'd in her breast.
Not youthful kings in battle seized alive,
Not scornful virgins who their charms survive,
Not ardent lovers robb'd of all their bliss,
Not ancient ladies when refused a kiss,
Not tyrants fierce that unrepenting die,
Not Cynthia when her manteau's pinn'd awry,
E'er felt such rage, resentment, and despair,
As thou, sad virgin! for thy ravish'd hair.
For, that sad moment, when the sylphs withdrew
And Ariel weeping from Belinda flew,
Umbriel, a dusky, melancholy sprite,
As ever sullied the fair face of light,
Down to the central earth, his proper scene,
Repair'd to search the gloomy Cave of Spleen.[43]
Swift on his sooty pinions flits the gnome,
And in a vapour reach'd the dismal dome.
No cheerful breeze this sullen region knows,
The dreaded east [44] is all the wind that blows.
Here in a grotto, shelter'd close from air,

[43] Like a journey to the underworld in a classical epic.
[44] Dreaded as source of ill health.

And screen'd in shades from day's detested glare,
She sighs for ever on her pensive bed,
Pain at her side, and Megrim [45] at her head.
Two handmaids wait the throne: alike in place,
But diff'ring far in figure and in face.
Here stood Ill-nature like an ancient maid,
Her wrinkled form in black and white array'd;
With store of prayers, for mornings, nights, and noons,
Her hand is fill'd; her bosom with lampoons.
  There Affectation, with a sickly mien,
Shows in her cheek the roses of eighteen,
Practised to lisp, and hang the head aside,
Faints into airs, and languishes with pride,
On the rich quilt sinks with becoming woe,
Wrapp'd in a gown, for sickness, and for show.
The fair ones feel such maladies as these,
When each new night-dress gives a new disease.
  A constant vapour o'er the palace flies;
Strange phantoms rising as the mists arise;
Dreadful, as hermits' dreams in haunted shades,
Or bright, as visions of expiring maids.
Now glaring fiends, and snakes on rolling spires,
Pale spectres, gaping tombs, and purple fires:
Now lakes of liquid gold, Elysian scenes,
And crystal domes, and angels in machines.[46]
  Unnumber'd throngs on every side are seen
Of bodies changed to various forms by Spleen.
Here living tea-pots stand, one arm held out,
One bent; the handle this, and that the spout:
A pipkin there, like Homer's tripod walks; [47]

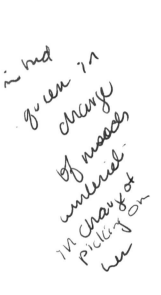

[45] Melancholy, a popular disease of the well-off, frequently brought on headache.

[46] Like a *deus ex machina* in classical drama, or perhaps like an angel in a masque or opera.

[47] A small pot or kettle; Homer's tripod refers to the project Hephaestus is working on in Bk. XVIII of *The Iliad* when Thetis comes to ask for the magic armor for Achilleus—the tripods were twenty, had wheels, and could move by themselves.

Here sighs a jar, and there a goose-pie talks:
Men prove with child, as powerful fancy works,
And maids turn'd bottles call aloud for corks.
  Safe pass'd the gnome through this fantastic band,
A branch of healing spleen-wort [48] in his hand.
Then thus address'd the power: "Hail, wayward Queen!
Who rule the sex to fifty from fifteen;
Parent of vapours,[49] and of female wit,
Who give th' hysteric or poetic fit;
On various tempers act by various ways,
Make some take physic, others scribble plays;
Who cause the proud their visits to delay,
And send the godly in a pet to pray;
A nymph there is, that all thy power disdains,
And thousands more in equal mirth maintains.
But oh! if e'er thy gnome could spoil a grace,
Or raise a pimple on a beauteous face,
Like citron waters [50] matrons' cheeks inflame,
Or change complexions at a losing game;
If e'er with airy horns [51] I planted heads,
Or rumpled petticoats, or tumbled beds,
Or caused suspicion when no soul was rude,
Or discomposed the head-dress of a prude,
Or e'er to costive lap-dog gave disease,
Which not the tears of brightest eyes could ease;
Hear me, and touch Belinda with chagrin,
That single act gives half the world the spleen."
  The Goddess with a discontented air
Seems to reject him, though she grants his prayer.
A wondrous bag with both her hands she binds,
Like that where once Ulysses held the winds; [52]

[48] A cure for melancholy.
[49] More melancholy.
[50] Fruit brandy or something akin.
[51] Horns of cuckoldry.
[52] Allusion to the bag of winds Aeolus gave Odysseus in Bk. X of *The Odyssey*.

There she collects the force of female lungs,
Sighs, sobs, and passions, and the war of tongues.
A vial next she fills with fainting fears,
Soft sorrows, melting griefs, and flowing tears.
The gnome rejoicing bears her gifts away,
Spreads his black wings, and slowly mounts to day.
    Sunk in Thalestris' [53] arms the nymph he found,
Her eyes dejected, and her hair unbound.
Full o'er their heads the swelling bag he rent,
And all the furies issued at the vent.
Belinda burns with more than mortal ire,
And fierce Thalestris fans the rising fire;
"O wretched maid!" she spread her hands, and cried,
(While Hampton's echoes, "Wretched maid!" replied)
"Was it for this you took such constant care
The bodkin, comb, and essence to prepare?
For this your locks in paper durance bound?
For this with torturing irons wreathed around?
For this with fillets strain'd your tender head,
And bravely bore the double loads of lead? [54]
Gods! shall the ravisher display your hair,
While the fops envy and the ladies stare?
Honour forbid! at whose unrivall'd shrine
Ease, pleasure, virtue, all our sex resign.
Methinks already I your tears survey,
Already hear the horrid things they say,
Already see you a degraded toast,
And all your honour in a whisper lost!
How shall I then your helpless fame defend?
'Twill then be infamy to seem your friend!
And shall this prize, th' inestimable prize,
Exposed through crystal to the gazing eyes,
And heighten'd by the diamond's circling rays,
On that rapacious hand for ever blaze?

[53] Belinda's friend.
[54] Hair curlers.

Sooner shall grass in Hyde Park Circus [55] grow,
And wits take lodgings in the sound of Bow; [56]
Sooner let earth, air, sea, to Chaos fall,
Men, monkeys, lap-dogs, parrots, perish all!"
   She said; then raging to Sir Plume [57] repairs,
And bids her beau demand the precious hairs:
(Sir Plume of amber snuff-box justly vain,
And the nice conduct of a clouded [58] cane)
With earnest eyes, and round, unthinking face,
He first the snuff-box open'd, then the case,
And then broke out—"My Lord, why, what the devil!
Z—ds! damn the lock! 'fore Gad, you must be civil!
Plague on't! 'tis past a jest—nay prithee, pox!
Give her the hair"—he spoke, and rapp'd his box.
"It grieves me much (replied the peer again)
Who speaks so well should ever speak in vain,
But by this lock, this sacred lock, I swear,
(Which never more shall join its parted hair;
Which never more its honours shall renew,
Clipp'd from the lovely head where late it grew)
That while my nostrils draw the vital air,
This hand, which won it, shall for ever wear."
He spoke, and speaking, in proud triumph spread
The long-contended honours of her head.
   But Umbriel, hateful gnome! forbears not so;
He breaks the vial whence the sorrows flow.
Then see! the nymph in beauteous grief appears,
Her eyes half-languishing, half-drowned in tears;
On her heaved bosom hung her drooping head,
Which, with a sigh, she raised; and thus she said:
   "For ever cursed be this detested day,
Which snatch'd my best, my fav'rite curl away!

[55] Because horses trot there constantly.
[56] A church in an unfashionable district.
[57] A reference to the only man who, in real life, took the affair seriously; here Pope really socks it to 'im.
[58] Multi-shaded.

Happy! ay ten times happy had I been,
If Hampton Court these eyes had never seen!
Yet am I not the first mistaken maid,
By love of courts to numerous ills betray'd,
Oh had I rather unadmired remain'd
In some lone isle, or distant northern land;
Where the gilt chariot never marks the way,
Where none learn ombre, none e'er taste bohea! [59]
There kept my charms conceal'd from mortal eye,
Like roses that in deserts bloom and die.
What moved my mind with youthful lords to roam?
Oh had I stayed, and said my prayers at home!
'Twas this the morning omens seem'd to tell:
Thrice from my trembling hand the patch-box [60] fell;
The tott'ring china shook without a wind;
Nay, Poll sat mute, and Shock was most unkind!
A sylph too warn'd me of the threats of Fate,
In mystic visions, now believed too late!
See the poor remnants of these slighted hairs!
My hands shall rend what e'en thy rapine spares:
These in two sable ringlets taught to break,
Once gave new beauties to the snowy neck;
The sister-lock now sits uncouth, alone,
And in its fellow's fate foresees its own;
Uncurl'd it hangs, the fatal shears demands,
And tempts, once more, thy sacrilegious hands.
Oh hadst thou, cruel! been content to seize
Hairs less in sight, or any hairs but these!"

CANTO V

She said: the pitying audience melt in tears;
But Fate and Love had stopp'd the baron's ears.
In vain Thalestris with reproach assails,
For who can move when fair Belinda fails?
Not half so fix'd the Trojan could remain,

[59] A rare tea.
[60] A container for "beauty patches."

165

While Anna begg'd and Dido raged in vain.[61]
Then grave Clarissa [62] graceful waved her fan;
Silence ensued, and thus the nymph began:
   "Say, why are beauties praised and honoured most,
The wise man's passion, and the vain man's toast?
Why deck'd with all that land and sea afford?
Why angels call'd, and angel-like adored?
Why round our coaches crowd the white-gloved beaux?
Why bows the side-box from its inmost rows?
How vain are all these glories, all our pains,
Unless good sense preserve what beauty gains;
That men may say, when we the front-box grace,
'Behold the first in virtue as in face!'
Oh! if to dance all night, and dress all day,
Charm'd the small-pox, or chased old age away;
Who would not scorn what housewife's cares produce,
Or who would learn one earthly thing of use?
To patch, nay, ogle, might become a saint,
Nor could it sure be such a sin to paint.
But since, alas! frail beauty must decay,
Curl'd or uncurl'd, since locks will turn to grey;
Since painted, or not painted, all shall fade,
And she who scorns a man must die a maid;
What then remains, but well our power to use,
And keep good-humour still, whate'er we lose?
And trust me, dear, good-humour can prevail,
When airs, and flights, and screams, and scolding fail.
Beauties in vain their pretty eyes may roll;
Charms strike the sight, but merit wins the soul."
   So spoke the dame, but no applause ensued;
Belinda frown'd, Thalestris call'd her prude.
"To arms, to arms!" the fierce virago cries,
And swift as lightning to the combat flies.
All side in parties, and begin th' attack:

[61] Dido's sister begged Aeneas to stay with Dido in Carthage.
[62] Literally "clear-minded," she here points out a moral to be gained from the experience—ironically, of course.

Fans clap, silks rustle, and tough whalebones crack;
Heroes' and heroines' shouts confusedly rise,
And bass and treble voices strike the skies.
No common weapons in their hands are found,
Like Gods they fight, nor dread a mortal wound.
  So when bold Homer makes the Gods engage,
And heavenly breasts with human passions rage;
'Gainst Pallas, Mars; Latona, Hermes arms; [63]
And all Olympus rings with loud alarms;
Jove's thunder roars, Heaven trembles all around,
Blue Neptune storms, the bellowing deeps resound:
Earth shakes her nodding towers, the ground gives way,
And the pale ghosts start at the flash of day!
  Triumphant Umbriel on a sconce's [64] height
Clapp'd his glad wings, and sate to view the fight:
Propp'd on their bodkin spears, the sprites survey
The growing combat, or assist the fray.
  While through the press enraged Thalestris flies,
And scatters death around from both her eyes,
A beau and witling perish'd in the throng,
One died in metaphor, and one in song.
"O cruel nymph! a living death I bear,"
Cried Dapperwit, and sunk beside his chair.
A mournful glance Sir Fopling [65] upwards cast,
"Those eyes are made so killing,"—was his last.
Thus on Mæander's [66] flowery margin lies
Th' expiring swan, and as he sings he dies.
  When bold Sir Plume had drawn Clarissa down,
Chloe stepp'd in, and kill'd him with a frown;
She smiled to see the doughty hero slain,
But, at her smile, the beau revived again.
  Now Jove suspends his golden scales in air,

[63] Athena and Ares (Minerva and Mars) fight, as do Latona (mother of Artemis or Diana and Apollo) and Hermes (Mercury).
[64] A high hanging or wall-mounted candle holder.
[65] Dapperwit and Sir Fopling were fops in Restoration comedies.
[66] A Trojan river.

Weighs the men's wits against the lady's hair:
The doubtful beam long nods from side to side;
At length the wits mount up, the hairs subside.
    See fierce Belinda on the baron flies,
With more than usual lightning in her eyes:
Nor fear'd the chief th' unequal fight to try,
Who sought no more than on his foe to die.
But this bold lord with manly strength endued,
She with one finger and a thumb subdued:
Just where the breath of life his nostrils drew,
A charge of snuff the wily virgin threw;
The gnomes direct, to every atom just,
The pungent grains of titillating dust.
Sudden, with starting tears each eye o'erflows,
And the high dome re-echoes to his nose.
    "Now meet thy fate," incensed Belinda cried,
And drew a deadly bodkin from her side.
(The same, his ancient personage to deck,
Her great-great-grandsire wore about his neck,
In three seal rings; which after, melted down,
Form'd a vast buckle for his widow's gown:
Her infant grandame's whistle next it grew,
The bells she jingled, and the whistle blew;
Then in a bodkin graced her mother's hairs,
Which long she wore, and now Belinda wears.)
    "Boast not my fall, (he cried) insulting foe!
Thou by some other shalt be laid as low.
Nor think, to die dejects my lofty mind:
All that I dread is leaving you behind!
Rather than so, ah let me still survive,
And burn in Cupid's flames—but burn alive."
    "Restore the lock!" she cries; and all around
"Restore the lock!" the vaulted roofs rebound.
Not fierce Othello in so loud a strain
Roar'd for the handkerchief that caused his pain.[67]

[67] Othello believes that a handkerchief he sees in Cassio's hand is evidence of
Desdemona's unfaithfulness.

But see how oft ambitious aims are cross'd,
And chiefs contend till all the prize is lost!
The lock, obtain'd with guilt, and kept with pain,
In every place is sought, but sought in vain:
With such a prize no mortal must be blest,
So Heaven decrees! with Heaven who can contest?
    Some thought it mounted to the lunar sphere,
Since all things lost on earth are treasured there.
There heroes' wits are kept in pond'rous vases,
And beaux' in snuff-boxes and tweezer-cases.
There broken vows, and death-bed alms are found,
And lovers' hearts with ends of riband bound,
The courtier's promises, and sick man's prayers,
The smiles of harlots, and the tears of heirs,
Cages for gnats, and chains to yoke a flea,
Dried butterflies, and tomes of casuistry.[68]
    But trust the Muse—she saw it upward rise,
Though mark'd by none but quick, poetic eyes:
(So Rome's great founder [69] to the heavens withdrew,
To Proculus [70] alone confess'd in view)
A sudden star it shot through liquid air,
And drew behind a radiant trail of hair.
Not Berenice's lock [71] first rose so bright,
The heavens bespangling with dishevell'd light.
The sylphs behold it kindling as it flies,
And pleased pursue its progress through the skies.
    This the beau-monde shall from the Mall [72] survey,
And hail with music its propitious ray.
This the blest lover shall for Venus take,
And send up vows from Rosamonda's lake.[73]

---

[68] Sophistry.
[69] Romulus.
[70] As Romulus left the world, he appeared to Proculus to tell him that Mars was calling him up to Olympus.
[71] The Egyptian queen Berenice's hair supposedly became a constellation.
[72] Pall Mall, a walkway in a London park.
[73] A London pond, known as a suicide spot for forlorn lovers.

This Partridge [74] soon shall view in cloudless skies,
When next he looks through Galileo's eyes; [75]
And hence th' egregious wizard shall foredoom
The fate of Louis, and the fall of Rome. [76]
    Then cease, bright nymph! to mourn thy ravish'd hair,
Which adds new glory to the shining sphere!
Not all the tresses that fair head can boast
Shall draw such envy as the lock you lost.
For, after all the murders of your eye,
When, after millions slain, yourself shall die;
When those fair suns shall set, as set they must,
And all those tresses shall be laid in dust;
This lock, the Muse shall consecrate to fame,
And 'midst the stars inscribe Belinda's name.

THE CHARACTER OF ATTICUS
from *The Epistle to Dr. Arbuthnot*

In the complete Epistle to Dr. Arbuthnot, *Pope defends himself against what he feels are unjust attacks, and he asserts his independence of court and patron. Arbuthnot, a royal physician and wit, is a friend of Swift, Pope, Gay, and others in the literary circle. Pope and Addison (Atticus) had been friends, but the friendship chilled when some of Addison's hangers-on ("his little Senate") attacked Pope. When Addison aided Thomas Tickell with an edition of the* Iliad *to rival Pope's translation, Pope saw an act of jealousy. This satiric character sketch of his one-time friend is the result.*

Peace to all such! but were there one whose fires
True Genius kindles, and fair Fame inspires,
Bless'd with each talent and each art to please,

[74] An almanac maker and quack, object of a famous Swift satire.
[75] A telescope.
[76] Louis XIV and the Papacy were targets of Partridge's predictions.

And born to write, converse, and live with ease;
Should such a man, too fond to rule alone,
Bear, like the Turk,[1] no brother near the throne;
View him with scornful, yet with jealous eyes,
And hate for arts that caus'd himself to rise;
Damn with faint praise, assent with civil leer,
And without sneering teach the rest to sneer;
Willing to wound, and yet afraid to strike,
Just hint a fault, and hesitate dislike;
Alike reserv'd to blame or to commend,
A tim'rous foe, and a suspicious friend;
Dreading ev'n fools; by flatterers besieged,
And so obliging that he ne'er obliged;
Like Cato,[2] give his little Senate laws,
And sit attentive to his own applause;
While Wits and Templars [3] ev'ry sentence raise,[4]
And wonder with a foolish face of praise—
Who but must laugh if such a man there be?
Who would not weep, if Atticus were he?

from SATIRES AND EPISTLES OF HORACE
IMITATED

*In Pope's Imitation of the First Epistle of the Second Book
of Horace, he presents a characteristic Neo-Classical defense
of the art of satire by suggesting how the function of satire
arose within society.*

Our rural ancestors, with little blest,
Patient of labour when the end was rest,

---

[1] The Turkish tyrants legendarily protected their positions by murdering all
their near kinsmen.

[2] Cato, Roman statesman and writer (234–194 B.C.), was the hero of Addison's tragedy (1713), for which Pope had written the prologue. To assure a
favorable reception Addison was said to have hired friends to applaud.

[3] Law students.

[4] Applaud.

Indulg'd the day that hous'd their annual grain
With feasts, and off'rings, and a thankful strain:
The joy their wives, their sons, their servants share,
Ease of their toil, and part'ners of their care:
The laugh, the jest, attendants on the bowl,
Smooth'd ev'ry brow, and open'd ev'ry soul;
With growing years the pleasing licence grew,
And taunts alternate innocently flew.
But times corrupt, and nature ill-inclin'd,
Produc'd the point that left a sting behind;
Till, friend with friend, and families at strife,
Triumphant malice rag'd thro' private life.
Who felt the wrong, or fear'd it, took th' alarm,
Appeal'd to law, and justice lent her arm.
At length, by wholesome dread of statutes bound,
The poets learn'd to please, and not to wound:
Most warp'd to flattery's side; but some, more nice,
Preserv'd the freedom, and forebore the vice.
Hence satire rose, that just the medium hit,
And heals with morals what it hurts with wit.

Jonathan Swift
FOUR SATIRES

The epitome of the Juvenalian satirist, Swift was born in Ireland, son of an English minor official, in 1667. His childhood was disillusioning, and his later efforts at escaping the repressive life of a minor Anglican ecclesiastic were similarly frustrating. For a time in the early 1700's he was a faithful servant, in England, of the Tory party, and friendly with Addison, Steele, and Pope. But about 1713 he was more or less exiled to the post of Dean of St. Patrick's Cathedral, Dublin, where he spent most of the rest of his life. From his disappointments and his deep rage about the treatment of Ireland came The Drapier's Letters (1724), Gulliver's Travels (1726), *and* A Modest Proposal (1729) *—three of the greatest satires in our language. No other satirist has ranged so widely in moral, political, and literary satire as Swift—nor written with such consistent intensity. One major reason he survives his time so well (many satirists do not) is that he so often managed to control his rage and convert it into art. He is the absolute master of irony and understatement. One sentence perhaps can illustrate this point. Imagine an English official visiting Dublin, chatting with a colleague over tea: "Last week I saw a woman flayed, and you will hardly believe how much it altered her person for the worse." So one finds in Swift both the self-discipline and the fury of the major artist. Perhaps the painter Goya can serve as an example of a kindred spirit in the visual arts. Part of Swift's own epitaph—"He has gone now where furious indignation can lacerate his heart no more"—suggests something of the moral anger which fueled his satiric impulse.*

A MEDITATION UPON A BROOMSTICK

According to the playwright Thomas Sheridan, Swift, on his yearly visits to London in the early eighteenth century, would act as chaplain and advisor to Lady Berkeley, who found inspiration in the Meditations *of Robert Boyle (1627–1691), the famous scientist often called "the father of chemistry." When Swift was asked repeatedly to read the meditations aloud, he found them insufferably tedious and platitudinous. He wrote the following parody, slipped it into the Boyle volume and gravely read it aloud. Lady Berkeley was taken in, to the amusement of visiting friends, and Swift was no longer asked to read from the work he had thus devastated.*

This single stick, which you now behold ingloriously lying in that neglected corner, I once knew in a flourishing state in a forest: it was full of sap, full of leaves, and full of boughs: but now, in vain does the busy art of man pretend to vie with nature, by tying that withered bundle of twigs to its sapless trunk: it is now, at best, but the reverse of what it was, a tree turned upside down, the branches on the earth, and the root in the air; it is now handled by every dirty wench, condemned to do her drudgery, and, by a capricious kind of fate, destined to make other things clean, and be nasty itself: at length, worn to the stumps in the service of the maids, it is either thrown out of doors, or condemned to the last use, of kindling a fire. When I beheld this, I sighed, and said within myself, *Surely man is a Broomstick!* Nature sent him into the world strong and lusty, in a thriving condition, wearing his own hair on his head, the proper branches of this reasoning vegetable, until the axe of intemperance has lopped off his green boughs, and left him a withered trunk: he then flies to art, and puts on a periwig, valuing himself upon an unnatural bundle of hairs (all covered with powder), that never grew on his head; but now, should this our broomstick pretend to enter the scene, proud of those birchen spoils it never bore, and all covered with dust, though the sweepings of the finest lady's chamber, we should be apt to ridicule and despise its vanity. Partial judges that we are of our own excellences and other men's defaults!

But a broomstick, perhaps you will say, is an emblem of a tree standing on its head; and pray what is man but a topsyturvy creature, his animal faculties perpetually mounted on his rational, his head where his heels should be, grovelling on the earth? And yet, with all his faults, he sets up to be a universal reformer and corrector of abuses, a remover of grievances, rakes into every slut's corner of nature, bringing hidden corruption to the light, and raises a mighty dust where there was none before; sharing deeply all the while in the very same pollutions he pretends to sweep away: his last days are spent in slavery to women, and generally the least deserving; till, worn out to the stumps, like his brother besom,[1] he is either kicked out of doors, or made use of to kindle flames for others to warm themselves by.

A SATIRICAL ELEGY
ON THE DEATH OF A LATE FAMOUS GENERAL

This elegy on the Duke of Marlborough, Churchill's ancestor who won the great victory at Blenheim, reveals that Swift's aversion to pomposity and military pride is as deeply felt and as pungently expressed as Erasmus' in his Militaria.

His Grace! impossible! what dead!
Of old age too, and in his bed!
And could that Mighty Warrior fall?
And so inglorious, after all!
Well, since he's gone, no matter how,
The last loud trump must wake him now:
And, trust me, as the noise grows stronger,
He'd wish to sleep a little longer.
And could he be indeed so old
As by the news-papers we're told?
Threescore, I think, is pretty high;
'Twas time in conscience he should die.
This world he cumber'd long enough;
He burnt his candle to the snuff;

[1] broom.

And that's the reason, some folks think,
He left behind *so great a s . . . k.*
Behold his funeral appears,
Nor widow's sighs, nor orphan's tears,
Wont at such times each heart to pierce,
Attend the progress of his herse.
But what of that, his friends may say,
He had those honours in his day.
True to his profit and his pride,
He made them weep before he dy'd.

Come hither, all ye empty things,
Ye bubbles [1] rais'd by breath of Kings;
Who float upon the tide of state,
Come hither, and behold your fate.
Let pride be taught by this rebuke,
How very mean a thing's a Duke;
From all his ill-got honours flung,
Turn'd to that dirt from whence he sprung.

THOUGHTS ON VARIOUS SUBJECTS

These epigrams, set down about 1706, are selected from a large number dealing with most aspects of man's life. The most frequently recurring theme is that of man's self-love. In this concern they resemble the Maxims of La Roche-foucauld.

We have just religion enough to make us hate, but not enough to make us love, one another.

No wise man ever wished to be younger.

Some people take more care to hide their wisdom than their folly.

When a true genius appears in the world, you may know him by this infallible sign: that the dunces are all in confederacy against him.

Censure is the tax a man pays to the public for being eminent.

[1] Ignoble people raised to the peerage.

A nice man is a man of nasty ideas.

If a man will observe as he walks the streets, I believe he will find the merriest countenances in mourning coaches.

The latter part of a wise man's life is taken up in curing the follies, prejudices, and false opinions he had contracted in the former.

The power of Fortune is confessed only by the miserable, for the happy impute all their success to prudence or merit.

Apollo was held the God of physick and sender of diseases. Both were originally the same trade, and still continue.

A MODEST PROPOSAL

FOR PREVENTING THE CHILDREN OF POOR PEOPLE FROM BEING A BURTHEN TO THEIR PARENTS OR COUNTRY, AND FOR MAKING THEM BENEFICIAL TO THE PUBLIC.

This tract, published in Dublin and London in 1729, results from Swift's profound despair over man's inhumanity to his fellows as it evidenced itself in Ireland. The country was ruled by the members of the Established Church (about one-twelfth the population) and an uncaring, distant government in England. In northern Ireland most of the English settlers were Presbyterian dissenters and were thus prohibited from any part in the government. The worst injustice came to the majority of Ireland's population, Catholics, who were treated as second-class foreigners in their own country. The masses of the people lived on the edge of starvation because of harshly repressive trade laws which had resulted in the ruin of Irish manufacture and agriculture. Swift's mood here is one of revulsion at the callous, statistical approach of the politician or social scientist who has lost sight of the human reality underlying the numbers. (Interested readers may enjoy hearing an especially good reading of Swift by Sir Alec Guiness on MGM recording E 3620.)

References in the text to "this great town" are to Dublin, from which large numbers of Irish went to France or Spain as mercenaries or sold themselves as indentured servants.

It is a melancholy object to those who walk through this great town, or
travel in the country, when they see the streets, the roads, and cabin-
doors crowded with beggars of the female sex, followed by three, four,
or six children, *all in rags*, and importuning every passenger for an
alms. These mothers, instead of being able to work for their honest
livelihood, are forced to employ all their time in strolling, to beg sustenance for their helpless infants, who, as they grow up, either turn thieves
for want of work, or leave their dear Native Country to fight for the
Pretender [1] in Spain, or sell themselves to the Barbadoes.

I think it is agreed by all parties that this prodigious number of children, in the arms, or on the backs, or at the heels of their mothers, and
frequently of their fathers, is in the present deplorable state of the kingdom a very great additional grievance; and therefore whoever could
find out a fair, cheap, and easy method of making these children sound
useful members of the commonwealth would deserve so well of the
public as to have his statue set up for a preserver of the nation.

But my intention is very far from being confined to provide only for
the children of professed beggars; it is of a much greater extent, and
shall take in the whole number of infants at a certain age who are born
of parents in effect as little able to support them as those who demand
our charity in the streets.

As to my own part, having turned my thoughts, for many years, upon
this important subject, and maturely weighed the several schemes of
other projectors, I have always found them grossly mistaken in their
computation. It is true a child, just dropped from its dam, may be supported by her milk for a solar year with little other nourishment, at
most not above the value of two shillings, which the mother may certainly get, or the value in scraps, by her lawful occupation of begging,
and it is exactly at one year old that I propose to provide for them, in
such a manner as, instead of being a charge upon their parents, or the
parish, or wanting food and raiment for the rest of their lives, they shall,
on the contrary, contribute to the feeding and partly to the clothing of
many thousands.

There is likewise another great advantage in my scheme that it will

[1] James Stuart, son of James II, claimed the throne lost by his father in 1688.
He landed an Army in 1715, but was defeated. In 1718, another attempt
failed.

prevent those voluntary abortions, and that horrid practice of women murdering their bastard children, alas, too frequent among us, sacrificing the poor innocent babes, I doubt, more to avoid the expense than the shame, which would move tears and pity in the most savage and inhuman breast.

The number of souls in this kingdom being usually reckoned one million and a half, of these I calculate there may be about two hundred thousand couples whose wives are breeders, from which number I subtract thirty thousand couples who are able to maintain their own children, although I apprehend there cannot be so many under the present distresses of the kingdom, but this being granted, there will remain an hundred and seventy thousand breeders. I again subtract fifty thousand for those women who miscarry, or whose children die by accident or disease within the year. There only remain an hundred and twenty thousand children of poor parents annually born: The question therefore is, how this number shall be reared, and provided for, which, as I have already said, under the present situation of affairs, is utterly impossible by all the methods hitherto proposed, for we can neither employ them in handicraft, or agriculture; we neither build houses (I mean in the country), nor cultivate land: they can very seldom pick up a livelihood by stealing till they arrive at six years old, except where they are of towardly parts,[2] although, I confess they learn the rudiments much earlier, during which time they can however be properly looked upon only as *probationers*, as I have been informed by a principal gentleman in the County of Cavan,[3] who protested to me that he never knew above one or two instances under the age of six, even in a part of the kingdom so renowned for the quickest proficiency in that art.

I am assured by our merchants that a boy or a girl, before twelve years old, is no saleable commodity, and even when they come to this age, they will not yield above three pounds, or three pounds and half-a-crown at most on the Exchange, which cannot turn to account either to the parents or the kingdom, the charge of nutriment and rags having been at least four times that value.

I shall now therefore humbly propose my own thoughts, which I hope will not be liable to the least objection.

[2] Precocious.
[3] In Northern Ireland.

I have been assured by a very knowing American of my acquaintance in London, that a young healthy child well nursed is at a year old a most delicious, nourishing, and wholesome food, whether stewed, roasted, baked, or boiled, and I make no doubt that it will equally serve in a fricassee, or a ragout.

I do therefore humbly offer it to public consideration, that of the hundred and twenty thousand children already computed, twenty thousand may be reserved for breed, whereof only one fourth part to be males, which is more than we allow to sheep, black-cattle, or swine, and my reason is that these children are seldom the fruits of marriage, a circumstance not much regarded by our savages, therefore one male will be sufficient to serve four females. That the remaining hundred thousand may at a year old be offered in sale to the persons of quality, and fortune, through the kingdom, always advising the mother to let them suck plentifully in the last month, so as to render them plump, and fat for a good table. A child will make two dishes at an entertainment for friends, and when the family dines alone, the fore or hind quarter will make a reasonable dish, and seasoned with a little pepper or salt will be very good boiled on the fourth day, especially in winter.

I have reckoned upon a medium,[4] that a child just born will weigh 12 pounds, and in a solar year if tolerably nursed increaseth to 28 pounds.

I grant this food will be somewhat dear, and therefore very proper for landlords, who, as they have already devoured most of the parents, seem to have the best title to the children.

Infants' flesh will be in season throughout the year, but more plentiful in March, and a little before and after, for we are told by a grave author, an eminent French physician,[5] that fish being a prolific diet, there are more children born in Roman Catholic countries about nine months after Lent than at any other season; therefore reckoning a year after Lent, the markets will be more glutted than usual, because the number of Popish infants is at least three to one in this kingdom, and therefore it will have one other collateral advantage by lessening the number of Papists among us.

I have already computed the charge of nursing a beggar's child (in

---

[4] Average.
[5] Rabelais, an earlier French satirist.

which list I reckon all cottagers,[6] labourers, and four-fifths of the farmers) to be about two shillings *per annum*, rags included, and I believe no gentleman would repine to give ten shillings for the carcass of a good fat child, which, as I have said, will make four dishes of excellent nutritive meat, when he hath only some particular friend or his own family to dine with him. Thus the Squire will learn to be a good landlord, and grow popular among his tenants, the mother will have eight shillings net profit, and be fit for work till she produces another child.

Those who are more thrifty (as I must confess the times require) may flay the carcass; the skin of which, artificially dressed, will make admirable gloves for ladies, and summer boots for fine gentlemen.

As to our City of Dublin, shambles [7] may be appointed for this purpose, in the most convenient parts of it, and butchers we may be assured will not be wanting, although I rather recommend buying the children alive, and dressing them hot from the knife, as we do roasting pigs.

A very worthy person, a true lover of this country, and whose virtues I highly esteem, was lately pleased, in discoursing on this matter, to offer a refinement upon my scheme. He said that many gentlemen of this kingdom, having of late destroyed their deer, he conceived that the want of venison might be well supplied by the bodies of young lads and maidens, not exceeding fourteen years of age, nor under twelve, so great a number of both sexes in every country being now ready to starve, for want of work and service: and these to be disposed of by their parents if alive, or otherwise by their nearest relations. But with due deference to so excellent a friend, and so deserving a patriot, I cannot be altogether in his sentiments; for as to the males, my American acquaintance assured me from frequent experience that their flesh was generally tough and lean, like that of our schoolboys, by continual exercise, and their taste disagreeable, and to fatten them would not answer the charge. Then as to the females, it would, I think with humble submission, be a loss to the public, because they soon would become breeders themselves: And besides, it is not improbable that some scrupulous people might be apt to censure such a practice (although indeed very unjustly) as a little bordering upon cruelty, which, I confess, hath al-

[6] Tenant-farmers.
[7] Slaughter houses.

ways been with me the strongest objection against any project, however so well intended.

But in order to justify my friend, he confessed that this expedient was put into his head by the famous Psalmanazar [8] a native of the island Formosa, who came from thence to London, above twenty years ago, and in conversation told my friend that in his country when any young person happened to be put to death, the executioner sold the carcass to persons of quality, as a prime dainty, and that, in his time, the body of a plump girl of fifteen, who was crucified for an attempt to poison the emperor, was sold to his Imperial Majesty's Prime Minister of State, and other great Mandarins of the Court, in joints from the gibbet, at four hundred crowns. Neither indeed can I deny that if the same use were made of several plump young girls in this town, who, without one single groat to their fortunes, cannot stir abroad without a chair, and appear at the playhouse, and assemblies in foreign fineries, which they never will pay for, the kingdom would not be the worse.

Some persons of a desponding spirit are in great concern about that vast number of poor people, who are aged, diseased, or maimed, and I have been desired to employ my thoughts what course may be taken to ease the nation of so grievous an encumbrance. But I am not in the least pain upon that matter, because it is very well known that they are every day dying, and rotting, by cold, and famine, and filth, and vermin, as fast as can be reasonably expected. And as to the younger labourers they are now in almost as hopeful a condition. They cannot get work, and consequently pine away for want of nourishment, to a degree, that if at any time they are accidentally hired to common labour, they have not strength to perform it; and thus the country and themselves are happily delivered from the evils to come.

I have too long digressed, and therefore shall return to my subject. I think the advantages by the proposal which I have made are obvious and many, as well as of the highest importance.

For first, as I have already observed, it would greatly lessen the number of Papists, with whom we are yearly over-run, being the principal breeders of the nation, as well as our most dangerous enemies, and who

[8] A Frenchman and famous imposter, who pretended to be Formosan. He confessed his plot in 1728, the year before publication of *A Modest Proposal.*

stay at home on purpose with a design to deliver the kingdom to the Pretender, hoping to take their advantage by the absence of so many good Protestants, who have chosen rather to leave their country than stay at home, and pay tithes against their conscience to an Episcopal curate.

Secondly, The poorer tenants will have something valuable of their own, which by law be made liable to distress, and help to pay their landlord's rent, their corn and cattle being already seized, and *money a thing unknown.*

Thirdly, Whereas the maintenance of an hundred thousand children, from two years old, and upwards, cannot be computed at less than ten shillings a piece *per annum,* the nation's stock will be thereby increased fifty thousand pounds *per annum,* besides the profit of a new dish, introduced to the tables of all gentlemen of fortune in the kingdom, who have any refinement in taste, and the money will circulate among ourselves, the goods being entirely of our own growth and manufacture.

Fourthly, The constant breeders, besides the gain of eight shillings sterling *per annum,* by the sale of their children, will be rid of the charge of maintaining them after the first year.

Fifthly, This food would likewise bring great custom to taverns, where the vintners will certainly be so prudent as to procure the best receipts for dressing it to perfection, and consequently have their houses frequented by all the fine gentlemen, who justly value themselves upon their knowledge in good eating; and a skilful cook, who understands how to oblige his guests, will contrive to make it as expensive as they please.

Sixthly, This would be a great inducement to marriage, which all wise nations have either encouraged by rewards, or enforced by laws and penalties. It would increase the care and tenderness of mothers toward their children, when they were sure of a settlement for life, to the poor babes, provided in some sort by the public to their annual profit instead of expense. We should see an honest emulation among the married women, which of them could bring the fattest child to the market, men would become as fond of their wives, during the time of their pregnancy, as they are now of their mares in foal, their cows in calf, or sows when they are ready to farrow, nor offer to beat or kick them (as it is too frequent a practice) for fear of a miscarriage.

Many other advantages might be enumerated: For instance, the addition of some thousand carcasses in our exportation of barrelled beef; the propagation of swine's flesh, and improvement in the art of making good bacon, so much wanted among us by the great destruction of pigs, too frequent at our tables, which are no way comparable in taste or magnificence to a well-grown, fat yearling child, which roasted whole will make a considerable figure at a Lord Mayor's feast, or any other public entertainment. But this and many others I omit, being studious of brevity.

Supposing that one thousand families in this city would be constant customers for infants' flesh, besides others who might have it at merry-meetings, particularly weddings and christenings, I compute that Dublin would take off annually about twenty thousand carcasses, and the rest of the kingdom (where probably they will be sold somewhat cheaper) the remaining eighty thousand.

I can think of no one objection that will possibly be raised against this proposal, unless it should be urged that the number of people will be thereby much lessened in the kingdom. This I freely own, and was indeed one principal design in offering it to the world. I desire the reader will observe, that I calculate my remedy for this one individual *Kingdom of Ireland, and for no other that ever was, is, or, I think, ever can be upon earth.* Therefore let no man talk to me of other expedients: *Of taxing our absentees at five shillings a pound: Of using neither clothes, nor household furniture, except what is of our own growth and manufacture: Of utterly rejecting the materials and instruments that promote foreign luxury: Of curing the expensiveness of pride, vanity, idleness, and gaming in our women: Of introducing a vein of parsimony, prudence, and temperance: Of learning to love our Country, wherein we differ even from* LAPLANDERS, *and the inhabitants of* TOPINAMBOO: *Of quitting our animosities and factions, nor act any longer like the Jews, who were murdering one another at the very moment their city was taken: Of being a little cautious not to sell our country and consciences for nothing: Of teaching landlords to have at least one degree of mercy toward their tenants. Lastly, of putting a spirit of honesty, industry, and skill into our shopkeepers, who, if a resolution could now be taken to buy only our native goods, would immediately unite to cheat and exact upon us in the price, the measure, and the good-*

184

*ness, nor could ever yet be brought to make one fair proposal of just
dealing, though often and earnestly invited to it.*

Therefore I repeat, let no man talk to me of these and the like expedients, till he hath at least some glimpse of hope that there will ever
be some hearty and sincere attempt to put them in practice.

But as to myself, having been wearied out for many years with offering vain, idle, visionary thoughts, and at length utterly despairing of
success, I fortunately fell upon this proposal, which as it is wholly new,
so it hath something solid and real, of no expense and little trouble,
full in our own power, and whereby we can incur no danger in *disoblig-
ing* ENGLAND. For this kind of commodity will not bear exportation,
the flesh being of too tender a consistence to admit a long continuance
in salt, *although perhaps I could name a country which would be glad
to eat up our whole nation without it.*

After all I am not so violently bent upon my own opinion as to reject
any offer, proposed by wise men, which shall be found equally innocent,
cheap, easy, and effectual. But before something of that kind shall be
advanced in contradiction to my scheme, and offering a better, I desire
the author, or authors, will be pleased maturely to consider two points.
First, as things now stand, how they will be able to find food and
raiment for an hundred thousand useless mouths and backs. And
secondly, there being a round million of creatures in human figure,
throughout this kingdom, whose whole subsistence put into a common
stock would leave them in debt two millions of pounds sterling; adding
those, who are beggars by profession, to the bulk of farmers, cottagers,
and labourers with their wives and children, who are beggars in effect.
I desire those politicians, who dislike my overture, and may perhaps be
so bold to attempt an answer, that they will first ask the parents of
these mortals whether they would not at this day think it a great happiness to have been sold for food at a year old, in the manner I prescribe,
and thereby have avoided such a perpetual scene of misfortunes as they
have since gone through, by the oppression of landlords, the impossibility of paying rent without money or trade, the want of common
sustenance, with neither house nor clothes to cover them from the in-
clemencies of the weather, and the most inevitable prospect of entailing
the like, or greater miseries upon their breed for ever.

I profess in the sincerity of my heart that I have not the least personal interest in endeavouring to promote this necessary work, having no other motive than the *public good of my country, by advancing our trade, providing for infants, relieving the poor, and giving some pleasure to the rich.* I have no children by which I can propose to get a single penny; the youngest being nine years old, and my wife past child-bearing.

Montesquieu
from
THE PERSIAN
LETTERS

Montesquieu (1689–1755) was both lawyer and writer, and he used the two vocations to criticize and help improve his own society. His most important work is The Spirit of the Law *(1748), dealing with the question of man-made laws versus "higher" or natural laws. His* Persian Letters *(1721) postulate the idea that an outsider can see things more clearly, more objectively than one's own countrymen, a technique as common to science fiction as to satire.*

LETTER 48
USBEK TO RHEDI, AT VENICE

Those who take pleasure in their own instruction are never idle. Although I am not employed on any business of importance, I am yet constantly occupied. I spend my time observing, and at night I write down what I have noticed, what I have seen, what I have heard, during the day. I am interested in everything, astonished at everything: I am like a child, whose organs, still over-sensitive, are vividly impressed by the merest trifles.

You would scarcely believe it, but we have been well received in all circles, and among all classes. This is largely owing to the quick wit and natural gaiety of Rica, which lead him to seek out everybody, and make him equally sought after. Our foreign aspect offends nobody;

indeed, we are delighted at the surprise which people show on finding us not altogether without manners; for the French imagine that men are not among the products of our country. Nevertheless, I must admit that they are well worth undeceiving.

I spent some days in the country near Paris at the house of a man of some note, who delights in having company with him. He has a very amiable wife, who, along with great modesty, possesses what the secluded life they lead stifles in our Persian women, a charming gaiety.

Stranger as I was, I had nothing better to do than to study the crowd of people who came and went without ceasing, affording me a constant change of subject for contemplation. I noticed at once one man, whose simplicity pleased me; I allied myself with him, and he with me, in such a manner that we were always together.

One day, as we were talking quietly in a large company, leaving the general conversation to the others, I said, "You will perhaps find in me more inquisitiveness than good manners; but I beg you to let me ask some questions, for I am wearied to death doing nothing, and of living with people with whom I have nothing in common. My thoughts have been busy these two days; there is not one among these men who has not put me to the torture two hundred times; in a thousand years I would never understand them; they are more invisible to me than the wives of our great king." "You have only to ask," replied he, "and I will tell you all you desire—the more willingly because I think you a discreet man, who will not abuse my confidence."

"Who is that man," said I, "who has told us so much about the banquets at which he has entertained the great, who is so familiar with your dukes, and who talks so often to your ministers, who, they tell me, are so difficult of access? He ought surely to be a man of quality; but his aspect is so mean that he is hardly an honour to the aristocracy; and, besides, I find him deficient in education. I am a stranger; but it seems to me that there is, generally speaking, a certain tone of good-breeding common to all nations, and I do not find it in him. Can it be that your upper classes are not so well trained as those of other nations?" "That man," answered he, laughing, "is a farmer-general; he is as much above others in wealth, as he is inferior to us all by birth. He might have the best people in Paris at his table, if he could make up his mind never to eat in his own house. He is very impertinent, as you see; but he excels in his cook, and is not ungrateful, for you heard how he praised him to-day."

"And that big man dressed in black," said I, "whom that lady has placed next her? How comes he to wear a dress so solemn, with so jaunty an air, and such a florid complexion? He smiles benignly when he is addressed; his attire is more modest, but not less carefully adjusted than that of your women." "That," answered he, "is a preacher, and, which is worse, a confessor. Such as he is, he knows more of their own affairs than the husbands; he is acquainted with the women's weak side, and they also know his." "Ha!" cried I, "he talks for ever of something he calls Grace?" "No, not always," was the reply; "in the ear of a pretty woman he speaks more willingly of the Fall: in public, he is a son of thunder; in private, as gentle as a lamb." "It seems to me," said I, "that he receives much attention, and is held in great respect."

"In great respect! Why! he is a necessity; he is the sweetener of solitude; then there are little lessons, officious cares, set visits; he cures a headache better than any man in the world; he is incomparable."

"But, if I may trouble you again, tell me who that ill-dressed person is opposite us? He makes occasional grimaces, and does not speak like the others; and without wit enough to talk, he talks that he may have wit." "That," answered he, "is a poet, the grotesquest of human kind. These sort of people declare that they are born what they are; and, I may add, what they will be all their lives, namely, almost always, the most ridiculous of men; and so nobody spares them; contempt is cast upon them from every quarter. Hunger has driven that one into this house. He is well received by its master and mistress, as their good-nature and courtesy are always the same to everybody. He wrote their epithalamium when they were married, and it is the best thing he has done, for the marriage has been as fortunate as he prophesied it would be.

"You will not believe, perhaps," added he, "prepossessed as you are in favour of the East, that there are among us happy marriages, and wives whose virtue is a sufficient guard. This couple, here, enjoy untroubled peace; everybody loves and esteems them; only one thing is amiss: in their good-nature they receive all kinds of people, which makes the company at their house sometimes not altogether unexceptionable. I, of course, have nothing to say against it; we must live

189

with people as we find them; those who are said to be well-bred are often only those who are exquisite in their vices; and perhaps it is with them as with poisons, the more subtle, the more dangerous."

"And that old man," I whispered, "who looks so morose? I took him at first for a foreigner; because, in addition to being dressed differently from the rest, he condemns everything that is done in France, and disapproves of your government." "He is an old soldier," said he, "who makes himself memorable to all his hearers by the tedious story of his exploits. He cannot endure the thought that France has gained any battles without him, nor hear a siege bragged of at which he did not mount the breach. He believes himself so essential to our history that he imagines it came to an end when he retired; some wounds he has received mean, simply, the dissolution of the monarchy; and, unlike the philosophers who maintain that enjoyment is only in the present, and that the past is as if it had not been, he, on the contrary, delights in nothing but the past, and exists only in his old campaigns; he breathes the air of the age that has gone by, just as heroes ought to live in that which is to come." "But why," I asked, "has he quitted the service?" "He has not quitted it, but it has quitted him. He has been employed in a small post, where he will retail his adventures for the rest of his days; but he will never get any further; the path of honour is closed to him." "And why?" asked I. "It is a maxim in France," replied he, "never to advance officers whose patience has been worn out as subalterns; we look upon them as men whose minds have been narrowed by detail; and who, through a constant application to small things, are become incapable of great ones. We believe that a man who, at thirty, has not the qualities of a general, will never have them; that he, whose glance cannot take in at once a tract of several leagues as if from every point of view, who is not possessed of that presence of mind which in victory leaves no advantage unimproved, and in defeat employs every resource, will never acquire such capacity. Therefore we employ in brilliant services those great, those sublime men, on whom Heaven has bestowed not only the courage, but the genius of the hero; and in inferior services those whose talents are inferior. Of this number are such as have grown old in obscure warfare; they can succeed only at what they have been doing all their lives; and it would be ill-advised to start them on fresh employment when age has weakened their powers."

A moment after, curiosity again seized me, and I said, "I promise not to ask another question if you will only answer this one. Who is that tall young man who wears his own hair, and has more impertinence than wit? How comes it that he speaks louder than the others, and is so charmed with himself for being in the world?" "That is a great lady-killer," he replied. With these words some people entered, others left, and all rose. Some one came to speak to my acquaintance, and I remained in my ignorance. But shortly after, I know not by what chance, the young man in question found himself beside me, and began to talk. "It is fine weather," he said. "Will you take a turn with me in the garden?" I replied as civilly as I could, and we went out together. "I have come to the country," said he, "to please the mistress of the house, with whom I am not on the worst of terms. There is a certain woman in the world who will be rather out of humour; but what can one do? I visit the finest women in Paris; but I do not confine my attentions to one; they have plenty to do to look after me, for, between you and me, I am a sad dog." "In that case, sir," said I, "you doubtless have some office or employment which prevents you from waiting on them more assiduously?" "No, sir; I have no other business than to provoke husbands, and drive fathers to despair; I delight in alarming a woman who thinks me hers, and in bringing her within an ace of losing me. A set of us young fellows divide up Paris among us in this pursuit, and keep it wondering at everything we do." "From what I understand," said I, "you make more stir than the most valorous warrior, and are more regarded than a grave magistrate. If you were in Persia, you would not enjoy all these advantages; you would be held fitter to guard our women than to please them." The blood mounted to my face; and I believe, had I gone on speaking, I could not have refrained from affronting him.

What say you to a country where such people are tolerated, and where a man who follows such a profession is allowed to live? Where faithlessness, treachery, rape, deceit, and injustice lead to distinction? Where a man is esteemed because he has bereaved a father of his daughter, a husband of his wife, and distresses the happiest and purest homes? Happy the children of Hali who protect their families from outrage and seduction! Heaven's light is not purer than the fire that burns in the hearts of our wives; our daughters think only with dread of the day when they will be deprived of that purity, in virtue of which they rank with the angels and the spiritual powers. My beloved land, on which the morning sun looks first, thou art unsoiled by those horrible crimes which compel that star to hide his beams as he approaches the dark West!

Paris, the 5th of the moon of
  Rhamazan, 1713.

Oliver Goldsmith
from
THE CITIZEN OF
THE WORLD

---

*Born (1730?) and educated in Ireland, Oliver Goldsmith
tried a variety of occupations before he settled on medicine,
at which he was never very successful. To support his medical practice he turned to writing, at which he was more
suited, whether as a poet, novelist, dramatist, or essayist.
These essays are directly descended from those of* The
Tatler *and* The Spectator; *they are graceful, pleasing, and
witty. Despite the success of his novel* The Vicar of Wake-
field *and his comedy* She Stoops to Conquer, *Goldsmith
died a debtor in 1774.*

LETTER 86
THE RACES OF NEWMARKET RIDICULED—
DESCRIPTION OF A CART RACE

The essays from The Citizen of the World *are gently amusing examples of the convention of having a foreign visitor,
often an Oriental, observe and comment on European practices.*

Of all the places of amusement where gentlemen and ladies are entertained, I have not been yet to visit Newmarket.[1] This, I am told, is a
large field where, upon certain occasions, three or four horses are

---

[1] *Newmarket:* the center of English racing, fourteen miles from Cambridge.

brought together, then set a-running, and that horse which runs fastest wins the wager.

This is reckoned a very polite and fashionable amusement here, much more followed by the nobility than partridge fighting at Java, or paper kites in Madagascar. Several of the great here, I am told, understand as much of farriery as their grooms; and a horse with any share of merit can never want a patron among the nobility.

We have a description of this entertainment almost every day in some of the gazettes, as for instance: "On such a day the Give and Take Plate was run for between his Grace's Crab, his Lordship's Periwinkle, and Squire Smackem's Slamerkin. All rode their own horses. There was the greatest concourse of nobility that has been known here for several seasons. The odds were in favor of Crab in the beginning; but Slamerkin, after the first heat, seemed to have the match hollow: however, it was soon seen that Periwinkle improved in wind, which at last turned out accordingly; Crab was run to a standstill, Slamerkin was knocked up, and Periwinkle was brought in with universal applause." Thus, you see, Periwinkle received universal applause, and, no doubt, his Lordship came in for some share of that praise which was so liberally bestowed upon Periwinkle. Sun of China! how glorious must the senator [2] appear in his cap and leather breeches, his whip crossed in his mouth, and thus coming to the goal, amongst the shouts of grooms, jockeys, pimps, stable-bred dukes, and degraded generals!

From the description of this princely amusement now transcribed, and from the great veneration I have for the characters of its principal promoters, I make no doubt but I shall look upon a horse race with becoming reverence, predisposed as I am by a similar amusement, of which I have lately been a spectator; for just now I happened to have an opportunity of being present at a cart race.

Whether this contention between three carts of different parishes was promoted by a subscription among the nobility, or whether the grand jury, in council assembled, had gloriously combined to encourage plaustral [3] merit, I cannot take upon me to determine; but certain it is, the whole was conducted with the utmost regularity and decorum, and the company, which made a brilliant appearance, were universally of

[2] *senator:* member of the House of Lords.
[3] *plaustral:* a jocose coinage by Goldsmith from Latin *plaustrum,* cart.

opinion that the sport was high, the running fine, and the riders influenced by no bribe.

It was run on the road from London to a village called Brentford, between a turnip cart, a dust cart [4] and a dung cart, each of the owners condescending to mount, and be his own driver. The odds, at starting, were Dust against Dung, five to four; but, after half a mile's going, the knowing ones found themselves all on the wrong side, and it was Turnip against the field, brass to silver.

Soon, however, the contest became more doubtful; Turnip indeed kept the way, but it was perceived that Dung had better bottom.[5] The road re-echoed with the shouts of the spectators—"Dung against Turnip! Turnip against Dung!" was now the universal cry; neck and neck; one rode lighter, but the other had more judgment. I could not but particularly observe the ardor with which the fair sex espoused the cause of the different riders on this occasion; one was charmed with the unwashed beauties of Dung; another was captivated with the patibulary [6] aspect of Turnip: while, in the meantime, unfortunate gloomy Dust, who came whipping behind, was cheered by the encouragement of some and pity of all.

The contention now continued for some time, without a possibility of determining to whom victory designed the prize. The winning post appeared in view, and he who drove the turnip cart assured himself of success; and successful he might have been, had his horse been as ambitious as he; but, upon approaching a turn from the road, which led homewards, the horse fairly stood still and refused to move a foot farther. The dung cart had scarce time to enjoy this temporary triumph, when it was pitched headlong into a ditch by the wayside, and the rider left to wallow in congenial mud. Dust, in the meantime, soon came up, and, not being far from the post, came in, amidst the shouts and acclamations of all the spectators, and greatly caressed by all the quality [7] of Brentford. Fortune was kind only to one, who ought to have been favorable to all; each had peculiar merit, each labored hard to earn the prize, and each richly deserved the cart he drove.

[4] *dust cart:* trash cart.
[5] *better bottom:* staying power.
[6] *patibulary:* another coinage; gallowslike.
[7] *quality:* upper class.

I do not know whether this description may not have anticipated that which I intended giving of Newmarket. I am told there is little else to be seen even there. There may be some minute differences in the dress of the spectators, but none at all in their understandings: the quality of Brentford are as remarkable for politeness and delicacy as the breeders of Newmarket. The quality of Brentford drive their own carts, and the honorable fraternity of Newmarket ride their own horses. In short, the matches in one place are as rational as those in the other; and it is more than probable that turnips, dust, and dung are all that can be found to furnish out description in either.

Forgive me, my friend; but a person like me, bred up in a philosophic seclusion, is apt to regard perhaps with too much asperity those occurrences which sink man below his station in nature, and diminish the intrinsic value of humanity. Adieu.

Benjamin Franklin
from
POOR RICHARD'S
ALMANACKS

In his earlier years, Franklin wrote occasional gentle satire as in The Silence Dogood Letters *and* Poor Richard's Almanacks *for the years 1733–1758. The handsomest edition of the Almanacks is that of the Heritage Press "Embellish'd with illustrations" by Norman Rockwell.*

for April, 1733

Kind Katherine to her husband kiss'd these words,
"Mine own sweet Will, how dearly I love thee!"
If true (quoth Will) the world no such affords.
And that it's true I durst his warrant be;
    For ne'er heard I of woman good or ill,
    But always loved best, her own sweet Will.

for May, 1734

Neither a fortress nor a maidenhead will hold out long after they begin to parley.

for December, 1734

Famine, plague, war, and an unnumber'd throng
Of guilt-avenging ills, to man belong;

Is't not enough plagues, wars, and famines rise
To lash our crimes, but must our wives be wise?

for May, 1735

Pain wastes the body, pleasures the understanding.

When ♂ and ♄ in ♀ lie,
then, maids, whate'er is asked of you, deny.

for January, 1736

Fish & visitors stink in 3 days.

for September, 1736

He that speaks much is much mistaken.

for September, 1738

I have never seen the philosopher's stone that turns lead into gold,
but I have known the pursuit of it turn a man's gold into lead.

for March, 1739

Historians relate not so much what is done as what they would have
believed.

for September, 1739

When man and woman die, as poets sung,
His head's the last part moves, her last, the tongue.

for September, 1749

All would live long, but none would be old.

THE SALE OF THE HESSIANS

As an old man, Franklin revealed a darker tone in his satires, a more Juvenalian tone, as in this fictional letter he wrote during his stay in France as he sought French aid for the Colonies. George III hired mercenary troops from various German princes to fight in America. Apparently the contracts called for a specific payment to the prince for each soldier killed, or so Franklin satirically implies.

Rome, February 18, 1777

Monsieur Le Baron:—On my return from Naples, I received at Rome your letter of the 27th December of last year. I have learned with unspeakable pleasure the courage our troops exhibited at Trenton, and you cannot imagine my joy on being told that of the 1,950 Hessians engaged in the fight, but 345 escaped. There were just 1,605 men killed, and I cannot sufficiently commend your prudence in sending an exact list of the dead to my minister in London. This precaution was the more necessary, as the report sent to the English ministry does not give but 1,455 dead. This would make 483,450 florins instead of 643,500 which I am entitled to demand under our convention. You will comprehend the prejudice which such an error would work in my finances, and I do not doubt you will take the necessary pains to prove that Lord North's list is false and yours correct.

The court of London objects that there were a hundred wounded who ought not to be included in the list, nor paid for as dead; but I trust you will not overlook my instructions to you on quitting Cassel, and that you will not have tried by human succor to recall the life of the unfortunates whose days could not be lengthened but by the loss of a leg or an arm. That would be making them a pernicious present, and I am sure they would rather die than live in a condition no longer fit for my service. I do not mean by this that you should assassinate them; we should be humane, my dear Baron, but you may insinuate to the surgeons with entire propriety that a crippled man is a reproach to their profession, and that there is no wiser course than to let every one of them die when he ceases to be fit to fight.

I am about to send to you some new recruits. Don't economize them.

Remember glory before all things. Glory is true wealth. There is nothing degrades the soldier like the love of money. He must care only for honour and reputation, but this reputation must be acquired in the midst of dangers. A battle gained without costing the conqueror any blood is an inglorious success, while the conquered cover themselves with glory by perishing with their arms in their hands. Do you remember that of the 300 Lacedæmonians who defended the defile of Thermopylæ, not one returned? How happy should I be could I say the same of my brave Hessians!

It is true that their king, Leonidas, perished with them: but things have changed, and it is no longer the custom for princes of the empire to go and fight in America for a cause with which they have no concern. And besides, to whom should they pay the thirty guineas per man if I did not stay in Europe to receive them? Then, it is necessary also that I be ready to send recruits to replace the men you lose. For this purpose I must return to Hesse. It is true, grown men are becoming scarce there, but I will send you boys. Besides, the scarcer the commodity the higher the price. I am assured that the women and little girls have begun to till our lands, and they get on not badly. You did right to send back to Europe that Dr. Crumerus who was so successful in curing dysentery. Don't bother with a man who is subject to looseness of the bowels. That disease makes bad soldiers. One coward will do more mischief in an engagement than ten brave men will do good. Better that they burst in their barracks than fly in a battle, and tarnish the glory of our arms. Besides, you know that they pay me as killed for all who die from disease, and I don't get a farthing for runaways. My trip to Italy, which has cost me enormously, makes it desirable that there should be a great mortality among them. You will therefore promise promotion to all who expose themselves; you will exhort them to seek glory in the midst of dangers; you will say to Major Maundorff: that I am not at all content with his saving the 345 men who escaped the massacre of Trenton. Through the whole campaign he has not had ten men killed in consequence of his orders. Finally, let it be your principal object to prolong the war and avoid a decisive engagement on either side, for I have made arrangements for a grand Italian opera, and I do not wish to be obliged to give it up. Meantime I pray God, my dear Baron de Hohendorf, to have you in his holy and gracious keeping.

Robert Burns
HOLY WILLIE'S PRAYER

In this dramatic monologue, Burns satirizes that bane of many churches, the zealous, meddlesome elder, self-appointed to look after everyone else's piety. The poem is based on an actual incident in which such an elder accused a truly decent member of the congregation with neglecting one or another of the church ordinances. The charge was heard by the church council and the accused exonerated to the great frustration of Holy Willie. As the poem opens, he is at his evening devotion.

O Thou, wha in the heavens dost dwell,
Wha, as it pleases best thysel',
Sends ane [1] to heaven and ten to hell,
    A' for thy glory,
And no for ony guid or ill
      They've done afore thee!

I bless and praise thy matchless might,
Whan thousands thou hast left in night,
That I am here afore thy sight,
    For gifts an' grace [2]
A burnin' an' a shinin' light,
      To a' this place.

What was I, or my generation,
That I should get sic [3] exaltation?

[1] One.
[2] Gifts and grace are outward signs of the Elect, those chosen by God for salvation.
[3] Such.

201

I, wha deserve most just damnation,
For broken laws,
Sax thousand years 'fore my creation,
Through Adam's cause.[4]

When frae my mither's womb I fell,
Thou might hae plungèd me in hell,
To gnash my gums, to weep and wail,
In burnin' lakes,
Where damnèd devils roar and yell,
Chained to their stakes;

Yet I am here a chosen sample,
To show thy grace is great and ample;
I'm here a pillar in thy temple,
Strong as a rock,
A guide, a buckler, an example
To a' thy flock.

O Lord, thou kens [5] what zeal I bear,
When drinkers drink, and swearers swear,
And singin' there and dancin' here,
Wi' great an' sma';
For I am keepit by thy fear
Free frae [6] them a'.

But yet, O Lord! confess I must
At times I'm fashed [7] wi' fleshy lust;
An' sometimes too, in warldly trust,
Vile self gets in;
But thou remembers we are dust,
Defiled in sin.

[4] Original sin; note that Willie places Adam's birth 6000 years before his own.
[5] Know.
[6] From.
[7] Troubled.

O Lord! yestreen, thou kens, wi' Meg—
Thy pardon I sincerely beg,
O! may it ne'er be a livin'plague
    To my dishonor!
An' I'll ne'er lift a lawless leg
    Again upon her.

Besides, I farther maun allow,[8]
Wi' Lizzie's lass, three times, I trow;
But, Lord, that Friday I was fou,[9]
    When I came near her,
Or else, thou kens, thy servant true
    Wad ne'er hae steer'd [10] her.

May be thou lets this fleshly thorn
Beset thy servant e'en and morn
Lest he owre [11] high and proud should turn,
    That he's sae gifted;
If sae, thy hand maun e'en be borne,
    Until thou lift it.

Lord, bless thy chosen in this place,
For here thou hast a chosen race;
But God confound their stubborn face,
    And blast their name,
Wha bring thy elders to disgrace
    An' public shame.

Lord, mind Gawn Hamilton's [12] deserts,
He drinks, an' swears, an' plays at cartes,
Yet has sae mony takin' arts [13]

[8] Must admit.
[9] Drunk.
[10] Stirred, touched, bothered.
[11] Too.
[12] The man accused by Willie.
[13] Has so many talking arts.

Wi' grit an' sma',[14]
Frae God's ain [15] priest the people's hearts
He steals awa'.

An' when we chastened him therefor,
Thou kens how he bred sic a splore [16]
As set the warld in a roar
O' laughin' at us;
Curse thou his basket and his store,
Kail and potatoes.

Lord, hear my earnest cry an' prayer,
Against that presbyt'ry o' Ayr; [17]
Thy strong right hand, Lord, make it bare
Upo' their heads;
Lord, weigh it down, and dinna spare,
For their misdeeds.

O Lord my God, that glib-tongued Aiken,[18]
My very heart and soul are quakin',
To think how we stood sweatin', shakin',
An' filled wi' dread,
While he, wi' hingin' lips and snakin',[19]
Held up his head.

Lord, in the day of vengeance try him;
Lord, visit them wha did employ him,
And pass not in thy mercy by them,
Nor hear their prayer;
But, for thy people's sake, destroy them,
And dinna spare.

[14] Great and small.
[15] Own.
[16] Made such a row.
[17] Those who heard the charge but voted acquittal.
[18] Hamilton's defender.
[19] Drooping lips and sneering.

But, Lord, remember me and mine
Wi' mercies temp'ral and divine,
That I for gear [20] and grace may shine
Excelled by nane,
And a' the glory shall be thine,
Amen, Amen!

[20] Goods, possessions.

Timothy Dwight
from
THE TRIUMPH OF
INFIDELITY

*The grandson of Jonathan Edwards, Timothy Dwight,
tutor and later President of Yale University, army chaplain,
Congregational minister, Calvinist, and Federalist, came to
be known as one of the "Connecticut Wits" late in the
eighteenth century. His heroic couplet satire is certainly no
match for that of his model Pope because it is generally
transparent and abusive, but it does sometimes rise to moments of light, thrusting caricature as in this passage describing a weak, self-seeking "modern" preacher, one who
falls far short of the Calvinist standard approved by Dwight.*

There smiled the smooth Divine, unused to wound
The sinner's heart with hell's alarming sound.
No terrors on his gentle tongue attend;
No grating truths the nicest ear offend.
That strange new-birth, that Methodistic grace,
Nor in his heart nor sermons found a place.
Plato's fine tales he clumsily retold,
Trite, fireside, moral seesaws, dull as old;
His Christ and Bible placed at good remove,
Guilt hell-deserving and forgiving love.
'Twas best, he said, mankind should cease to sin:
Good fame required it; so did peace within. ·
Their honors, well he knew, would ne'er be driven;
But hoped they still would please to go to heaven.
Each week he paid his visitation dues:

Coaxed, jested, laughed; rehearsed the private news;
Smoked with each goody,[1] thought her cheese excelled;
Her pipe he lighted, and her baby held.
Or placed in some great town, with lacquered shoes,
Trim wig and trimmer gown, and glistening hose,
He bowed, talked politics, learned manners mild,
Most meekly questioned, and most smoothly smiled;
At rich men's jests laughed loud, their stories praised;
Their wives new patterns gazed, and gazed, and gazed;
Most daintily on pampered turkeys dined;
Nor shrunk with fasting, nor with study pined:
Yet from their churches saw his brethren driven,
Who thundered truth, and spoke the voice of heaven,
Chilled trembling guilt in Satan's headlong path,
Charmed their feet back, and roused the ear of death.
"Let fools," he cried, "starve on, while prudent I
Snug in my nest shall live, and snug shall die."

[1] A polite term applied to a wife of humble rank.

Robert Browning
TWO POEMS

MY LAST DUCHESS

*In this dramatic monologue set in Ferrara during the Italian
Renaissance, the poet lets the speaker, the Duke of Ferrara,
ironically reveal himself to an envoy from a neighboring
Count, who has come to offer the Count's daughter in marriage to the Duke. As the poem opens, the two pause in
their walk through the Duke's quarters to study the portrait
of his "last duchess," whose fate, though ambiguous, is
clearly sinister.*

FERRARA

That's my last Duchess painted on the wall,
Looking as if she were alive. I call
That piece a wonder, now: Frà Pandolf's [1] hands
Worked busily a day, and there she stands.
Will 't please you sit and look at her? I said
"Frà Pandolf" by design, for never read
Strangers like you that pictured countenance,
The depth and passion of its earnest glance,
But to myself they turned (since none puts by
The curtain I have drawn for you, but I)
And seemed as they would ask me, if they durst,
How such a glance came there; so, not the first
Are you to turn and ask thus. Sir, 't was not
Her husband's presence only, called that spot
Of joy into the Duchess' cheek: perhaps

[1] An imaginary painter.

Frà Pandolf chanced to say "Her mantle laps
Over my lady's wrist too much," or "Paint
Must never hope to reproduce the faint
Half-flush that dies along her throat"; such stuff
Was courtesy, she thought, and cause enough
For calling up that spot of joy. She had
A heart—how shall I say?—too soon made glad,
Too easily impressed; she liked whate'er
She looked on, and her looks went everywhere.
Sir, 't was all one! My favour at her breast,
The dropping of the daylight in the West,
The bough of cherries some officious fool
Broke in the orchard for her, the white mule
She rode with round the terrace—all and each
Would draw from her alike the approving speech,
Or blush, at least. She thanked men,—good! but thanked
Somehow—I know not how—as if she ranked
My gift of a nine-hundred-years-old name
With anybody's gift. Who'd stoop to blame
This sort of trifling? Even had you skill
In speech—(which I have not)—to make your will
Quite clear to such an one, and say, "Just this
Or that in you disgusts me; here you miss,
Or there exceed the mark"—and if she let
Herself be lessoned so, nor plainly set
Her wits to yours, forsooth, and made excuse,
—E'en then would be some stooping; and I choose
Never to stoop. Oh, sir, she smiled, no doubt,
Whene'er I passed her; but who passed without
Much the same smile? This grew; I gave commands;
Then all smiles stopped together. There she stands
As if alive. Will 't please you rise? We'll meet
The company below, then, I repeat,
The Count your master's known munificence
Is ample warrant that no just pretence
Of mine for dowry will be disallowed;
Though his fair daughter's self, as I avowed

At starting, is my object. Nay, we'll go
Together down, sir! Notice Neptune, though,
Taming a sea-horse, thought a rarity,
Which Claus of Innsbruck [2] cast in bronze for me!

SOLILOQUY OF THE SPANISH CLOISTER

In this interior monologue, the speaker's frustrations with cloister life and his own petty nature are revealed in a satiric series of juxtapositions.

Gr—r—r— there go, my heart's abhorrence!
    Water your damned flower-pots, do!
If hate killed men, Brother Lawrence,
    God's blood, would not mine kill you!
What? your myrtle-bush wants trimming?
    Oh, that rose has prior claims—
Needs its leaden vase filled brimming?
    Hell dry you up with its flames!

At the meal we sit together:
    Salve tibi.[3] I must hear
Wise talk of the kind of weather,
    Sort of season, time of year:
Not a plenteous cork-crop: scarcely
    Dare we hope oak-galls,[4] *I doubt:*
What's the Latin name for "parsley"?
    What's the Greek name for Swine's Snout?

Whew! We'll have our platter burnished,
    Laid with care on our own shelf!

[2] An imaginary sculptor.
[3] Greeting used in the cloister.
[4] Oak galls or oak apples are tree swellings caused by wasp larvae and are useful for tanning leather.

With a fire-new spoon we're furnished,
    And a goblet for ourself,
Rinsed like something sacrificial
    Ere 'tis fit to touch our chaps—
Marked with L. for our initial!
    (He-he! There his lily snaps!)

Saint, forsooth! While brown Dolores
    Squats outside the Convent bank
With Sanchicha, telling stories,
    Steeping tresses in the tank,
Blue-black, lustrous, thick like horsehairs,
    —Can't I see his dead eye glow,
Bright as 'twere a Barbary corsair's?
    (That is, if he'd let it show!)

When he finishes refection,
    Knife and fork he never lays
Cross-wise, to my recollection,
    As do I, in Jesu's praise.
I, the Trinity illustrate,
    Drinking watered orange pulp—
In three sips the Arian frustrate;
    While he drains his at one gulp!

Oh, those melons! If he's able
    We're to have a feast! so nice!
One goes to the Abbot's table,
    All of us get each a slice.
How go on your flowers? None double?
    Not one fruit-sort can you spy?
Strange!—And I, too, at such trouble,
    Keep them close-nipped on the sly!

There's a great text in Galatians,
    Once you trip on it, entails
Twenty-nine distinct damnations,

One sure, if another fails:
If I trip him just a-dying,
    Sure of heaven as sure can be,
Spin him round and send him flying
    Off to hell, a Manichee?

Or, my scrofulous French novel
    On grey paper with blunt type!
Simply glance at it, you grovel
    Hand and foot in Belial's gripe:
If I double down its pages
    At the woeful sixteenth print,
When he gathers his greengages,[5]
    Ope a sieve and slip it in't?

Or, there's Satan!—one might venture
    Pledge one's soul to him, yet leave
Such a flaw in the indenture
    As he'd miss till, past retrieve,
Blasted lay that rose-acacia
    We're so proud of! *Hy, Zy, Hine* . . .[6]
'St, there's Vespers! *Plena gratia,*
    Ave, Virgo! [7] G—r—r—you swine!

[5] Plums.
[6] Beginning of a formula for conjuring up the devil.
[7] Part of the Hail Mary.

James Fenimore Cooper
from
HOME AS FOUND

This short section of Cooper's 1838 novel is interesting for two reasons. It contains a satiric sketch—or "character" like those of Earle and Overbury and Pope printed earlier in the Reader—of Aristabulus Bragg the lawyer, who becomes a type of that little political figure we all know. But the very setting of the sketch also adds to the satire, because Bragg, when ushered into the presence of people with real quality, is clearly rendered inferior. We include this selection for a third reason. Having read Cooper's rather precious little satire, one might find it fun to turn to Clemens' classic rough burlesque, "Fenimore Cooper's Literary Offenses."

"Ask him for his card,—there must be a mistake, I think."

While this short conversation took place, Grace Van Cortlandt was sketching a cottage with a pen, without attending to a word that was said. But, when Eve received the card from Pierre and read aloud, with the tone of surprise that the name would be apt to excite in a novice in the art of American nomenclature, the words "Aristabulus Bragg," her cousin began to laugh.

"Who can this possibly be, Grace?—Did you ever hear of such a person, and what right can he have to wish to see me?"

"Admit him, by all means; it is your father's land agent, and he may wish to leave some message for my uncle. You will be obliged to make his acquaintance, sooner or later, and it may as well be done now as at another time."

"You have shown this gentleman into the front drawing-room, Pierre?"

"Oui, Mademoiselle."

"I will ring when you are wanted."

Pierre withdrew, and Eve opened her secretaire, out of which she took a small manuscript book, over the leaves of which she passed her fingers rapidly.

"Here it is," she said, smiling, " 'Mr. Aristabulus Bragg, Attorney and Counsellor at Law, and the agent of the Templeton estate.' This precious little work, you must understand, Grace, contains sketches of the characters of such persons as I shall be the most likely to see, by John Effingham, A.M. It is a sealed volume, of course, but there can be no harm in reading the part that treats of our present visitor, and, with your permission, we will have it in common. —'Mr. Aristabulus Bragg was born in one of the western counties of Massachusetts, and emigrated to New York, after receiving his education, at the mature age of nineteen; at twenty-one he was admitted to the bar, and for the last seven years he has been a successful practitioner in all the courts of Otsego, from the justice's to the circuit. His talents are undeniable, as he commenced his education at fourteen and terminated it at twenty-one, the law course included. This man is an epitome of all that is good and all that is bad, in a very large class of his fellow citizens. He is quick-witted, prompt in action, enterprising in all things in which he has nothing to lose, but wary and cautious in all things in which he has a real stake, and ready to turn not only his hand, but his heart and his principles, to anything that offers an advantage. With him, literally, "nothing is too high to be aspired to, nothing too low to be done." He will run for Governor, or for town clerk, just as opportunities occur, is expert in all the practices of his profession, has had a quarter's dancing, with three years in the classics, and turned his attention towards medicine and divinity, before he finally settled down into the law. Such a compound of shrewdness, impudence, common-sense, pretension, humility, cleverness, vulgarity, kind-heartedness, duplicity, selfishness, law-honesty, moral fraud and mother wit, mixed up with a smattering of learning and much penetration in practical things, can hardly be described, as any one of his prominent qualities is certain to be met by another quite as obvious that is almost its converse. Mr. Bragg, in short, is purely a creature of circumstances, his qualities pointing him out for either a member of congress or a deputy sheriff, offices that he is equally ready to fill. I have employed him to watch over the estate of your father, in the absence of the latter, on the principle that one practised in tricks is the best qualified to detect and expose them, and with the certainty that no man will trespass with impunity, so long as the courts continue to tax bills of costs with their present liberality.' You appear to know the gentleman, Grace; is this character of him faithful?"

"I know nothing of bills of costs and deputy sheriffs, but I do know that Mr. Aristabulus Bragg is an amusing mixture of strut, humility, roguery, and cleverness. He is waiting all this time in the drawing-room, and you had better see him, as he may now be almost considered part of the family. You know he has been living in the house at Templeton, ever since he was installed by Mr. John Effingham. It was there I had the honor first to meet him."

"First!—Surely you have never seen him anywhere else!"

"Your pardon, my dear. He never comes to town without honoring me with a call. This is the price I pay for having had the honor of being an inmate of the same house with him for a week."

Eve rang the bell, and Pierre made his appearance.

"Desire Mr. Bragg to walk into the library."

Grace looked demure while Pierre was gone to usher in their visitor, and Eve was thinking of the medley of qualities John Effingham had assembled in his description, as the door opened, and the subject of her contemplation entered.

"Monsieur Aristabule," said Pierre, eyeing the card, but sticking at the first name.

Mr. Aristabulus Bragg was advancing with an easy assurance to make his bow to the ladies, when the more finished air and quiet dignity of Miss Effingham, who was standing, so far disconcerted him, as completely to upset his self-possession. As Grace had expressed it, in consequence of having lived three years in the old residence at Templeton, he had begun to consider himself a part of the family, and at home he never spoke of the young lady without calling her "Eve," or "Eve Effingham." But he found it a very different thing to affect familiarity among his associates, and to practise it in the very face of its subject; and, although seldom at a loss for words of some sort or another, he was now actually dumbfounded. Eve relieved his awkwardness by directing Pierre, with her eye, to hand a chair, and first speaking.

Samuel Clemens
FIVE SATIRES

*Certainly the greatest American satirist is Clemens. He is
our Juvenal, our Cervantes, our Swift, our Voltaire. Like
them, he was a man of wide practical experience. Writing
journalistic humor at first, he gradually darkened his satire
as he broadened his experience. For sheer range, no other
American satirist is close to him. He exploits the satiric
potential of the travel book in such early works as* The In-
nocents Abroad *(1869) and* Roughing It *(1872). In* The
Gilded Age *(1873) he wrote a full-scale satiric novel
which gave America an ironic phrase for the period and a
character, Colonel Sellers, who became as much a symbol as
Sinclair Lewis' Babbitt in the 1920's and 1930's. A Connecticut Yankee in King Arthur's Court (1889) is an epic
double-edged satire, attacking not only modern values but
those European corruptions Clemens traces back to the
world of Camelot itself. In* Following the Equator *(1897),*
The Man That Corrupted Hadleyburg *(1900),* What Is
Man? *(1906),* The Mysterious Stranger *(1916), and* Letters from the Earth *(published posthumously in 1963),
the dark pessimism of his satire is more evident. An irony
of our time is that Clemens, like Swift, has come to be
known as a kindly old humorist.* Huckleberry Finn, *his
most popular work, is considered by many to be simply an
amusing children's book; yet it is one of the most thorough
satires ever produced in America, attacking many social, religious, and philosophical attitudes and practices. The satirist's dilemma was well expressed by Clemens in a letter to
William Dean Howells in 1879: "A man can't write successful satire unless he be in a calm judicial good humor. I
don't ever seem to be in a good enough humor with* ANY-
thing to satirize *it; no, I want to stand up before it and
curse it, and foam at the mouth—or take a club and pound*

*it to rags and pulp." It is self discipline—control of that
fierce indignation—which a writer must have to write satire
and not mere invective, abuse, and sarcasm.*

from A TRAMP ABROAD

*Anyone who has through the complexitiesimpossible of
the Germanlanguage studying suffered will surely Clemens
light, telling, and well-sustained burlesque of that very
problem enjoy. Although the lightness of the treatment to
make the reader move through this satire quickly tends, one
a further level of delight in closelyreading, the nuances of
Clemens' 1880 travesty savoring, finds.*

THE AWFUL GERMAN LANGUAGE

A little learning makes the whole world kin.—Proverbs xxxii, 7.

I went often to look at the collection of curiosities in Heidelberg
Castle, and one day I surprised the keeper of it with my German. I
spoke entirely in that language. He was greatly interested; and after
I had talked a while he said my German was very rare, possibly a
"unique;" and wanted to add it to his museum.

If he had known what it had cost me to acquire my art, he would
also have known that it would break any collector to buy it. Harris
and I had been hard at work on our German during several weeks
at that time, and although we had made good progress, it had been
accomplished under great difficulty and annoyance, for three of our
teachers had died in the mean time. A person who has not studied
German can form no idea of what a perplexing language it is.

Surely there is not another language that is so slip-shod and system-
less, and so slippery and elusive to the grasp. One is washed about in
it, hither and thither, in the most helpless way; and when at last he
thinks he has captured a rule which offers firm ground to take a rest
on amid the general rage and turmoil of the ten parts of speech, he

turns over the page and reads, "Let the pupil make careful note of the following *exceptions.*" He runs his eye down and finds that there are more exceptions to the rule than instances of it. So overboard he goes again, to hunt for another Ararat and find another quicksand. Such has been, and continues to be, my experience. Every time I think I have got one of these four confusing "cases" where I am master of it, a seemingly insignificant preposition intrudes itself into my sentence, clothed with an awful and unsuspected power, and crumbles the ground from under me. For instance, my book inquires after a certain bird—(it is always inquiring after things which are of no sort of consequence to anybody): "Where is the bird?" Now the answer to this question,—according to the book,—is that the bird is waiting in the blacksmith shop on account of the rain. Of course no bird would do that, but then you must stick to the book. Very well, I begin to cipher out the German for that answer. I begin at the wrong end, necessarily, for that is the German idea, I say to myself, *"Regen,* (rain), is masculine—or maybe it is feminine—or possibly neuter—it is too much trouble to look, now. Therefore, it is either *der* (the) Regen, or *die* (the) Regen, or *das* (the) Regen, according to which gender it may turn out to be when I look. In the interest of science, I will cipher it out on the hypothesis that it is masculine. Very well—then *the* rain is *der* Regen, if it is simply in the quiescent state of being *mentioned,* without enlargement or discussion—Nominative case; but if this rain is lying around, in kind of a general way on the ground, it is then definitely located, it is *doing something*—that is, *resting,* (which is one of the German grammar's ideas of doing something,) and this throws the rain into the Dative case, and makes it *dem* Regen. However, this rain is not resting, but is doing something *actively,*—it is falling,— to interfere with the bird, likely,—and this indicates *movement,* which has the effect of sliding it into the Accusative case and changing *dem* Regen into *den* Regen." Having completed the grammatical horoscope of this matter, I answer up confidently and state in German that the bird is staying in the blacksmith shop "wegen (on account of) *den* Regen." Then the teacher lets me softly down with the remark that whenever the word "wegen" drops into a sentence, it *always* throws that subject into the *Genitive* case, regardless of consequences—and that therefore this bird staid in the blacksmith shop "wegen *des* Regens."

N.B. I was informed, later, by a higher authority, that there was an "exception" which permits one to say "wegen *den* Regen" in certain peculiar and complex circumstances, but that this exception is not extended to anything *but* rain.

There are ten parts of speech, and they are all troublesome. An average sentence, in a German newspaper, is a sublime and impressive curiosity; it occupies a quarter of a column; it contains all the ten parts of speech—not in regular order, but mixed; it is built mainly of compound words constructed by the writer on the spot, and not to be found in any dictionary—six or seven words compacted into one, without joint or seam—that is, without hyphens; it treats of fourteen or fifteen different subjects, each inclosed in a parenthesis of its own, with here and there extra parentheses which reinclose three or four of the minor parentheses, making pens within pens: finally, all the parentheses and reparentheses are massed together between a couple of king-parentheses, one of which is placed in the first line of the majestic sentence and the other in the middle of the last line of it—*after which comes the* VERB, and you find out for the first time what the man has been talking about; and after the verb—merely by way of ornament, as far as I can make out,—the writer shovels in *"haben sind gewesen gehabt haben geworden sein,"* or words to that effect, and the monument is finished. I suppose that this closing hurrah is in the nature of the flourish to a man's signature—not necessary, but pretty. German books are easy enough to read when you hold them before the looking-glass or stand on your head,—so as to reverse the construction,—but I think that to learn to read and understand a German newspaper is a thing which must always remain an impossibility to a foreigner.

Yet even the German books are not entirely free from attacks of the Parenthesis distemper—though they are usually so mild as to cover only a few lines, and therefore when you at last get down to the verb it carries some meaning to your mind because you are able to remember a good deal of what has gone before.

Now here is a sentence from a popular and excellent German novel,—with a slight parenthesis in it. I will make a perfectly literal translation, and throw in the parenthesis-marks and some hyphens for the assistance of the reader,—though in the original there are no parenthesis-marks or hyphens, and the reader is left to flounder through to the remote verb the best way he can:

"But when he, upon the street, the (in-satin-an-silk-covered-now-very-unconstrainedly-after-the-newest-fashion-dressed) government counselor's wife *met,*" etc., etc.[1]

That is from "The Old Mamselle's Secret," by Mrs. Marlitt. And that sentence is constructed upon the most approved German model. You observe how far that verb is from the reader's base of operations; well, in a German newspaper they put their verb away over on the next page; and I have heard that sometimes after stringing along on exciting preliminaries and parentheses for a column or two, they get in a hurry and have to go to press without getting to the verb at all. Of course, then, the reader is left in a very exhausted and ignorant state.

We have the Parenthesis disease in our literature, too; and one may see cases of it every day in our books and newspapers; but with us it is the mark and sign of an unpractised writer or a cloudy intellect, whereas with the Germans it is doubtless the mark and sign of a practised pen and of the presence of that sort of luminous intellectual fog which stands for clearness among these people. For surely it is *not* clearness,—it necessarily can't be clearness. Even a jury would have penetration enough to discover that. A writer's ideas must be a good deal confused, a good deal out of line and sequence, when he starts out to say that a man met a counsellor's wife in the street, and then right in the midst of this so simple undertaking halts these approaching people and makes them stand still until he jots down an inventory of the woman's dress. That is manifestly absurd. It reminds a person of those dentists who secure your instant and breathless interest in a tooth by taking a grip on it with the forceps, and then stand there and drawl through a tedious anecdote before they give the dreaded jerk. Parentheses in literature and dentistry are in bad taste.

The Germans have another kind of parenthesis, which they make by splitting a verb in two and putting half of it at the beginning of an exciting chapter and the *other half* at the end of it. Can any one conceive

---

[1] "Wenn er aber auf der Strasse der in Sammt und Seide gehüllten jetz sehr ungenirt nach der neusten mode gekleideten Regierungsrathin begegnet."

cf anything more confusing than that? These things are called "separable verbs." The German grammar is blistered all over with separable verbs; and the wider the two portions of one of them are spread apart, the better the author of the crime is pleased with his performance. A favorite one is *reiste ab*,—which means, *departed*. Here is an example which I culled from a novel and reduced to English:

"The trunks being now ready, he De- after kissing his mother and sisters, and once more pressing to his bosom his adored Gretchen, who, dressed in simple white muslin, with a single tuberose in the ample folds of her rich brown hair, had tottered feebly down the stairs, still pale from the terror and excitement of the past evening, but longing to lay her poor aching head yet once again upon the breast of him whom she loved more dearly than life itself, PARTED."

However, it is not well to dwell too much on the separable verbs. One is sure to lose his temper early; and if he sticks to the subject, and will not be warned, it will at last either soften his brain or petrify it. Personal pronouns and adjectives are a fruitful nuisance in this language, and should have been left out. For instance, the same sound, *sie* means *you*, and it means *she*, and it means *her*, and it means *it*, and it means *they*, and it means *them*. Think of the ragged poverty of a language which has to make one word do the work of six,—and a poor little weak thing of only three letters at that. But mainly, think of the exasperation of never knowing which of these meanings the speaker is trying to convey. This explains why, whenever a person says *sie* to me, I generally try to kill him, if a stranger.

Now observe the Adjective. Here was a case where simplicity would have been an advantage; therefore, for no other reason, the inventor of this language complicated it all he could. When we wish to speak of our "good friend or friends," in our enlightened tongue, we stick to the one form and have no trouble or hard feeling about it; but with the German tongue it is different. When a German gets his hands on an adjective, he declines it, and keeps on declining it until the common sense is all declined out of it. It is as bad as Latin. He says, for instance:

SINGULAR.

Nominative—Mein gut*er* Freund, my good friend.
Genitive—Mein*es* gut*en* Freund*es*, of my good friend.
Dative—Mein*em* gut*en* Freund, to my good friend.
Accusative—Mein*en* gut*en* Freund, my good friend.

PLURAL.

N.—Mein*e* gut*en* Freund*e*, my good friends.
G.—Mein*er* gut*en* Freund*e*, of my good friends.
D.—Mein*en* gut*en* Freund*en*, to my good friends.
A.—Mein*e* gut*en* Freund*e*, my good friends.

Now let the candidate for the asylum try to memorize those variations, and see how soon he will be elected. One might better go without friends in Germany than take all this trouble about them. I have shown what a bother it is to decline a good (male) friend; well, this is only a third of the work, for there is a variety of new distortions of the adjective to be learned when the object is feminine, and still another when the object is neuter. Now there are more adjectives in this language than there are black cats in Switzerland, and they must all be as elaborately declined as the examples above suggested. Difficult?—troublesome?—these words cannot describe it. I heard a Californian student in Heidelberg, say, in one of his calmest moods, that he would rather decline two drinks than one German adjective.

The inventor of the language seems to have taken pleasure in complicating it in every way he could think of. For instance, if one is casually referring to a house, *Haus,* or a horse, *Pferd,* or a dog, *Hund,* he spells these words as I have indicated; but if he is referring to them in the Dative case, he sticks on a foolish and unnecessary *e* and spells them *Hause, Pferde, Hunde.* So, as an added *e* often signifies the plural, as the *s* does with us, the new student is likely to go on for a month making twins out of a Dative dog before he discovers his mistake; and on the other hand, many a new student who could ill afford loss, has bought and paid for two dogs and only got one of them, because he ignorantly bought that dog in the Dative singular when he really supposed he was talking plural,—which left the law on the seller's side, of course, by the strict rules of grammar, and therefore a suit for recovery could not lie.

In German, all the Nouns begin with a capital letter. Now that is a good idea; and a good idea, in this language, is necessarily conspicuous from its lonesomeness. I consider this capitalizing of nouns a good idea, because by reason of it you are almost always able to tell a noun the minute you see it. You fall into error occasionally, because you mistake the name of a person for the name of a thing, and waste a good deal of time trying to dig a meaning out of it. German names almost always do mean something, and this helps to deceive the student. I translated a passage one day, which said that "the infuriated tigress broke loose and utterly ate up the unfortunate fir forest," (*Tannenwald.*) When I was girding up my loins to doubt this, I found out that Tannenwald, in this instance, was a man's name.

Every noun has a gender, and there is no sense or system in the distribution; so the gender of each must be learned separately and by heart. There is no other way. To do this, one has to have a memory like a memorandum book. In German, a young lady has no sex, while a turnip has. Think what overwrought reverence that shows for the turnip, and what callous disrespect for the girl. See how it looks in print—I translate this from a conversation in one of the best of the German Sunday-school books:

"*Gretchen.* Wilhelm, where is the turnip?

"*Wilhelm.* She has gone to the kitchen.

"*Gretchen.* Where is the accomplished and beautiful English maiden?

"*Wilhelm.* It has gone to the opera."

To continue with the German genders: a tree is male, its buds are female, its leaves are neuter; horses are sexless, dogs are males, cats are female,—Tom-cats included, of course; a person's mouth, neck, bosom, elbows, fingers, nails, feet, and body, are of the male sex, and his head is male or neuter according to the word selected to signify it, and *not* according to the sex of the individual who wears it,—for in Germany all the women wear either male heads or sexless ones; a person's nose, lips, shoulders, breast, hands, and toes are of the female sex; and his hair, ears, eyes, chin, legs, knees, heart, and conscience haven't any sex at all. The inventor of the language probably got what he knew about a conscience from hearsay.

Now, by the above dissection, the reader will see that in Germany a man may *think* he is a man, but when he comes to look into the matter closely, he is bound to have his doubts; he finds that in sober truth he is a most ridiculous mixture; and if he ends by trying to comfort himself with the thought that he can at least depend on a third of this mess as being manly and masculine, the humiliating second thought will quickly remind him that in this respect he is no better off than any woman or cow in the land.

In the German it is true that by some oversight of the inventor of the language, a Woman is a female; but a Wife, (*Weib,*) is not,—which is unfortunate. A Wife, here, has no sex; she is neuter; so, according to the grammar, a fish is *he,* his scales are *she,* but a fishwife is neither. To describe a wife as sexless, may be called under-description; that is bad enough, but over-description is surely worse. A German speaks of an Englishman as the *Engländer;* to change the sex, he adds *inn,* and that stands for Englishwoman—*Engländerinn.* That seems descriptive enough, but still it is not exact enough for a German; so he precedes the word with that article which indicates that the creature to follow is feminine, and writes it down thus: *"die* Engländer*inn,"*—which means "the *she-Englishwoman."* I consider that that person is over-described.

Well, after the student has learned the sex of a great number of nouns, he is still in a difficulty, because he finds it impossible to persuade his tongue to refer to things as *"he"* and *"she,"* and *"him"* and *"her,"* which it has been always accustomed to refer to as *"it."* When he even frames a German sentence in his mind, with the hims and hers in the right places, and then works up his courage to the utterance-point, it is no use,—the moment he begins to speak his tongue flies the track and all those labored males and females come out as *"its."* And even when he is reading German to himself, he always calls those things *"it,"* whereas he ought to read in this way:

TALE OF THE FISHWIFE AND ITS SAD FATE [2]

It is a bleak Day. Hear the Rain, how he pours, and the Hail, how he rattles; and see the Snow, how he drifts along, and oh the Mud, how

[2] I capitalize the nouns, in the German (and ancient English) fashion.

deep he is! Ah the poor Fishwife, it is stuck fast in the Mire; it has dropped its Basket of Fishes; and its Hands have been cut by the Scales as it seized some of the falling Creatures; and one Scale has even got into its Eye, and it cannot get her out. It opens its Mouth to cry for Help; but if any Sound comes out of him, alas he is drowned by the raging of the Storm. And now a Tomcat has got one of the Fishes and she will surely escape with him. No, she bites off a Fin, she holds her in her Mouth,—will she swallow her? No, the Fishwife's brave Mother-Dog deserts his Puppies and rescues the Fin,—which he eats, himself, as his Reward. O, horror, the Lightning has struck the Fishbasket; he sets him on Fire; see the Flame, how she licks the doomed Utensil with her red and angry Tongue; now she attacks the helpless Fishwife's Foot, —she burns him up, all but the big Toe, and even *she* is partly consumed; and still she spreads, still she waves her fiery Tongues; she attacks the Fishwife's Leg and destroys *it;* she attacks its Hand and destroys *her;* she attacks its poor worn Garment and destroys *her* also; she attacks its Body and consumes *him;* she wreaths herself about its Heart and *it* is consumed; next about its Breast, and in a Moment *she* is a Cinder; now she reaches its Neck—*he* goes; now its Chin—*it* goes; now its Nose,—*she* goes. In another Moment, except Help come, the Fishwife will be no more. Time presses,—is there none to succor and save? Yes! Joy, joy, with flying Feet the she-Englishwoman comes! But alas, the generous she-Female is too late: where now is the fated Fishwife? It has ceased from its Sufferings, it has gone to a better Land; all that is left of it for its loved Ones to lament over, is this poor smoldering Ash-heap. Ah, woeful, woeful Ash-heap! Let us take him up tenderly, reverently, upon the lowly Shovel, and bear him to his long Rest, with the Prayer that when he rises again it will be in a Realm where he will have one good square responsible Sex, and have it all to himself, instead of assorted Sexes scattered all over him in Spots.

There, now, the reader can see for himself that this pronoun business is a very awkward thing for the unaccustomed tongue.

I suppose that in all languages the similarities of look and sound between words which have no similarity in meaning are a fruitful source of perplexity to the foreigner. It is so in our tongue, and it is notably the case in the German. Now there is that troublesome word *vermählt:*

226

to me it has so close a resemblance,—either real or fancied,—to three or four other words, that I never know whether it means despised, painted, suspected, or married; until I look in the dictionary, and then I find it means the latter. There are lots of such words and they are a great torment. To increase the difficulty there are words which *seem* to resemble each other, and yet do not; but they make just as much trouble as if they did. For instance, there is the word *vermiethen*, (to let, to lease, to hire); and the word *verheirathen*, (another way of saying to marry). I heard of an Englishman who knocked at a man's door in Heidelberg and proposed; in the best German he could command, to "verheirathen" that house. Then there are some words which mean one thing when you emphasize the first syllable, but mean something very different if you throw the emphasis on the last syllable. For instance, there is a word which means a runaway, or the act of glancing through a book, according to the placing of the emphasis; and another word which signifies to *associate* with a man, or to *avoid* him, according to where you put the emphasis,—and you can generally depend on putting it in the wrong place and getting into trouble.

There are some exceedingly useful words in this language. *Schlag,* for example; and *Zug*. There are three-quarters of a column of *Schlags* in the dictionary, and a column and a half of *Zugs*. The word *Schlag* means Blow, Stroke, Dash, Hit, Shock, Clap, Slap, Time, Bar, Coin, Stamp, Kind, Sort, Manner, Way, Apoplexy, Wood-cutting, Inclosure, Field, Forest-clearing. This is its simple and *exact* meaning,—that is to say, its restricted, its fettered meaning; but there are ways by which you can set it free, so that it can soar away, as on the wings of the morning, and never be at rest. You can hang any word you please to its tail, and make it mean anything you want to. You can begin with *Schlag-ader,* which means artery, and you can hang on the whole dictionary, word by word, clear through the alphabet to *Schlag-wasser,* which means bilge-water,—and including *Schlag-mutter,* which means mother-in-law.

Just the same with *Zug*. Strictly speaking, *Zug* means Pull, Tug, Draught, Procession, March, Progress, Flight, Direction, Expedition, Train, Caravan, Passage, Stroke, Touch, Line, Flourish, Trait of Character, Feature, Lineament, Chess-move, Organ-stop, Team, Whiff, Bias, Drawer, Propensity, Inhalation, Disposition: but that thing which it does *not* mean,—when all its legitimate pennants have been hung on, has not been discovered yet.

One cannot overestimate the usefulness of Schlag and Zug. Armed just with these two, and the word *Also,* what cannot the foreigner on German soil accomplish? The German word *Also* is the equivalent of the English phrase "You know," and does not mean anything at all,— in *talk,* though it sometimes does in print. Every time a German opens his mouth an *Also* falls out; and every time he shuts it he bites one in two that was trying to *get* out.

Now, the foreigner, equipped with these three noble words, is master of the situation. Let him talk right along, fearlessly; let him pour his indifferent German forth, and when he lacks for a word, let him heave a *Schlag* into the vacuum; all the chances are that it fits it like a plug, but if it doesn't let him promptly heave a *Zug* after it; the two together can hardly fail to bung the hole; but if, by a miracle, they *should* fail, let him simply say *Also!* and this will give him a moment's chance to think of the needful word. In Germany, when you load your conversational gun it is always best to throw in a *Schlag* or two and a *Zug* or two, because it doesn't make any difference how much the rest of the charge may scatter, you are bound to bag something with *them.* Then you blandly say *Also,* and load up again. Nothing gives such an air of grace and elegance and unconstraint to a German or an English conversation as to scatter it full of "Also's" or "You-knows."

In my note-book I find this entry:

July 1.—In the hospital yesterday, a word of thirteen syllables was successfully removed from a patient—a North-German from near Hamburg; but as most unfortunately the surgeons had opened him in the wrong place, under the impression that he contained a panorama, he died. The sad event has cast a gloom over the whole community.

That paragraph furnishes a text for a few remarks about one of the most curious and notable features of my subject—the length of German words. Some German words are so long that they have a perspective. Observe these examples:

Freundschaftsbezeigungen.
Dilettantenaufdringlichkeiten.
Stadtverordnetenversammlungen.

These things are not words, they are alphabetical processions. And they are not rare; one can open a German newspaper any time and see them marching majestically across the page,—and if he has any imagination he can see the banners and hear the music, too. They impart a martial thrill to the meekest subject. I take a great interest in these curiosities. Whenever I come across a good one, I stuff it and put it in my museum. In this way I have made quite a valuable collection. When I get duplicates, I exchange with other collectors, and thus increase the variety of my stock. Here are some specimens which I lately bought at an auction sale of the effects of a bankrupt bric-a-brac hunter:

GENERALSTAATSVERORDNETENVERSAMMLUNGEN.
ALTERTHUMSWISSENSCHAFTEN.
KINDERBEWAHRUNGSANSTALTEN.
UNABHAENGIGKEITSERKLAERUNGEN.
WIEDERERSTELLUNGSBESTREBUNGEN.
WAFFENSTILLSTANDSUNTERHANDLUNGEN.

Of course when one of these grand mountain ranges goes stretching across the printed page, it adorns and ennobles that literary landscape, —but at the same time it is a great distress to the new student, for it blocks up his way; he cannot crawl under it, or climb over it, or tunnel through it. So he resorts to the dictionary for help, but there is no help there. The dictionary must draw the line somewhere,—so it leaves this sort of words out. And it is right, because these long things are hardly legitimate words, but are rather combinations of words, and the inventor of them ought to have been killed. They are compound words with the hyphens left out. The various words used in building them are in the dictionary, but in a very scattered condition; so you can hunt the materials out, one by one, and get at the meaning at last, but it is a tedious and harassing business. I have tried this process upon some of the above examples. "Freundschaftsbezeigungen" seems to be "Friendship demonstrations," which is only a foolish and clumsy way of saying "demonstrations of friendship." "Unabhaengigkeitserklaerungen" seems to be "Independencedeclarations," which is no improvement upon "Declarations of Independence," so far as I can see. "Generalstaatsverordnetenversammlungen" seems to be "Generalstatesrepresentativesmeetings," as nearly as I can get it,—a mere rhythmical, gushy euphuism

229

for "meetings of the legislature," I judge. We used to have a good deal of this sort of crime in our literature, but it has gone out now. We used to speak of a thing as a "never-to-be-forgotten" circumstance, instead of cramping it into the simple and sufficient word "memorable" and then going calmly about our business as if nothing had happened. In those days we were not content to embalm the thing and bury it decently, we wanted to build a monument over it.

But in our newspapers the compounding-disease lingers a little to the present day, but with the hyphens left out, in the German fashion. This is the shape it takes; instead of saying "Mr. Simmons, clerk of the county and district courts, was in town yesterday," the new form puts it thus: "Clerk of the County and District Courts Simmons was in town yesterday." This saves neither time nor ink, and has an awkward sound besides. One often sees a remark like this in our papers: "*Mrs.* Assistant District Attorney Johnson returned to her city residence yesterday for the season." That is a case of really unjustifiable compounding; because it not only saves no time or trouble, but confers a title on Mrs. Johnson which she has no right to. But these little instances are trifles indeed, contrasted with the ponderous and dismal German system of piling jumbled compounds together. I wish to submit the following local item, from a Mannheim journal, by way of illustration:

"In the daybeforeyesterdayshortlyaftereleveno'clock Night, the inthistownstandingtavern called 'The Wagoner' was downburnt. When the fire to the onthedownburninghouseresting Stork's Nest reached, flew the parent Storks away. But when the bytheraging, firesurrounded Nest *itself* caught Fire, straightway plunged the quickreturning Mother-stork into the Flames and died, her Wings over her young ones outspread."

Even the cumbersome German construction is not able to take the pathos out of that picture,—indeed, it somehow seems to strengthen it. This item is dated away back yonder months ago. I could have used it sooner, but I was waiting to hear from the Father-stork. I am still waiting.

"*Also!*" If I have not shown that the German is a difficult language, I have at least intended to do it. I have heard of an American student who was asked how he was getting along with his German, and who answered promptly: "I am not getting along at all. I have worked at it hard for three level months, and all I have got to show for it is one solitary German phrase—'*Zwei glas'*," (two glasses of beer). He paused a moment, reflectively; then added with feeling: "But I've got that *solid!*"

And if I have not also shown that German is a harassing and infuriating study, my execution has been at fault, and not my intent. I heard lately of a worn and sorely tried American student who used to fly to a certain German word for relief when he could bear up under his aggravations no longer,—the only word in the whole language whose sound was sweet and precious to his ear and healing to his lacerated spirit. This was the word *Damit*. It was only the *sound* that helped him, not the meaning; [3] and so, at last, when he learned that the emphasis was not on the first syllable, his only stay and support was gone, and he faded away and died.

I think that a description of any loud, stirring, tumultuous episode must be tamer in German than in English. Our descriptive words of this character have such a deep, strong, resonant sound, while their German equivalents do seem so thin and mild and energyless. Boom, burst, crash, roar, storm, bellow, blow, thunder, explosion; howl, cry, shout, yell, groan; battle, hell. These are magnificent words; they have a force and magnitude of sound befitting the things which they describe. But their German equivalents would be ever so nice to sing the children to sleep with, or else my awe-inspiring ears were made for display and not for superior usefulness in analyzing sounds. Would any man want to die in a battle which was called by so tame a term as a *Schlacht?* Or would not a consumptive feel too much bundled up, who was about to go out, in a shirt-collar, and a seal-ring, into a storm which the bird-song word *Gewitter* was employed to describe? And observe the strongest of the several German equivalents for explosion,—*Ausbruch*. Our word Toothbrush is more powerful than that. It seems to me that the Germans could do worse than import it into their language to describe particularly tremendous explosions with. The German word for hell,— Hölle,—sounds more like *helly* than anything else; therefore, how necessarily chipper, frivolous, and unimpressive it is. If a man were told in German to go there, could he really rise to the dignity of feeling insulted?

Having pointed out, in detail, the several vices of this language, I

[3] It merely means, in its general sense, *"herewith."*

SAMUEL CLEMENS

now come to the brief and pleasant task of pointing out its virtues. The capitalizing of the nouns, I have already mentioned. But far before this virtue stands another,—that of spelling a word according to the sound of it. After one short lesson in the alphabet, the student can tell how any German word is pronounced without having to ask; whereas in our language if a student should inquire of us "What does B, O, W, spell!" we should be obliged to reply, "Nobody can tell what it spells when you see it off by itself,—you can only tell by referring to the context and finding out what it signifies,—whether it is a thing to shoot arrows with, or a nod of one's head, or the forward end of a boat."

There are some German words which are singularly and powerfully effective. For instance, those which describe lowly, peaceful, and affectionate home life; those which deal with love, in any and all forms, from mere kindly feeling and honest good will toward the passing stranger, clear up to courtship; those which deal with outdoor Nature, in its softest and loveliest aspects,—with meadows, and forests, and birds and flowers, the fragrance and sunshine of summer, and the moonlight of peaceful winter nights; in a word, those which deal with any and all forms of rest, repose, and peace; those also which deal with the creatures and marvels of fairyland; and lastly and chiefly, in those words which express pathos, is the language surpassingly rich and effective. There are German songs which can make a stranger to the language cry. That shows that the *sound* of the words is correct,—it interprets the meanings with truth and with exactness; and so the ear is informed, and through the ear, the heart.

The Germans do not seem to be afraid to repeat a word when it is the right one. They repeat it several times, if they choose. That is wise. But in English, when we have used a word a couple of times in a paragraph, we imagine we are growing tautological, and so we are weak enough to exchange it for some other word which only approximates exactness, to escape what we wrongly fancy is a greater blemish. Repetition may be bad, but surely inexactness is worse.

There are people in the world who will take a great deal of trouble to point out the faults in a religion or a language, and then go blandly about their business without suggesting any remedy. I am not that kind of a person. I have shown that the German language needs reforming.

232

Very well, I am ready to reform it. At least I am ready to make the proper suggestions. Such a course as this might be immodest in another; but I have devoted upward of nine full weeks, first and last, to a careful and critical study of this tongue, and thus have acquired a confidence in my ability to reform it which no mere superficial culture could have conferred upon me.

In the first place, I would leave out the Dative Case. It confuses the plurals; and, besides, nobody ever knows when he is in the Dative case, except he discover it by accident,—and then he does not know when or where it was that he got into it, or how long he has been in it, or how he is ever going to get out of it again. The Dative Case is but an ornamental folly,—it is better to discard it.

In the next place, I would move the Verb further up to the front. You may load up with ever so good a Verb, but I notice that you never really bring down a subject with it at the present German range—you only cripple it. So I insist that this important part of speech should be brought forward to a position where it may be easily seen with the naked eye.

Thirdly, I would import some strong words from the English tongue, —to swear with, and also to use in describing all sorts of vigorous things in a vigorous way.[4]

Fourthly, I would reorganize the sexes, and distribute them according to the will of the Creator. This as a tribute of respect, if nothing else.

Fifthly, I would do away with those great long compounded words; or require the speaker to deliver them in sections, with intermissions for refreshments. To wholly do away with them would be best, for ideas are

[4] *"Verdammt,"* and its variations and enlargements, are words which have plenty of meaning, but the *sounds* are so mild and ineffectual that German ladies can use them without sin. German ladies who could not be induced to commit a sin by any persuasion or compulsion, promptly rip out one of these harmless little words when they tear their dresses or don't like the soup. It sounds about as wicked as our "My gracious." German ladies are constantly saying, "Ach! Gott!" "Mein Gott!" "Gott in Himmel!" "Herr Gott!" "Der Herr Jesus!" etc. They think our ladies have the same custom, perhaps; for I once heard a gentle and lovely old German lady say to a sweet young American girl: "The two languages are so alike—how pleasant that is; we say 'Ach! Gott!' you say *'Goddam.'* "

233

more easily received and digested when they come one at a time than when they come in bulk. Intellectual food is like any other; it is pleasanter and more beneficial to take it with a spoon than with a shovel.

Sixthly, I would require a speaker to stop when he is done, and not hang a string of those useless "haben sind gewesen gehabt haben geworden seins" to the end of his oration. This sort of gew-gaws undignify a speech, instead of adding a grace. They are, therefore, an offense, and should be discarded.

Seventhly, I would discard the Parenthesis. Also the reparenthesis, the rereparenthesis, and the re-re-re-re-re-re-parentheses, and likewise the final wide-reaching all-inclosing king-parenthesis. I would require every individual, be he high or low, to unfold a plain straightforward tale, or else coil it and sit on it and hold his peace. Infractions of this law should be punishable with death.

And eighthly and last, I would retain *Zug* and *Schlag*, with their pendants, and discard the rest of the vocabulary. This would simplify the language.

I have now named what I regard as the most necessary and important changes. These are perhaps all I could be expected to name for nothing; but there are other suggestions which I can and will make in case my proposed application shall result in my being formally employed by the government in the work of reforming the language.

My philological studies have satisfied me that a gifted person ought to learn English (barring spelling and pronouncing), in thirty hours, French in 30 days, and German in 30 years. It seems manifest, then, that the latter tongue ought to be trimmed down and repaired. If it is to remain as it is, it ought to be gently and reverently set aside among the dead languages, for only the dead have time to learn it.

FENIMORE COOPER'S LITERARY OFFENSES

Always the enemy of pomposity and dishonesty, Clemens here singles out for his scorn the "learned opinions" of three men of letters. His first sentence launches the satire, which does not let up until the reductio ad absurdum *is completed in his last. Here one finds many of the classic devices of satire—the witty title, the opening quotation from authority, the employment of a mask or* persona, *the shattering accusation, exaggeration, allusion to a fictitious standard, piling up of selected evidence, catalogs, burlesque, irony, invective, sarcasm, and those final two sentences which bite like the twist of the embedded barb. Perhaps Clemens' 1885 example can encourage each of us to be less docile in accepting the judgments of the so-called critical experts. Students, especially, should be encouraged to accept cliché critical opinions, including ours, very reluctantly and to read carefully for themselves.*

The Pathfinder and *The Deerslayer* stand at the head of Cooper's novels as artistic creations. There are others of his works which contain parts as perfect as are to be found in these, and scenes even more thrilling. Not one can be compared with either of them as a finished whole.

The defects in both of these tales are comparatively slight. They were pure works of art. —PROF. LOUNSBURY

The five tales reveal an extraordinary fullness of invention.

. . . One of the very greatest characters in fiction, Natty Bumppo. . . .

The craft of the woodsman, the tricks of the trapper, all the delicate art of the forest, were familiar to Cooper from his youth up.
—PROF. BRANDER MATTHEWS

Cooper is the greatest artist in the domain of romantic fiction yet produced by America. —WILKIE COLLINS

It seems to me that it was far from right for the Professor of English Literature in Yale, the Professor of English Literature in Columbia, and Wilkie Collins to deliver opinions on Cooper's literature without having read some of it. It would have been much more decorous to keep silent and let persons talk who have read Cooper.

Cooper's art has some defects. In one place in *Deerslayer,* and in the restricted space of two-thirds of a page, Cooper has scored 114 offenses against literary art out of a possible 115. It breaks the record.

There are nineteen rules governing literary art in the domain of romantic fiction—some say twenty-two. In *Deerslayer* Cooper violated eighteen of them. These eighteen require:

1. That a tale shall accomplish something and arrive somewhere. But the *Deerslayer* tale accomplishes nothing and arrives in the air.

2. They require that the episodes of a tale shall be necessary parts of

the tale, and shall help to develop it. But as the *Deerslayer* tale is not a tale, and accomplishes nothing and arrives nowhere, the episodes have no rightful place in the work, since there was nothing for them to develop.

3. They require that the personages in a tale shall be alive, except in the case of corpses, and that always the reader shall be able to tell the corpses from the others. But this detail has often been overlooked in the *Deerslayer* tale.

4. They require that the personages in a tale, both dead and alive, shall exhibit a sufficient excuse for being there. But this detail also has been overlooked in the *Deerslayer* tale.

5. They require that when the personages of a tale deal in conversation, the talk shall sound like human talk, and be talk such as human beings would be likely to talk in the given circumstances, and have a discoverable meaning, also a discoverable purpose, and a show of relevancy, and remain in the neighborhood of the subject in hand, and be interesting to the reader, and help out the tale, and stop when the people cannot think of anything more to say. But this requirement has been ignored from the beginning of the *Deerslayer* tale to the end of it.

6. They require that when the author describes the character of a personage in his tale, the conduct and conversation of that personage shall justify said description. But this law gets little or no attention in the *Deerslayer* tale, as Natty Bumppo's case will amply prove.

7. They require that when a personage talks like an illustrated, gilt-edged, tree-calf, hand-tooled, seven-dollar Friendship's Offering in the beginning of a paragraph, he shall not talk like a negro minstrel in the end of it. But this rule is flung down and danced upon in the *Deerslayer* tale.

8. They require that crass stupidities shall not be played upon the reader as "the craft of the woodsman, the delicate art of the forest," by either the author or the people in the tale. But this rule is persistently violated in the *Deerslayer* tale.

9. They require that the personages of a tale shall confine themselves to possibilities and let miracles alone; or, if they venture a miracle, the author must so plausibly set it forth as to make it look possible and reasonable. But these rules are not respected in the *Deerslayer* tale.

10. They require that the author shall make the reader feel a deep

interest in the personages of his tale and in their fate; and that he shall make the reader love the good people in the tale and hate the bad ones. But the reader of the *Deerslayer* tale dislikes the good people in it, is indifferent to the others, and wishes they would all get drowned together.

11. They require that the characters in a tale shall be so clearly defined that the reader can tell beforehand what each will do in a given emergency. But in the *Deerslayer* this rule is vacated.

In addition to these large rules there are some little ones. These require that the author shall

12. *Say* what he is proposing to say, not merely come near it.

13. Use the right word, not its second cousin.

14. Eschew surplusage.

15. Not omit necessary details.

16. Avoid slovenliness of form.

17. Use good grammar.

18. Employ a simple and straightforward style.

Even these seven are coldly and persistently violated in the *Deerslayer* tale.

Cooper's gift in the way of invention was not a rich endowment; but such as it was he liked to work it, he was pleased with the effects, and indeed he did some quite sweet things with it. In his little box of stage-properties he kept six or eight cunning devices, tricks, artifices for his savages and woodsmen to deceive and circumvent each other with, and he was never so happy as when he was working these innocent things and seeing them go. A favorite one was to make a moccasined person tread in the tracks of the moccasined enemy, and thus hide his own trail. Cooper wore out barrels and barrels of moccasins in working that trick. Another stage-property that he pulled out of his box pretty frequently was his broken twig. He prized his broken twig above all the rest of his effects, and worked it the hardest. It is a restful chapter in any book of his when somebody doesn't step on a dry twig and alarm all the reds and whites for two hundred yards around. Every time a Cooper person is in peril, and absolute silence is worth four dollars a minute, he is sure to step on a dry twig. There may be a hundred handier things to step on, but that wouldn't satisfy Cooper. Cooper requires him to turn out and find a dry twig; and if he can't do it, go and borrow one. In fact, the Leatherstocking Series ought to have been called the Broken Twig Series.

I am sorry there is not room to put in a few dozen instances of the delicate art of the forest, as practised by Natty Bumppo and some of the other Cooperian experts. Perhaps we may venture two or three samples. Cooper was a sailor—a naval officer; yet he gravely tells us how a vessel, driving toward a lee shore in a gale, is steered for a particular spot by her skipper because he knows of an *undertow* there which will hold her back against the gale and save her. For just pure woodcraft, or sailorcraft, or whatever it is, isn't that neat? For several years Cooper was daily in the society of artillery, and he ought to have noticed that when a cannon-ball strikes the ground it either buries itself or skips a hundred feet or so; skips again a hundred feet or so—and so on, till finally it gets tired and rolls. Now in one place he loses some "females"—as he always calls women—in the edge of a wood near a plain at night in a fog, on purpose to give Bumppo a chance to show off the delicate art of the forest before the reader. These mislaid people are hunting for a fort. They hear a cannon-blast, and a cannon-ball presently comes rolling into the wood and stops at their feet. To the females this suggests nothing. The case is very different with the admirable Bumppo. I wish I may never know peace again if he doesn't strike out promptly and *follow the track* of that cannon-ball across the plain through the dense fog and find the fort. Isn't it a daisy? If Cooper had any real knowledge of Nature's way of doing things, he had a most delicate art in concealing the fact. For instance: one of his acute Indian experts, Chingachgook (pronounced Chicago, I think), has lost the trail of a person he is tracking through the forest. Apparently that trail is hopelessly lost. Neither your nor I could ever have guessed out the way to find it. It was very different with Chicago. Chicago was not stumped for long. He turned a running stream out of its course, and there, in the slush in its old bed, were that person's moccasin tracks. The current did not wash them away, as it would have done in all other like cases—no, even the eternal laws of Nature have to vacate when Cooper wants to put up a delicate job of woodcraft on the reader.

We must be a little wary when Brander Matthews tells us that Cooper's books "reveal an extraordinary fullness of invention." As a rule, I am quite willing to accept Brander Matthews's literary judgments and applaud his lucid and graceful phrasing of them; but that particular statement needs to be taken with a few tons of salt. Bless your heart, Cooper hasn't any more invention than a horse; and, I don't mean a high class horse, either; I mean a clotheshorse. It would be very difficult to find a really clever "situation" in Cooper's books, and still more difficult to find one of any kind which he has failed to render absurd by his handling of it. Look at the episodes of "the caves"; and at the celebrated scuffle between Maqua and those others on the tableland a few days later; and at Hurry Harry's queer water-transit from the castle to the ark; and at Deerslayer's half-hour with his first corpse; and at the quarrel between Hurry Harry and Deerslayer later; and at—but choose for yourself; you can't go amiss.

If Cooper had been an observer his inventive faculty would have worked better; not more interestingly, but more rationally, more plausibly. Cooper's proudest creations in the way of "situations" suffer noticeably from the absence of the observer's protecting gift. Cooper's eye was splendidly inaccurate. Cooper seldom saw anything correctly. He saw nearly all things as through a glass eye, darkly. Of course a man who cannot see the commonest little everyday matters accurately is working at a disadvantage when he is constructing a "situation." In the *Deerslayer* tale Cooper has a stream which is fifty feet wide where it flows out of a lake; it presently narrows to twenty as it meanders along for no given reason, and yet when a stream acts like that it ought to be required to explain itself. Fourteen pages later the width of the brook's outlet from the lake has suddenly shrunk thirty feet, and become "the narrowest part of the stream." This shrinkage is not accounted for. The stream has bends in it, a sure indication that it has alluvial banks and cuts them; yet these bends are only thirty and fifty feet long. If Cooper had been a nice and punctilious observer he would have noticed that the bends were oftener nine hundred feet long than short of it.

Cooper made the exit of that stream fifty feet wide, in the first place, for no particular reason; in the second place, he narrowed it to less than twenty to accommodate some Indians. He bends a "sapling" to the form of an arch over this narrow passage, and conceals six Indians in its foliage. They are "laying" for a settler's scow or ark which is coming up the stream on its way to the lake; it is being hauled against the stiff current by a rope whose stationary end is anchored in the lake; its rate of progress cannot be more than a mile an hour. Cooper describes the ark, but pretty obscurely. In the matter of dimensions "it was little more than a modern canal-boat." Let us guess, then, that it was about one hundred and forty feet long. It was of "greater breadth than common." Let us guess, then, that it was about sixteen feet wide. This leviathan had been prowling down bends which were but a third as long as itself, and scraping between banks where it had only two feet of space to spare on each side. We cannot too much admire this miracle. A low-roofed log dwelling occupies "two-thirds of the ark's length"—a dwelling ninety feet long and sixteen feet wide, let us say—a kind of vestibule train. The dwelling has two rooms—each forty-five feet long and sixteen feet wide, let us guess. One of them is the bedroom of the Hutter girls, Judith and Hetty; the other is the parlor in the daytime, at night it is papa's bedchamber. The ark is arriving at the stream's exit now, whose width has been reduced to less than twenty feet to accommodate the Indians—say to eighteen. There is a foot to spare on each side of the boat. Did the Indians notice that there was going to be a tight squeeze there? Did they notice that they could make money by climbing down out of that arched sapling and just stepping aboard when the ark scraped by? No, other Indians would have noticed these things, but Cooper's Indians never notice anything. Cooper thinks they are marvelous creatures for noticing, but he was almost always in error about his Indians. There was seldom a sane one among them.

The ark is one hundred and forty feet long; the dwelling is ninety feet long. The idea of the Indians is to drop softly and secretly from the arched sapling to the dwelling as the ark creeps along under it at the rate of a mile an hour, and butcher the family. It will take the ark a minute and a half to pass under. It will take the ninety-foot dwelling a minute to pass under. Now, then, what did the six Indians do? It would take you thirty years to guess, and even then you would have to give it up, I believe. Therefore, I will tell you what the Indians did. Their chief, a person of quite extraordinary intellect for a Cooper Indian, warily watched the canal-boat as it squeezed along under him, and when he had got his calculations fined down to exactly the right shade, as he judged, he let go and dropped. *And missed the house!* That is actually what he did. He missed the house, and landed in the stern of the scow. It was not much of a fall, yet it knocked him silly. He lay there unconscious. If the house had been ninety-seven feet long he would have made the trip. The fault was Cooper's, not his. The error lay in the construction of the house. Cooper was no architect.

There still remained in the roost five Indians. The boat has passed under and is now out of their reach. Let me explain what the five did —you would not be able to reason it out for yourself. No. 1 jumped for the boat, but fell in the water astern of it. Then No. 2 jumped for the boat, but fell in the water still farther astern of it. Then No. 3 jumped for the boat, and fell a good way astern of it. Then No. 4 jumped for the boat, and fell in the water *away* astern. Then even No. 5 made a jump for the boat—for he was a Cooper Indian. In the matter of intellect, the difference between a Cooper Indian and the Indian that stands in front of the cigar-shop is not spacious. The scow episode is really a sublime burst of invention; but it does not thrill, because the inaccuracy of the details throws a sort of air of fictitiousness and general improbability over it. This comes of Cooper's inadequacy as an observer.

The reader will find some examples of Cooper's high talent for inaccurate observation in the account of the shooting-match in *The Pathfinder.*

A common wrought nail was driven lightly into the target, its head having been first touched with paint.

The color of the paint is not stated—an important omission, but Cooper deals freely in important omissions. No, after all, it was not an important omission; for this nail-head is *a hundred yards from* the marksmen, and could not be seen by them at that distance, no matter what its color might be. How far can the best eyes see a common house-fly? A hundred yards? It is quite impossible. Very well; eyes that cannot see a house-fly that is a hundred yards away cannot see an ordinary nail-head at that distance, for the size of the two objects is the same. It takes a keen eye to see a fly or a nail-head at fifty yards—one hundred and fifty feet. Can the reader do it?

The nail was lightly driven, its head painted, and game called. Then the Cooper miracles began. The bullet of the first marksman chipped an edge of the nail-head; the next man's bullet drove the nail a little way into the target—and removed all the paint. Haven't the miracles gone far enough now? Not to suit Cooper; for the purpose of this whole scheme is to show off his prodigy, Deerslayer-Hawkeye-Long-Rifle-Leatherstocking-Pathfinder-Bumppo before the ladies.

"Be all ready to clench it, boys!" cried out Pathfinder, stepping into his friend's tracks the instant they were vacant. "Never mind a new nail; I can see that, though the paint is gone, and what I can see I can hit a hundred yards, though it were only a mosquito's eye. Be ready to clench!" The rifle cracked, the bullet sped its way, and the head of the nail was buried in the wood, covered by the piece of flattened lead.

There, you see, is a man who could hunt flies with a rifle, and command a ducal salary in a Wild West show to-day if we had him back with us.

The recorded feat is certainly surprising just as it stands; but it is not surprising enough for Cooper. Cooper adds a touch. He has made Pathfinder do this miracle with another man's rifle; and not only that, but Pathfinder did not have even the advantage of loading it himself. He had everything against him, and yet he made that impossible shot; and not only made it, but did it with absolute confidence, saying, "Be ready to clench." Now a person like that would have undertaken that same feat with a brickbat, and with Cooper to help he would have achieved it, too.

Pathfinder showed off handsomely that day before the ladies. His very first feat was a thing which no Wild West show can touch. He was standing with the group of marksmen, observing—a hundred yards from the target, mind; one Jasper raised his rifle and drove the center of the bull's-eye. Then the Quartermaster fired. The target exhibited no result this time. There was a laugh. "It's a dead miss," said Major Lundie. Pathfinder waited an impressive moment or two; then said, in that calm, indifferent, know-it-all way of his, "No, Major, he has covered Jasper's bullet, as will be seen if any one will take the trouble to examine the target."

Wasn't it remarkable? How *could* he see that little pellet fly through the air and enter that distant bullet-hole? Yet that is what he did; for nothing is impossible to a Cooper person. Did any of those people have any deep-seated doubts about this thing? No; for that would imply sanity, and these were all Cooper people.

The respect for Pathfinder's skill and for his *quickness and accuracy of sight* [the italics are mine] was so profound and general, that the instant he made this declaration the spectators began to distrust their own opinions, and a dozen rushed to the target in order to ascertain the fact. There, sure enough, it was found that the Quartermaster's bullet had gone through the hole made by Jasper's, and that, too, so accurately as to require a minute examination to be certain of the circumstance, which, however, was soon clearly established by discovering one bullet over the other in the stump against which the target was placed.

They made a "minute" examination; but never mind, how could they know that there were two bullets in that hole without digging the latest one out? for neither probe nor eyesight could prove the presence of any more than one bullet. Did they dig? No; as we shall see. It is the Pathfinder's turn now; he steps out before the ladies, takes aim, and fires.

But, alas! here is a disappointment; an incredible, an unimaginable disappointment—for the target's aspect is unchanged; there is nothing there but that same old bullet-hole!

"If one dared to hint at such a thing," cried Major Duncan, "I should say that the Pathfinder has also missed the target!"

As nobody had missed it yet, the "also" was not necessary; but never mind about that, for the Pathfinder is going to speak.

"No, no, Major," said he, confidently, "that *would* be a risky declaration. I didn't load the piece, and can't say what was in it; but if it was lead, you will find the bullet driving down those of the Quartermaster and Jasper, else is not my name Pathfinder."

A shout from the target announced the truth of this assertion.

Is the miracle sufficient as it stands? Not for Cooper. The Pathfinder speaks again, as he "now slowly advances toward the stage occupied by the females":

"That's not all, boys, that's not all; if you find the target touched at all, I'll own to a miss. The Quartermaster cut the wood, but you'll find no wood cut by that last messenger."

The miracle is at last complete. He knew—doubtless *saw*—at the distance of a hundred yards—that his bullet had passed into the hole *without fraying the edges.* There were now three bullets in that one hole—three bullets embedded processionally in the body of the stump back of the target. Everybody knew this—somehow or other—and yet nobody had dug any of them out to make sure. Cooper is not a

---

close observer, but he is interesting. He is certainly always that, no matter what happens. And he is more interesting when he is not noticing what he is about than when he is. This is a considerable merit.

The conversations in the Cooper books have a curious sound in our modern ears. To believe that such talk really ever came out of people's mouths would be to believe that there was a time when time was of no value to a person who thought he had something to say; when it was the custom to spread a two-minute remark out to ten; when a man's mouth was a rolling-mill, and busied itself all day long in turning four-foot pigs of thought into thirty-foot bars of conversational railroad iron by attenuation; when subjects were seldom faithfully stuck to, but the talk wandered all around and arrived nowhere; when conversations consisted mainly of irrelevancies, with here and there a relevancy, a relevancy with an embarrassed look, as not being able to explain how it got there.

Cooper was certainly not a master in the construction of dialogue. Inaccurate observation defeated him here as it defeated him in so many other enterprises of his. He even failed to notice that the man who talks corrupt English six days in the week must and will talk it on the seventh, and can't help himself. In the *Deerslayer* story he lets Deerslayer talk the showiest kind of book-talk sometimes, and at other times the basest of base dialects. For instance, when some one asks him if he has a sweetheart, and if so, where she abides, this is his majestic answer:

"She's in the forest—hanging from the boughs of the trees, in a soft rain —in the dew on the open grass—the clouds that float about in the blue heaven—the birds that sing in the woods—the sweet springs where I slake my thirst—and in all the other glorious gifts that come from God's Providence!"

And he preceded that, a little before, with this:

"It consarns me as all things that touches a fri'nd consarns a fri'nd."

And this is another of his remarks:

"If I was Injun born, now, I might tell of this, or carry in the scalp and boast of the expl'ite afore the whole tribe; or if my inimy had only been a bear"—[and so on].

We cannot imagine such a thing as a veteran Scotch Commander-in-Chief comporting himself in the field like a windy melodramatic actor, but Cooper could. On one occasion Alice and Cora were being chased by the French through a fog in the neighborhood of their father's fort:

"Point de quartier aux coquins!" cried an eager pursuer, who seemed to direct the operations of the enemy.

"Stand firm and be ready, my gallant 60ths!" suddenly exclaimed a voice above them; "wait to see the enemy; fire low, and sweep the glacis."

"Father! father!" exclaimed a piercing cry from out of the mist; "it is I! Alice! thy own Elsie! spare, O! save your daughters!"

"Hold!" shouted the former speaker, in the awful tones of parental agony, the sound reaching even to the woods, and rolling back in solemn echo. " 'Tis she! God has restored me my children! Throw open the sally-port; to the field, 60ths, to the field! pull not a trigger, lest ye kill my lambs! Drive off these dogs of France with your steel!"

Cooper's word-sense was singularly dull. When a person has a poor ear for music he will flat and sharp right along without knowing it. He keeps near the tune, but it is *not* the tune. When a person has a poor ear for words, the result is a literary flatting and sharping; you perceive what he is intending to say, but you also perceive that he doesn't *say* it. This is Cooper. He was not a word-musician. His ear was satisfied with the *approximate* word. I will furnish some circumstantial evidence in support of this charge. My instances are gathered from half a dozen pages of the tale called *Deerslayer*. He uses "verbal" for "oral"; "precision" for "facility"; "phenomena" for "marvels"; "necessary" for "predetermined"; "unsophisticated" for "primitive"; "preparation" for "expectancy"; "rebuked" for "subdued"; "dependent on" for "resulting from"; "fact" for "condition"; "fact" for "conjecture"; "precaution" for "caution"; "explain" for "determine"; "mortified" for "disappointed"; "meretricious" for "factitous"; "materially" for "considerably"; "decreasing" for "deepening"; "increasing" for "disappearing"; "embedded" for "enclosed"; "treacherous" for "hostile"; "stood" for "stooped"; "softened" for "replaced"; "rejoined" for "remarked"; "situation" for "condition"; "different" for "differing"; "insensible" for "unsentient"; "brevity" for "celerity"; "distrusted" for "suspicious";

"mental imbecility" for "imbecility"; "eyes" for "sight"; "counteracting" for "opposing"; "funeral obsequies" for "obsequies."

There have been daring people in the world who claimed that Cooper could write English, but they are all dead now—all dead but Lounsbury. I don't remember that Lounsbury makes the claim in so many words, still he makes it, for he says that *Deerslayer* is a "pure work of art." Pure, in that connection, means faultless—faultless in all details—and language is a detail. If Mr. Lounsbury had only compared Cooper's English with the English which he writes himself—but it is plain that he didn't; and so it is likely that he imagines until this day that Cooper's is as clean and compact as his own. Now I feel sure, deep down in my heart, that Cooper wrote about the poorest English that exists in our language, and that the English of *Deerslayer* is the very worst that even Cooper ever wrote.

I may be mistaken, but it does seem to me that *Deerslayer* is not a work of art in any sense; it does seem to me that it is destitute of every detail that goes to the making of a work of art; in truth, it seems to me that *Deerslayer* is just simply a literary *delirium tremens*.

A work of art? It has no invention; it has no order, system, sequence, or result; it has no life-likeness, no thrill, no stir, no seeming of reality; its characters are confusedly drawn, and by their acts and words they prove that they are not the sort of people the author claims that they are; its humor is pathetic; its pathos is funny; its conversations are—oh! indescribable; its love-scenes odious; its English a crime against the language.

Counting these out, what is left is Art. I think we must all admit that.

from
A DOUBLE-BARRELLED DETECTIVE STORY

Clemens planted the following paragraph in his 1901 detective story—which also contains a parody of Sherlock Holmes—to trap the unwary reader. The first danger is concentrating on the odd use of esophagus *near the close of the paragraph. Check words like* laburnum *and* larch *in a dictionary. Try visualizing, or better, sketching the scene as Clemens describes it.*

It was a crisp and spicy morning in early October. The lilacs and la-
burnums, lit with the glory-fires of autumn, hung burning and flashing
in the upper air, a fairy bridge provided by kind Nature for the wingless
wild things that have their homes in the tree tops and would visit together; the larch and the pomegranate flung their purple and yellow
flames in brilliant broad splashes along the slanting sweep of the wood-
land; the sensuous fragrance of innumerable deciduous flowers rose
upon the swooning atmosphere; far in the empty sky a solitary esophagus slept upon motionless wing; everywhere brooded stillness, serenity,
and the peace of God.

TO THE PERSON SITTING IN DARKNESS

*One of the classic functions of the satirist is to break
through the walls of ignorance and indifference and shake
his reader awake by shocking him. Seldom is Clemens better
at this shock technique than in this 1901 North American
Review article, in which he takes as his text a sickeningly
optimistic passage from the Christmas Eve edition of a New
York newspaper.*

"Christmas will dawn in the United States over a people full of hope and
aspiration and good cheer. Such a condition means contentment and happiness. The carping grumbler who may here and there go forth will find
few to listen to him. The majority will wonder what is the matter with him
and pass on."—*New York Tribune*, on Christmas Eve.

From *The Sun*, of New York:

"The purpose of this article is not to describe the terrible offenses against
humanity committed in the name of Politics in some of the most notorious
East Side districts. *They could not be described, even verbally.* But it is the
intention to let the great mass of more or less careless citizens of this beautiful metropolis of the New World get some conception of the havoc and
ruin wrought to man, woman, and child in the most densely populated and
least-known section of the city. Name, date, and place can be supplied to
those of little faith—or to any man who feels himself aggrieved. It is a plain

247

statement of record and observation, written without license and without garnish.

"Imagine, if you can, a section of the city territory completely dominated by one man, without whose permission neither legitimate nor illegitimate business can be conducted; *where illegitimate business is encouraged and legitimate business discouraged*; where the respectable residents have to fasten their doors and windows summer nights and sit in their rooms with asphyxiating air and 100-degree temperature, rather than try to catch the faint whiff of breeze in their natural breathing places, the stoops of their homes; *where naked women dance by night in the streets, and unsexed men prowl like vultures through the darkness on "business"* not only permitted but encouraged by the police; *where the education of infants begins with the knowledge of prostitution* and the training of little girls is training in the arts of Phyrne; where *American* girls brought up with the refinements of *American* homes are imported from small towns upstate, Massachusetts, Connecticut, and New Jersey, and kept as virtually prisoners as if they were locked up behind jail bars until they have lost all semblance of womanhood; *where small boys are taught to solicit for the women of disorderly houses*; where there is an organized society of young men *whose sole business in life is to corrupt young girls and turn them over to bawdy houses*; where men walking with their wives along the street are openly insulted; *where children that have adult diseases are the chief patrons of the hospitals and dispensaries;* where it is the rule, rather than the exception, that *murder, rape, robbery, and theft go unpunished*—in short where the Premium of the most awful forms of Vice is the Profit of the politicians."

The following news from China appeared in *The Sun*, of New York, on Christmas Eve. The italics are mine:

"The Rev. Mr. Ament, of the American Board of Foreign Missions, has returned from a trip which he made for the purpose of collecting indemnities for damages done by Boxers. *Everywhere he went he compelled the Chinese to pay.* He says that all his native Christians are now provided for. He had 700 of them under his charge, and 300 were killed. He has *collected 300 taels for each* of these murders, and has *compelled full payment for all the property belonging to Christians* that was destroyed. He also assessed *fines* amounting to THIRTEEN TIMES the amount of the indemnity. *This money will be used for the propagation of the Gospel.*

"Mr. Ament declares that the compensation he has collected is *moderate* when compared with the amount secured by the Catholics, who demand, in addition to money, *head for head.* They collect 500 taels for each murder of a Catholic. In the Wenchiu country, 680 Catholics were killed, and for this the European Catholics here demand 750,000 strings of cash and 680 *heads.*

"In the course of a conversation Mr. Ament referred to the attitude of the missionaries toward the Chinese. He said:

"I deny emphatically that the missionaries are *vindictive*, that they *generally* looted, or that they have done anything *since* the siege that *the circumstances did not demand.* I criticize the Americans. *The soft hand of the Americans is not as good as the mailed fist of the Germans.* If you deal with the Chinese with a soft hand they will take advantage of it.

"The statement that the French Government will return the loot taken by the French soldiers is the source of the greatest amusement here. The French soldiers were more systematic looters than the Germans, and it is a fact that to-day *Catholic Christians,* carrying French flags and armed with modern guns, *are looting villages* in the Province of Chili."

By happy luck, we get all these glad tidings on Christmas Eve—just in time to enable us to celebrate the day with proper gaiety and enthusiasm. Our spirits soar, and we find we can even make jokes: Taels I win, Heads you lose.

Our Reverend Ament is the right man in the right place. What we want of our missionaries out there is, not that they shall merely represent in their acts and persons the grace and gentleness and charity and loving kindness of our religion, but that they shall also represent the American spirit. The oldest Americans are the Pawnees. Macallum's History says:

When a white Boxer kills a Pawnee and destroys his property, the other Pawnees do not trouble to seek *him* out, they kill any white person that comes along; also, they make some white village pay deceased's heirs the full cash value of deceased, together with full cash value of the property destroyed; they also make the village pay, in addition, *thirteen times* the value of that property into a fund for the dissemination of the Pawnee religion, which they regard as the best of all religions for the softening and humanizing of the heart of man. It is their idea that it is only fair and right that the innocent should be made to suffer for the guilty, and that it is better that ninety and nine innocent should suffer than that one guilty person should escape.

Our Reverend Ament is justifiably jealous of those enterprising Catholics, who not only get big money for each lost convert, but get "head for head" besides. But he should soothe himself with the reflection that the entirety of their exactions are for their own pockets, whereas he, less selfishly, devotes only 300 taels per head to that service, and gives the whole vast thirteen repetitions of the property-indemnity to the service of propagating the Gospel. His magnanimity has won him the approval of his nation, and will get him a monument. Let him be content with these rewards. We all hold him dear for manfully defending his fellow missionaries from exaggerated charges which were beginning to distress us, but which his testimony has so considerably modified that we can now contemplate them without noticeable pain. For now we know that, even before the siege, the missionaries were not "generally" out looting, and that, "since the siege," they have acted quite handsomely, except when "circumstances" crowded them. I am arranging for the monument. Subscriptions for it can be sent to the American Board; designs for it can be sent to me. Designs must allegorically set forth the Thirteen Reduplications of the Indemnity, and the Object for which they were exacted; as Ornaments, the designs must exhibit 680 Heads, so disposed, as to give a pleasing and pretty effect; for the Catholics have done nicely, and are entitled to notice in the monument. Mottoes may be suggested, if any shall be discovered that will satisfactorily cover the ground.

Mr. Ament's financial feat of squeezing a thirteen-fold indemnity out of the pauper peasants to square other people's offenses, thus condemning them and their women and innocent little children to inevitable starvation and lingering death, in order that the blood money so acquired might be *"used for the propagation of the Gospel,"* does not flutter my serenity; although the act and the words, taken together, concrete a blasphemy so hideous and so colossal that, without doubt, its mate is not findable in the history of this or of any other age. Yet, if a layman had done that thing and justified it with those words, I should have shuddered, I know. Or, if I had done the thing and said the words myself—however, the thought is unthinkable, irreverent as some imperfectly informed people think me. Sometimes an ordained minister sets out to be blasphemous. When this happens, the layman is out of the running; he stands no chance.

We have Mr. Ament's impassioned assurance that the missionaries are not "vindictive." Let us hope and pray that they will never become so, but will remain in the almost morbidly fair and just and gentle temper which is affording so much satisfaction to their brother and champion to-day.

The following is from the *New York Tribune* of Christmas Eve. It comes from that journal's Tokio correspondent. It has a strange and impudent sound, but the Japanese are but partially civilized as yet. When they become wholly civilized they will not talk so:

The missionary question, of course, occupies a foremost place in the discussion. It is now felt as essential that the Western Powers take cognizance of the sentiment here, that religious invasions of Oriental countries by powerful Western organizations are tantamount to filibustering expeditions, and should not only be discountenanced, but that stern measures should be adopted for their suppression. The feeling here is that the missionary organizations constitute a constant menace to peaceful international relations.

Shall we? That is, shall we go on conferring our Civilization upon the peoples that sit in darkness, or shall we give those poor things a rest? Shall we bang right ahead in our old-time, loud, pious way, and commit the new century to the game; or shall we sober up and sit down and think it over first? Would it not be prudent to get our Civilization-tools together, and see how much stock is left on hand in the way of Glass Beads and Theology, and Maxim Guns and Hymn Books, and Trade Gin and Torches of Progress and Enlightenment (patent adjustable ones, good to fire villages with, upon occasion), and balance the books, and arrive at the profit and loss, so that we may intelligently decide whether to continue the business or sell out the property and start a new Civilization Scheme on the proceeds?

Extending the Blessings of Civilization to our Brother who Sits in Darkness has been a good trade and has paid well, on the whole; and there is money in it yet, if carefully worked—but not enough, in my judgment, to make any considerable risk advisable. The People that Sit in Darkness are getting to be too scarce—too scarce and too shy.

And such darkness as is now left is really of but an indifferent quality, and not dark enough for the game. The most of those People that Sit in Darkness have been furnished with more light than was good for them or profitable for us. We have been injudicious.

The Blessings-of-Civilization Trust, wisely and curiously administered, is a Daisy. There is more money in it, more territory, more sovereignty, and other kinds of emolument, than there is in any other game that is played. But Christendom has been playing it badly of late years, and must certainly suffer by it, in my opinion. She has been so eager to get every stake that appeared on the green cloth, that the People who Sit in Darkness have noticed it—they have noticed it, and have begun to show alarm. They have become suspicious of the Blessings of Civilization. More—they have begun to examine them. This is not well. The Blessings of Civilization are all right, and a good commercial property; there could not be a better, in a dim light. In the right kind of a light, and at a proper distance, with the goods a little out of focus, they furnish this desirable exhibit to the Gentlemen who Sit in Darkness:

LOVE,	LAW AND ORDER,
JUSTICE,	LIBERTY,
GENTLENESS,	EQUALITY,
CHRISTIANITY,	HONORABLE DEALING,
PROTECTION TO THE WEAK,	MERCY,
TEMPERANCE,	EDUCATION,

—and so on.

There. Is it good? Sir, it is pie. It will bring into camp any idiot that sits in darkness anywhere. But not if we adulterate it. It is proper to be emphatic upon that point. This brand is strictly for Export—apparently. *Apparently.* Privately and confidentially, it is nothing of the kind. Privately and confidentially, it is merely an outside cover, gay and pretty and attractive, displaying the special patterns of our Civilization which we reserve for Home Consumption, while *inside* the bale is the Actual Thing that the Customer Sitting in Darkness buys with his blood and tears and land and liberty. That Actual Thing is, indeed, Civilization, but it is only for Export. Is there a difference between the two brands? In some of the details, yes.

We all know that the Business is being ruined. The reason is not far to seek. It is because our Mr. McKinley, and Mr. Chamberlain, and the Kaiser, and the Tsar and the French have been exporting the Actual Thing *with the outside cover left off.* This is bad for the Game. It shows that these new players of it are not sufficiently acquainted with it.

It is a distress to look on and note the mismoves, they are so strange and so awkward. Mr. Chamberlain manufactures a war out of materials so inadequate and so fanciful that they make the boxes grieve and the gallery laugh, and he tries hard to persuade himself that it isn't purely a private raid for cash, but has a sort of dim, vague respectability about it somewhere, if he could only find the spot; and that, by and by, he can scour the flag clean again after he has finished dragging it through the mud, and make it shine and flash in the vault of heaven once more as it had shone and flashed there a thousand years in the world's respect until he laid his unfaithful hand upon it. It is bad play—bad. For it exposes the Actual Thing to Them that Sit in Darkness, and they say: "What! Christian against Christian? And only for money? Is *this* a case of magnanimity, forbearance, love, gentleness, mercy, protection of the weak—this strange and over-showy onslaught of an elephant upon a nest of field-mice, on the pretext that the mice had squeaked an insolence at him—conduct which 'no self-respecting government could allow to pass unavenged'? as Mr. Chamberlain said. Was that a good pretext in a small case, when it had not been a good pretext in a large one?—for only recently Russia had affronted the elephant three times and survived alive and unsmitten. Is this Civilization and Progress? Is it something better than we already possess? These harryings and burnings and desert-makings in the Transvaal—is this an improvement on our darkness? Is it, perhaps, possible that there are two kinds of Civilization—one for home consumption and one for the heathen market?"

Then They that Sit in Darkness are troubled, and shake their heads; and they read this extract from a letter of a British private, recounting his exploits in one of Methuen's victories, some days before the affair of Magersfontein, and they are troubled again:

We tore up the hill and into the intrenchments, and the Boers saw we had them; so they dropped their guns and went down on their knees and

put up their hands clasped, and begged for mercy. And we gave it them—
with the long spoon.

The long spoon is the bayonet. See *Lloyd's Weekly,* London, of
those days. The same number—and the same column—contained
some quite unconscious satire in the form of shocked and bitter upbraid-
ings of the Boers for their brutalities and inhumanities!

Next, to our heavy damage, the Kaiser went to playing the game
without first mastering it. He lost a couple of missionaries in a riot in
Shantung, and in his account he made an overcharge for them. China
had to pay a hundred thousand dollars apiece for them, in money;
twelve miles of territory, containing several millions of inhabitants
and worth twenty million dollars; and to build a monument, and also
a Christian church; whereas the people of China could have been
depended upon to remember the missionaries without the help of these
expensive memorials. This was all bad play. Bad, because it would
not, and could not, and will not now or ever, deceive the Person Sitting
in Darkness. He knows that it was an overcharge. He knows that a
missionary is like any other man: he is worth merely what you can
supply his place for, and no more. He is useful, but so is a doctor, so is
a sheriff, so is an editor; but a just Emperor does not charge war prices
for such. A diligent, intelligent, but obscure missionary, and a diligent,
intelligent country editor are worth much, and we know it; but they
are not worth the earth. We esteem such an editor, and we are sorry
to see him go; but, when he goes, we should consider twelve miles
of territory, and a church, and a fortune, overcompensation for his loss.
I mean, if he was a Chinese editor, and we had to settle for him. It is
no proper figure for an editor or a missionary; one can get shop-worn
kings for less. It was bad play on the Kaiser's part. It got this property,
true; but it *produced the Chinese revolt,* the indignant uprising of
China's traduced patriots, the Boxers. The results have been expensive
to Germany, and to the other Disseminators of Progress and the Blessings of Civilization.

The Kaiser's claim was paid, yet it was bad play, for it could not
fail to have an evil effect upon Persons Sitting in Darkness in China.
They would muse upon the event, and be likely to say: "Civilization
is gracious and beautiful, for such is its reputation; but can we afford
it? There are rich Chinamen, perhaps they can afford it; but this tax

is not laid upon them, it is laid upon the peasants of Shantung; it is they that must pay this mighty sum, and their wages are but four cents a day. Is this a better civilization than ours, and holier and higher and nobler? Is not this rapacity? Is not this extortion? Would Germany charge America two hundred thousand dollars for two missionaries, and shake the mailed fist in her face, and send warships, and send soldiers, and say: 'Seize twelve miles of territory, worth twenty millions of dollars, as additional pay for the missionaries; and make those peasants build a monument to the missionaries, and a costly Christian church to remember them by?' And later would Germany say to her soldiers: 'March through America and slay, *giving no quarter;* make the German face there, as has been our Hun-face here, a terror for a thousand years; march through the Great Republic and slay, slay, slay, carving a road for our offended religion through its heart and bowels?' Would Germany do like this to America, to England, to France, to Russia? Or only to China the helpless—imitating the elephant's assault upon the field-mice? Had we better invest in this Civilization—this Civilization which called Napoleon a buccaneer for carrying off Venice's bronze horses, but which steals our ancient astronomical instruments from our walls, and goes looting like common bandits—that is, all the alien soldiers except America's; and (Americans again excepted) storms frightened villages and cables the result to glad journals at home every day: 'Chinese losses, 450 killed; ours, *one officer and two men wounded.* Shall proceed against neighboring village to-morrow, where a *massacre* is reported.' Can we afford Civilization?"

And, next, Russia must go and play the game injudiciously. She affronts England once or twice—with the Person Sitting in Darkness observing and noting; by moral assistance of France and Germany, she robs Japan of her hard-earned spoil, all swimming in Chinese blood —Port Arthur—with the Person again observing and noting; then she seizes Manchuria, raids its villages, and chokes its great river with the swollen corpses of countless massacred peasants—that astonished Person still observing and noting. And perhaps he is saying to himself: "It is yet *another* Civilized Power, with its banner of the Prince of Peace in one hand and its loot-basket and its butcher knife in the other. Is there no salvation for us but to adopt Civilization and lift ourselves down to its level?"

And by and by comes America, and our Master of the Game plays it badly—plays it as Mr. Chamberlain was playing it in South Africa. It was a mistake to do that; also, it was one which was quite unlooked for in a Master who was playing it so well in Cuba. In Cuba, he was playing the usual and regular *American* game, and it was winning, for there is no way to beat it. The Master, contemplating Cuba, said: "Here is an oppressed and friendless little nation which is willing to fight to be free; we go partners, and put up the strength of seventy million sympathizers and the resources of the United States: play!" Nothing but Europe combined could call that hand: and Europe cannot combine on anything. There, in Cuba, he was following our great traditions in a way which made us very proud of him, and proud of the deep dissatisfaction which his play was provoking in continental Europe. Moved by a high inspiration, he threw out those stirring words which proclaimed that forcible annexation would be "criminal aggression"; and in that utterance fired another shot heard round the world." The memory of that fine saying will be outlived by the remembrance of no act of his but one—that he forgot it within the twelvemonth, and its honorable gospel along with it.

For, presently, came the Philippine temptation. It was strong; it was too strong, and he made that bad mistake: he played the European game, the Chamberlain game. It was a pity; it was a great pity, that error; that one grievous error, that irrevocable error. For it was the very place and time to play the American game again. And at no cost. Rich winnings to be gathered in, too; rich and permanent; indestructible; a fortune transmissible forever to the children of the flag. Not land, not money, not dominion—no, something worth many times more than that dross: our share, the spectacle of a nation of long harassed and persecuted slaves set free through our influence; our posterity's share, the golden memory of that fair deed. The game was in our hands. If it had been played according to the American rules, Dewey would have sailed away from Manila as soon as he had destroyed the Spanish fleet—after putting up a sign on shore guaranteeing foreign property and life against damage by the Filipinos, and warning the Powers that interference with the emancipated patriots would be regarded as an act unfriendly to the United States. The Powers cannot combine, in even a bad cause, and the sign would not have been molested.

Dewey could have gone about his affairs elsewhere, and left the competent Filipino army to starve out the little Spanish garrison and send it home, and the Filipino citizens to set up the form of government they might prefer, and deal with the friars and their doubtful acquisitions according to Filipino ideas of fairness and justice—ideas which have since been tested and found to be of as high an order as any that prevail in Europe or America.

But we played the Chamberlain game, and lost the chance to add another Cuba and another honorable deed to our good record.

The more we examine the mistake, the more clearly we perceive that it is going to be bad for the Business. The Person Sitting in Darkness is almost sure to say: "There is something curious about this—curious and unaccountable. There must be two Americas: one that sets the captive free, and one that takes a once-captive's new freedom away from him, and picks a quarrel with him with nothing to found it on; then kills him to get his land."

The truth is, the Person Sitting in Darkness *is* saying things like that; and for the sake of the Business we must persuade him to look at the Philippine matter in another and healthier way. We must arrange his opinions for him. I believe it can be done; for Mr. Chamberlain has arranged England's opinion of the South African matter, and done it most cleverly and successfully. He presented the facts—some of the facts—and showed those confiding people what the facts meant. He did it statistically, which is a good way. He used the formula: "Twice 2 are 14, and 2 from 9 leaves 35." Figures are effective; figures will convince the elect.

Now, my plan is a still bolder one than Mr. Chamberlain's, though apparently a copy of it. Let us be franker than Mr. Chamberlain; let us audaciously present the whole of the facts, shirking none, then explain them according to Mr. Chamberlain's formula. This daring truthfulness will astonish and dazzle the Person Sitting in Darkness, and he will take the Explanation down before his mental vision has had time to get back into focus. Let us say to him:

"Our case is simple. On the 1st of May, Dewey destroyed the Spanish fleet. This left the Archipelago in the hands of its proper and rightful owners, the Filipino nation. Their army numbered 30,000 men, and they were competent to whip out or starve out the little Spanish garrison; then the people could set up a government of their own devising. Our traditions required that Dewey should now set up his warning sign, and go away. But the Master of the Game happened to think of another plan—the European plan. He acted upon it. This was, to send out an army—ostensibly to help the native patriots put the finishing touch upon their long and plucky struggle for independence, but really to take their land away from them and keep it. That is, in the interest of Progress and Civilization. The plan developed, stage by stage, and quite satisfactorily. We entered into a military alliance with the trusting Filipinos, and they hemmed in Manila on the land side, and by their valuable help the place, with its garrison of 8,000 or 10,000 Spaniards, was captured—a thing which we could not have accomplished unaided at that time. We got their help by—by ingenuity. We knew they were fighting for their independence, and that they had been at it for two years. We knew they supposed that we also were fighting in their worthy cause—just as we had helped the Cubans fight for Cuban independence—and we allowed them to go on thinking so. *Until Manila was ours and we could get along without them.* Then we showed our hand. Of course, they were surprised—that was natural; surprised and disappointed; disappointed and grieved. To them it looked un-American; uncharacteristic; foreign to our established traditions. And this was natural, too; for we were only playing the American Game in public—in private it was the European. It was neatly done, very neatly, and it bewildered them. They could not understand it; for we had been so friendly—so affectionate, even—with those simple-minded patriots! We, our own selves, had brought back out of exile their leader, their hero, their hope, their Washington—Aguinaldo; brought him in a warship, in high honor, under the sacred shelter and hospitality of the flag; brought him back and restored him to his people, and got their moving and eloquent gratitude for it. Yes, we had been so friendly to them, and had heartened them up in so many ways! We had lent them guns and ammunition; advised with them; exchanged pleasant courtesies with them; placed our sick and wounded in their kindly care; intrusted our Spanish prisoners to their humane and honest hands; fought shoulder to shoulder with them against "the common enemy" (our own phrase); praised their courage, praised their gallantry, praised their mercifulness, praised their fine and honorable conduct; borrowed their trenches, borrowed strong positions which they had previously captured from the Spaniards; petted them, lied to them—officially proclaiming that our land and naval forces came to give them their freedom and displace the bad Spanish Government—fooled them, used them until we needed them no longer; then derided the sucked orange and threw it away. We kept the positions which we had beguiled them of; by and by, we moved a force forward and overlapped patriot ground—a clever thought, for we needed trouble, and this would produce it. A Filipino soldier, crossing the ground, where no one had a right to forbid him, was shot by our sentry. The badgered patriots resented this with arms, without waiting to know whether Aguinaldo, who was absent, would approve or not. Aguinaldo did not approve; but that availed nothing. What we wanted, in the interest of Progress and Civilization, was the Archipelago, unencumbered by patriots struggling for independence; and War was what we needed. We clinched our opportunity. It is Mr. Chamberlain's case over again—at least in its motive and intention; and we played the game as adroitly as he played it himself."

At this point in our frank statement of fact to the Person Sitting in Darkness, we should throw in a little trade-taffy about the Blessings of Civilization—for a change, and for the refreshment of his spirit—then go on with our tale:

"We and the patriots having captured Manila, Spain's ownership of the Archipelago and her sovereignty over it were at an end—obliterated—annihilated—not a rag or shred of either remaining behind. It was then that we conceived the divinely humorous idea of *buying* both of these specters from Spain! [It is quite safe to confess this to the Person Sitting in Darkness, since neither he nor any other sane person will believe it.] In buying those ghosts for twenty millions, we also contracted to take care of the friars and their accumulations. I think we also agreed to propagate leprosy and smallpox, but as to this there is doubt. But it is not important; persons afflicted with the friars do not mind other diseases.

"With our Treaty ratified, Manila subdued, and our Ghosts secured, we had no further use for Aguinaldo and the owners of the Archipelago. We forced a war, and we have been hunting America's guest and ally through the woods and swamps ever since."

At this point in the tale, it will be well to boast a little of our warwork and our heroisms in the field, so as to make our performance look as fine as England's in South Africa; but I believe it will not be best to emphasize this too much. We must be cautious. Of course, we must read the war telegrams to the Person, in order to keep up our frankness; but we can throw an air of humorousness over them, and that will modify their grim eloquence a little, and their rather indiscreet exhibitions of gory exultation. Before reading to him the following display heads of the dispatches of November 18, 1900, it will be well to practice on them in private first, so as to get the right tang of lightness and gaiety into them:

ADMINISTRATION WEARY OF PROTRACTED HOSTILITIES!

REAL WAR AHEAD FOR FILIPINO REBELS! [5]

WILL SHOW NO MERCY!

KITCHENER'S PLAN ADOPTED!

Kitchener knows how to handle disagreeable people who are fighting for their homes and their liberties, and we must let on that we are merely imitating Kitchener, and have no national interest in the matter, further than to get ourselves admired by the Great Family of Nations, in which august company our Master of the Game has bought a place for us in the back row.

Of course, we must not venture to ignore our General MacArthur's reports—oh, why do they keep on printing those embarrassing things? —we must drop them trippingly from the tongue and take the chances:

"During the last ten months our losses have been 268 killed and 750 wounded; Filipino loss, *three thousand two hundred and twenty-seven killed,* and 694 wounded."

We must stand ready to grab the Person Sitting in Darkness, for he

[5] "Rebels!" Mumble that funny word—don't let the Person catch it distinctly.

will swoon away at this confession, saying: "Good God! those 'niggers' spare their wounded, and the Americans massacre theirs!" We must bring him to, and coax him and coddle him, and assure him that the ways of Providence are best, and that it would not become us to find fault with them; and then, to show him that we are only imitators, not originators, we must read the following passage from the letter of an American soldier lad in the Philippines to his mother, published in *Public Opinion*, of Decorah, Iowa, describing the finish of a victorious battle:

"WE NEVER LEFT ONE ALIVE. IF ONE WAS WOUNDED, WE WOULD RUN OUR BAYONETS THROUGH HIM."

Having now laid all the historical facts before the Person Sitting in Darkness, we should bring him to again, and explain them to him. We should say to him:

"They look doubtful, but in reality they are not. There have been lies; yes, but they were told in a good cause. We have been treacherous; but that was only in order that real good might come out of apparent evil. True, we have crushed a deceived and confiding people; we have turned against the weak and the friendless who trusted us; we have stamped out a just and intelligent and well-ordered republic; we have stabbed an ally in the back and slapped the face of a guest; we have bought a Shadow from an enemy that hadn't it to sell; we have robbed a trusting friend of his land and his liberty; we have invited our clean young men to shoulder a discredited musket and do bandits' work under a flag which bandits have been accustomed to fear, not to follow; we have debauched America's honor and blackened her face before the world; but each detail was for the best. We know this. The Head of every State and Sovereignty in Christendom and ninety per cent. of every legislative body in Christendom, including our Congress and our fifty state legislatures, are members not only of the church, but also of the Blessings-of-Civilization Trust. This world-girdling accumulation of trained morals, high principles, and justice cannot do an unright thing, an unfair thing, an ungenerous thing, an unclean thing. It knows what it is about. Give yourself no uneasiness; it is all right."

Now then, that will convince the Person. You will see. It will restore the Business. Also, it will elect the Master of the Game to the vacant place in the Trinity of our national gods; and there on their high thrones the Three will sit, age after age, in the people's sight, each bearing the Emblem of his service: Washington, the Sword of the Liberator; Lincoln, the Slave's Broken Chains; the Master, the Chains Repaired. It will give the Business a splendid new start. You will see.

Everything is prosperous, now; everything is just as we should wish it. We have got the Archipelago, and we shall never give it up. Also, we have every reason to hope that we shall have an opportunity before very long to slip out of our congressional contract with Cuba and give her something better in the place of it. It is a rich country, and many of us are already beginning to see that the contract was a sentimental mistake. But now—right now—is the best time to do some profitable rehabilitating work—work that will set us up and make us comfortable, and discourage gossip. We cannot conceal from ourselves that, privately, we are a little troubled about our uniform. It is one of our prides; it is acquainted with honor; it is familiar with great deeds and noble; we love it, we revere it; and so this errand it is on makes us uneasy. And our flag—another pride of ours, our chiefest! We have worshiped it so; and when we have seen it in far lands—glimpsing it unexpectedly in that strange sky, waving its welcome and benediction to us—we have caught our breath, and uncovered our heads, and couldn't speak, for a moment, for the thought of what it was to us and the great ideals it stood for. Indeed, we *must* do something about these things; we must not have the flag out there, and the uniform. They are not needed there; we can manage in some other way. England manages, as regards the uniform, and so can we. We have to send soldiers—we can't get out of that—but we can disguise them. It is the way England does in South Africa. Even Mr. Chamberlain himself takes pride in England's honorable uniform, and makes the army down there wear an ugly and odious and appropriate disguise, of yellow stuff such as quarantine flags are made of, and which are hoisted to warn the healthy away from unclean disease and repulsive death. This cloth is called khaki. We could adopt it. It is light, comfortable, grotesque, and deceives the enemy, for he cannot conceive of a soldier being concealed in it.

And as for a flag for the Philippine Province, it is easily managed. We can have a special one—our States do it: we can just have our usual flag, with the white stripes painted black and the stars replaced by the skull and cross-bones.

And we do not need the Civil Commission out there. Having no powers, it has to invent them, and that kind of work canot be effectively done by just anybody; an expert is required. Mr. Croker can be spared. We do not want the United States represented there, but only the Game.

By help of these suggested amendments, Progress and Civilization in that country can have a boom, and it will take in the Persons who are Sitting in Darkness, and we can resume Business at the old stand.

from EUROPE AND ELSEWHERE

This black ironic prayer shows Clemens looking fiercely into the human heart, finding there that animal urge to kill which is hidden by the hypocritical, patriotic, outwardly pious veil of our words. Although he apparently wrote this prayer in 1905, he withheld it from publication until after his death, telling a friend "I have told the whole truth in that, and only dead men can tell the truth in this word."

THE WAR PRAYER

It was a time of great and exalting excitement. The country was up in arms, the war was on, in every breast burned the holy fire of patriotism; the drums were beating, the bands playing, the toy pistols popping, the bunched firecrackers hissing and spluttering; on every hand and far down the receding and fading spread of roofs and balconies a fluttering wilderness of flags flashed in the sun; daily the young volunteers marched down the wide avenue gay and fine in their new uniforms, the proud fathers and mothers and sisters and sweethearts cheering them with voices choked with happy emotion as they swung by; nightly the packed mass meetings listened, panting, to patriot oratory which stirred the deepest deeps of their hearts, and which they interrupted at briefest intervals with cyclones of applause, the tears running down their cheeks the while; in the churches the pastors preached devotion to flag and country, and invoked the God of Battles, beseeching His aid in our good cause in outpouring of fervid eloquence which moved every listener. It was indeed a glad and gracious time, and the half dozen rash spirits that ventured to disapprove of the war and cast a doubt upon its righteousness straightway got such a stern and angry warning that for their personal safety's sake they quickly shrank out of sight and offended no more in that way.

Sunday morning came—next day the battalions would leave for the front; the church was filled; the volunteers were there, their young faces alight with martial dreams—visions of the stern advance, the gathering momentum, the rushing charge, the flashing sabers, the flight of the foe, the tumult, the enveloping smoke, the fierce pursuit, the surrender!— then home from the war, bronzed heroes, welcomed, adored, submerged in golden seas of glory! With the volunteers sat their dear ones, proud, happy, and envied by the neighbors and friends who had no sons and brothers to send forth to the field of honor, there to win for the flag, or, failing, die the noblest of deaths. The service proceeded; a war chapter from the Old Testament was read; the first prayer was said; it was followed by an organ burst that shook the building, and with one impulse the house rose, with glowing eyes and beating hearts, and poured out that tremendous invocation—

God the all-terrible! Thou who ordainest,
Thunder thy clarion and lightning thy sword!

Then came the "long" prayer. None could remember the like of it for passionate pleading and moving and beautiful language. The burden of its supplication was, that an ever-merciful and benignant Father of us all would watch over our noble young soldiers, and aid, comfort, and encourage them in their patriotic work; bless them, shield them in the day of battle and the hour of peril, bear them in His mighty hand, make them strong and confident, invincible in the bloody onset; help them to crush the foe, grant to them and to their flag and country imperishable honor and glory—

An aged stranger entered and moved with slow and noiseless step up the main aisle, his eyes fixed upon the minister, his long body clothed in a robe that reached to his feet, his head bare, his white hair descending in a frothy cataract to his shoulders, his seamy face unnaturally pale, pale even to ghastliness. With all eyes following him and wondering, he made his silent way; without pausing, he ascended to the preacher's side and stood there, waiting. With shut lids the preacher, unconscious of his presence, continued his moving prayer, and at last finished it with the words, uttered in fervent appeal, "Bless our arms, grant us the victory, O Lord our God, Father and Protector of our land and flag!"

The stranger touched his arm, motioned him to step aside—which the startled minister did—and took his place. During some moments he surveyed the spellbound audience with solemn eyes, in which burned an uncanny light; then in a deep voice he said:

"I come from the Throne—bearing a message from Almighty God!" The words smote the house with a shock; if the stranger perceived it he gave no attention. "He has heard the prayer of His servant your shepherd, and will grant it if such shall be your desire after I, His messenger, shall have explained to you its import—that is to say, its full import. For it is like unto many of the prayers of men, in that it asks for more than he who utters it is aware of—except he pause and think.

"God's servant and yours has prayed his prayer. Has he paused and taken thought? Is it one prayer? No, it is two—one uttered, the other not. Both have reached the ear of Him Who heareth all supplications, the spoken and the unspoken. Ponder this—keep it in mind. If you would beseech a blessing upon yourself, beware! lest without intent you invoke a curse upon a neighbor at the same time. If you pray for the blessing of rain upon your crop which needs it, by that act you are possibly praying for a curse upon some neighbor's crop which may not need rain and can be injured by it.

"You have heard your servant's prayer—the uttered part of it. I am commissioned of God to put into words the other part of it—that part which the pastor—and also you in your hearts—fervently prayed silently. And ignorantly and unthinkingly? God grant that it was so! You heard these words: 'Grant us the victory, O Lord our God!' That is sufficient. The *whole* of the uttered prayer is compact into those pregnant words. Elaborations were not necessary. When you have prayed for victory you have prayed for many unmentioned results which follow victory—*must* follow it, cannot help but follow it. Upon the listening spirit of God the Father fell also the unspoken part of the prayer. He commandeth me to put it into words. Listen!

"O Lord our Father, our young patriots, idols of our hearts, go forth to battle—be Thou near them! With them—in spirit—we also go forth from the sweet peace of our beloved firesides to smite the foe. O Lord our God, help us to tear their soldiers to bloody shreds with our shells; help us to cover their smiling fields with the pale forms of their patriot dead; help us to drown the thunder of the guns with the shrieks of their wounded, writhing in pain; help us to lay waste their humble homes with a hurricane of fire; help us to wring the hearts of their unoffending widows with unavailing grief; help us to turn them out roofless with their little children to wander unfriended the wastes of their desolated land in rags and hunger and thirst, sports of the sun flames of summer and the icy winds of winter, broken in spirit, worn with travail, imploring Thee for the refuge of the grave and denied it—for our sakes who adore Thee, Lord, blast their hopes, blight their lives, protract their bitter pilgrimage, make heavy their steps, water their way with their tears, stain the white snow with the blood of their wounded feet! We ask it, in the spirit of love, of Him Who is the Source of Love, and Who is the ever-faithful refuge and friend of all that are sore beset and seek His aid with humble and contrite hearts. Amen."

(*After a pause.*) "Ye have prayed it; if ye still desire it, speak! The messenger of the Most High waits."

It was believed afterward that the man was a lunatic, because there was no sense in what he said.

Charles Dickens
from THE LIFE AND ADVENTURES OF MARTIN CHUZZLEWIT

As a result of misunderstandings at home in England, young Martin Chuzzlewit goes to America to be an architect for the Eden Land Corporation, a shady land development in a swampy lagoon. With him is his chipper servant, Mark Tapley, who nurses Martin through a serious fever acquired in Eden. In this passage, American character, taste, and intelligence are assaulted from a British perspective of about 1844.

"There's one good thing in this place, sir," said Mr. Tapley, scrubbing away at the linen, "as disposes me to be jolly; and that is, that it's a reg'lar little United States in itself. There's two or three American settlers left; and they coolly comes over one even here, sir, as if it was the wholesomest and loveliest spot in the world. But they're like the cock that went and hid himself to save his life, and was found out by the noise he made. They can't help crowing. They was born to do it, and do it they must, whatever comes of it."

Glancing from his work out at the door as he said these words, Mark's eyes encountered a lean person in a blue frock and a straw hat, with a short black pipe in his mouth, and a great hickory stick, studded all over with knots, in his hand; who smoking and chewing as he came along, and spitting frequently, recorded his progress by a train of decomposed tobacco on the ground.

"Here's one on 'em," cried Mark, "Hannibal Chollop."

"Don't let him in," said Martin, feebly.

"He won't want any letting in," replied Mark. "He'll come in, sir." Which turned out to be quite true, for he did. His face was almost as hard and knobby as his stick; and so were his hands. His head was like an old black hearth-broom. He sat down on the chest with his hat on; and crossing his legs and looking up at Mark, said without removing his pipe:

"Well, Mr. Co.! and how do you git along, sir?"

It may be necessary to observe that Mr. Tapley had gravely introduced himself to all strangers, by that name.

"Pretty well, sir; pretty well," said Mark.

"If this ain't Mr. Chuzzlewit, ain't it!" exclaimed the visitor. "How do *you* git along, sir?"

Martin shook his head, and drew the blanket over it involuntarily; for he felt that Hannibal was going to spit; and his eye, as the song says, was upon him.

"You need not regard me, sir," observed Mr. Chollop, complacently. "I am fever-proof, and likewise agur."

"Mine was a more selfish motive," said Martin, looking out again. "I was afraid you were going to—"

"I can calc'late my distance, sir," returned Mr. Chollop, "to an inch."

With a proof of which happy faculty he immediately favoured him.

"I re-quire, sir," said Hannibal, "two foot clear in a circ'lar di-rection, and can engage my-self toe keep within it. I *have* gone ten foot, in a circ'lar direction, but that was for a wager."

"I hope you won it, sir," said Mark.

"Well, sir, I realised the stakes," said Chollop. "Yes, sir."

He was silent for a time, during which he was actively engaged in the formation of a magic circle round the chest on which he sat. When it was completed, he began to talk again.

"How do you like our country, sir?" he inquired, looking at Martin.

"Not at all," was the invalid's reply.

Chollop continued to smoke without the least appearance of emotion, until he felt disposed to speak again. That time at length arriving, he took his pipe from his mouth, and said:

"I am not surprised to hear you say so. It re-quires An elevation, and A preparation of the intellect. The mind of man must be prepared for Freedom, Mr. Co."

He addressed himself to Mark: because he saw that Martin, who wished him to go, being already half-mad with feverish irritation, which the droning voice of this new horror rendered almost insupportable, had closed his eyes, and turned on his uneasy bed.

"A little bodily preparation wouldn't be amiss, either, would it, sir," said Mark, "in the case of a blessed old swamp like this?"

"Do you con-sider this a swamp, sir?" inquired Chollop gravely.

"Why yes, sir," returned Mark. "I haven't a doubt about it myself."

"The sentiment is quite Europian," said the major, "and does not surprise me: what would your English millions say to such a swamp in England, sir?"

"They'd say it was an uncommon nasty one, I should think," said Mark; "and that they would rather be inoculated for fever in some other way."

"Europian!" remarked Chollop, with sardonic pity. "Quite Europian!"

And there he sat. Silent and cool, as if the house were his; smoking away like a factory chimney.

Mr. Chollop was, of course, one of the most remarkable men in the country; but he really was a notorious person besides. He was usually described by his friends, in the South and West, as "a splendid sample of our na-tive raw material, sir," and was much esteemed for his devotion to rational Liberty; for the better propagation whereof he usually carried a brace of revolving pistols in his coat pocket, with seven barrels a-piece. He also carried, amongst other trinkets, a sword-stick, which he called his "Tickler"; and a great knife, which (for he was a man of a pleasant turn of humour) he called "Ripper," in allusion to its usefulness as a means of ventilating the stomach of any adversary in a close contest. He had used these weapons with distinguished effect in several instances, all duly chronicled in the newspapers; and was greatly beloved for the gallant manner in which he had "jobbed out" the eye of one gentleman, as he was in the act of knocking at his own street-door.

Mr. Chollop was a man of a roving disposition; and, in any less advanced community, might have been mistaken for a violent vagabond. But his fine qualities being perfectly understood and appreciated in those regions where his lot was cast, and where he had many kindred spirits to consort with, he may be regarded as having been born under a fortunate star, which is not always the case with a man so much before the age in which he lives. Preferring, with a view to the gratification of his tickling and ripping fancies, to dwell upon the outskirts of society, and in the more remote towns and cities, he was in the habit of emigrating from place to place, and establishing in each some business—usually a newspaper—which he presently sold: for the most part closing the bargain by challenging, stabbing, pistoling, or gouging the new editor, before he had quite taken possession of the property.

He had come to Eden on a speculation of this kind, but had abandoned it, and was about to leave. He always introduced himself to strangers as a worshipper of Freedom; was the consistent advocate of Lynch law, and slavery; and invariably recommended, both in print and speech, the "tarring and feathering" of any unpopular person who differed from himself. He called this "planting the standard of civilisation in the wilder gardens of My country."

There is little doubt that Chollop would have planted this standard in Eden at Mark's expense, in return for his plainness of speech (for the genuine Freedom is dumb, save when she vaunts herself), but for the utter desolation and decay prevailing in the settlement, and his own approaching departure from it. As it was, he contented himself with showing Mark one of the revolving-pistols, and asking him what he thought of that weapon.

"It ain't long since I shot a man down with that, sir, in the State of Illin*oy*," observed Chollop.

"D:d you, indeed!" said Mark, without the smallest agitation. "Very free of you. And very independent!"

"I shot him down, sir," pursued Chollop, "for asserting in the Spartan Portico, a tri-weekly journal, that the ancient Athenians went a-head of the present Locofoco Ticket."

"And what's that?" asked Mark.

"Europian not to know," said Chollop, smoking placidly. "Europian quite!"

After a short devotion to the interests of the magic circle, he resumed the conversation by observing:

"You won't half feel yourself at home in Eden, now?"

"No," said Mark, "I don't."

"You miss the imposts of your country. You miss the house dues?" observed Chollop.

"And the houses—rather," said Mark.

"No window dues here, sir," observed Chollop.

"And no windows to put 'em on," said Mark.

"No stakes, no dungeons, no blocks, no racks, no scaffolds, no thumb-screws, no pikes, no pillories," said Chollop.

"Nothing but rewolvers and bowie-knives," returned Mark. "And what are they? Not worth mentioning!"

The man who had met them on the night of their arrival came crawling up at this juncture, and looked in at the door.

"Well, sir," said Chollop. "How do *you* git along?"

He had considerable difficulty in getting along at all, and said as much in reply.

"Mr. Co. And me, sir," observed Chollop, "are disputating a piece. He ought to be slicked up pretty smart to disputate between the Old World and the New, I do expect?"

"Well!" returned the miserable shadow. "So he had."

"I was merely observing, sir," said Mark, addressing this new visitor, "that I looked upon the city in which we have the honour to live, as being swampy. What's your sentiments?"

"I opinionate it's moist perhaps, at certain times," returned the man.

"But not as moist as England, sir?" cried Chollop, with a fierce expression in his face.

"Oh! Not as moist as England; let alone its Institutions," said the man.

"I should hope there ain't a swamp in all Americay, as don't whip *that* small island into mush and molasses," observed Chollop, decisively. "You bought slick, straight, and right away, of Scadder, sir?" to Mark.

He answered in the affirmative. Mr. Chollop winked at the other citizen.

"Scadder is a smart man, sir? He is a rising man? He is a man as will come up'ards, right side up, sir?" Mr. Chollop winked again at the other citizen.

"He should have his right side very high up, if I had my way," said Mark. "As high up as the top of a good tall gallows, perhaps."

Mr. Chollop was so delighted at the smartness of his excellent countryman having been too much for the Britisher, and at the Britisher's resenting it, that he could contain himself no longer, and broke forth in a shout of delight. But the strangest exposition of this ruling passion was in the other: the pestilence-stricken, broken, miserable shadow of a man: who derived so much entertainment from the circumstance that he seemed to forget his own ruin in thinking of it, and laughed outright when he said "that Scadder was a smart man, and had draw'd a lot of British capital that way, as sure as sun-up."

After a full enjoyment of this joke, Mr. Hannibal Chollop sat smoking and improving the circle, without making any attempts either to converse or to take leave; apparently labouring under the not uncommon delusion that for a free and enlightened citizen of the United States to convert another man's house into a spittoon for two or three hours together, was a delicate attention, full of interest and politeness, of which nobody could ever tire. At last he rose.

"I am a-going easy," he observed.

Mark entreated him to take particular care of himself.

"Afore I go," he said sternly, "I have got a leetle word to say to you. You are darnnation 'cute, you are."

Mark thanked him for the compliment.

"But you are much too 'cute to last. I can't con-ceive of any spotted Painter in the bush, as ever was so riddled through and through as you will be, I bet."

"What for?" asked Mark.

"We must be cracked-up, sir," retorted Chollop, in a tone of menace. "You are not now in A despotic land. We are a model to the airth, and must be jist cracked-up, I tell you."

"What! I speak too free, do I?" cried Mark.

"I have draw'd upon A man, and fired upon A man for less," said Chollop, frowning. "I have know'd strong men obleeged to make themselves uncommon skase for less. I have know'd men Lynched for less, and beaten into punkin'-sarse for less, by an enlightened people. We are the intellect and virtue of the airth, the cream Of human natur', and the flower Of moral force. Our backs is easy ris. We must be cracked-up, or they rises, and we snarls. We shows our teeth, I tell you, fierce. You'd better crack us up, you had!"

After the delivery of this caution, Mr. Chollop departed; with Ripper, Tickler, and the revolvers, all ready for action on the shortest notice.

Lewis Carroll
from
THROUGH THE
LOOKING-GLASS AND
WHAT ALICE FOUND
THERE

Through the Looking-Glass is a dream fantasy, purportedly written for children but of course speaking clearly to adults as well. Alice, having stepped through her mirror into Looking-Glass House, experiences a marvelous series of misadventures. In her encounter with Humpty-Dumpty, Alice must respond to a unique linguistic system and a most unusual sort of reasoning. All this is part of Carroll's satire of the entrenched logic systems of 1871. A lecturer in mathematics at Oxford for a quarter century, he maintained enough wit to poke fun at the absurdities of mathematical and logical theory often passed off for a genuine philosophical speculation at the time. This wit is behind Humpty Dumpty's declaration that proper names have general meaning and common words mean exactly what he chooses them to mean. Humpty Dumpty not only brings private bias or connotation to words whenever he feels like it but also arbitrarily reacts to the literal denotation of a word in a fashion most unpredictable. Alice, fortunately, is a very bright, quick intellect, able to follow most of Humpty Dumpty's quick and occasionally petulant logical leapings. She is also young, therefore not walled off from his wild inventiveness by an accretion of habits of thought and prejudice as an older person probably would be. It is this chapter of Through the Looking-Glass which has given the world that mod poem "Jabberwocky" and the expression "portmanteau word." Lewis Carroll admirers should certainly read The Annotated Alice, *an edition of* Alice's Adventures in Wonderland *and* Through the Looking-Glass *complete with John Tenniel's illustrations and a most thorough set of running annotations by Martin Gardner, which clarifies the several levels of Carroll's wit and imagination.*

Chapter VI
HUMPTY-DUMPTY

However, the egg only got larger and larger, and more and more human: when she had come within a few yards of it, she saw that it had eyes and a nose and mouth, and, when she had come close to it, she saw clearly that it was HUMPTY DUMPTY himself. "It can't be anybody else!" she said to herself. "I'm as certain of it, as if his name were written all over his face!"

It might have been written a hundred times, easily, on that enormous face. Humpty Dumpty was sitting, with his legs crossed like a Turk, on the top of a high wall—such a narrow one that Alice quite wondered how he could keep his balance—and, as his eyes were steadily fixed in the opposite direction, and he didn't take the least notice of her, she thought he must be a stuffed figure, after all.

"And how exactly like an egg he is!" she said aloud, standing with her hands ready to catch him, for she was every moment expecting him to fall.

"It's *very* provoking," Humpty Dumpty said after a long silence, looking away from Alice as he spoke, "to be called an egg,—*very!*"

"I said you *looked* like an egg, Sir," Alice gently explained. "And some eggs are very pretty, you know," she added, hoping to turn her remark into a sort of compliment.

"Some people," said Humpty Dumpty, looking away from her as usual, "have no more sense than a baby!"

Alice didn't know what to say to this: it wasn't at all like conversation, she thought, as he never said anything to *her;* in fact, his last remark was evidently addressed to a tree—so she stood and softly repeated to herself:—

> Humpty Dumpty sat on a wall:
> Humpty Dumpty had a great fall.
> All the King's horses and all the
> King's men
> Couldn't put Humpty Dumpty in his
> place again.

"That last line is much too long for the poetry," she added, almost out loud, forgetting that Humpty Dumpty would hear her.

"Don't stand chattering to yourself like that." Humpty Dumpty said, looking at her for the first time, "but tell me your name and your business."

"My *name* is Alice, but—"

"It's a stupid name enough!" Humpty Dumpty interrupted impatiently. "What does it mean?"

"*Must* a name mean something?" Alice asked doubtfully.

"Of course it must," Humpty Dumpty said with a short laugh: "*my* name means the shape I am—and a good handsome shape it is, too. With a name like yours, you might be any shape, almost."

"Why do you sit out here all alone?" said Alice, not wishing to begin an argument.

"Why, because there's nobody with me!" cried Humpty Dumpty. "Did you think I didn't know the answer to *that?* Ask another."

"Don't you think you'd be safer down on the ground?" Alice went on, not with any idea of making another riddle, but simply in her good-natured anxiety for the queer creature. "That wall is so *very* narrow!"

"What tremendously easy riddles you ask!" Humpty Dumpty growled out. "Of course I don't think so! Why, if ever I *did* fall off— which there's no chance of—but *if* I did—" Here he pursed up his lips, and looked so solemn and grand that Alice could hardly help laughing. "*If* I *did* fall," he went on, "*the King has promised me*—ah, you may turn pale, if you like! You didn't think I was going to say that, did you? *The King has promised me—with his very own mouth—to—to—*"

"To send all his horses and all his men," Alice interrupted, rather unwisely.

"Now I declare that's too bad!" Humpty Dumpty cried, breaking into a sudden passion. "You've been listening at doors—and behind trees— and down chimneys—or you couldn't have known it!"

"I haven't, indeed!" Alice said very gently. "It's in a book."

"Ah, well! They may write such things in a *book,*" Humpty Dumpty said in a calmer tone. "That's what you call a History of England, that is. Now, take a good look at me! I'm one that has spoken to a King, *I* am: mayhap you'll never see such another: and, to show you I'm not proud, you may shake hands with me!" And he grinned almost from ear to ear, as he leant forwards (and as nearly as possible fell off the wall in doing so) and offered Alice his hand. She watched him a little anxiously as she took it. "If he smiled much more the ends of his mouth might meet behind," she thought: "and then I don't know *what* would happen to his head! I'm afraid it would come off!"

"Yes, all his horses and all his men," Humpty Dumpty went on. "They'd pick me up again in a minute, *they* would! However, this con- versation is going on a little too fast: let's go back to the last remark but one."

"I'm afraid I can't quite remember it," Alice said, very politely.

"In that case we start afresh," said Humpty Dumpty, "and it's my turn to choose a subject—" ("He talks about it just as if it was a game!" thought Alice.) "So here's a question for you. How old did you say you were?"

Alice made a short calculation, and said "Seven years and six months."

"Wrong!" Humpty Dumpty exclaimed triumphantly. "You never said a word like it!"

"I though you meant 'How old *are* you?' " Alice explained.

"If I'd meant that, I'd have said it," said Humpty Dumpty.

Alice didn't want to begin another argument, so she said nothing.

"Seven years and six months!" Humpty Dumpty repeated thought- fully. "An uncomfortable sort of age. Now if you'd asked *my* advice, I'd have said 'Leave off at seven'—but it's too late now."

"I never ask advice about growing," Alice said indignantly.

"Too proud?" the other enquired.

Alice felt even more indignant at this suggestion. "I mean," she said, "that one can't help growing older."

"One can't, perhaps," said Humpty Dumpty; "but *two* can. With proper assistance, you might have left off at seven."

"What a beautiful belt you've got on!" Alice suddenly remarked. (They had had quite enough of the subject of age, she thought: and, if they really were to take turns in choosing subjects, it was *her* turn now.) "At least," she corrected herself on second thoughts, "a beautiful cravat, I should have said—no, a belt, I mean—I beg your pardon!" she added in dismay, for Humpty Dumpty looked thoroughly offended, and she began to wish she hadn't chosen that subject. "If only I knew," she thought to herself, "which was neck and which was waist!"

Evidently Humpty Dumpty was very angry, though he said nothing for a minute or two. When he *did* speak again, it was in a deep growl.

"It is a—*most—provoking*—thing," he said at last, "when a person doesn't know a cravat from a belt!"

"I know it's very ignorant of me," Alice said, in so humble a tone that Humpty Dumpty relented.

"It's a cravat, child, and a beautiful one, as you say. It's a present from the White King and Queen. There now!"

"Is it really?" said Alice, quite pleased to find that she *had* chosen a good subject, after all.

"They gave it me," Humpty Dumpty continued thoughtfully, as he crossed one knee over the other and clasped his hands round it, "they gave it me—for an unbirthday present."

"I beg your pardon?" Alice said with a puzzled air.

"I'm not offended," said Humpty Dumpty.

"I mean, what *is* an un-birthday present?"

"A present given when it isn't your birthday, of course."

Alice considered a little. "I like birthday presents best," she said at last.

"You don't know what you're talking about!" cried Humpty Dumpty. "How many days are there in a year?"

"Three hundred and sixty-five," said Alice.

"And how many birthdays have you?"

"One."

"And if you take one from three hundred and sixty-five, what remains?"

"Three hundred and sixty-four, of course."

Humpty Dumpty looked doubtful. "I'd rather see that done on paper," he said.

Alice couldn't help smiling as she took out her memorandum-book, and worked the sum for him:

$$\begin{array}{r} 365 \\ 1 \\ \hline 364 \\ \hline \end{array}$$

Humpty Dumpty took the book, and looked at it carefully. "That seems to be done right—" he began.

"You're holding it upside down!" Alice interrupted.

"To be sure I was!" Humpty Dumpty said gaily, as she turned it round for him. "I thought it looked a little queer. As I was saying, that *seems* to be done right—though I haven't time to look it over thoroughly just now—and that shows that there are three hundred and sixty-four days when you might get un-birthday presents—"

"Certainly," said Alice.

"And only *one* for birthday presents, you know. There's glory for you!"

"I don't know what you mean by 'glory,' " Alice said.

Humpty Dumpty smiled contemptuously. "Of course you don't—till I tell you. I meant 'there's a nice knock-down argument for you!' "

"But 'glory' doesn't mean 'a nice knock-down argument,' " Alice objected.

"When *I* use a word," Humpty Dumpty said, in rather a scornful tone, "it means just what I choose it to mean—neither more nor less."

"The question is," said Alice, "whether you *can* make words mean so many different things."

"The question is," said Humpty Dumpty, "which is to be master—that's all."

Alice was too much puzzled to say anything; so after a minute Humpty Dumpty began again. "They've a temper, some of them—particularly verbs: they're the proudest—adjectives you can do anything with, but not verbs—however, *I* can manage the whole lot of them! Impenetrability! That's what *I* say!"

"Would you tell me, please," said Alice, "what that means?"

"Now you talk like a reasonable child," said Humpty Dumpty, looking very much pleased. "I meant by 'impenetrability' that we've had enough of that subject, and it would be just as well if you'd mention what you mean to do next, as I suppose you don't mean to stop here all the rest of your life."

"That's a great deal to make one word mean," Alice said in a thoughtful tone.

"When I make a word do a lot of work like that," said Humpty Dumpty, "I always pay it extra."

"Oh!" said Alice. She was too much puzzled to make any other remark.

"Ah, you should see 'em come round me of a Saturday night," Humpty Dumpty went on, wagging his head gravely from side to side, "for to get their wages, you know."

(Alice didn't venture to ask what he paid them with; and so you see I can't tell *you*.)

"You seem very clever at explaining words, Sir," said Alice. "Would you kindly tell me the meaning of the poem called 'Jabberwocky'?"

"Let's hear it," said Humpty Dumpty. "I can explain all the poems that ever were invented—and a good many that haven't been invented just yet."

This sounded very hopeful, so Alice repeated the first verse:—

> 'Twas brillig, and the slithy toves
> Did gyre and gimble in the wabe:
> All mimsy were the borogoves,
> And the mome raths outgrabe.

"That's enough to begin with," Humpty Dumpty interrupted: "there are plenty of hard words there. '*Brillig*' means four o'clock in the afternoon—the time when you begin *broiling* things for dinner."

"That'll do very well," said Alice: "and '*slithy*'?"

"Well, '*slithy*' means 'lithe and slimy.' 'Lithe' is the same as 'active.' You see it's like a portmanteau—there are two meanings packed up into one word."

"I see it now," Alice remarked thoughtfully: "and what are '*toves*'?"

"Well, *'toves'* are something like badgers—they're something like lizards—and they're something like corkscrews."

"They must be very curious-looking creatures."

"They are that," said Humpty Dumpty; "also they make their nests under sundials—also they live on cheese."

"And what's to *'gyre'* and to *"gimble'?"*

"To *'gyre'* is to go round and round like a gyroscope. To *'gimble'* is to make holes like a gimlet."

"And *'the wabe'* [1] is the grass-plot round a sun-dial, I suppose?" said Alice, surprised at her own ingenuity.

"Of course it is. It's called *'wabe,'* you know, because it goes a long way before it, and a long way behind it—"

"And a long way beyond it on each side," Alice added.

"Exactly so. Well then, *'mimsy'* is 'flimsy and miserable' (there's another portmanteau for you). And a *'borogove'* is a thin shabby-looking bird with its feathers sticking out all round—something like a live mop."

"And then *'mome raths'?"* said Alice. "I'm afraid I'm giving you a great deal of trouble."

"Well, a *'rath'* is a sort of green pig: but *'mome'* I'm not certain about. I think it's short for 'from home'—meaning that they'd lost their way, you know."

"And what does *'outgrabe'* mean?"

"Well, *'outgribing'* is something between bellowing and whistling, with a kind of sneeze in the middle: however, you'll hear it done, maybe —down in the wood yonder—and, when you've once heard it, you'll be *quite* content. Who's been repeating all that hard stuff to you?"

"I read it in a book," said Alice. "But I *had* some poetry repeated to me much easier than that, by—Tweedledee, I think it was."

"As to poetry, you know," said Humpty Dumpty, stretching out one of his great hands, *"I* can repeat poetry as well as other folk, if it comes to that—"

"Oh, it needn't come to that!" Alice hastily said, hoping to keep him from beginning.

"The piece I'm going to repeat," he went on without noticing her remark, "was written entirely for your amusement."

[1] *Wabe* should be pronounced *way-be.*

Alice felt that in that case she really *ought* to listen to it; so she sat down, and said "Thank you" rather sadly.

> In winter, when the fields are white,
> I sing this song for your delight—

only I don't sing it," he added, as an explanation.

"I see you don't," said Alice.

"If you can *see* whether I'm singing or not, you've sharper eyes than most," Humpty Dumpty remarked severely. Alice was silent.

> In spring, when woods are getting
>   green,
> I'll try and tell you what I mean:

"Thank you very much," said Alice.

> In summer when the days are long
> Perhaps you'll understand the song.

> In autumn, when the leaves are
>   brown,
> Take pen and ink, and write it
>   down.

"I will, if I can remember it so long," said Alice.

"You needn't go on making remarks like that," Humpty Dumpty said: "they're not sensible, and they put me out."

> I sent a message to the fish:
> I told them 'This is what I wish.'

> The little fishes of the sea,
> They sent an answer back to me.

> The little fishes' answer was
> 'We cannot do it, Sir, because—'

"I'm afraid I don't quite understand," said Alice.

"It gets easier further on," Humpty Dumpty replied.

> I sent to them again to say
> 'It will be better to obey.'

The fishes answered, with a grin,
'Why, what a temper you are in!'

I told them once, I told them twice:
They would not listen to advice.

I took a kettle large and new,
Fit for the deed I had to do.

My heart went hop, my heart went
    thump:
I filled the kettle at the pump.

Then some one came to me and said
'The little fishes are in bed.'

I said to him, I said it plain,
'Then you must wake them up again.'

I said it very loud and clear:
I went and shouted in his ear.

Humpty Dumpty raised his voice almost to a scream as he repeated this verse, and Alice thought, with a shudder, "I wouldn't have been the messenger for *anything!*"

But he was very stiff and proud:
He said 'You needn't shout so loud!"

And he was very proud and stiff:
He said 'I'd go and wake them, if—'

I took a corkscrew from the shelf:
I went to wake them up myself.

And when I found the door was
    locked,
I pulled and pushed and kicked and
    knocked.

And when I found the door was shut,
I tried to turn the handle, but—

There was a long pause.

"Is that all?" Alice timidly asked.

"That's all," said Humpty Dumpty. "Good-bye."

This was rather sudden, Alice thought: but, after such a *very* strong hint that she ought to be going, she felt that it would hardly be civil to stay. So she got up, and held out her hand. "Good-bye, till we meet again!" she said as cheerfully as she could.

"I shouldn't know you again if we *did* meet," Humpty Dumpty replied in a discontented tone, giving her one of his fingers to shake: "you're so exactly like other people."

"The face is what one goes by, generally," Alice remarked in a thoughtful tone.

"That's just what I complain of," said Humpty Dumpty. "Your face is the same as everybody has—the two eyes, so—" (marking their places in the air with his thumb) "nose in the middle, mouth under. It's always the same. Now if you had the two eyes on the same side of the nose, for instance—or the mouth at the top—that would be *some* help."

"It wouldn't look nice," Alice objected. But Humpty Dumpty only shut his eyes, and said "Wait till you've tried."

Alice waited a minute to see if he would speak again, but, as he never opened his eyes or took any further notice of her, she said "Good-bye!" once more, and, getting no answer to this, she quietly walked away: but she couldn't help saying to herself, as she went, "Of all the unsatisfactory—" (she repeated this aloud, as it was a great comfort to have such a long word to say) "of all the unsatisfactory people I *ever* met—" She never finished the sentence, for at this moment a heavy crash shook the forest from end to end.

Emily Dickinson
FIVE POEMS

---

*Dickinson's short lyrics concentrate on aphorism, irony, and
paradox. Pretending to be small in scope, they raise universal questions about life and religion. She deliberately uses
an imperfect rhyme or "slant rhyme," as it is often called,
to surprising effect, almost as if she is trying to echo in the
convention of rhyme the imperfection she sees about her in
the world. One of her verses actually begins "Tell all the
truth but tell it slant." The third poem is a good example of
slant rhyme. In each of the first four poems, her ironic wit
enables her to write satire, not mere invective. The fifth
poem is "straight," that is, not satiric. It is characteristic of
hundreds of Dickinson's poems. That her poetry lends itself to parody should be evident from Peterson's "After
Great Drink," which follows.*

ABRAHAM TO KILL HIM

Abraham to kill him
Was distinctly told—
Isaac was an Urchin—
Abraham was old—

Not a hesitation
Abraham complied—
Flattered by Obeisance
Tyranny demurred—

Isaac—to his children
Lived to tell the tale—

Moral—with a Mastiff
Manners may prevail.

APPARENTLY WITH NO SURPRISE

Apparently with no surprise
To any happy Flower
The Frost beheads it at its play—
In accidental power—
The blonde Assassin passes on—
The Sun proceeds unmoved
To measure off another Day
For an Approving God.

GOD IS INDEED A JEALOUS GOD

God is indeed a jealous God—
He cannot bear to see
That we had rather not with Him
But with each other play.

MUCH MADNESS IS DIVINEST SENSE

Much Madness is divinest Sense—
To a discerning Eye—
Much Sense—the starkest Madness—
'Tis the Majority
In this, as All, prevail—
Assent—and you are sane—
Demur—you're straightway dangerous—
And handled with a Chain—

AFTER GREAT PAIN, A FORMAL FEELING COMES

After great pain, a formal feeling comes—
The Nerves sit ceremonious, like Tombs—

The stiff Heart questions was it He, that bore,
And Yesterday, or Centuries before?

The Feet, mechanical, go round—
Of Ground, or Air, or Ought—
A Wooden way
Regardless grown,
A Quartz contentment, like a stone—

This is the Hour of Lead—
Remembered, if outlived,
As Freezing persons, recollect the Snow—
First—Chill—then Stupor—then the letting go—

Nils Peterson
AFTER GREAT DRINK

from *Satire Newsletter*, Spring, 1968.

After great drink, a formal feeling comes—
The Nerves sit ceremonious, like Tombs,—
The hurt Head questions was it I that drank
And Yesterday, and Centuries before?

The Feet, mechanical, go round—
A Wooden way
Of Floor, or Chair, or Desk
Regardless grown,
A Quart resentment, like a stone—

Beneath this Hour of Dread—
Dismembered, as if lived out,
The Sobering person recollects the Flow—
First One—then Several—then the letting go—

Algernon Swinburne
NEPHELIDIA

Rare indeed is that serious poet with objectivity and sense
of humor enough to parody himself. Swinburne, often the
victim of parody because of his individualistic, mannered
verse, decided in 1880 to have his own try, just possibly
because he felt he could do a better job than anyone else.
The result, "Nephelidia"—which means "little clouds"—is
a classic. The rhythm, the meter, the onomatopoeia, the
alliteration, all typical of Swinburne, are wittingly rendered.
In fact, the poem is so well rendered for sound patterns, it
has no meaning.

From the depth of the dreamy decline of the dawn through a notable
    nimbus of nebulous noonshine,
Pallid and pink as the palm of the flag-flower that flickers with
    fear of the flies as they float,
Are the looks of our lovers that lustrously lean from a marvel of
    mystic miraculous moonshine,
These that we feel in the blood of our blushes that thicken and
    threaten with throbs through the throat?
Thicken and thrill as a theatre thronged at appeal of an actor's appalled
    agitation,
Fainter with fear of the fires of the future than pale with the
    promise of pride in the past;
Flushed with the famishing fullness of fever that reddens with radiance
    of rathe [1] recreation,
Gaunt as the ghastliest of glimpses that gleam through the gloom
    of the gloaming when ghosts go aghast?
Nay, for the nick of the tick of the time is a tremulous touch on the
    temples of terror,

[1] Rapid.

Strained as the sinews yet strenuous with strife of the dead who is
dumb as the dust-heaps of death:
Surely no soul is it, sweet as the spasm of erotic emotional exquisite
error,
Bathed in the balms of beatified bliss, beatific itself by beatitude's
breath.
Surely no spirit or sense of a soul that was soft to the spirit and soul
of our senses
Sweetens the stress of suspiring suspicion that sobs in the semblance
and sound of a sigh;
Only this oracle opens Olympian, in mystical moods and triangular
tenses—
"Life is the lust of a lamp for the light that is dark till the dawn
of the day when we die."
Mild is the mirk and monotonous music of memory, melodiously
mute as it may be,
While the hope in the heart of a hero is bruised by the breach of
men's rapiers, resigned to the rod;
Made meek as a mother whose bosom-beats bound with the bliss-
bringing bulk of a balm-breathing baby,
As they grope through the graveyard of creeds, under skies growing
green at a groan for the grimness of God.
Blank is the book of his bounty beholden of old, and its binding is
blacker than bluer:
Out of blue into black is the scheme of the skies, and their dews
are the wine of the bloodshed of things;
Till the darkling desire of delight shall be free as a fawn that is freed
from the fangs that pursue her,
Till the heart-beats of hell shall be hushed by a hymn from the
hunt that has harried the kennel of kings.

Oscar Wilde
EPIGRAMS

Wilde's popular witty comedies, all written in the 1890's, are studded with epigrams like those which follow.

—England has done one thing; it has invented and established Public Opinion, which is an attempt to organize the ignorance of the community, and to elevate it to the dignity of physical force.

—The only difference between a caprice and a lifelong passion is that the caprice lasts a little longer.

—I am but too conscious of the fact that we are born in an age when only the dull are treated seriously, and I live in terror of not being misunderstood.

—When a woman marries again, it is because she detested her first husband. When a man marries again, it is because he adored his first wife. Women try their luck; men risk theirs.

—Seriousness is the only refuge of the shallow.

—There is no sin except stupidity.

—It is a curious fact that the worst work is always done with the best intentions, and that people are never so trivial as when they take themselves seriously.

—Truth is never pure, and rarely simple.

—As long as war is regarded as wicked, it will always have its fascination. When it is looked upon as vulgar, it will cease to be popular.

—To believe is very dull. To doubt is intensely engrossing. To be on the alert is to live; to be lulled into security is to die.

—It is enough that our fathers have believed. They have exhausted the faith-faculty of the species. Their legacy to us is the scepticism of which they were afraid.

—Women are a decorative sex. They never have anything to say, but they say it charmingly. Women represent the triumph of matter over mind, just as men represent the triumph of mind over morals.

—Twenty years of romance make a woman look like a ruin; but twenty years of marriage make her look like a public building.

—The English country gentleman galloping after a fox—the unspeakable in full pursuit of the uneatable.

—[A cynic is] a man who knows the price of everything and the value of nothing.

—I can resist everything except temptation.

John Collins Bossidy
ON THE ARISTOCRACY
OF HARVARD

This famous old four-liner is a variety of the epigram.

And this is good old Boston,
The home of the bean and the cod,
Where the Lowells talk only to Cabots
And the Cabots talk only to God.

Sarah Cleghorn
QUATRAIN

The quiet surface irony of this piece masks the rather bitter
social satire beneath.

The golf links lie so near the mill
That almost every day
The laboring children can look out
And see the men at play.

Arthur Hugh Clough
THE LATEST DECALOGUE

Clough's decalogue is an ironic parody of the Christian one.
It combines irony with a sense of epigram in much the
same way as the Bossidy and Cleghorn verses just before it.

Thou shalt have one God only; who
Would be at the expense of two?
No graven images may be
Worshipped, except the currency:
Swear not at all; for, for thy curse
Thine enemy is none the worse:
At church on Sunday to attend
Will serve to keep the world thy friend:
Honour thy parents; that is, all
From whom advancement may befall:
Thou shalt not kill; but need'st not strive
Officiously to keep alive:
Do not adultery commit;
Advantage rarely comes of it:
Thou shalt not steal; an empty feat,
When it's so lucrative to cheat:
Bear not false witness; let the lie
Have time on its own wings to fly:
Thou shalt not covet, but tradition
Approves all forms of competition.

Finley Peter Dunne
TWO COLUMNS

Finley Peter Dunne was a reporter and editor for Chicago newspapers for many years. As a device for satire, he hit upon the creation of Mr. Dooley, a Chicago bartender, who chatted with his friend and customer, Hennessy, a local workingman, about the news of the day. Mr. Dooley was an extremely popular figure for many years about the turn of the century. He speaks in an Irish-American dialect, a mask for the great urban majority of the day, evidently not silent and clearly not effete. The two selections involve satire of our war with the Spanish. The first deals with preparations for the invasion of Cuba; the second is a reaction to Theodore Roosevelt's book The Rough Riders. *It may be interesting to compare Dunne's satire (setting the dialect aside) with that of Art Buchwald in our time.*

ON PREPARING FOR THE INVASION OF CUBA

"Well," Mr. Hennessy asked, "how goes th' war?" "Splendid, thank ye," said Mr. Dooley. "Fine, fine. It makes me heart throb with pride that I'm a citizen iv th' Sixth Wa-ard."

"Has th' ar-rmy started f'r Cuba yet?"

"Wan ar-rmy, says ye? Twinty! Las' Choosdah an advance ar-rmy iv wan hundherd an' twinty thousand men landed fr'm th' *Gussie,* with tin thousand cannons hurlin' projick-tyles weighin' eight hundherd pounds sivinteen miles. Winsdah night a second ar-rmy iv injineers, miners, plumbers, an' lawn tinnis experts, numberin' in all four hundherd an' eighty thousan' men, ar-rmed with death-dealin' canned goods, was hurried to Havana to storm th' city.

"Thursdah mornin' three thousand full rigimints acrost to Matoonzas, an' afther a spirited battle captured th' Rainy Christiny golf

293

links, two up an' hell to play, an' will hold thim again all comers. Th' same afthernoon th' reg'lar cavalry, consistin' iv four hundherd an' eight thousan' well-mounted men, was loaded aboord th' tug *Lucy J.,* and departed on their earend iv death amidst th' cheers iv eight millyon sojers left behind at Chickamaha. These cavl'ry'll co-operate with Commodore Schlow; an' whin he desthroys th' Spanish fleet, as he does ivry Sundah an' holy day except in Lent, an' finds out where they ar-re an' desthroys thim, afther batterin' down th' forts where they ar-re con-cealed so that he can't see thim, but thinks they ar-re on their way f'r to fight Cousin George Dooley, th' cav'lry will make a dash back to Tampa, where Gin-ral Miles is preparin' to desthroy th' Spanish at wan blow—an' he's th' boy to do it.

"The gin'ral arrived th' other day, fully prepared f'r th' bloody wurruk iv war. He had his intire fam'ly with him. He r-rode recklessly into camp, mounted on a superb specyal ca-ar. As himsilf an' Uncle Mike Miles, an' Cousin Hennery Miles, an' Master Miles, aged eight years, dismounted fr'm th' specyal train, they were received with wild cheers be eight millyon iv th' bravest sojers that iver give up their lives f'r their counthry. Th' press cinchorship is so pow'rful that no news is allowed to go out; but I have it fr'm th' specyal corryspondint iv Mesilf, Clancy th' Butcher, Mike Casey, an' th' City Direchtry that Gin'ral Miles instantly repaired himsilf to th' hotel, where he made his plans f'r cr-rushin' th' Spanyards at wan blow. He will equip th' ar-rmy with blowguns at wanst. His uniforms ar-re comin' down in specyal steel protected bullyon trains fr'm th' mint, where they've kept f'r a year. He has ordhered out th' gold resarve f'r to equip his staff, numberin' eight thousan' men, manny iv whom ar-re clubmen; an' as soon as he can have his pitchers took, he will cr-rush th' Spanish with wan blow. Th' pur-pose iv th' gin'ral is to permit no delay. Decisive action is de-manded be th' people. An', whin th' hot air masheens has been sint to th' front, Gin'ral Miles will strike wan blow that'll be th' damdest blow since th' year iv th' big wind in Ireland.

"Iv coorse, they'se dissinsions in th' cabinet; but they don't amount to nawthin'. Th' Sicrety iv War is in favor iv sawin' th' Spanish ar-rmy into two-be-four joists. Th' Sicrety iv th' Threeasury has a scheme f'r roonin' thim be lindin' thim money. Th' Sicrety iv th' Navy wants to sue thim before th' Mattsachusetts Supreme Coort. I've heerd that th'

Prisident is arrangin' a knee dhrill, with th' idee iv prayin' th' villyans to th' divvil. But these diff'rences don't count. We're all wan people, an' we look to Gin-ral Miles to desthroy th' Spanish with wan blow. Whin it comes, trees will be lifted out be th' roots. Morro Castle'll cave in, an' th' air'll be full iv Spanish whiskers. A long blow, a sthrong blow, an' a blow all together."

"We're a gr-reat people," said Mr. Hennessy, earnestly.

"We ar-re," said Mr. Dooley. "We ar-re that. An' th' best iv it is, we know we ar-re."

ON ROOSEVELT'S *The Rough Riders*

"Well, sir," said Mr. Dooley, "I jus' got hold iv a book, Hinnissy, that suits me up to th' handle, a gran' book, th' grandest iver seen. Ye know I'm not much throubled be lithrachoor, havin' manny worries iv me own, but I'm not prejudiced agin books. I am not. Whin a rale good book comes along I'm as quick as anny wan to say it isn't so bad, an' this here book is fine. I tell ye 'tis fine."

"What is it?" Mr. Hennessy asked languidly.

" 'Tis 'Th' Biography iv a Hero be Wan Who Knows.' 'Tis 'Th' Darin' Exploits iv a Brave Man be an Actual Eye Witness.' 'Tis 'Th' Account iv th' Desthruction iv Spanish Power in th' Ant Hills,' as it fell fr'm th' lips iv Tiddy Rosenfelt an' was took down be his own hands. Ye see 'twas this way, Hinnissy, as I r-read th' book. Whin Tiddy was blowed up in th' harbor iv Havana he instantly concluded they must be war. He debated th' question long an' earnestly an' fin'lly passed a jint resolution declarin' war. So far so good. But there was no wan to carry it on. What shud he do? I will lave th' janial author tell th' story in his own wurruds.

" 'Th' sicrety iv war had offered me,' he says, 'th' command of a rig-mint,' he says, 'but I cud not consint to remain in Tampa while less audacious heroes was at th' front,' he says. 'Besides,' he says, 'I felt I was incompetent f'r to command a rig'mint raised be another,' he says. 'I determined to raise wan iv me own,' he says. 'I selected fr'm me acquaintances in th' West,' he says, 'men that had thravelled with me acrost th' desert an' th' storm-wreathed mountain,' he says, 'sharin' me burdens an' at times confrontin' perils almost as gr-reat as anny that beset me path,' he says. 'Together we had faced th' turrors iv th' large but vilent West,' he says, 'an' these brave men had seen me with me trusty rifle shootin' down th' buffalo, th' elk, th' moose, th' grizzly bear, th' mountain goat,' he says, 'th' silver man, an' otther ferocious beasts iv thim parts,' he says. 'An' they niver flinched,' he says. 'In a few days I had thim perfectly tamed,' he says, 'an' ready to go annywhere I led,' he says. 'On th' thransport goin' to Cubia,' he says, 'I wud stand beside wan iv these r-rough men threatin' him as an ankel, which he was in ivrything but birth, education, rank, an' courage, an' together we wud look up at th' admirable stars iv that tolerable southern sky an' quote th' Bible fr'm Walt Whitman,' he says. 'Honest, loyal, thrue-hearted la-ads, how kind I was to thim,' he says.

" 'We had no sooner landed in Cubia than it becomes nicissry f'r me to take command iv th' ar-rmy which I did at wanst. A number iv days was spint be me in reconnoitring, attinded on'y be me brave an' fluent body guard, Richard Harding Davis. I discovered that th' inimy was heavily inthrenched on th' top iv San Joon hill immejiately in front iv me. At this time it become apparent that I was handicapped be th' prisence iv th' ar-rmy,' he says. 'Wan day whin I was about to charge a block house sturdily defined by an ar-rmy corps undher Gin'ral Tamale, th' brave Castile that I aftherwards killed with a small ink-eraser that I always carry, I r-ran into th' entire military force iv th' United States lying on its stomach. 'If ye won't fight,' says I, 'let me go through,' I says. 'Who are ye?' says they. 'Colonel Rosenfelt,' says I. 'Oh, excuse me,' says th' gin-ral in command (if me mimry serves me thrue it was Miles) r-risin' to his knees an' salutin'. This showed me 'twud be impossible f'r to carry th' war to a successful conclusion unless I was free, so I sint th' ar-rmy home an' attacked San Joon hill. Arrmed on'y with a small thirty-two which I used in th' West to shoot th' fleet priarie dog, I climbed that precipitous ascent in th' face iv th' most gallin' fire I iver knew or heerd iv. But I had a few r-rounds iv gall mesilf an' what cared I? I dashed madly on cheerin' as I wint. Th' Spanish troops was dhrawn up in a long line in th' formation known among military men as a long line. I fired at th' man nearest to me an' I knew be th' expression iv his face that th' trusty bullet wint home. It passed through his frame, he fell, an' wan little home in far-off Catalonia was made happy be th' thought that their riprisintative had been kilt be th' future governor iv New York. Th' bullet sped on its mad flight an' passed through th' intire line fin'lly imbeddin' instelf in th' abdomen iv th' Ar-ch-bishop iv Santago eight miles away. This ended th' war.'

" 'They has been some discussion as to who was th' first man to r-reach th' summit iv San Joon hill. I will not attempt to dispute th' merits iv th' manny gallant sojers, statesmen, corryspondints, an' kinetoscope men who claim th' distinction. They ar-re all brave men an' if they wish to wear me laurels they may. I have so manny annyhow that it keeps me broke havin' thim blocked an' irned. But I will say f'r th' binifit iv posterity that I was th' on'y man I see. An' I had a tillyscope.'

"I have thried, Hinnissy," Mr. Dooley continued, "to give you a fair idee iv th' contints iv this remarkable book, but what I've tol' ye is on'y what Hogan calls an outline iv th' principal pints. Ye'll have to r-read th' book ye'ersilf to get a thrue conciption. I haven't time f'r to tell ye th' wurruk Tiddy did in ar-rmin' an' equippin' himsilf, how he fed himsilf, how he steadied himsilf in battle an' encouraged himsilf with a few well-chosen wurruds whin th' sky was darkest. Ye'll have to stake a squint into th' book ye'ersilf to larn thim things."

"I won't do it," said Mr. Hennessy. "I think Tiddy Rosenfelt is all r-right an' if he wants to blow his hor-nn lave him do it."

"Thrue f'r ye," said Mr. Dooley, "an' if his valliant deeds didn't get into this book 'twud be a long time befure they appeared in Shafter's histhry iv th' war. No man bears a gredge agin' himsilf'll iver be governor iv a state. An' if Tiddy done it all he ought to say so an' relieve th' suspinse. But if I was him I'd call th' book 'Alone in Cubia.' "

Stephen Crane
SEVEN POEMS

In the 1890's Crane wrote a large number of brief verses somewhat like those of Emily Dickinson written earlier in the century. Perhaps fifty were satiric, of which these are among the best. The first is a classic war protest poem, balancing images of the battlefield against reactions by those at home—a lover, a child, a mother—who have lost someone in the war, and interspersing ironic commentary. The second sustains a skeptical perspective on that bastion of society and social prejudices, the newspaper. It closes with an echo of Macbeth's "sound and fury" speech and an ironic suggestion of what the newspaper may actually achieve. The third and fourth comment upon the energetic pomposity of man and the grand indifference of the universe. The final three are basically satires on man's religious and philosophical absurdities. As such, they bear reading with the Thomas Hardy poems which follow.

DO NOT WEEP, MAIDEN, FOR WAR IS KIND

Do not weep, maiden, for war is kind.
Because your lover threw wild hands toward the sky
And the affrighted steed ran on alone,
Do not weep.
War is kind.

Hoarse, booming drums of the regiment,
Little souls who thirst for fight,
These men were born to drill and die.
The unexplained glory flies above them,

Great is the battle-god, great, and his kingdom—
A field where a thousand corpses lie.

Do not weep, babe, for war is kind.
Because your father tumbled in the yellow trenches,
Raged at his breast, gulped and died,
Do not weep.
War is kind.

Swift blazing flag of the regiment,
Eagle with crest of red and gold,
These men were born to drill and die.
Point for them the virtue of slaughter,
Make plain to them the excellence of killing
And a field where a thousand corpses lie.

Mother whose heart hung humble as a button
On the bright splendid shroud of your son,
Do not weep.
War is kind.

A NEWSPAPER IS A COLLECTION OF HALF-INJUSTICES

A newspaper is a collection of half-injustices
Which, bawled by boys from mile to mile,
Spreads its curious opinion
To a million merciful and sneering men,
While families cuddle the joys of the fireside
When spurred by tale of dire lone agony.
A newspaper is a court
Where everyone is kindly and unfairly tried
By a squalor of honest men.
A newspaper is a market
Where wisdom sells its freedom
And melons are crowned by the crowd.

A newspaper is a game
Where his error scores the player victory
While another's skill wins death.
A newspaper is a symbol;
It is feckless life's chronicle,
A collection of loud tales
Concentrating eternal stupidities,
That in remote ages lived unhaltered,
Roaming through a fenceless world.

A MAN SAID TO THE UNIVERSE

A man said to the universe:
"Sir, I exist!"
"However," replied the universe,
"The fact has not created in me
A sense of obligation."

I SAW A MAN PURSUING THE HORIZON

I saw a man pursuing the horizon;
Round and round they sped.
I was disturbed at this;
I accosted the man.
"It is futile," I said,
"You can never—"
"You lie," he cried,
And ran on.

GOD FASHIONED THE SHIP OF THE WORLD
CAREFULLY

God fashioned the ship of the world carefully.
With the infinite skill of an All-Master
Made He the hull and the sails,

Held He the rudder
Ready for adjustment.
Erect stood He, scanning his work proudly.
Then—at a fateful time—a wrong called,
And God turned, heeding.
Lo, the ship, at this opportunity, slipped slyly,
Making cunning noiseless travel down the ways.
So that, forever rudderless, it went upon the seas
Going ridiculous voyages,
Making quaint progress,
Turning as with serious purpose
Before stupid winds.
And there were many in the sky
Who laughed at this thing.

IF THERE IS A WITNESS

If there is a witness to my little life,
To my tiny throes and struggles,
He sees a fool;
And it is not fine for gods to menace fools.

A GOD IN WRATH

A god in wrath
Was beating a man;
He cuffed him loudly
With thunderous blows
That rang and rolled over the earth.
All people came running.
The man screamed and struggled,
And bit madly at the feet of the god.
The people cried,
"Ah, what a wicked man!"
And—
"Ah, what a redoubtable god!"

Thomas Hardy
FOUR POEMS

After a long career as novelist in the late nineteenth cen-
tury, Hardy concentrated on poetry and drama in the early
twentieth. Like most of his other works, his poetry ex-
presses with wit and detachment his perception of man's
helplessness and folly amid the mighty forces of a vast and
indifferent universe.

AH, ARE YOU DIGGING ON MY GRAVE?

"Ah, are you digging on my grave
    My loved one?—planting rue?"
—"No: yesterday he went to wed
One of the brightest wealth has bred.
'It cannot hurt her now,' he said,
    'That I should not be true.' "

"Then who is digging on my grave?
    My nearest dearest kin?"
—"Ah, no: they sit and think, 'What use!
What good will planting flowers produce?
No tendance of her mound can loose
    Her spirit from Death's gin.' "

"But some one digs upon my grave?
    My enemy?—prodding sly?"
—"Nay: when she heard you had passed the Gate
That shuts on all flesh soon or late,
She thought you no more worth her hate,
    And cares not where you lie."

"Then, who is digging on my grave?
　　　Say—since I have not guessed!"
—"O it is I, my mistress dear,
Your little dog, who still lives near,
And much I hope my movements here
　　　Have not disturbed your rest?"

"Ah, yes! *You* dig upon my grave . . .
　　　Why flashed it not on me
That one true heart was left behind!
What feeling do we ever find
To equal among human kind
　　　A dog's fidelity!"

"Mistress, I dug upon your grave
　　　To bury a bone, in case
I should be hungry near this spot
When passing on my daily trot.
I am sorry, but I quite forgot
　　　It was your resting-place."

NEW YEAR'S EVE

"I have finished another year," said God,
　　　"In grey, green, white, and brown;
I have strewn the leaf upon the sod,
Sealed up the worm within the clod,
　　　And let the last sun down."

"And what's the good of it?" I said,
　　　"What reasons made you call
From formless void this earth we tread,
When nine-and-ninety can be read
　　　Why nought should be at all?

"Yea, Sire: why shaped you us, 'who in
　　　This tabernacle groan'—

303

If ever a joy be found herein,
Such joy no man had wished to win
   If he had never known!"

Then he: "My labours—logicless—
   You may explain; not I:
Sense-sealed I have wrought, without a guess
That I evolved a Consciousness
   To ask for reasons why.

"Strange that ephemeral creatures who
   By my own ordering are,
Should see the shortness of my view,
Use ethic tests I never knew,
   Or made provision for!"

He sank to raptness as of yore,
   And opening New Year's Day
Wove it by rote as theretofore,
And went on working evermore
   In his unweeting way.

CHANNEL FIRING

That night your great guns, unawares,
Shook all our coffins as we lay,
And broke the chancel [1] window-squares,
We thought it was the Judgment-day

And sat upright. While drearisome
Arose the howl of wakened hounds:
The mouse let fall the altar-crumb,
The worms drew back into the mounds,

[1] Area about the altar in a church.

The glebe [2] cow drooled. Till God called, "No;
It's gunnery practice out at sea
Just as before you went below;
The world is as it used to be:

"All nations striving strong to make
Red war yet redder. Mad as hatters
They do no more for Christés sake
Than you who are helpless in such matters.

"That this is not the judgment-hour
For some of them's a blessed thing,
For if it were they'd have to scour
Hell's floor for so much threatening. . . .

"Ha, ha. It will be warmer when
I blow the trumpet (if indeed
I ever do; for you are men,
And rest eternal sorely need)."

So down we lay again. "I wonder,
Will the world ever saner be,"
Said one, "than when He sent us under
In our indifferent century!"

And many a skeleton shook his head.
"Instead of preaching forty year,"
My neighbour Parson Thirdly said,
"I wish I had stuck to pipes and beer."

Again the guns disturbed the hour,
Roaring their readiness to avenge,
As far inland as Stourton Tower,
And Camelot, and starlit Stonehenge. [3]

[2] Plot of land granted a clergyman by a parish.
[3] Symbols of England's ancient glory.

IN CHURCH

"And now to God the Father," he ends,
And his voice thrills up to the topmost tiles:
Each listener chokes as he bows and bends,
And emotion pervades the crowded aisles.
Then the preacher glides to the vestry-door,
And shuts it, and thinks he is seen no more.

The door swings softly ajar meanwhile,
And a pupil of his in the Bible class,
Who adores him as one without gloss or guile,
Sees her idol stand with a satisfied smile
And re-enact at the vestry-glass
Each pulpit gesture in deft dumb-show
That had moved the congregation so.

Ambrose Bierce
from
FANTASTIC FABLES

Bierce was a newspaperman with a waspish tongue, whose columns, fables, and satiric definitions were popular in the late nineteenth and early twentieth centuries. His brief fables usually satirize entrenched popular attitudes in religion, politics, and social affairs. He even satirizes satirists. His definitions, collected in The Devil's Dictionary, *are consistently acerbic, unlike the gently humorous ones found in numerous small newspapers throughout the country today. Bierce was evidently killed in Mexico in 1914 while covering Pancho Villa for the Hearst papers.*

THE DEVOTED WIDOW

A Widow weeping on her husband's grave was approached by an Engaging Gentleman who, in a respectful manner, assured her that he had long entertained for her the most tender feelings.

"Wretch!" cried the Widow. "Leave me this instant! Is this a time to talk to me of love?"

"I assure you, madam, that I had not intended to disclose my affection," the Engaging Gentleman humbly explained, "but the power of your beauty has overcome my discretion."

"You should see me when I have not been weeping," said the Widow.

A RADICAL PARALLEL

The correct title is possibly "A Racial Parallel" as printed in the table of contents of The Collected Works of Ambrose Bierce, *Vol. VI.*

Some White Christians engaged in driving Chinese Heathens out of an American town found a newspaper published in Peking in the Chinese tongue and compelled one of their victims to translate an editorial. It turned out to be an appeal to the people of the province of Pang Ki to drive the foreign devils out of the country and burn their dwellings and churches. At this evidence of Mongolian barbarity the White Christians were so greatly incensed that they carried out their original design.

THE HOLY DEACON

An Itinerant Preacher who had wrought hard in the moral vineyard for several hours whispered to a Holy Deacon of the local church:

"Brother, these people know you, and your active support will bear fruit abundantly. Please pass the plate for me, and you shall have one fourth."

The Holy Deacon did so, and putting the money into his pocket waited till the congregation was dismissed, then said good-night.

"But the money, brother, the money that you collected!" said the Itinerant Preacher.

"Nothing is coming to you," was the reply; "the Adversary has hardened their hearts and one fourth is all they gave."

A CALL TO QUIT

Seeing that his audiences were becoming smaller every Sunday, a Minister of the Gospel broke off in the midst of a sermon, descended the pulpit stairs and walked on his hands down the central aisle of the church. He then remounted his feet, ascended to the pulpit and resumed his discourse, making no allusion to the incident.

"Now," said he to himself, as he went home, "I shall have, henceforth, a large attendance and no snoring."

But on the following Friday he was waited upon by the Pillars of the Church, who informed him that in order to be in harmony with the New Theology and get full advantage of modern methods of Gospel interpretation they had deemed it advisable to make a change. They had therefore sent a call to Brother Jowjeetum-Fallal, the world-renowned

Hindoo human pin-wheel, then holding forth in Hoopitup's circus. They were happy to say that the reverend gentleman had been moved by the Spirit to accept the call, and on the ensuing Sabbath would break the bread of life for the brethren or break his neck in the attempt.

OFFICER AND THUG

A Chief of Police who had seen an Officer beating a Thug was very indignant, and said he must not do so any more on pain of dismissal.

"Don't be too hard on me," said the Officer, smiling; "I was beating him with a stuffed club."

"Nevertheless," persisted the Chief of Police, "it was a liberty that must have been very disagreeable, though it may not have hurt. Please do not repeat it."

"But," said the Officer, still smiling, "it was a stuffed Thug."

In attempting to express his gratification the Chief of Police thrust out his right hand with such violence that his skin was ruptured at the arm-pit and a stream of sawdust poured from the wound. He was a stuffed Chief of Police.

THE FABULIST

An Illustrious Satirist was visiting a traveling menagerie with a view to collecting literary materials. As he was passing near the Elephant that animal said:

"How sad that so justly famous a censor should mar his work by ridicule of persons with pendulous noses—who are the salt of the earth!"

The Kangaroo said:

"I do so enjoy that great man's censure of the ridiculous—particularly his attacks on the proboscidæ; but, alas! he has no reverence for the marsupials, and laughs at our way of carrying our young in a pouch."

The Camel said:

"If he would only respect the Sacred Hump, he would be faultless. As it is, I can not permit his work to be read in the presence of my family."

The Ostrich, seeing his approach, thrust her head into the straw, saying:

"If I do not conceal myself, he may be reminded to write something disagreeable about my lack of a crest, or my appetite for scrap-iron; and although he is inexpressibly brilliant when he devotes himself to ridicule of folly and greed, his dulness is matchless when he transcends the limits of legitimate comment."

"That," said the Buzzard to his mate, "is the distinguished author of that glorious fable, 'The Ostrich and the Keg of Raw Nails.' I regret to add, that he wrote also, 'The Buzzard's Feast,' in which a carrion diet is contumeliously disparaged. A carrion diet is the foundation of sound health. If nothing but corpses were eaten, death would be unknown."

Seeing an attendant approaching, the Illustrious Satirist passed out of the tent and mingled with the crowd. It was afterward discovered that he had crept in under the canvas without paying.

from
THE DEVIL'S
DICTIONARY

corporation, n.   An ingenious device for obtaining individual profit without individual responsibility.

cynic, n.   A blackguard whose faulty vision sees things as they are, not as they ought to be. Hence the custom among the Scythians of plucking out a cynic's eyes to improve his vision.

duel, n.   A formal ceremony preliminary to the reconciliation of two enemies. Great skill is necessary to its satisfactory observance; if awkwardly performed the most unexpected and deplorable consequences sometimes ensue. A long time ago a man lost his life in a duel.

edible, adj. Good to eat, and wholesome to digest, as a worm to a toad, a toad to a snake, a snake to a pig, a pig to a man, and a man to a worm.

embalm, v.t. To cheat vegetation by locking up the gases upon which it feeds. By embalming their dead and thereby deranging the natural balance between animal and vegetable life, the Egyptians made their once fertile and populous country barren and incapable of supporting more than a meagre crew. The modern metallic burial casket is a step in the same direction, and many a dead man who ought now to be ornamenting his neighbor's lawn as a tree, or enriching his table as a bunch of radishes, is doomed to a long inutility. We shall get him after awhile if we are spared, but in the meantime the violet and rose are languishing for a nibble at his *gluteus maximus.*

impale, v.t. In popular usage to pierce with any weapon which remains fixed in the wound. This, however, is inaccurate; to impale is, properly, to put to death by thrusting an upright sharp stake into the body, the victim being left in a sitting posture. This was a common mode of punishment among many of the nations of antiquity, and is still in high favor in China and other parts of Asia. Down to the beginning of the fifteenth century it was widely employed in "churching" heretics and schismatics. Wolecraft calls it the "stoole of repentynge," and among the common people it was jocularly known as "riding the one legged horse." Ludwig Salzmann informs us that in Thibet impalement is considered the most appropriate punishment for crimes against religion; and although in China it is sometimes awarded for secular offences, it is most frequently adjudged in cases of sacrilege. To the person in actual experience of impalement it must be a matter of minor importance by what kind of civil or religious dissent he was made acquainted with its discomforts; but doubtless he would feel a certain satisfaction if able to contemplate himself in the character of a weathercock on the spire of the True Church.

impiety, n. Your irreverence toward my deity.

impunity, n. Wealth.

lawyer, n. One skilled in circumvention of the law.

noise, n. A stench in the ear. Undomesticated music. The chief product and authenticating sign of civilization.

Occident, n.   The part of the world lying west (or east) of the Orient. It is largely inhabited by Christians, a powerful sub-tribe of the Hypocrites, whose principal industries are murder and cheating, which they are pleased to call "war" and "commerce." These, also, are the principal industries of the Orient.

patriotism, n.   Combustible rubbish ready to the torch of any one ambitious to illuminate his name. In Dr. Johnson's famous dictionary *patriotism* is defined as the last resort of a scoundrel. With all due respect to an enlightened but inferior lexicographer, I beg to submit that it is the first.

politics, n.   A strife of interests masquerading as a contest of principles. The conduct of public affairs for private advantage.

positive, adj.   Mistaken at the top of one's voice.

radicalism, n.   The conservatism of tomorrow injected into the affairs of today.

retaliation, n.   The natural rock upon which is reared the Temple of Law.

A. E. Housman
FRAGMENT OF A GREEK
TRAGEDY

This parody, written by an English lyric poet and classical scholar, will be best appreciated by those who have suffered through studies of ancient Greek drama in a dull, bookish, too literal, and unimaginative translation. The parody improves when read aloud.

CHORUS   O suitably-attired-in-leather-boots
Head of a traveler, wherefore seeking whom
Whence by what way how purposed art thou come
To this well-nightingaled vicinity?
My object in inquiring is to know.
But if you happen to be deaf and dumb
And do not understand a word I say,
Then wave your hand, to signify as much.
   ALC   I journeyed hither a Boetian road.
   CHORUS   Sailing on horseback, or with feet for oars?
   ALC   Plying with speed my partnership of legs.
   CHORUS   Beneath a shining or a rainy Zeus?
   ALC   Mud's sister, not himself, adorns my shoes.
   CHORUS   To learn your name would not displease me much.
   ALC   Not all that men desire do they obtain.
   CHORUS   Might I then hear at what your presence shoots?
   ALC   A shepherd's questioned mouth informed me that—
   CHORUS   What? for I know not yet what you will say.
   ALC   Nor will you ever, if you interrupt.
   CHORUS   Proceed, and I will hold my speechless tongue.
   ALC   This house was Eriphyla's, no one's else.

CHORUS   Nor did he shame his throat with shameful lies.
ALC   May I then enter, passing through the door?
CHORUS   Go chase into the house a lucky foot.
And, O my son, be, on the one hand, good,
And do not, on the other hand, be bad;
For that is very much the safest plan.
ALC   I go into the house with heels and speed.

CHORUS

Strophe

In speculation
I would not willingly acquire a name
   For ill-digested thought;
   But after pondering much
To this conclusion I at last have come:
   Life is uncertain.
   This truth I have written deep
   In my reflective midriff
   On tablets not of wax,
Nor with a pen did I inscribe it there,
For many reasons: *Life,* I say, *is not*
   A stranger to uncertainty.
Not from the flight of omen-yelling fowls
   This fact did I discover,
Nor did the Delphine tripod bark it out,
   Nor yet Dodona.
Its native ingenuity sufficed
   My self-taught diaphragm.

   Antistrophe

   Why should I mention
The Inachean daughter, loved of Zeus?
   Her whom of old the gods,
   More provident than kind,
Provided with four hoofs, two horns, one tail,

A gift not asked for,
And sent her forth to learn
The unfamiliar science
Of how to chew the cud.
She therefore, all about the Argive fields,
Went cropping pale green grass and nettle-tops,
   Nor did they disagree with her.
But yet, howe'er nutritious, such repasts
   I do not hanker after:
Never may Cypris for her seat select
   My dappled liver!
Why should I mention Io? Why indeed?
   I have no notion why.

   Epode

But now does my boding heart,
Unhired, unaccompanied, sing
A strain not meet for the dance.
Yea even the palace appears
To my yoke of circular eyes
(The right, nor omit I the left)
Like a slaughterhouse, so to speak,
Garnished with woolly deaths
And many shipwrecks of cows.
I therefore in a Cissian strain lament;
   And to the rapid
Loud, linen-tattering thumps upon my chest
   Resounds in concert
The battering of my unlucky head.

   ERI (*within*):   O, I am smitten with a hatchet's jaw;
And that in deed and not in word alone.
   CHORUS   I thought I heard a sound within the house
Unlike the voice of one that jumps for joy.
   ERI   He splits my skull, not in a friendly way,
Once more: he purposes to kill me dead
   CHORUS   I would not be reputed rash, but yet

I doubt if all be gay within the house.

ERI   O! O! another stroke! that makes the third.
He stabs me to the heart against my wish.

CHORUS   If that be so, thy state of health is poor;
But thine arithmetic is quite correct.

Anatole France
from
PENGUIN ISLAND

In Penguin Island (*1908*), *France constructs a large satiri-cal allegory of the development of modern France. Chris-tianity, civilization, and government are introduced among the penguins, who quickly master the sophisticated human arts of intolerance, barbarism, and anarchy. Eventually they manage to blow up Paris and destroy their civilization. The chapter printed here uses the image of clothing as a meta-phor for the religious and moral "clothing" which mankind devises to corrupt itself.*

Book II, Chapter One
THE FIRST CLOTHES

One day St. Maël was sitting by the seashore on a warm stone that he found. He thought it had been warmed by the sun and he gave thanks to God for it, not knowing that the Devil had been resting on it. The apostle was waiting for the monks of Yvern who had been commis-sioned to bring a freight of skins and fabrics to clothe the inhabitants of the island of Alca.

Soon he saw a monk called Magis coming ashore and carrying a chest upon his back. This monk enjoyed a great reputation for holiness.

When he had drawn near to the old man he laid the chest on the ground and wiping his forehead with the back of his sleeve, he said:

"Well, father, you wish then to clothe these penguins?"

"Nothing is more needful, my son," said the old man. "Since they have been incorporated into the family of Abraham these penguins share the curse of Eve, and they know that they are naked, a thing of which they were ignorant before. And it is high time to clothe them, for they are losing the down that remained on them after their metamorphosis."

"It is true," said Magis as he cast his eyes over the coast where the penguins were to be seen looking for shrimps, gathering mussels, singing, or sleeping, "they are naked. But do you not think, father, that it would be better to leave them naked? Why clothe them? When they wear clothes and are under the moral law they will assume an immense pride, a vile hypocrisy, and an excessive cruelty."

"Is it possible, my son," sighed the old man, "that you understand so badly the effects of the moral law to which even the heathen submit?"

"The moral law," answered Magis, "forces men who are beasts to live otherwise than beasts, a thing that doubtless puts a constraint upon them, but that also flatters and reassures them; and as they are proud, cowardly, and covetous of pleasure, they willingly submit to restraints that tickle their vanity and on which they found both their present security and the hope of their future happiness. That is the principle of all morality. . . . But let us not mislead ourselves. My companions are unloading their cargo of stuffs and skins on the island. Think, father, while there is still time! To clothe the penguins is a very serious business. At present when a penguin desires a penguin he knows precisely what he desires and his lust is limited by an exact knowledge of its object. At this moment two or three couples of penguins are making love on the beach. See with what simplicity! No one pays any attention and the actors themselves do not seem to be greatly preoccupied. But when the female penguins are clothed, the male penguin will not form so exact a notion of what it is that attracts him to them. His indeterminate desires will fly out into all sorts of dreams and illusions; in short, father, he will know love and its mad torments. And all the time the female penguins will cast down their eyes and bite their lips, and take on airs as if they kept a treasure under their clothes! . . . what a pity!

"The evil will be endurable as long as these people remain rude and poor; but only wait for a thousand years and you will see, father, with what powerful weapons you have endowed the daughters of Alca. If you will allow me, I can give you some idea of it beforehand. I have some old clothes in this chest. Let us take at hazard one of these female penguins to whom the male penguins give such little thought, and let us dress her as well as we can.

"Here is one coming towards us. She is neither more beautiful nor uglier than the others; she is young. No one looks at her. She strolls indolently along the shore, scratching her back and with her finger at her nose as she walks. You cannot help seeing, father, that she has narrow shoulders, clumsy breasts, a stout figure, and short legs. Her reddish knees pucker at every step she takes, and there is, at each of her joints, what looks like a little monkey's head. Her broad and sinewy feet cling to the rock with their four crooked toes, while the great toes stick up like the heads of two cunning serpents. She begins to walk, all her muscles are engaged in the task, and, when we see them working, we think of her as a machine intended for walking rather than as a machine intended for making love, although visibly she is both, and contains within herself several other pieces of machinery besides. Well, venerable apostle, you will see what I am going to make of her."

With these words the monk, Magis, reached the female penguin in three bounds, lifted her up, carried her in his arms with her hair trailing behind her, and threw her, overcome with fright, at the feet of the holy Maël.

And whilst she wept and begged him to do her no harm, he took a pair of sandals out of his chest and commanded her to put them on.

"Her feet," observed the old man, "will appear smaller when squeezed in by the woollen cords. The soles, being two fingers high, will give an elegant length to her legs and the weight they bear will seem magnified."

As the penguin tied on her sandals she threw a curious look towards the open coffer, and seeing that it was full of jewels and finery, she smiled through her tears.

The monk twisted her hair on the back of her head and covered it with a chaplet of flowers. He encircled her wrist with golden bracelets and making her stand upright, he passed a large linen band beneath her breasts, alleging that her bosom would thereby derive a new dignity and that her sides would be compressed to the greater glory of her hips.

He fixed this band with pins, taking them one by one out of his mouth.

"You can tighten it still more," said the penguin.

When he had, with much care and study, enclosed the soft parts of her bust in this way, he covered her whole body with a rose-coloured tunic which gently followed the lines of her figure.

"Does it hang well?" asked the penguin.

And bending forward with her head on one side and her chin on her shoulder, she kept looking attentively at the appearance of her toilet.

Magis asked her if she did not think the dress a little long, but she answered with assurance that it was not—she would hold it up.

Immediately, taking the back of her skirt in her left hand, she drew it obliquely across her hips, taking care to disclose a glimpse of her heels. Then she went away, walking with short steps and swinging her hips.

She did not turn her head, but as she passed near a stream she glanced out of the corner of her eye at her own reflection.

A male penguin, who met her by chance, stopped in surprise, and retracing his steps began to follow her. As she went along the shore, others coming back from fishing went up to her, and after looking at her, walked behind her. Those who were lying on the sand got up and joined the rest.

Unceasingly, as she advanced, fresh penguins, descending from the paths of the mountain, coming out of clefts of the rocks, and emerging from the water, added to the size of her retinue.

And all of them, men of ripe age with vigorous shoulders and hairy breasts, agile youths, old men shaking the multitudinous wrinkles of their rosy and white-haired skins, or dragging their legs thinner and drier than the juniper staff that served them as a third leg, hurried on, panting and emitting an acrid odour and hoarse gasps. Yet she went on peacefully and seemed to see nothing.

"Father," cried Magis, "notice how each one advances with his nose pointed towards the centre of gravity of that young damsel now that the centre is covered by a garment. The sphere inspires the meditations of geometers by the number of its properties. When it proceeds from a physical and living nature it acquires new qualities, and in order that the interest of that figure might be fully revealed to the penguins it was necessary that, ceasing to see it distinctly with their eyes, they should be led to represent it to themselves in their minds. I myself feel at this moment irresistibly attracted towards that penguin. Whether it be because her skirt gives more importance to her hips, and that in its simple magnificence it invests them with a synthetic and general character and allows only the pure idea, the divine principle, of them to be seen, whether this be the cause I cannot say, but I feel that if I embraced her I would hold in my hands the heaven of human pleasure. It is certain that modesty communicates an invincible attraction to women. My uneasiness is so great that it would be vain for me to try to conceal it."

He spoke, and, gathering up his habit, he rushed among the crowd of penguins, pushing, jostling, trampling, and crushing, until he reached the daughter of Alca, whom he seized and suddenly carried in his arms into a cave that had been hollowed out by the sea.

Then the penguins felt as if the sun had gone out. And the holy Maël knew that the Devil had taken the features of the monk, Magis, in order that he might give clothes to the daughter of Alca. He was troubled in spirit, and his soul was sad. As with slow steps he went towards his hermitage he saw the little penguins of six and seven years of age tightening their waists with belts made of sea-weed and walking along the shore to see if anybody would follow them.

Don Marquis
from
THE OLD SOAK'S
HISTORY OF THE WORLD

*In the same tradition as Finley Peter Dunne's Mr. Dooley,
Don Marquis' Old Soak is a dialect mask through which he
satirizes issues of the day. Using one of the oldest satiric
tricks—defense of an issue by the wrong person for the
wrong reason in the wrong way—Marquis "defends" the
Bible against an "athyiss" attack. Marquis, a newspaper
columnist in Atlanta and New York from 1902–1922, is
also the creator of archy the free-lance-writing cockroach
and his feline girl friend mehitabel.*

Chapter I
MEN ARE NOT DESSENDED OFF OF MONKEYS

Well, what people want to find out about the histry of the world is
mostly how people acted at different times and what they et and drunk
and thought about, which it is my idea that from the garden of Eden
down the present times it has all been about the same.

But the Eighteenth Commandment has come along and things have
changed and from the garden of Eden down to today is one area, and
from now on is another area, with a great gulf fixed, as the Good
Book says.

Well, one of the most prominent men in the old days was Sampson
he never liked to work none but use to loaf around with his hair long

and show how stout he was and as far as taking a drink was concerned it never hurt him none but he would liquor up and slay more Phillippines drunk than one of these here Prohibitionists was ever man enough to do sober.

If you had said to him he was descended off of a monkey he would of beaned you with anything that was handy. And in my histry of the World it will be proved that men is not descended off of monkeys for if so why did not all the monkeys turn into men. You can't get back of the Good Book in them things, and for my part I don't hanker to.

There use to hang around Jake Smith's place a smart alec couisin of his by the name of Hennery Withers and every time this here Hennery Withers got too much to drink he use to say, Well, then, you tell me now, "Where did Cain get his wife?"

I says to Jake more than oncet, Well you tell Hennery to leave the Good Book alone or I will bean him one of these days with a bottle he is a dam little athyiss, and if there is anything I hate it is a dam little athyiss.

Well, Jake says, you leave him alone Clem, I keep a respectible place and I don't want a word of religion or any other trouble in here or no fuss for they will take away my lisence.

This feller Hennery Withers was proud of being an athyiss. You go and be one I says to him and keep your mouth shut about it and nobody will give a dam but I never saw one of these athyisses yet he didn't want to blah blah it around so the whole town would know it. It made him feel like he was important. He knowed he wasn't worth nothing and he's got to feel important some faked up way or he wouldn't have no reason to keep on living.

One difference of the old days in the early times of world whose histry I am going to write is that they didn't have no glass bottles, they kept it in jugs and skins which they was bladders I guess like they keep oil and putty in nowadays and they drunk it right out of the jug. Well, I have drunk cider that a way, and oncet I run onto a gang of Scandinavians building a barn and them fellows was drinking equival parts of sweet cider and straight alkohawl mixed right out of a jug and Oh boy! what a head ache you can get out of that stuff.

In Sampson's time they didn't have no alkohawl and it come into the

323

world in recent years, what they had in the old days was wine and liquors.

He says the little foxes spoils the grapes, you can read it in the Good Book, and that made him sore and he went out and caught a hunderd of them foxes and tied all their tales together and set fire to them and turned them loose against the Phillippines.

Well, they finally got him, he married a new wife and she says you gotto cut that hair and he says bob your own and she slipped some nock out drops into his hootch and when he come to he was bob haired and it disturbed his balance.

Afore he got his hair cut when he wanted to set his self for a good lick his hair balanced him like the tale onto a kite, but when his balance was disturbed he couldn't set his self for a good lick and finally the enimy got him because he couldn't set him self for a good lick.

They took him and conkered him they bored his eyes out and they says now you gotto go to work.

Work, hell, he says, I won't do it, I never done nothing but drink liquor and fight and run with the women and I won't work.

You can see work was quite a come down to a gent that has always lived free and easy like that, but when they bored his eyes out they hooked him to a kind of a dog churn thing and he had to keep stepping or he would get his heels barked and he had to turn that mill.

But one day he notis his hair is down to his neck again and he says to his self these coots is got a big surprise coming to them some day. If I could get a jug of the old stuff I would show them.

Well, them Phillippines was an unreligious set. On Sundays they would play baseball and go fishing and have big parties. They had some kind of a church, but it wasn't a reg'lar orthydox church, neither Baptis or Methodis nor none of the churches we know about in this country. It was an idle church full of them heathen idles all carved out of elephants tushes and things and on Sundays they would have like a street fair in front of the church so one Sunday they says let us bring out this Sampson to the street fair and make him do stunts and we will thrown orange peel and tomatoes at him and mebby eggs that aint so young as they use to be. Well he got some of that grubbage in his face and he fetched one roar like a bull and he pulled that church full of idles down on top of the whole kit and biling of them and they perished.

Offen Jake Smith an me have argued wether he could of licked John Sullivan, and Jake says John would of out boxed him but with the old london prise ring rules Sampson would of licked him.

Well I see John L. oncet in Boston I was into his place and shook the hand that knocked Charlie michell cold.

H. L. Mencken
THE HILLS OF ZION

*No satirist was more famous in America in the 1920's and
1930's than H. L. Mencken, an editor and columnist for
Baltimore newspapers and founder, critic, and editor of two
important periodicals,* The Smart Set *and* The American
Mercury. *Mencken was an amazingly prolific and wide-
ranging writer for fifty years, producing among other works
a volume of poetry, several critical studies of literary figures,
two plays, a travel book, the monumental linguistic study*
The American Language, *numerous collections of columns
and essays, and a dictionary of quotations based on historical principles. But his popularity still rests largely on six
collections of satiric essays published from 1919–1927 called*
Prejudices. *The selection here was written for the Baltimore*
Sun *in July, 1925, and published in* Prejudices: Fifth Series. *It is Mencken's reaction to the famous Scopes trial in
Tennessee, which provided him the opportunity to see
"evangelical Christianity as a going concern." Mencken
probably resembles Addison or Samuel Johnson more than
any other American satirist and man of letters. Yet he is
somehow less Horatian than either, more Juvenalian. He
characteristically operates without a satiric mask, writing
directly, revealing directly. His pose is that of a lofty, incisive mind, partly amused, partly disgusted by what he sees
and driven to write about it in a style and vocabulary likewise lofty and incisive.*

It was hot weather when they tried the infidel Scopes at Dayton, but I
went down there very willingly, for I had good reports of the sub-
Potomac bootleggers, and moreover I was eager to see something of
evangelical Christianity as a going concern. In the big cities of the Re-

326

public, despite the endless efforts of consecrated men, it is laid up with a wasting disease. The very Sunday-school superintendents, taking jazz from the stealthy radio, shake their fireproof legs; their pupils, moving into adolescence, no longer respond to the proliferating hormones by enlisting for missionary service in Africa, but resort to necking and petting instead. I know of no evangelical church from Oregon to Maine that is not short of money: the graft begins to peter out, like wiretapping and three-card monte before it. Even in Dayton, though the mob was up to do execution upon Scopes, there was a strong smell of antinomianism. The nine churches of the village were all half empty on Sunday, and weeds choked their yards. Only two or three of the resident pastors managed to sustain themselves by their ghostly science; the rest had to take orders for mail-order pantaloons or work in the adjacent strawberry fields; one, I heard, was a barber. On the courthouse green a score of sweating theologians debated the darker passages of Holy Writ day and night, but I soon found that they were all volunteers, and that the local faithful, while interested in their exegesis as an intellectual exercise, did not permit it to impede the indigenous debaucheries. Exactly twelve minutes after I reached the village I was taken in tow by a Christian man and introduced to the favorite tipple of the Cumberland Range: half corn liquor and half coca-cola. It seemed a dreadful dose to me, spoiled as I was by the bootleg light wines and beers of the Eastern seaboard, but I found that the Dayton illuminati got it down with gusto, rubbing their tummies and rolling their eyes. I include among them the chief local proponents of the Mosaic cosmogony. They were all hot for Genesis, but their faces were far too florid to belong to teetotalers, and when a pretty girl came tripping down the main street, which was very often, they reached for the places where their neckties should have been with all the amorous enterprise of movie actors. It seemed somehow strange.

An amiable newspaper woman of Chattanooga, familiar with those uplands, presently enlightened me. Dayton, she explained, was simply a great capital like any other great capital. That is to say, it was to Rhea County what Atlanta was to Georgia or Paris to France. That is to say, it was predominantly epicurean and sinful. A country girl from some remote valley of the county, coming into town for her semi-annual bottle of Lydia Pinkham's Vegetable Compound, shivered on approaching

Robinson's drug-store quite as a country girl from up-state New York might shiver on approaching the Metropolitan Opera House or the Ritz Hotel. In every village lout she saw a potential white-slaver. The hard sidewalks hurt her feet. Temptations of the flesh bristled to all sides of her, luring her to hell. This newspaper woman told me of a session with just such a visitor, holden a few days before. The latter waited outside one of the town hot-dog and coca-cola shops while her husband negotiated with a hardware merchant across the street. The newspaper woman, idling along and observing that the stranger was badly used by the heat, invited her to step into the shop for a glass of coca-cola. The invitation brought forth only a gurgle of terror. Coca-cola, it quickly appeared, was prohibited by the country lady's pastor, as a levantine and hell-sent narcotic. He also prohibited coffee and tea—and pies! He had his doubts about white bread and boughten meat. The newspaper woman, interested, inquired about ice-cream. It was, she found, not specifically prohibited, but going into a coca-cola shop to get it would be clearly sinful. So she offered to get a saucer of it and bring it out to the sidewalk. The visitor vacillated—and came near being lost. But God saved her in the nick of time. When the newspaper woman emerged from the place she was in full flight up the street! Later on, her husband, mounted on a mule, overtook her four miles out the mountain pike.

This newspaper woman, whose kindness covered city infidels as well as Alpine Christians, offered to take me back in the hills to a place where the old-time religion was genuinely on tap. The Scopes jury, she explained, was composed mainly of its customers, with a few Dayton sophisticates added to leaven the mass. It would thus be instructive to climb the heights and observe the former at their ceremonies. The trip, fortunately, might be made by automobile. There was a road running out of Dayton to Morgantown, in the mountains to the westward, and thence beyond. But foreigners, it appeared, would have to approach the sacred grove cautiously, for the upland worshippers were very shy, and at the first sight of a strange face they would adjourn their orgy and slink into the forest. They were not to be feared, for God had long since forbidden them to practice assassination, or even assault, but if they were alarmed a rough trip would go for naught. So, after dreadful bumpings up a long and narrow road, we parked our car in a little

328

wood-path a mile or two beyond the tiny village of Morgantown and made the rest of the approach on foot, deployed like skirmishers. Far off in a dark, romantic glade a flickering light was visible, and out of the silence came the rumble of exhortation. We could distinguish the figure of the preacher only as a moving mote in the light: it was like looking down the tube of a dark-field microscope. Slowly and cautiously we crossed what seemed to be a pasture, and then we crouched down along the edge of a cornfield and stealthily edged further and further. The light now grew larger and we could begin to make out what was going on. We went ahead on all fours, like snakes in the grass.

From the great limb of a mighty oak hung a couple of crude torches of the sort that car inspectors thrust under Pullman cars when a train pulls in at night. In the guttering glare was the preacher, and for a while we could see no one else. He was an immensely tall and thin mountaineer in blue jeans, his collarless shirt open at the neck and his hair a tousled mop. As he preached he paced up and down under the smoking flambeaux, and at each turn he thrust his arms into the air and yelled: "Glory to God!" We crept nearer in the shadow of the cornfield and began to hear more of his discourse. He was preaching on the Day of Judgment. The high kings of the earth, he roared, would all fall down and die; only the sanctified would stand up to receive the Lord God of Hosts. One of these kings he mentioned by name, the King of what he called Greece-y. The King of Greece-y, he said, was doomed to hell. We crawled forward a few more yards and began to see the audience. It was seated on benches ranged round the preacher in a circle. Behind him sat a row of elders, men and women. In front were the younger folk. We crept on cautiously, and individuals rose out of the ghostly gloom. A young mother sat suckling her baby, rocking as the preacher paced up and down. Two scared little girls hugged each other, their pigtails down their backs. An immensely huge mountain woman, in a gingham dress, cut in one piece, rolled on her heels at every "Glory to God!" To one side, and but half visible, was what appeared to be a bed. We found afterwards that half a dozen babies were asleep upon it.

The preacher stopped at last, and there arose out of the darkness a woman with her hair pulled back into a little tight knot. She began so quietly that we couldn't hear what she said, but soon her voice rose resonantly and we could follow her. She was denouncing the reading of books. Some wandering book-agent, it appeared, had come to her cabin and tried to sell her a specimen of his wares. She refused to touch it. Why, indeed, read a book? If what was in it was true, then everything in it was already the Bible. If it was false, then reading it would imperil the soul. This syllogism from Caliph Omar complete, she sat down. There followed a hymn, led by a somewhat fat brother wearing silver-rimmed country spectacles. It droned on for half a dozen stanzas, and then the first speaker resumed the floor. He argued that the gift of tongues was real and that education was a snare. Once his children could read the Bible, he said, they had enough. Beyond lay only infidelity and damnation. Sin stalked the cities. Dayton itself was a Sodom. Even Morgantown had begun to forget God. He sat down, and a female aurochs in gingham got up. She began quietly, but was soon leaping and roaring, and it was hard to follow her. Under cover of the turmoil we sneaked a bit closer.

A couple of other discourses followed, and there were two or three hymns. Suddenly a change of mood began to make itself felt. The last hymn ran longer than the others, and dropped gradually into a monotonous, unintelligible chant. The leader beat time with his book. The faithful broke out with exultations. When the singing ended there was a brief palaver that we could not hear, and two of the men moved a bench into the circle of light directly under the flambeaux. Then a half-grown girl emerged from the darkness and threw herself upon it. We noticed with astonishment that she had bobbed hair. "This sister," said the leader, "has asked for prayers." We moved a bit closer. We could now see faces plainly, and hear every word. What followed quickly reached such heights of barbaric grotesquerie that it was hard to believe it real. At a signal all the faithful crowded up to the bench and began to pray—not in unison, but each for himself! At another they all fell on their knees, their arms over the penitent. The leader kneeled facing us, his head alternately thrown back dramatically or buried in his hands. Words spouted from his lips like bullets from a machine-gun —appeals to God to pull the penitent back out of hell, defiances of the demons of the air, a vast impassioned jargon of apocalyptic texts. Suddenly he rose to his feet, threw back his head and began to speak in the tongues—blub-blub-blub, gurgle-gurgle-gurgle. His voice rose to a higher register. The climax was a shrill, inarticulate squawk, like that of a man throttled. He fell headlong across the pyramid of suppliants. A comic scene? Somehow, no. The poor half-wits were too horribly in earnest. It was like peeping through a knothole at the writings of people in pain. From the squirming and jabbering mass a young woman gradually detached herself—a woman not uncomely, with a pathetic home-made cap on her head. Her head jerked back, the veins of her neck swelled, and her fists went to her throat as if she were fighting for breath. She bent backward until she was like half a hoop. Then she suddenly snapped forward. We caught a flash of the whites of her eyes. Presently her whole body began to be convulsed—great throes that began at the shoulders and ended at the hips. She would leap to her feet, thrust her arms in air, and then hurl herself upon the heap. Her praying flattened out into a mere delirious caterwauling, like that of a tomcat on a petting party. I describe the thing discreetly, and as a strict behaviorist. The lady's subjective sensations I leave to infidel pathologists, privy to the works of Ellis, Freud, and Moll. Whatever they were, they were obviously not painful, for they were accompanied by vast heavings and gurglings of a joyful and even ecstatic nature. And they seemed to be contagious, too, for soon a second penitent, also female, joined the first, and then came a third, and a fourth, and a fifth. The last one had an extraordinary violent attack. She began with mild enough jerks of the head, but in a moment she was bounding all over the place, like a chicken with its head cut off. Every time her head came up, a stream of hosannas would issue out of it. Once she collided with a dark, undersized brother, hitherto silent and stolid. Contact with her set him off as if he had been kicked by a mule. He leaped into the air, threw back his head, and began to gargle as if with a mouthful of BB shot. Then he loosed one tremendous, stentorian sentence in the tongues, and collapsed.

By this time the performers were quite oblivious of the profane universe and so it was safe to go still closer. We left our hiding and came up to the little circle of light. We slipped into the vacant seats on one of the rickety benches. The heap of mourners was directly before us. They bounced into us as they cavorted. The smell that they radiated, sweating there in that obscene heap, half suffocated us. Not all of them, of course, did the thing in the grand manner. Some merely moaned and rolled their eyes. The female ox in gingham flung her great bulk on the ground and jabbered an unintelligible prayer. One of the men, in the intervals between fits, put on his spectacles and read his Bible. Beside me on the bench sat the young mother and her baby. She suckled it through the whole orgy, obviously fascinated by what was going on, but never venturing to take any hand in it. On the bed just outside the light half a dozen other babies slept peacefully. In the shadows, suddenly appearing and as suddenly going away, were vague figures, whether of believers or of scoffers I do not know. They seemed to come and go in couples. Now and then a couple at the ringside would step out and vanish into the black night. After a while some came back, the males looking somewhat sheepish. There was whispering outside the circle of vision. A couple of Fords lurched up the road, cutting holes in the darkness with their lights. Once someone out of sight loosed a bray of laughter.

All this went on for an hour or so. The original penitent, by this time, was buried three deep beneath the heap. One caught a glimpse, now and then, of her yellow bobbed hair, but then she would vanish again. How she breathed down there I don't know; it was hard enough six feet away, with a strong five-cent cigar to help. When the praying brothers would rise up for a bout with the tongues, their faces were streaming with perspiration. The fat harridan in gingham sweated like a longshoreman. Her hair got loose and fell down over her face. She fanned herself with her skirt. A powerful old gal she was, plainly equal in her day to a bout with obstetrics and a week's washing on the same morning, but this was worse than a week's washing. Finally she fell into a heap, breathing in great, convulsive gasps.

Finally we got tired of the show and returned to Dayton. It was nearly eleven o'clock—an immensely late hour for those latitudes—but the whole town was still gathered in the courthouse yard, listening to the disputes of theologians. The Scopes trial had brought them in from all directions. There was a friar wearing a sandwich sign announcing that he was the Bible champion of the world. There was a Seventh Day Adventist arguing that Clarence Darrow was the beast with seven heads and ten horns described in Revelation xiii, and that the end of the world was at hand. There was an evangelist made up like Andy Gump, with the news that atheists in Cincinnati were preparing to descend upon Dayton, hang the eminent Judge Raulston, and burn the town. There was an ancient who maintained that no Catholic could be a Christian. There was the eloquent Dr. T. T. Martin, of Blue Mountain, Miss., come to town with a truck-load of torches and hymn-books to put Darwin in his place. There was a singing brother bellowing apocalyptic hymns. There was William Jennings Bryan, followed everywhere by a gaping crowd. Dayton was having a roaring time. It was better than the circus. But the note of devotion was simply not there; the Daytonians, after listening awhile, would slip away to Robinson's drug-store to regale themselves with coca-cola, or to the lobby of the Aqua Hotel, where the learned Raulston sat in state, judicially picking his teeth. The real religion was not present. It began at the bridge over the town creek, where the road makes off for the hills.

T. S. Eliot
TWO POEMS

One of the most learned and difficult poets of our time, Eliot reveres tradition and hopes to see it revitalized. In his mock "love song," he scorns the figure of modern man. Prufrock is an arid mutation of what a man ought to be. His world is shallow, full of triviality, inconsequential. He is timid, fated to die without tasting manhood, glory, or love. The opening Italian lines are from Dante's Divine Comedy. *They are the words of one of the damned who, assuming that Dante is also dead, agrees to speak the truth to him. The implication, of course, is that Prufrock, too, is dead, although this is not evident until one reads the entire poem. The satire itself clearly begins in the third English line, as the opening simile turns grotesque. In "The Hippopotamus," Eliot uses an amusing four-stress line, ironic paradox, and, above all, a monstrous metaphor to carry his satire on the sterility of twentieth-century religion.*

THE LOVE SONG OF J. ALFRED PRUFROCK

S'io credesse che mia risposta fosse
A persona che mai tornasse al mondo,
Questa fiamma staria senza piu scosse.
Ma perciocche giammai di questo fondo
Non torno vivo alcun, s'i'odo il vero,
Senza tema d'infamia ti rispondo.

Let us go then, you and I,
When the evening is spread out against the sky
Like a patient etherized upon a table;

Let us go, through certain half-deserted streets,
The muttering retreats
Of restless nights in one-night cheap hotels
And sawdust restaurants with oyster-shells:
Streets that follow like a tedious argument
Of insidious intent
To lead you to an overwhelming question . . .
Oh, do not ask, "What is it?"
Let us go and make our visit.

In the room the women come and go
Talking of Michelangelo.

The yellow fog that rubs its back upon the window-panes,
The yellow smoke that rubs its muzzle on the window-panes
Licked its tongue into the corners of the evening,
Lingered upon the pools that stand in drains,
Let fall upon its back the soot that falls from chimneys,
Slipped by the terrace, made a sudden leap,
And seeing that it was a soft October night,
Curled once about the house, and fell asleep.

And indeed there will be time
For the yellow smoke that slides along the street,
Rubbing its back upon the window-panes;

There will be time, there will be time
To prepare a face to meet the faces that you meet;
There will be time to murder and create,
And time for all the works and days of hands
That lift and drop a question on your plate;
Time for you and time for me,
And time yet for a hundred indecisions,
And for a hundred visions and revisions,
Before the taking of a toast and tea.

335

In the room the women come and go
Talking of Michelangelo.

And indeed there will be time
To wonder, "Do I dare?" and, "Do I dare?"
Time to turn back and descend the stair,
With a bald spot in the middle of my hair—
[They will say: "How his hair is growing thin!"]
My morning coat, my collar mounting firmly to the chin,
My necktie rich and modest, but asserted by a simple pin—
[They will say: "But how his arms and legs are thin!"]
Do I dare
Disturb the universe?
In a minute there is time
For decisions and revisions which a minute will reverse.

For I have known them all already, known them all:
Have known the evenings, mornings, afternoons,
I have measured out my life with coffee spoons;
I know the voices dying with a dying fall
Beneath the music from a farther room.
      So how should I presume?

And I have known the eyes already, known them all—
The eyes that fix you in a formulated phrase,
And when I am formulated, sprawling on a pin,
When I am pinned and wriggling on the wall,
Then how should I begin
To spit out all the butt-ends of my days and ways?
      And how should I presume?

And I have known the arms already, known them all—
Arms that are braceleted and white and bare
(But in the lamplight, downed with light brown hair!)
Is it perfume from a dress
That makes me so digress?
Arms that lie along a table, or wrap about a shawl.

And should I then presume?
And how should I begin?

● ● ●

Shall I say, I have gone at dusk through narrow streets
And watched the smoke that rises from the pipes.
Of lonely men in shirt-sleeves, leaning out of windows? . . .

I should have been a pair of ragged claws
Scuttling across the floors of silent seas.

● ● ●

And the afternoon, the evening, sleeps so peacefully!
Smoothed by long fingers,
Asleep . . . tired . . . or it malingers,
Stretched on the floor, here beside you and me.
Should I, after tea and cakes and ices,
Have the strength to force the moment to its crisis?
But though I have wept and fasted, wept and prayed,
Though I have seen my head (grown slightly bald) brought in upon
        a platter,
I am no prophet—and here's no great matter;
I have seen the moment of my greatness flicker,
And I have seen the eternal Footman hold my coat, and snicker,
And in short, I was afraid.

And would it have been worth it, after all,
After the cups, the marmalade, the tea,
Among the porcelain, among some talk of you and me,
Would it have been worth while,
To have bitten off the matter with a smile,
To have squeezed the universe into a ball
To roll it toward some overwhelming question,
To say: "I am Lazarus, come from the dead,
Come back to tell you all, I shall tell you all"—

If one, settling a pillow by her head,
  Should say: "That is not what I meant at all,
  That is not it, at all."

And would it have been worth it, after all,
Would it have been worth while,
After the sunsets and the dooryards and the sprinkled streets,
After the novels, after the teacups, after the skirts that trail along
    the floor—
And this, and so much more?—
It is impossible to say just what I mean!
But as if a magic lantern threw the nerves in patterns on a screen:
Would it have been worth while
If one, settling a pillow or throwing off a shawl,
And turning toward the window, should say:
  "That is not it at all,
  That is not what I meant, at all."

•   •   •

No! I am not Prince Hamlet, nor was meant to be,
Am an attendant lord, one that will do
To swell a progress, start a scene or two,
Advise the prince; no doubt, an easy tool,
Deferential, glad to be of use,
Politic, cautious, and meticulous;
Full of high sentence, but a bit obtuse;
At times, indeed, almost ridiculous—
Almost, at times, the Fool.

I grow old . . . I grow old . . .
I shall wear the bottoms of my trousers rolled.

Shall I part my hair behind? Do I dare to eat a peach?
I shall wear white flannel trousers, and walk upon the beach.
I have heard the mermaids singing, each to each.

I do not think that they will sing to me.

I have seen them riding seaward on the waves
Combing the white hair of the waves blown back
When the wind blows the water white and black.

We have lingered in the chambers of the sea
By sea-girls wreathed with seaweed red and brown
Till human voices wake us, and we drown.

THE HIPPOPOTAMUS

The broad-backed hippopotamus
Rests on his belly in the mud;
Although he seems so firm to us
He is merely flesh and blood.

Flesh and blood is weak and frail,
Susceptible to nervous shock;
While the True Church can never fail
For it is based upon a rock.

The hippo's feeble steps may err
In compassing material ends,
While the True Church need never stir
To gather in its dividends.

The 'potamus can never reach
The mango on the mango-tree;
But fruits of pomegranate and peach
Refresh the Church from over sea.

At mating time the hippo's voice
Betrays inflexions hoarse and odd,
But every week we hear rejoice
The Church, at being one with God.

The hippopotamus's day
Is passed in sleep; at night he hunts;
God works in a mysterious way—
The Church can sleep and feed at once.

I saw the 'potamus take wing
Ascending from the damp savannas,
And quiring angels round him sing
The praise of God, in loud hosannas.

Blood of the Lamb shall wash him clean
And him shall heavenly arms enfold,
Among the saints he shall be seen
Performing on a harp of gold.

He shall be washed as white as snow,
By all the martyr'd virgins kist,
While the True Church remains below
Wrapt in the old miasmal mist.

Robert Frost
THREE POEMS

Frost almost never satirizes specific people, events, or institutions. He prefers to remain general and to understate, to suggest his case rather than declaim it. In "Departmental" he treats bureaucracy with low burlesque. In "The Bear" he ridicules a certain attitude of mind through ironic contrast of bear and man. In "Forgive, O Lord" the pose is all.

DEPARTMENTAL

An ant on the tablecloth
Ran into a dormant moth
Of many times his size.
He showed not the least surprise.
His business wasn't with such.
He gave it scarcely a touch,
And was off on his duty run.
Yet if he encountered one
Of the hive's enquiry squad
Whose work is to find out God
And the nature of time and space,
He would put him onto the case.
Ants are a curious race:
One crossing with hurried tread
The body of one of their dead
Isn't given a moment's arrest—
Seems not even impressed.
But he no doubt reports to any
With whom he crosses antennae,

And they no doubt report
To the higher up at court.
Then word goes forth in Formic:
"Death's come to Jerry McCormic,
Our selfless forager Jerry.
Will the special Janizary
Whose office it is to bury
The dead of the commissary
Go bring him home to his people.
Lay him in state on a sepal.
Wrap him for shroud in a petal.
Embalm him with ichor of nettle.
This is the word of your Queen."
And presently on the scene
Appears a solemn mortician;
And taking formal position
With feelers calmly atwiddle,
Seizes the dead by the middle,
And heaving him high in air,
Carries him out of there.
No one stands round to stare.
It is nobody else's affair.
It couldn't be called ungentle.
But how thoroughly departmental.

THE BEAR

The bear puts both arms around the tree above her
And draws it down as if it were a lover
And its choke cherries lips to kiss good-by,
Then lets it snap back upright in the sky.
Her next step rocks a boulder on the wall
(She's making her cross-country in the fall).
Her great weight creaks the barbed-wire in its staples
As she flings over and off down through the maples,
Leaving on one wire tooth a lock of hair.

Such is the uncaged progress of the bear.
The world has room to make a bear feel free;
The universe seems cramped to you and me.
Man acts more like the poor bear in a cage
That all day fights a nervous inward rage,
His mood rejecting all his mind suggests.
He paces back and forth and never rests
The toe-nail click and shuffle of his feet,
The telescope at one end of his beat,
And at the other end the microscope,
Two instruments of nearly equal hope,
And in conjunction giving quite a spread.
Or if he rests from scientific tread,
'Tis only to sit back and sway his head
Through ninety odd degrees of arc, it seems
Between two metaphysical extremes.
He sits back on his fundamental butt
With lifted snout and eyes (if any) shut,
(He almost looks religious but he's not),
And back and forth he sways from cheek to cheek,
At one extreme agreeing with one Greek,
At the other agreeing with another Greek
Which may be thought, but only so to speak.
A baggy figure, equally pathetic
When sedentary and when peripatetic.

FORGIVE, O LORD

Forgive, O Lord, my little jokes on Thee
And I'll forgive Thy great big one on me.

E. E. Cummings
THREE POEMS

Cummings is very difficult at first appearance. He arranges words in a puzzling way. He coins words like trig *in line four of "I Sing of Olaf." He uses little punctuation. He creates wild metaphors like* furnished souls *in line one of "The Cambridge Ladies," and wild similes like* a fragment of angry candy *in line fourteen of the same poem. He puns. He plays with capitalization, as in the final* Etcetera *of "My Sweet Old Etcetera." His technique fits Pope's definition of true wit: "what oft was thought, but ne'er so well expressed." The first poem, a product of Cummings' World War I experience, deals with the brutality of an "in" group toward an outsider. The second, ironically a sonnet, satirizes the shallow* unawareness and trivial activities *of ladies in a Massachusetts university city. The third contrasts the thoughts of relatives at home with those of the soldier at the front. Cummings is often easier to understand if one regards his poems as scripts to be read aloud; just let the pauses and emphases fall where the script indicates.*

I SING OF OLAF

i SING of Olaf glad and big
whose warmest heart recoiled at war:
a conscientious object-or

his wellbelovéd colonel(trig
westpointer most succinctly bred)
took erring Olaf soon in hand;
but—though an host of overjoyed

344

noncoms(first knocking on the head
him)do through icy waters roll
that helplessness which others stroke
with brushes recently employed
anent this muddy toiletbowl,
while kindred intellects evoke
allegiance per blunt instruments—
Olaf(being to all intents
a corpse and wanting any rag
upon what God unto him gave)
responds,without getting annoyed
"I will not kiss your f.ing flag"

straightway the silver bird looked grave
(departing hurriedly to shave)

but—though all kinds of officers
(a yearning nation's blueeyed pride)
their passive prey did kick and curse
until for wear their clarion
voices and boots were much the worse,
and egged the firstclassprivates on
his rectum wickedly to tease
by means of skilfully applied
bayonets roasted hot with heat—
Olaf(upon what were once knees)
does almost ceaselessly repeat
"there is some s. I will not eat"

our president, being of which
assertions duly notified
threw the yellowsonofabitch
into a dungeon, where he died

Christ(of His mercy infinite)
i pray to see;and Olaf, too

preponderatingly because
unless statistics lie he was
more brave than me:more blond than you.

THE CAMBRIDGE LADIES

the Cambridge ladies who live in furnished souls
are unbeautiful and have comfortable minds
(also, with the church's protestant blessings
daughters, unscented shapeless spirited)
they believe in Christ and Longfellow, both dead,
are invariably interested in so many things—
at the present writing one still finds
delighted fingers knitting for the is it Poles?
perhaps. While permanent faces coyly bandy
scandal of Mrs. N and Professor D
. . . . the Cambridge ladies do not care, above
Cambridge if sometimes in its box of
sky lavender and cornerless, the
moon rattles like a fragment of angry candy

MY SWEET OLD ETCETERA

my sweet old etcetera
aunt lucy during the recent

war could and what
is more did tell you just
what everybody was fighting

for,
my sister

isabel created hundreds
(and

346

hundreds) of socks not to
mention shirts fleaproof earwarmers

etcetera wristers etcetera, my
mother hoped that

i would die etcetera
bravely of course my father used
to become hoarse talking about how it was
a privilege and if only he
could meanwhile my

self etcetera lay quietly
in the deep mud et

cetera
(dreaming,
et
    cetera, of
Your smile
eyes knees and of your Etcetera)

Dorothy Parker
THREE POEMS

These three poems are typical of the witty, irreverent, worldly wise reactions to common situations in life by a very "cool" lady who has obviously been around.

UNFORTUNATE COINCIDENCE

By the time you swear you're his,
Shivering and sighing,
And he vows his passion is
    Infinite, undying—
Lady, make a note of this:
    One of you is lying.

RESUMÉ

Razors pain you;
Rivers are damp;
Acids stain you;
And drugs cause cramp.
Guns aren't lawful;
Nooses give;
Gas smells awful;
You might as well live.

life is perfect. live w/it

348

INDIAN SUMMER

In youth, it was a way I had
   To do my best to please,
And change, with every passing lad,
   To suit his theories.

But now I know the things I know,
   And do the things I do;
And if you do not like me so,
   To hell, my love, with you!

Robert Benchley
OPERA SYNOPSIS

The opera synopsis is a kind of program note handed out to the audience at a performance of grand opera. It is supposed to inform opera goers of what it is they have come to hear. Because operas are often performed in foreign languages, such a synopsis can be a useful aid to the listener, who can read it over before the curtain goes up or between acts and then, theoretically, relax and enjoy the production. However, many operas have plots that defy synopsis. And many synopses are so badly written that even simple plots can be rendered unrecognizable. Here, Benchley offers a parody of the opera synopsis which does for Wagnerian opera what Housman's "Fragment" does for Greek drama.

DIE MEISTER-GENOSSENSCHAFT

SCENE: *The Forests of Germany.*
TIME: *Antiquity.*

Cast

STRUDEL, *God of Rain*	Basso
SCHMALZ, *God of Slight Drizzle*	Tenor
IMMERGLÜCK, *Goddess of the Six Primary Colors*	Soprano
LUDWIG DAS EIWEISS, *the Knight of the Iron Duck*	Baritone
THE WOODPECKER	Soprano

Argument

The basis of "Die Meister-Genossenschaft" is an old legend of Germany which tells how the Whale got his Stomach.

ACT 1

The Rhine at Low Tide Just Below Weldschnoffen.—Immerglück has grown weary of always sitting on the same rock with the same fishes swimming by every day, and sends for Schwül to suggest something to do. Schwül asks her how she would like to have pass before her all the wonders of the world fashioned by the hand of man. She says, rotten. He then suggests that Ringblattz, son of Pflucht, be made to appear before her and fight a mortal combat with the Iron Duck. This pleases Immerglück and she summons to her the four dwarfs: Hot Water, Cold Water, Cool, and Cloudy. She bids them bring Ringblattz to her. They refuse, because Pflucht has at one time rescued them from being buried alive by acorns, and, in a rage, Immerglück strikes them all dead with a thunderbolt.

ACT 2

A Mountain Pass.—Repenting of her deed, Immerglück has sought advice of the giants, Offen and Besitz, and they tell her that she must procure the magic zither which confers upon its owner the power to go to sleep while apparently carrying on a conversation. This magic zither has been hidden for three hundred centuries in an old bureau drawer, guarded by the Iron Duck, and, although many have attempted to rescue it, all have died of a strange ailment just as success was within their grasp.

But Immerglück calls to her side Dampfboot, the tinsmith of the gods, and bids him make for her a tarnhelm or invisible cap which will enable her to talk to people without their understanding a word she says. For a dollar and a half extra Dampfboot throws in a magic ring which renders its wearer insensible. Thus armed, Immerglück starts out for Walhalla, humming to herself.

ACT 3

The Forest Before the Iron Duck's Bureau Drawer.—Merglitz, who has up till this time held his peace, now descends from a balloon and demands the release of Betty. It has been the will of Wotan that Merglitz and Betty should meet on earth and hate each other like poison, but Zweiback, the druggist of the gods, has disobeyed and concocted a love-potion which has rendered the young couple very unpleasant company. Wotan, enraged, destroys them with a protracted heat spell.

Encouraged by this sudden turn of affairs, Immerglück comes to earth in a boat drawn by four white Holsteins, and, seated alone on a rock, remembers aloud to herself the days when she was a girl. Pilgrims from Augenblick, on their way to worship at the shrine of Schmürr, hear the sound of reminiscence coming from the rock and stop in their march to sing a hymn of praise for the drying-up of the crops. They do not recognize Immerglück, as she has her hair done differently, and think that she is a beggar girl selling pencils.

In the meantime, Ragel, the papercutter of the gods, has fashioned himself a sword on the forge of Schmalz, and has called the weapon "Assistance-in-Emergency." Armed with "Assistance-in-Emergency" he comes to earth, determined to slay the Iron Duck and carry off the beautiful Irma.

But Frimsel overhears the plan and has a drink brewed which is given to Ragel in a golden goblet and which, when drunk, makes him forget his past and causes him to believe that he is Schnorr, the God of Fun. While laboring under this spell, Ragel has a funeral pyre built on the summit of a high mountain and, after lighting it, climbs on top of it with a mandolin which he plays until he is consumed.

Immerglück never marries.

Sinclair Lewis
from BABBITT

The first American to win the Nobel Prize for literature (1930), Lewis waged a relentless attack against Puritanism, social hypocrisy, and the false ideals of economic success and bourgeois respectability. Like lawyer Bragg in Fenimore Cooper's Home As Found, Babbitt *is a man for whom "nothing is too high to be aspired to, nothing too low to be done." In Chapter XIV, he is seen speaking in the Sixteenth Ward of Zenith, Lewis' fictional midwestern city, for the candidate of the solid citizenry and against the Labor candidate, then later addressing the Zenith Real Estate Board after "the victory of righteousness" in the election.*

Chapter XIV

I

This autumn a Mr. W. G. Harding, of Marion, Ohio, was appointed President of the United States, but Zenith was less interested in the national campaign than in the local election. Seneca Doane, though he was a lawyer and a graduate of the State University, was candidate for mayor of Zenith on an alarming labor ticket. To oppose him the Democrats and Republicans united on Lucas Prout, a mattress-manufacturer with a perfect record for sanity. Mr. Prout was supported by the banks, the Chamber of Commerce, all the decent newspapers, and George F. Babbitt.

Babbitt was precinct-leader on Floral Heights, but his district was safe and he longed for stouter battling. His convention paper had given him the beginning of a reputation for oratory, so the Republican-Democratic Central Committee sent him to the Seventh Ward and South

Zenith, to address small audiences of workmen and clerks, and wives uneasy with their new votes. He acquired a fame enduring for weeks. Now and then a reporter was present at one of his meetings, and the headlines (though they were not very large) indicated that George F. Babbitt had addressed Cheering Throng, and Distinguished Man of Affairs had pointed out the Fallacies of Doane. Once, in the rotogravure section of the Sunday *Advocate-Times,* there was a photograph of Babbitt and a dozen other business men, with the caption "Leaders of Zenith Finance and Commerce Who Back Prout."

He deserved his glory. He was an excellent campaigner. He had faith; he was certain that if Lincoln were alive, he would be electioneering for Mr. W. G. Harding—unless he came to Zenith and electioneered for Lucas Prout. He did not confuse audiences by silly subtleties; Prout represented honest industry, Seneca Doane represented whining laziness, and you could take your choice. With his broad shoulders and vigorous voice, he was obviously a Good Fellow; and, rarest of all, he really liked people. He almost liked common workmen. He wanted them to be well paid, and able to afford high rents—though, naturally, they must not interfere with the reasonable profits of stockholders. Thus nobly endowed, and keyed high by the discovery that he was a natural orator, he was popular with audiences, and he raged through the campaign, renowned not only in the Seventh and Eighth Wards but even in parts of the Sixteenth.

II

Crowded in his car, they came driving up to Turnverein Hall, South Zenith—Babbitt, his wife, Verona, Ted, and Paul and Zilla Riesling. The hall was over a delicatessen shop, in a street banging with trolleys and smelling of onions and gasoline and fried fish. A new appreciation of Babbitt filled all of them, including Babbitt.

"Don't know how you keep it up, talking to three bunches in one evening. Wish I had your strength," said Paul; and Ted exclaimed to Verona, "The old man certainly does know how to kid these roughnecks along!"

Men in black sateen shirts, their faces new-washed but with a hint of grime under their eyes, were loitering on the broad stairs up to the hall.

354

Babbitt's party politely edged through them and into the whitewashed room, at the front of which was a dais with a red-plush throne and a pine altar painted watery blue, as used nightly by the Grand Masters and Supreme Potentates of innumerable lodges. The hall was full. As Babbitt pushed through the fringe standing at the back, he heard the precious tribute, "That's him!" The chairman bustled down the center aisle with an impressive, "The speaker? All ready, sir! Uh—let's see— what was the name, sir?"

Then Babbitt slid into a sea of eloquence:

"Ladies and gentlemen of the Sixteenth Ward, there is one who can- not be with us here to-night, a man than whom there is no more stalwart Trojan in all the political arena—I refer to our leader, the Honorable Lucas Prout, standard-bearer of the city and county of Zenith. Since he is not here, I trust that you will bear with me if, as a friend and neigh- bor, as one who is proud to share with you the common blessing of be- ing a resident of the great city of Zenith, I tell you in all candor, hon- esty, and sincerity how the issues of this critical campaign appear to one plain man of business—to one who, brought up to the blessings of pov- erty and of manual labor, has, even when Fate condemned him to sit at a desk, yet never forgotten how it feels, by heck, to be up at five-thirty and at the factory with the ole dinner-pail in his hardened mitt when the whistle blew at seven, unless the owner sneaked in ten minutes on us and blew it early! (Laughter.) To come down to the basic and fun- damental issues of this campaign, the great error, insincerely promul- gated by Seneca Doane—"

There were workmen who jeered—young cynical workmen, for the most part foreigners, Jews, Swedes, Irishmen, Italians—but the older men, the patient, bleached, stooped carpenters and mechanics, cheered him; and when he worked up to his anecdote of Lincoln their eyes were wet.

Modestly, busily, he hurried out of the hall on delicious applause, and sped off to his third audience of the evening. "Ted, you better drive," he said. "Kind of all in after that spiel. Well, Paul, how'd it go? Did I get 'em?"

"Bully! Corking! You had a lot of pep."

Mrs. Babbitt worshiped, "Oh, it was fine! So clear and interesting, and such nice ideas. When I hear you orating I realize I don't appreciate how profoundly you think and what a splendid brain and vocabulary you have. Just—splendid."

But Verona was irritating. "Dad," she worried, "how do you know that public ownership of utilities and so on and so forth will always be a failure?"

Mrs. Babbitt reproved, "Rone, I should think you could see and realize that when your father's all worn out with orating, it's no time to expect him to explain these complicated subjects. I'm sure when he's rested he'll be glad to explain it to you. Now let's all be quiet and give Papa a chance to get ready for his next speech. Just think! Right now they're gathering in Maccabee Temple, and *waiting* for us!"

III

Mr. Lucas Prout and Sound Business defeated Mr. Seneca Doane and Class Rule, and Zenith was again saved. Babbitt was offered several minor appointments to distribute among poor relations, but he preferred advance information about the extension of paved highways, and this a grateful administration gave to him. Also, he was one of only nineteen speakers at the dinner with which the Chamber of Commerce celebrated the victory of righteousness.

His reputation for oratory established, at the dinner of the Zenith Real Estate Board he made the Annual Address. The *Advocate-Times* reported this speech with unusual fullness:

"One of the livest banquets that has recently been pulled off occurred last night in the annual Get-Together Fest of the Zenith Real Estate Board, held in the Venetian Ball Room of the O'Hearn House. Mine host Gil O'Hearn had as usual done himself proud and those assembled feasted on such an assemblage of plates as could be rivaled nowhere west of New York, if there, and washed down the plenteous feed with the cup which inspired but did not inebriate in the shape of cider from the farm of Chandler Mott, president of the board and who acted as witty and efficient chairman.

"As Mr. Mott was suffering from slight infection and sore throat, G. F. Babbitt made the principal talk. Besides outlining the progress of Torrensing real estate titles, Mr. Babbitt spoke in part as follows:

"'In rising to address you, with my impromptu speech carefully

356

tucked into my vest pocket, I am reminded of the story of the two Irishmen, Mike and Pat, who were riding on the Pullman. Both of them, I forgot to say, were sailors in the Navy. It seems Mike had the lower berth and by and by he heard a terrible racket from the upper, and when he yelled up to find out what the trouble was, Pat answered, "Shure an' bedad an' how can I ever get a night's sleep at all, at all? I been trying to get into this darned little hammock ever since eight bells!"

" 'Now, gentlemen, standing up here before you, I feel a good deal like Pat, and maybe after I've spieled along for a while, I may feel so darn small that I'll be able to crawl into a Pullman hammock with no trouble at all, at all!

" 'Gentlemen, it strikes me that each year at this annual occasion when friend and foe get together and lay down the battle-ax and let the waves of good-fellowship waft them up the flowery slopes of amity, it behooves us, standing together eye to eye and shoulder to shoulder as fellow-citizens of the best city in the world, to consider where we are both as regards ourselves and the common weal.

" 'It is true that even with our 361,000, or practically 362,000, population, there are, by the last census, almost a score of larger cities in the United States. But, gentlemen, if by the next census we do not stand at least tenth, then I'll be the first to request any knocker to remove my shirt and to eat the same, with the compliments of G. F. Babbitt, Esquire! It may be true that New York, Chicago, and Philadelphia will continue to keep ahead of us in size. But aside from these three cities, which are notoriously so overgrown that no decent white man, nobody who loves his wife and kiddies and God's good out-o'-doors and likes to shake the hand of his neighbor in greeting, would want to live in them —and let me tell you right here and now, I wouldn't trade a high-class Zenith acreage development for the whole length and breadth of Broadway or State Street!—aside from these three, it's evident to any one with a head for facts that Zenith is the finest example of American life and prosperity to be found anywhere.

" 'I don't mean to say we're perfect. We've got a lot to do in the way of extending the paving of motor boulevards, for, believe me, it's the fellow with four to ten thousand a year, say, and an automobile and a nice little family in a bungalow on the edge of town, that makes the wheels of progress go round!

" 'That's the type of fellow that's ruling America to-day; in fact, it's the ideal type to which the entire world must tend, if there's to be a decent, well-balanced, Christian, go-ahead future for this little old planet! Once in a while I just naturally sit back and size up this Solid American Citizen, with a whale of a lot of satisfaction.

" 'Our Ideal Citizen—I picture him first and foremost as being busier than a bird-dog, not wasting a lot of good time in day-dreaming or going to sassiety teas or kicking about things that are none of his business, but putting the zip into some store or profession or art. At night he lights up a good cigar, and climbs into the little old 'bus, and maybe cusses the carburetor, and shoots out home. He mows the lawn, or sneaks in some practice putting, and then he's ready for dinner. After dinner he tells the kiddies a story, or takes the family to the movies, or plays a few fists of bridge, or reads the evening paper, and a chapter or two of some good lively Western novel if he has a taste for literature, and maybe the folks next-door drop in and they sit and visit about their friends and the topics of the day. Then he goes happily to bed, his conscience clear, having contributed his mite to the prosperity of the city and to his own bank-account.

" 'In politics and religion this Sane Citizen is the canniest man on earth; and in the arts he invariably has a natural taste which makes him pick out the best, every time. In no country in the world will you find so many reproductions of the Old Masters and of well-known paintings on parlor walls as in these United States. No country has anything like our number of phonographs, with not only dance records and comic but also the best operas, such as Verdi, rendered by the world's highest-paid singers.

" 'In other countries, art and literature are left to a lot of shabby bums living in attics and feeding on booze and spaghetti, but in America the successful writer or picture-painter is indistinguishable from any other decent business man; and I, for one, am only too glad that the man who has the rare skill to season his message with interesting reading matter and who shows both purpose and pep in handling his literary wares has a chance to drag down his fifty thousand bucks a year, to mingle with the biggest executives on terms of perfect equality, and to show as big a house and as swell a car as any Captain of Industry! But, mind you, it's the appreciation of the Regular Guy who I have been depicting which has made this possible, and you got to hand as much credit to him as to the authors themselves.

" 'Finally, but most important, our Standardized Citizen, even if he is a bachelor, is a lover of the Little Ones, a supporter of the hearthstone which is the basic foundation of our civilization, first, last, and all the time, and the thing that most distinguishes us from the decayed nations of Europe.

" 'I have never yet toured Europe—and as a matter of fact, I don't know that I care to such an awful lot, as long as there's our own mighty cities and mountains to be seen—but, the way I figure it out, there must be a good many of our own sort of folks abroad. Indeed, one of the most enthusiastic Rotarians I ever met boosted the tenets of one-hundred-per-cent pep in a burr that smacked o' bonny Scutlond and all ye bonny braes o' Bobby Burns. But same time, one thing that distinguishes us from our good brothers, the hustlers over there, is that they're willing to take a lot off the snobs and journalists and politicians, while the modern American business man knows how to talk right up for himself, knows how to make it good and plenty clear that he intends to run the works. He doesn't have to call in some highbrow hired-man when it's necessary for him to answer the crooked critics of the sane and efficient life. He's not dumb, like the old-fashioned merchant. He's got a vocabulary and a punch.

" 'With all modesty, I want to stand up here as a representative business man and gently whisper, "Here's our kind of folks! Here's the specifications of the Standardized American Citizen! Here's the new generation of Americans: fellows with hair on their chests and smiles in their eyes and adding-machines in their offices. We're not doing any boasting, but we like ourselves first-rate, and if you don't like us, look out—better get under cover before the cyclone hits town!"

" 'So! In my clumsy way I have tried to sketch the Real He-man, the fellow with Zip and Bang. And it's because Zenith has so large a proportion of such men that it's the most stable, the greatest of our cities. New York also has its thousands of Real Folks, but New York is cursed with unnumbered foreigners. So are Chicago and San Francisco. Oh, we have a golden roster of cities—Detroit and Cleveland with their renowned factories, Cincinnati with its great machine-tool and soap products, Pittsburg and Birmingham with their steel, Kansas City and

Minneapolis and Omaha that open their bountiful gates on the bosom of the ocean-like wheatlands, and countless other magnificent sister-cities, for, by the last census, there were no less than sixty-eight glorious American burgs with a population of over one hundred thousand! And all these cities stand together for power and purity, and against foreign ideas and communism—Atlanta with Hartford, Rochester with Denver, Milwaukee with Indianapolis, Los Angeles with Scranton, Portland, Maine, with Portland, Oregon. A good live wire from Baltimore or Seattle or Duluth is the twin-brother of every like fellow booster from Buffalo or Akron, Fort Worth or Oskaloosa!

" 'But it's here in Zenith, the home for manly men and womanly women and bright kids, that you find the largest proportion of these Regular Guys, and that's what sets it in a class by itself; that's why Zenith will be remembered in history as having set the pace for a civilization that shall endure when the old time-killing ways are gone forever and the day of earnest efficient endeavor shall have dawned all round the world!

" 'Some time I hope folks will quit handing all the credit to a lot of moth-eaten, mildewed, out-of-date, old, European dumps, and give proper credit to the famous Zenith spirit, that clean fighting determination to win Success that has made the little old Zip City celebrated in every land and clime, wherever condensed milk and pasteboard cartons are known! Believe me, the world has fallen too long for these worn-out countries that aren't producing anything but boot-blacks and scenery and booze, that haven't got one bathroom per hundred people, and that don't know a loose-leaf ledger from a slip-cover; and it's just about time for some Zenithite to get his back up and holler for a show-down!

" 'I tell you, Zenith and her sister-cities are producing a new type of civilization. There are many resemblances between Zenith and these other burgs, and I'm darn glad of it! The extraordinary, growing, and sane standardization of stores, offices, streets, hotels, clothes, and newspapers throughout the United States shows how strong and enduring a type is ours.

" 'I always like to remember a piece that Chum Frink wrote for the newspapers about his lecture-tours. It is doubtless familiar to many of you, but if you will permit me, I'll take a chance and read it. It's one of the classic poems, like "If" by Kipling, or Ella Wheeler Wilcox's "The

Man Worth While"; and I always carry this clipping of it in my note-book:

When I am out upon the road, a poet with a pedler's load I mostly sing a hearty song, and take a chew and hike along, a-handing out my samples fine of Cheero Brand of sweet sunshine, and peddling optimistic pokes and stable lines of japes and jokes to Lyccums and other folks, to Rotarys, Kiwanis' Clubs, and feel I ain't like other dubs. And then old Major Silas Satan, a brainy cuss who's always waitin', he gives his tail a lively quirk, and gets in quick his dirty work. He fills me up with mully-grubs; my hair the backward way he rubs; he makes me lonelier than a hound, on Sunday when the folks ain't round. And then b' gosh, I would prefer to never be a lecturer, a-ridin' round in classy cars and smoking fifty-cent cigars, and never more I want to roam; I simply want to be back home, a-eatin' flap-jacks, hash, and ham, with folks who savvy whom I am!

But when I get that lonely spell, I simply seek the best hotel, no mat-ter in what town I be—St. Paul, Toledo, or K.C., in Washington, Sche-nectady, in Louisville or Albany. And at that inn it hits my dome that I again am right at home. If I should stand a lengthy spell in front of that first-class hotel, that to the drummers loves to cater, across from some big film theayter; if I should look around and buzz, and wonder in what town I was, I swear that I could never tell! For all the crowd would be so swell, in just the same fine sort of jeans they wear at home, and all the queens with spiffy bonnets on their beans, and all the fellows standing round a-talkin' always, I'll be bound, the same good jolly kind of guff, 'bout autos, politics and stuff and baseball players of renown that Nice Guys talk in my home town!

Then when I entered that hotel, I'd look around and say, "Well, well!" For there would be the same news-stand, same magazines and candies grand, same smokes of famous standard brand, I'd find at home, I'll tell! And when I saw the jolly bunch come waltzing in for eats at lunch, and squaring up in natty duds to platters large of French Fried spuds, why then I'd stand right up and bawl, "I've never left my home at all!" And all replete I'd sit me down beside some guy in derby brown upon a lobby chair of plush, and murmur to him in a rush, "Hello, Bill, tell me, good old scout, how is your stock a-holdin' out?" Then we'd be off, two solid pals, a-chatterin' like giddy gals of flivvers, weather, home,

*and wives, lodge-brothers then for all our lives! So when Sam Satan
makes you blue, good friend, that's what I'd up and do, for in these
States where'er you roam, you never leave your home sweet home.*

" 'Yes, sir, these other burgs are our true partners in the great game
of vital living. But let's not have any mistake about this. I claim that
Zenith is the best partner and the fastest-growing partner of the whole
caboodle. I trust I may be pardoned if I give a few statistics to back up
my claims. If they are old stuff to any of you, yet the tidings of prosperity, like the good news of the Bible, never become tedious to the ears
of a real hustler, no matter how oft the sweet story is told! Every intelligent person knows that Zenith manufactures more condensed milk
and evaporated cream, more paper boxes, and more lighting-fixtures,
than any other city in the United States, if not in the world. But it is
not so universally known that we also stand second in the manufacture
of package-butter, sixth in the giant realm of motors and automobiles,
and somewhere about third in cheese, leather findings, tar roofing,
breakfast food, and overalls!

" 'Our greatness, however, lies not alone in punchful prosperity but
equally in that public spirit, that forward-looking idealism and brother-
hood, which has marked Zenith ever since its foundation by the Fathers.
We have a right, indeed we have a duty toward our fair city, to announce broadcast the facts about our high schools, characterized by their
complete plants and the finest school-ventilating systems in the country, bar none; our magnificent new hotels and banks and the paintings
and carved marble in their lobbies; and the Second National Tower,
the second highest business building in any inland city in the entire
country. When I add that we have an unparalleled number of miles of
paved streets, bathrooms, vacuum cleaners, and all the other signs of
civilization; that our library and art museum are well supported and
housed in convenient and roomy buildings; that our park-system is more
than up to par, with its handsome driveways adorned with grass, shrubs,
and statuary, then I give but a hint of the all-round unlimited greatness
of Zenith!

" 'I believe, however, in keeping the best to the last. When I remind
you that we have one motor car for every five and seven-eighths persons in the city, then I give a rock-ribbed practical indication of the kind
of progress and braininess which is synonymous with the name Zenith!

" 'But the way of the righteous is not all roses. Before I close I must call your attention to a problem we have to face, this coming year. The worst menace to sound government is not the avowed socialists but a lot of cowards who work under cover—the long-haired gentry who call themselves "liberals" and "radicals" and "non-partisan" and "intelligentsia" and God only knows how many other trick names! Irresponsible teachers and professors constitute the worst of this whole gang, and I am ashamed to say that several of them are on the faculty of our great State University! The U. is my own Alma Mater, and I am proud to be known as an alumni, but there are certain instructors there who seem to think we ought to turn the conduct of the nation over to hoboes and roustabouts.

" 'Those profs are the snakes to be scotched—they and all their milk-and-water ilk! The American business man is generous to a fault, but one thing he does demand of all teachers and lecturers and journalists: if we're going to pay them our good money, they've got to help us by selling efficiency and whooping it up for rational prosperity! And when it comes to these blab-mouth, fault-finding, pessimistic, cynical University teachers, let me tell you that during this golden coming year it's just as much our duty to bring influence to have those cusses fired as it is to sell all the real estate and gather in all the good shekels we can.

" 'Not till that is done will our sons and daughters see that the ideal of American manhood and culture isn't a lot of cranks sitting around chewing the rag about their Rights and their Wrongs, but a God-fearing, hustling, successful, two-fisted Regular Guy, who belongs to some church with pep and piety to it, who belongs to the Boosters or the Rotarians or the Kiwanis, to the Elks or Moose or Red Men or Knights of Columbus or any one of a score of organizations of good, jolly, kidding, laughing, sweating, upstanding, lend-a-handing Royal Good Fellows, who plays hard and works hard, and whose answer to his critics is a square-toed boot that'll teach the grouches and smart alecks to respect the He-man and get out and root for Uncle Samuel, U.S.A.!' "

IV

Babbitt promised to become a recognized orator. He entertained a Smoker of the Men's Club of the Chatham Road Presbyterian Church with Irish, Jewish, and Chinese dialect stories.

But in nothing was he more clearly revealed as the Prominent Citizen than in his lecture on "Brass Tacks Facts on Real Estate," as delivered before the class in Sales Methods at the Zenith Y.M.C.A.

The *Advocate-Times* reported the lecture so fully that Vergil Gunch said to Babbitt, "You're getting to be one of the classiest spellbinders in town. Seems 's if I couldn't pick up a paper without reading about your well-known eloquence. All this guff ought to bring a lot of business into your office. Good work! Keep it up!"

"Go on, quit your kidding," said Babbitt feebly, but at this tribute from Gunch, himself a man of no mean oratorical fame, he expanded with delight and wondered how, before his vacation, he could have questioned the joys of being a solid citizen.

Franklin P. Adams
PILGRIM DADS LAND ON
MASS. COAST TOWN

In a modern variation of an old satiric trick, Adams gives us a new perspective on a familiar topic. The effect is two-edged; we not only look differently on the Pilgrim Landing, but we also laugh at the stylized approach of the modern newspaper.

PILGRIM DADS
LAND ON MASS.
COAST TOWN
Intrepid Band of Britons, Seeking Faith's
Pure Shrine, Reach Rock-Bound
Coast, Singing Amid Storm

PROVINCETOWN, MASS., Dec. 21—Poking her nose through the fog, the ship *Mayflower,* of Southampton, Jones, Master, limped into port tonight.

On board were men with hoary hair and women with fearless eyes, 109 in all.

Asked why they made the journey, they alleged that religious freedom was the goal they sought here.

The *Mayflower* carried a cargo of antique furniture.

Among those on board were William Bradford, M. Standish, Jno. Alden, Peregrine White, John Carver and others.

Steps are being taken to organize a society of Mayflower Descendants.

THE RICH MAN

Adams again sets us up for the unexpected.

The rich man has his motorcar,
His country and his town estate.
He smokes a fifty-cent cigar
And jeers at Fate.

He frivols through the livelong day,
He knows not Poverty her pinch.
His lot seems light, his heart seems gay.
He has a cinch.

Yet though my lamp burns low and dim,
Though I must slave for livelihood—
Think you that I would change with him?
You bet I would!

John Betjeman
IN WESTMINSTER ABBEY

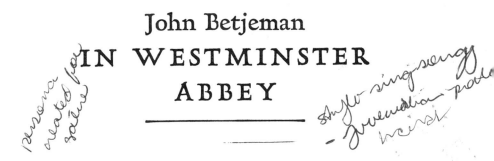

John Betjeman (b. 1906) often writes apparently light verse for a deadly serious satiric purpose. In much of his writing, as in this poem, he uses a geographical or architectural setting as a vehicle for his social or satirical point.

Let me take this other glove off
   As the *vox humana* swells,
And the beauteous fields of Eden
   Bask beneath the Abbey bells.
Here, where England's statesmen lie,
Listen to a lady's cry.

Gracious Lord, oh bomb the Germans.
   Spare their women for Thy Sake,
And if that is not too easy
   We will pardon Thy Mistake.
But, gracious Lord, whate'er shall be,
Don't let anyone bomb me.

Keep our Empire undismembered
   Guide our Forces by Thy Hand,
Gallant blacks from far Jamaica,
   Honduras and Togoland;
Protect them Lord in all their fights,
And, even more, protect the whites.

Think of what our Nation stands for,
  Books from Boots' and country lanes,
Free speech, free passes, class distinction,
  Democracy and proper drains.
Lord, put beneath Thy special care
One-eighty-nine Cadogan Square.

Although dear Lord I am a sinner,
  I have done no major crime;
Now I'll come to Evening Service
  Whensoever I have the time.
So, Lord, reserve for me a crown,
And do not let my shares go down.

I will labour for Thy Kingdom,
  Help our lads to win the war,
Send white feathers to the cowards
  Join the Women's Army Corps,
Then wash the Steps around Thy Throne
In the Eternal Safety Zone.

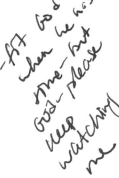

Now I feel a little better,
  What a treat to hear Thy Word,
Where the bones of leading statesmen,
  Have so often been interr'd.
And now, dear Lord, I cannot wait
Because I have a luncheon date.

W. H. Auden
THE UNKNOWN
CITIZEN

W. H. Auden (b. 1907), British born and educated, has also lived, taught, and written in the United States. One critic has called him the "extremely unofficial Anglo-American laureate." The social concerns implicit in this poem—the loss of identity, the disappearance of a sense of humanity, the effects of technocracy—have long been a part of his poetic make-up.

(To JS/07/M/378
This Marble Monument
Is Erected by the State)

He was found by the Bureau of Statistics to be
One against whom there was no official complaint,
And all the reports on his conduct agree
That, in the modern sense of an old-fashioned word, he was a saint,
For in everything he did he served the Greater Community.
Except for the War till the day he retired
He worked in a factory and never got fired,
But satisfied his employers, Fudge Motors Inc.
Yet he wasn't a scab or odd in his views,
For his Union reports that he paid his dues,
(Our report on his Union shows it was sound)
And our Social Psychology workers found
That he was popular with his mates and liked a drink.
The Press are convinced that he bought a paper every day

369

And that his reactions to advertisements were normal in every way.
Policies taken out in his name prove that he was fully insured,
And his Health-card shows he was once in hospital but left it cured.
Both Producers Research and High-Grade Living declare
He was fully sensible to the advantages of the Instalment Plan
And had everything necessary to the Modern Man,
A phonograph, a radio, a car and a frigidaire.
Our researchers into Public Opinion are content
That he held the proper opinions for the time of year;
When there was peace, he was for peace; when there was war, he
      went.
He was married and added five children to the population,
Which our Eugenist says was the right number for a parent of his
      generation,
And our teachers report that he never interfered with their educa-
      tion.
Was he free? Was he happy? The question is absurd:
Had anything been wrong, we should certainly have heard.

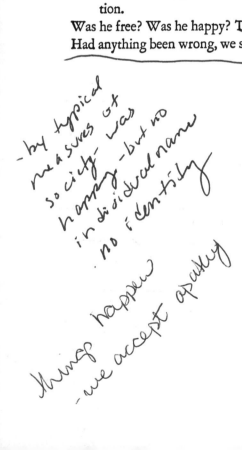

370

Kenneth Fearing
DIRGE

Kenneth Fearing (1902–1961) was preoccupied in his prose and poetry with the human effects of the American Depression. His "Dirge" is for the faceless, nameless businessman, victim of forces he helped create and could not control.

1–2–3 was the number he played but today the number came 3–2–1;
Bought his Carbide at 30 and it went to 29; had the favorite at Bowie
but the track was slow—

O executive type, would you like to drive a floating-power, knee-action,
silk-upholstered six? Wed a Hollywood star? Shoot the course in
58? Draw to the ace, king, jack?
O fellow with a will who won't take no, watch out for three cigarettes
on the same, single match; O democratic voter born in August
under Mars, beware of liquidated rails—

Denouement to denouement, he took a personal pride in the certain,
certain way he lived his own, private life,
But nevertheless, they shut off his gas; nevertheless, the bank fore-
closed; nevertheless, the landlord called; nevertheless, the radio
broke,

And twelve o'clock arrived just once too often,
Just the same he wore one gray tweed suit, bought one straw hat, drank
one straight Scotch, walked one short step, took one long look,
drew one deep breath,
Just one too many,

And wow he died as wow he lived,
Going whop to the office and blooie home to sleep and biff got married
and bam had children and oof got fired,
Zowie did he live and zowie did he die,

With who the hell are you at the corner of his casket, and where the
hell're we going on the right-hand silver knob, and who the hell
cares walking second from the end with an American Beauty
wreath from why the hell not,

Very much missed by the circulation staff of the New York Evening
Post; deeply, deeply mourned by the B.M.T.
Wham, Mr. Roosevelt; pow, Sears Roebuck; awk, big dipper; bop,
summer rain;
Bong, Mr., bong, Mr., bong, Mr., bong.

Henry Reed
NAMING OF PARTS

In this poem Reed uses a parody of the mechanically repeti-
tive training lecture to satirize the madness of war and of
its victims. The bored trainee is more interested in the com-
ing season, as the play on Spring *in line 24 suggests,*
than in mastering the nomenclature being disseminated.
(Or is it promulgated?)

To-day we have naming of parts. Yesterday,
We had daily cleaning. And to-morrow morning,
We shall have what to do after firing. But to-day,
To-day we have naming of parts. Japonica
Glistens like coral in all of the neighbouring gardens,
    And to-day we have naming of parts.

This is the lower sling swivel. And this
Is the upper sling swivel, whose use you will see,
When you are given your slings. And this is the piling swivel,
Which in your case you have not got. The branches
Hold in the gardens their silent, eloquent gestures,
    Which in our case we have not got.

This is the safety-catch, which is always released
With an easy flick of the thumb. And please do not let me
See anyone using his finger. You can do it quite easy
If you have any strength in your thumb. The blossoms
Are fragile and motionless, never letting anyone see
    Any of them using their finger.

And this you can see is the bolt. The purpose of this
Is to open the breech, as you see. We can slide it

Rapidly backwards and forwards: we call this
Easing the spring. And rapidly backwards and forwards
The early bees are assaulting and fumbling the flowers:
    They call it easing the Spring.

They call it easing the Spring: it is perfectly easy
If you have any strength in your thumb: like the bolt,
And the breech, and the cocking-piece, and the point of balance,
Which in our case we have not got; and the almond-blossom
Silent in all of the gardens and the bees going backwards and forwards,
    For to-day we have naming of parts.

A. D. Hope
THE KINGS

With a theme like Eliot's in The Love Song of J. Alfred
Prufrock, *Hope uses the symbol of the parasitic tapeworm
to attack the loss of social consciousness and responsibility
in modern technocratic man.*

The lion in deserts royally takes his prey;
Gaunt crags cast back the hunting eagle's scream.
The King of Parasites, delicate, white and blind,
Ruling his world of fable even as they,
Dreams out his greedy and imperious dream
Immortal in the bellies of mankind.

In a rich bath of pre-digested soup,
Warm in the pulsing bowel, safely shut
From the bright ambient horror of sun and air,
His slender segments ripening loop by loop,
Broods the voluptuous monarch of the gut,
The Tapeworm, the prodigious Solitaire.

Alone among the royal beasts of prey
He takes no partner, no imperial mate
Seeks his embrace and bears his clamorous brood;
Within himself, in soft and passionate play,
Two sexes in their vigour celebrate
The raptures of helminthine solitude.

From the barbed crown that hooks him to his host,
The limbless ribbon, a fecund, flat and wet,
Sways as the stream's delicious juices move;

And, as the ripe joints rupture and are lost,
Quivers in the prolonged, delirious jet
And spasm of unremitting acts of love.

And Nature no less prodigal in birth
In savage profusion spreads his royal sway:
Herds are his nurseries till the mouths of men,
At public feasts, or the domestic hearth,
Or by the hands of children at their play,
Transmit his line to human flesh again.

The former times, as emblems of an age,
Graved the gier-eagle's pride, the lion's great heart,
Leviathan sporting in the perilous sea;
Pictured on History's or the Muse's page,
All knew the King, the Hero, set apart
To stand up stiff against calamity,

Breed courage amid a broken nation's groans,
Cherish the will in men about to die,
To chasten with just rule a barbarous tribe
And guard, at last, the earth that kept his bones.
And still the Muse, who does not flatter or lie,
Finds for our age a symbol to describe

The secret life of Technocratic Man,
Abject desire, base fear that shape his law,
His idols of the cave, the mart, the stye—
No lion at bay for a beleaguered clan,
No eagle with the serpent in his claw,
Nor dragon soter [1] with his searing eye,

But the great, greedy, parasitic worm,
Sucking the life of nations from within,
Blind and degenerate, snug in excrement.
"Behold your dream!" she says, "View here the form
And mirror of Time, the Shape you trusted in
While your world crumbled and my heavens were rent."

[1] One who delivers from a dragon's clutches.

Philip Wylie
from
GENERATION OF
VIPERS

Diatribe, vituperation, invective, jeremiad—these are the terms most commonly used to describe Generation of Vipers, Wylie's abusive satire on American types, attitudes, and institutions, first published in 1942 and now an American classic. In 1955, for the twentieth printing of the book, Wylie wrote an Introduction and about fifty footnotes, many of them pointing out how his prophecies had, in fact, come about. The Introduction is especially fascinating to students of satire because in it Wylie reveals that odd combination of love, anger, and frustration which, in the right person at the right time, leads to satire. The Introduction is not itself satiric, but it shows in his own words how the author of as strong a frontal attack upon our cherished myths as has ever been written is motivated by surprisingly humane and civilized drives.

INTRODUCTION TO THE TWENTIETH PRINTING

Some while ago my publishers informed me that the twentieth printing of "Generation of Vipers" would soon go to press. They asked me if I would like to amend it in such a way as to bring it up to date. "Vipers," as the book is called by its fans, was written thirteen years ago. It is not "dated" but it does exhibit the lapse of time: much that is mere prediction in the text as it stands has become history.

However, I feel that the re-writing of a book of opinion is a kind of cheating; it is not comparable, for instance, to the revision of a scientific

377

work. What an author asserted in 1942 shows, in 1955, how wise (or foolish!) he was in the past; so he ought now to stand (or fall) on the fact of what he wrote then. The continuous revision of history to suit the insights or prejudices of the present is craven and nefarious—an enterprise suited to characters in "1984" or to demagogues.

I told my publishers I would read "Vipers" (I had not read fifty pages in a decade) and thereafter, if any comments came to my mind, I would make them—as footnotes. Somewhat to my surprise, it turned out that I wanted to add or to exclaim about something at fifty-odd points. A number of these "exclamations" relate to the now-demonstrated accuracy of predictions regarded, at the time "Vipers" first appeared, as bordering on insanity. It is, of course, "human" (in a low sense of the word) to take pleasure in saying, "I told you so." But I have a better reason for drawing attention to my record as a Jeremiah, which I shall explain later in this introduction.

"Vipers" has had and is still having a strange history. It was written —I should say it was dashed off—between the twelfth of May and the fourth of July in 1942. That was the year after Pearl Harbor. World War II had commenced. But the period of "phony war" prevailed in Europe, action in the Pacific had hardly begun, and the American people were apathetic. I had come home to Miami Beach after a stretch in "government war information"—ill, discouraged and frustrated. This book represented private catharsis, a catalogue of what I felt to be wrong morally, spiritually and intellectually with my fellow citizens. Since it did not enter my head that millions shared my vexations and anxieties, that they would read the list and remark over it to this day, I did not make—alas!—that careful literary effort such an audience has the right to expect.

Indeed, my principal feeling on re-reading the book was one of regret that I had not gone over a hasty manuscript with patience and with care—to make it easier to understand, more "definitive" and better documented with the sources of theories and ideas.

My publishers (then Farrar and Rinehart, now Rinehart and Company) reacted to the manuscript with some shock. I have since been asked, hundreds and hundreds of times, how I "managed" to get so much "criticism and truth published in America." The question has always discomfited me. It implies that a great many persons take it for granted that our country enjoys no actual freedom of speech. It should be pointed out, then, that such haunted notions are false and disclose the very kind of fears which, if held widely enough, *do* lead to censorship—by general default.

While my publishers did not by any means agree with every contentious and dissenting opinion in my manuscript, they asked only that I delete one or two libelous passages and one scandalous item. I was not an "important" author to them in the sense that my past books had enjoyed large sales. But Stanley Rinehart and John Farrar, for all the blood flowing from their personal icons, published my book without tremor or quibble. They knew it would mightily offend many highly placed individuals and many powerful minority groups. They thought, perhaps, (as I thought) that it might offend *everybody*. But they brought it out with utter aplomb and their usual skill—in January of 1943.

They did this, I might add, in the face of doubt expressed by some of their readers and the violent assertion (made by a famous "liberal" who was shown the manuscript) that the book was "fascist" and should be suppressed. My publishers, as much as I, were annoyed that a "liberal" would suddenly clamor for book suppression!

The first edition was of four thousand copies, a number commensurate with sales of my previous books and one I thought high for the current treatise. Even before publication, however, I began to have an inkling of what was to come. An extraordinarily praiseful letter was written to Farrar and Rinehart by Taylor Caldwell, who had been sent a pre-publication copy. A wire also came from Earnest Hooton, the late Harvard anthropologist, which wound up: PUT OUT THE LANTERN OF DIOGENES FOR HERE BY GOD IN THE PLAIN LIGHT OF DAY IS AN HONEST MAN. And, on the Sunday before publication, Walter Winchell (with whom I had long labored in the "Stop Hitler" movement) highly recommended "Vipers" in his evening broadcast. The four thousand copies melted fast enough.

The book has now sold more than one hundred and eighty thousand copies and its recent annual sales have approximated five thousand.

Criticisms were mixed but never neutral; reviewers went out of their way to commend the book or to seek terms of scorn that matched my own. The response of *readers,* however, was awesome—and remains so.

This may be partly owing to the fact that I invited correspondence in the forematter of the book. People possibly hesitate to write to authors for fear of being snubbed by silence; if so, my casual invitation undid that restraint. In the first year after publication I answered more than ten thousand letters.

They came from every sort of American—from soldiers and sailors and marines overseas, from ministers of the Gospel and Middle Western farmers' wives, from day laborers who "read the book five times over with the help of a dictionary," from young people in college and high school, from moms and pops—the very people I had indicted— from industrial tycoons and newspaper publishers and the presidents of banks, from college deans and generals and admirals, from Aldous Huxley and the late Harold Ickes and Hedy LaMarr. And more than ninety-five in every hundred *liked* "Vipers"!

In the years that have passed since then I have heard from fifty or sixty thousand people. "Vipers" has become a kind of "standard work" for Americans who love liberty, detest smugness and are anxious about the prospects of our nation. It has been studied by scores of Bible classes. It has also been proscribed by Catholics. It has been quoted in unrecorded dozens of other books; it is "compulsory reading" in hundreds of college English and journalism classes. In 1950 it was selected by The American Library Association as one of the major nonfiction works of the first half century. It was used, during the war, as an instrument for "briefing" those British officers who were to have contact with our troops, on the nature and neuroses of *genus homo, race Americanus.* And it no longer seems possible for any author, lay or scientific, to discuss motherhood and mom without noting that the dark side of that estate was defined earlier by me.

Those are but a few of the vicissitudes of "Vipers." I daresay this new, annotated edition will augment their number and their bewildering nature.

Two reactions to "Vipers" are common enough to warrant brief discussion here.

A great many people have asked me, often with evident anguish, this question: Are you sincere?

It is easy enough to reply, "Lord, yes!"

A far larger number of people appreciated my sincerity. And that number increases hourly, in potential, as it dawns on one American at a time that our situation in the Atomic Age is progressively of so dreadful a danger as to make it certain that, somewhere, somehow, we Americans have failed to achieve even a vestige of our goal of security. But the people who thought or feared that I was insincere are worthy of particular scrutiny.

Some may be, of course, merely literal-minded: persons who cannot believe that a man who will make a joke is really serious about anything —especially if his joke partakes of gallows humor. I suspect, however, on the good grounds of myriads of communications, that many are people who have so often felt themselves fooled or kidded or betrayed— by politicians and by supercilious authors—that they have grown skeptical of everybody's integrity. They would *like* to believe that, when a man lambastes hypocrisy, he is disgusted and deliberate—not just having private fun. They would *like* to feel that when a man stands up in their midst and yells, "To hell with it!" he is morally indignant—and not just trying to attract attention to himself. But they dare not. It is sad to learn that many Americans evidently feel within themselves a sense of being so often "sold out" that the most passionate sincerity puts them in quandary: they want to believe it—but they hate to risk being made suckers one more sorry time.

They are discouraged people, cynical without knowing it, robbed of self-confidence, intimidated, not very capable as citizens—and they are numerous.

A commoner and even more sobering reaction to "Vipers" concerned its concentration upon criticism and derogation. That was intended to stimulate constructive thought. I would not damn a traditional idea or circumstance or attitude that I did not believe could be improved: if I will not re-write history neither will I resent or regret the past, as do so many frantic authors these days. But to criticize or anathematize what men believe *now*, and are doing and saying *now*, is another matter: it is the *only* way to bring to the future any hope of betterment.

For a little thought will show that no improvement can be made in any object or idea until a criticism has first been made. If there is no criticism, if no fault is found, the object or idea will be regarded as perfect, or as not subject to favorable alteration; its status quo will thus be assured automatically. A better mousetrap, or a better automobile, or a better concept of freedom, may *seem* to occur as inspiration; but no such "inspiration" is possible unless the inspired mind has first perceived the existing mousetrap, automobile or concept to be inadequate.

Criticism, that is to say, and the *doubt* out of which it arises, are the prior conditions to progress of any sort. The intent of "Vipers" was and is to provide a body of exactly that sort of criticism, that sort of doubt and self-doubt.

The *critical attitude,* however, is mistrusted in America, for all its fundamental place in any pattern of progress. Formal criticism as such, while allowable, is regarded as an exercise of "longhairs" or "eggheads." All criticism is thought by millions to border on subversion especially when it becomes criticism of America or of popular American attitudes. "Boost, don't knock," has replaced the Golden Rule as the allegedly proper means to the American Way of Life.

That is partly the result of the infinite boosting of advertising along with the "chamber-of-commerce mentality" of most businessmen, and partly the by-product of censorship imposed from within (and often from without, by minority pressures) on our mass media of communication. Three whole categories of national behavior are very nearly immune to criticism in mass media—as I have proven by a sociological experiment performed since the writing of "Vipers." These "sacred" areas are: *sex, business* and *religion!* Such extensive "sanctity" leaves very little room for the critical function in the press, radio, TV, movies and magazines.

The result is to keep the American majority not just intellectually *un*critical but *anti*-critical. This situation means that to progress even a little, Americans must behave in a somewhat schizoid manner: hiding from themselves that they are "knocking" and not "boosting" wherever they find a need for improvement. We do not even say, "Chicago is a big slum," when we want to clear its slums; we say, "Let's make Chicago even *more* magnificent." In such ways, even when we are self-critical, we delude ourselves about the value of the critical function. A poisonous self-infatuation ensues—a blind bullheadedness, unwarranted by reality.

To people with that orientation—people who imagine that the "right" approach to any problem *must* involve optimism—"Vipers" was a great shock. For "Vipers" suggests that downright pessimism, in this day and age, may be a more fruitful source of national improvement (and even a surer road to mere survival) than all the compulsive optimism the public can pump up concerning its wonderful self. In this book I am plainly out looking for "what's wrong" and, during that pursuit, not interested in "what's right" or "what's magnificent"—whether about Chicago, or USA or common man himself. That many things are "right" is acknowledged—and ignored. For if the "wrongs" I see be great enough (left unexamined) to undo us all (and I believe they may be), they deserve our concentrated attention.

That *deliberate* fixation of my mind appalled many readers. They could see no "hope" in a book written to indicate *which way real hope lay.* "If what you say is true," a great many wrote me, "there is no use going on." And those same people often continued with the statement that they agreed with what I said! Three or four times, in the past thirteen years I have had to rush to the telephone or the telegraph office to get in touch with correspondents whose despondency, after reading this book, was so great that I honestly feared they meant to carry out plans for suicide described in their letters. I talked to one young lady for an hour while she sat on the window sill of a high floor of a Manhattan skyscraper with a copy of "Vipers" on her lap!

It was necessary to persuade such people that a mere vista of difficulties, however huge and horrid, is not an excuse for abandoning human effort—let alone life itself. Such reactions are extremely *childish.* Unfortunately, many people are just that infantile. A great many Americans have given up moral and intellectual effort in behalf of their country simply because it is hard to be moral and to reason.

The way most such persons "give up" is to decide they are "for" everything they consider "American," just as it stands, and "against" whatever they deem "un-American," and to demand that all of us conform to their particular set of delusions. On the high level of subjectivity, such people are traitors to America: they have not fallen asleep but *put themselves to sleep,* while standing guard over liberty. For if liberty has any meaning it means freedom to improve—i.e., that the right to knock is equal to the right to boost.

To people who became enraged by what they called the "negativism" of this book, I usually gave short shrift. Quite often—to my astonishment—they took my bitter words to heart, re-read the book more thoughtfully, and went forth in their communities to tilt with local dragons! Where the book struck home to individuals, they often wrote to say as much. I have on file, for instance, the confessions of numbers of "moms" who learned here how they had perverted motherhood to selfish ends and who pledged reform.

So much, then, for the vicissitudes of "Vipers" and so much for the responses of people who have read the book and written to or talked with me afterward.

I would wish—if I were a wishful person—that I'd had the foresight to estimate the interest in this random work. It is one thing to sit down in a mood of disappointment (mixed at times with toxic glee) to write, for one's private satisfaction, a bill of particulars against the antics of one's fellows. It is quite another to have that intemperate version of sincere heresies receive such a profound response from a huge, perpetual audience. Had I been able to foretell my future as an author I would surely have been a better one in the pages ahead!

"Vipers" is an important book to many because it looks into a variety of truths often overlooked. To other people, it has importance because it tends to keep open the franchise of freedom: "If Philip Wylie can say thus-and-so in print, why then, before God and as a sincere American, so can I." It has helped many to learn to *think*, for thinking involves the critical method employed here, before it can become "creative thinking" —as I have explained. It has had value as a continuing counterbalance to our dangerous American habit of thinking too well of ourselves—of making self-infatuation the pre-condition of what is deemed "patriotism."

But to me, the main value of this effort is usually disregarded. I said, earlier, that the new footnotes often point to a "prophesy" now proven accurate; and I said I had a better reason than gloating for those notes. I have.

Most of the observations and criticisms in the book derive from the application of the theories of "dynamic psychology"—that is, from a use of the psychological insights of Sigmund Freud and Carl Jung. Those theories concern man, his nature, his motives, his personality and the way his "mind works." They are well understood and highly regarded by some people. Modern medicine is coming more and more to appreciate, for example, how right Freud was in postulating the effect of inner conflict on bodily health. Arnold Toynbee, for another instance, has illuminated the whole of history by showing how men have followed psycho-dynamic laws which were discovered by Jung through studies of the individual. But the average layman, however intelligent, however well-educated, has little understanding of the *philosophical* implications and intellectual values of this very new and not yet very exact branch of science.

It is my hope that by noting here some few of the places in "Vipers" where I showed an insight in 1942 that was not commonplace, but that proved to be correct, I may draw attention not to me but to my *method*.

The test of *any* scientific theory is its accuracy in predictability. A theory is first "given," then "checked" by experiments; if they "come out" as predicted by the theory, the theory itself is accorded credence: it becomes "scientific," a "law of science."

Using the American scene and the state of the world for "experimental material" thirteen years ago, I applied psychodynamic laws. That so many of my "experiments" tallied with, or approximated, subsequent reality (when the great bulk of "prediction" in identical areas was different or contrary—hence fallacious) tends to show, I believe, not that I am a peculiarly bright, prophetic, intuitive or mystically gifted author but that the theory by which I guided myself was far more "correct" than the theories commonly employed. Since "predictability" is a scientific, rational or logical test of *any* method, I hope here to bring new attention to *psychodynamic* methods. For today's hideous history was made by the attitudes of yesterday, the attitudes of 1942 and attitudes a thousand years older than that: much of it was predictable when the attitudes were properly understood.

In 1955—a year far more threatening to American freedom, American security and even to American existence than the year 1942—I would like more people to come to understand a science by which useful insight into what may happen tomorrow may be had, through a special scrutiny of what we are doing—and thinking—right now.

There are numbers of dire predictions in this book which have not come true—*yet*. If enough of us understand the logical concepts which make such disasters foreseeable, I think the lot of us might be led to avoid them. It is this thought, that hope, about which I am *most* sincere:

The learning of science, logic, reason and especially the logics of dynamic psychology, by enough men and women to prevent the needless squandering of a great nation, in which I am one citizen, and the needless death of a great, free people, to whom I belong and whom I try to serve because I love them.

from Chapter XI

COMMON WOMEN

Generation of Vipers *must be read completely to be understood fully. However, the following excerpts from Chapter XI give a fair idea of Wylie's powerful denunciatory technique, a little reminiscent of Juvenal's in his satire on wives. It is in this chapter that Wylie gave the word* momism *to our language.*

Mom, however, is a great little guy. Pulling pants onto her by these words, let us look at mom.

She is a middle-aged puffin with an eye like a hawk that has just seen a rabbit twitch far below. She is about twenty-five pounds overweight, with no sprint, but sharp heels and a hard backhand which she does not regard as a foul but a womanly defense. In a thousand of her there is not sex appeal enough to budge a hermit ten paces off a rock ledge. She none the less spends several hundred dollars a year on permanents and transformations, pomades, cleansers, rouges, lipsticks, and the like—and fools nobody except herself. If a man kisses her with any earnestness, it is time for mom to feel for her pocketbook, and this occasionally does happen.

She smokes thirty cigarettes a day, chews gum, and consumes tons of bonbons and petits fours. The shortening in the latter, stripped from pigs, sheep and cattle, shortens mom. She plays bridge with the stupid voracity of a hammerhead shark, which cannot see what it is trying to gobble but never stops snapping its jaws and roiling the waves with its tail. She drinks moderately, which is to say, two or three cocktails before dinner every night and a brandy and a couple of highballs afterward. She doesn't count the two cocktails she takes before lunch when she lunches out, which is every day she can. On Saturday nights, at the club or in the juke joint, she loses count of her drinks and is liable to get a little tiddly,

386

which is to say, shot or blind. But it is her man who worries about where to acquire the money while she worries only about how to spend it, so he has the ulcers and colitis and she has the guts of a bear; she can get pretty stiff before she topples.

Her sports are all spectator sports.

She was graduated from high school or a "finishing" school or even a college in her distant past and made up for the unhappiness of compulsory education by sloughing all that she learned so completely that she could not pass the final examinations of a fifth grader. She reads the fiction in three women's magazines each month and occasionally skims through an article, which usually angers her so that she gets other moms to skim through it, and then they have a session on the subject over a canister of spiked coffee in order to damn the magazine, the editors, the author, and the silly girls who run about these days. She reads two or three motion-picture fan magazines also, and goes to the movies about two nights a week. If a picture does not coincide precisely with her attitude of the moment, she converses through all of it and so whiles away the time. She does not appear to be lecherous toward the moving photographs as men do, but that is because she is a realist and a little shy on imagination. However, if she gets to Hollywood and encounters the flesh-and-blood article known as a male star, she and her sister moms will run forward in a mob, wearing a joint expression that must make God rue his invention of bisexuality, and tear the man's clothes from his body, yea, verily, down to his B.V.D.'s.

Mom is organization-minded. Organizations, she has happily discovered, are intimidating to all men, not just to mere men. They frighten politicians to sniveling servility and they terrify pastors; they bother bank presidents and they pulverize school boards. Mom has many such organizations, the real purpose of which is to compel an abject compliance of her environs to her personal desires. With these associations and committees she has double parking ignored, for example. With them she drives out of the town and the state, if possible, all young harlots and all proprietors of places where "questionable" young women (though why they are called that—being of all women the least in question) could possibly foregather, not because she competes with such creatures but because she contrasts so unfavorably with them. With her clubs (a solid term!) she causes bus lines to run where they are convenient for her rather than for workers, plants flowers in sordid spots that would do better with sanitation, snaps independent men out of office and replaces them with clammy castrates, throws prodigious fairs and parties for charity and gives the proceeds, usually about eight dollars, to the janitor to buy the committee some beer for its headache on the morning after, and builds clubhouses for the entertainment of soldiers where she succeeds in persuading thousands of them that they are momsick and would rather talk to her than take Betty into the shrubs. All this, of course, is considered social service, charity, care of the poor, civic reform, patriotism, and self-sacrifice.

As an interesting sidelight, clubs afford mom an infinite opportunity for nosing into other people's business. Nosing is not a mere psychological ornament of her; it is a basic necessity. Only by nosing can she uncover all incipient revolutions against her dominion and so warn and assemble her co-cannibals.

Knowing nothing about medicine, art, science, religion, law, sanitation, civics, hygiene, psychology, morals, history, geography, poetry, literature, or any other topic except the all-consuming one of momism, she seldom has any especial interest in *what*, exactly, she is doing as a member of any of these endless organizations, so long as it is *something*.

• • •

Mom also has patriotism. If a war comes, this may even turn into a genuine feeling and the departure of her son may be her means to grace in old age. Often, however, the going of her son is only an occasion for more show. She has, in that case, no deep respect for him. What he has permitted her to do to him has rendered him unworthy of consideration—and she has shown him none since puberty. She does not miss him—only his varletry—but over that she can weep interminably. I have seen the unmistakable evidence in a blue star mom of envy of a gold star mom: and I have a firsthand account by a woman of unimpeachable integrity, of the doings of a shipload of these supermoms-of-the-gold-star, en route at government expense to France to visit the graves of their sons, which I forbear to set down here, because it is a document of such naked awfulness that, by publishing it, I would be inciting to riot, and the printed thing might even rouse the dead soldiers and set them tramping like Dunsany's idol all the way from Flanders to hunt and haunt their archenemy progenitrices—who loved them—to death.

But, peace or war, the moms have another kind of patriotism that, in the department of the human spirit, is identical to commercialized vice, because it captures a good thing and doles it out for the coin of unctuous pride—at the expense of deceased ancestors rather than young female offspring. By becoming a Daughter of this historic war or that, a woman makes herself into a sort of madam who fills the coffers of her ego with the prestige that has accrued to the doings of others. A frantic emptiness of those coffers provides the impulse for the act. There are, of course, other means of filling them, but they are difficult, and mom never does anything that is difficult—either the moving of a piano or the breaking of a nasty habit.

Some legionnaires accept, in a similar way, accolade due their associates only. But legionnaires learned a little wisdom, since they still can function in ways that have some resemblance to normality. Furthermore, competition with the legions from the new war will probably make veritable sages out of thousands.

But mom never meets competition. Like Hitler, she betrays the people who would give her a battle before she brings up her troops. Her whole personal life, so far as outward expression is concerned, is, in consequence, a mopping-up action. Traitors are shot, yellow stars are slapped on those beneath notice, the good-looking men and boys are rounded up and beaten or sucked into pliability, a new slave population continually goes to work at making more munitions for momism, and mom herself sticks up her head, or maybe the periscope of the woman next door, to find some new region that needs taking over. This technique pervades all she does.

In the matter of her affiliation of herself with the Daughters of some war the Hitler analogue especially holds, because these sororities of the sword often constitute her Party—her shirtism. Ancestor worship, like all other forms of religion, contained an instinctual reason and developed rituals thought to be germane to the reason. People sedulously followed those rituals, which were basically intended to remind them that they, too, were going to be ancestors someday and would have to labor for personal merit in order to be worthy of veneration. But mom's reverence for her bold forebears lacks even a ritualistic significance, and so instructs her in nothing. She is peremptory about historical truth, mandates, custom, fact, and point. She brushes aside the ideals and concepts for which her forebears perished fighting, as if they were the crumbs of melba toast. Instead, she attributes to the noble dead her own immediate and selfish attitudes. She "knows full well what they would have thought and done," and in that whole-cloth trumpery she goes busting on her way.

• • •

Young men whose natures are attuned to a female image with more feelings than mom possesses and different purposes from those of our synthetic archetype of Cinderella-the-go-getter bounce anxiously away from their first few brutal contacts with modern young women, frightened to find their shining hair is vulcanized, their agate eyes are embedded in cement, and their ruby lips casehardened into pliers for the bending males like wire. These young men, fresh-startled by learning that She is a chrome-plated afreet, but not able to discern that the condition is mom's unconscious preparation of somebody's sister for a place in the gynecocracy—are, again, presented with a soft and shimmering resting place, the bosom of mom.

J. F. Powers
THE VALIANT WOMAN

*In this witty story about the infuriating effect of a domi-
neering housekeeper on a long suffering Catholic priest,
Powers makes use of a clever image, the mosquito. Watch
for its innocent appearance in the middle of the story and
its devilish reemergence at the close.*

They had come to the dessert in a dinner that was a shambles. "Well,
John," Father Nulty said, turning away from Mrs. Stoner and to Father
Firman, long gone silent at his own table. "You've got the bishop com-
ing for confirmations next week."

"Yes," Mrs. Stoner cut in, "and for dinner. And if he don't eat any
more than he did last year—"

Father Firman, in a rare moment, faced it. "Mrs. Stoner, the bishop is
not well. You know that."

"And after I fixed that fine dinner and all." Mrs. Stoner pouted in
Father Nulty's direction.

"I wouldn't feel bad about it, Mrs. Stoner," Father Nulty said. "He
never eats much anywhere."

"It's funny. And that new Mrs. Allers said he ate just fine when he
was there," Mrs. Stoner argued, and then spit out, "but she's a damned
liar!"

Father Nulty, unsettled but trying not to show it, said, "Who's Mrs.
Allers?"

"She's at Holy Cross," Mrs. Stoner said.

"She's the housekeeper," Father Firman added, thinking Mrs. Stoner
made it sound as though Mrs. Allers were the pastor there.

"I swear I don't know what to do about the dinner this year," Mrs.
Stoner said.

Father Firman moaned. "Just do as you've always done, Mrs. Stoner."

"Huh! And have it all to throw out! Is that any way to do?"

"Is there any dessert?" Father Firman asked coldly.

Mrs. Stoner leaped up from the table and bolted into the kitchen, mumbling. She came back with a birthday cake. She plunged it in the center of the table. She found a big wooden match in her apron pocket and thrust it at Father Firman.

"I don't like this bishop," she said. "I never did. And the way he went and cut poor Ellen Kennedy out of Father Doolin's will!"

She went back into the kitchen.

"Didn't they talk a lot of filth about Doolin and the housekeeper?" Father Nulty asked.

"I should think they did," Father Firman said. "All because he took her to the movies on Sunday night. After he died and the bishop cut her out of the will, though I hear he gives her a pension privately, they talked about the bishop."

"I don't like this bishop at all," Mrs. Stoner said, appearing with a cake knife. "Bishop Doran—there was the man!"

"We know," Father Firman said. "All man and all priest."

"He did know real estate," Father Nulty said.

Father Firman struck the match.

"Not on the chair!" Mrs. Stoner cried, too late.

Father Firman set the candle burning—it was suspiciously large and yellow, like a blessed one, but he could not be sure. They watched the fluttering flame.

"I'm forgetting the lights!" Mrs. Stoner said, and got up to turn them off. She went into the kitchen again.

The priests had a moment of silence in the candlelight.

"Happy birthday, John," Father Nulty said softly. "Is it fifty-nine you are?"

"As if you didn't know, Frank," Father Firman said, "and you the same but one."

Father Nulty smiled, the old gold of his incisors shining in the flickering light, his collar whiter in the dark, and raised his glass of water, which would have been wine or better in the bygone days, and toasted Father Firman.

"Many of 'em, John."

"Blow it out," Mrs. Stoner said, returning to the room. She waited by the light switch for Father Firman to blow out the candle.

Mrs. Stoner, who ate no desserts, began to clear the dishes into the kitchen, and the priests, finishing their cake and coffee in a hurry, went to sit in the study.

Father Nulty offered a cigar.

"John?"

"My ulcers, Frank."

"Ah, well, you're better off." Father Nulty lit the cigar and crossed his long black legs. "Fish Frawley has got him a Filipino, John. Did you hear?"

Father Firman leaned forward, interested. "He got rid of the woman he had?"

"He did. It seems she snooped."

"Snooped, eh?"

"She did. And gossiped. Fish introduced two town boys to her, said, 'Would you think these boys were my nephews?' That's all, and the next week the paper had it that his two nephews were visiting him from Erie. After that, he let her believe he was going East to see his parents, though both are dead. The paper carried the story. Fish returned and made a sermon out of it. Then he got the Filipino."

Father Firman squirmed with pleasure in his chair. "That's like Fish, Frank. He can do that." He stared at the tips of his fingers bleakly. "You could never get a Filipino to come to a place like this."

"Probably not," Father Nulty said. "Fish is pretty close to Minneapolis. Ah, say, do you remember the trick he played on us all in Marmion Hall!"

"That I'll not forget!" Father Firman's eyes remembered. "Getting up New Year's morning and finding the toilet seats all painted!"

"*Happy Circumcision!* Hah!" Father Nulty had a coughing fit.

When he had got himself together again, a mosquito came and sat on his wrist. He watched it a moment before bringing his heavy hand down. He raised his hand slowly, viewed the dead mosquito, and sent it spinning with a plunk of his middle finger.

"Only the female bites," he said.

"I didn't know that," Father Firman said.

"Ah, yes . . ."

Mrs. Stoner entered the study and sat down with some sewing—Father Firman's black socks.

She smiled pleasantly at Father Nulty. "And what do you think of the atom bomb, Father?"

"Not much," Father Nulty said.

Mrs. Stoner had stopped smiling. Father Firman yawned.

Mrs. Stoner served up another: "Did you read about this communist convert, Father?"

"He's been in the Church before," Father Nulty said, "and so it's not a conversion, Mrs. Stoner."

"No? Well, I already got him down on my list of Monsignor's converts."

"It's better than a conversion, Mrs. Stoner, for there is more rejoicing in heaven over the return of . . . uh, he that was lost, Mrs. Stoner, is found.

"And that congresswoman, Father?"

"Yes. A convert—she."

"And Henry Ford's grandson, Father. I got him down."

"Yes, to be sure."

Father Firman yawned, this time audibly, and held his jaw.

"But he's one only by marriage, Father," Mrs. Stoner said. "I always say you got to watch those kind."

"Indeed you do, but a convert nonetheless, Mrs. Stoner. Remember, Cardinal Newman himself was one."

Mrs. Stoner was unimpressed. "I see where Henry Ford's making steering wheels out of soybeans, Father."

"I didn't see that."

"I read it in the *Reader's Digest* or some place."

"Yes, well . . ." Father Nulty rose and held his hand out to Father Firman. "John," he said. "It's been good."

"I heard Hirohito's next," Mrs. Stoner said, returning to converts.

"Let's wait and see, Mrs. Stoner," Father Nulty said.

The priests walked to the door.

"You know where I live, John."

"Yes. Come again, Frank. Good night."

Father Firman watched Father Nulty go down the walk to his

car at the curb. He hooked the screen door and turned off the porch light. He hesitated at the foot of the stairs, suddenly moved to go to bed. But he went back into the study.

"Phew!" Mrs. Stoner said. "I thought he'd never go. Here it is after eight o'clock."

Father Firman sat down in his rocking chair. "I don't see him often," he said.

"I give up!" Mrs. Stoner exclaimed, flinging the holey socks upon the horsehair sofa. "I'd swear you had a nail in your shoe."

"I told you I looked."

"Well, you ought to look again. And cut your toenails, why don't you? Haven't I got enough to do?"

Father Firman scratched in his coat pocket for a pill, found one; swallowed it. He let his head sink back against the chair and closed his eyes. He could hear her moving about the room, making the preparations; and how he knew them—the fumbling in the drawer for a pencil with a point, the rip of the page from his daily calendar, and finally the leg of the card table sliding up against his leg.

He opened his eyes. She yanked the floor lamp alongside the table, setting the bead fringe tinkling on the shade, and pulled up her chair on the other side. She sat down and smiled at him for the first time that day. Now she was happy.

She swept up the cards and began to shuffle with the abandoned virtuosity of an old river-boat gambler, standing them on end, fanning them out, whirling them through her fingers, dancing them halfway up her arms, cracking the whip over them. At last they lay before him tamed into a neat deck.

"Cut?"

"Go ahead," he said. She liked to go first.

She gave him her faint, avenging smile and drew a card, cast it aside for another which he thought must be an ace from the way she clutched it face down.

She was getting all the cards, as usual, and would have been invincible if she had possessed his restraint and if her cunning had been of a higher order. He knew a few things about leading and lying back that she would never learn. Her strategy was attack, forever attack, with one baffling departure: she might sacrifice certain tricks as expendable if only she could have the last ones, the heartbreaking ones, if she could slap them down one after another, shatteringly.

She played for blood, no bones about it, but for her there was no other way; it was her nature, as it was the lion's, and for this reason he found her ferocity pardonable, more a defect of the flesh, venial, while his own trouble was all in the will, mortal. He did not sweat and pray over each card as she must, but he did keep an eye out for reneging and demanded a cut now and then just to aggravate her, and he was always secretly hoping for aces.

With one card left in her hand, the telltale trick coming next, she delayed playing it, showing him first the smile, the preview of defeat. She laid it on the table—so! She held one more trump than he had reasoned possible. Had she palmed it from somewhere? No, she would not go that far; that would not be fair, was worse than reneging, which so easily and often happened accidentally, and she believed in being fair. Besides he had been watching her.

God smote the vines with hail, the sycamore trees with frost, and offered up the flocks to the lightning—but Mrs. Stoner! What a cross Father Firman had from God in Mrs. Stoner! There were other housekeepers as bad, no doubt, walking the rectories of the world, yes, but . . . yes. He could name one and maybe two priests who were worse off. One, maybe two. Cronin. His craggly blonde of sixty—take her, with her everlasting banging on the grand piano, the gift of the pastor; they were all in the game together. She was worse. She was something her proud talk about the goiter operation at the Mayo Brothers', also a gift; her honking the parish Buick at passing strange priests because to keep the home fires burning. Yes sir. And Cronin said she was not a bad person really, but what was he? He was quite a freak himself.

For that matter, could anyone say that Mrs. Stoner was a bad person? No. He could not say it himself, and he was no freak. She had her points, Mrs. Stoner. She was clean. And though she cooked poorly, could not play the organ, would not take up the collection in an emergency, and went to card parties, and told all—even so, she was clean. She washed everything. Sometimes her underwear hung down beneath her dress like a paratrooper's pants, but it and everything she touched was clean. She washed constantly. She was clean.

She had her other points, to be sure—her faults, you might say. She snooped—no mistake about it—but it was not snooping for snooping's sake; she had a reason. She did other things, always with a reason. She overcharged on rosaries and prayer books, but that was for the sake of the poor. She censored the pamphlet rack, but that was to prevent scandal. She pried into the baptismal and matrimonial records, but there was no other way if Father was out, and in this way she had once uncovered a bastard and flushed him out of the rectory, but that was the perverted decency of the times. She held her nose over bad marriages in the presence of the victims, but that was her sorrow and came from having her husband buried in a mine. And he had caught her telling a bewildered young couple that there was only one good reason for their wanting to enter into a mixed marriage—the child had to have a name, and that—that was what?

She hid his books, kept him from smoking, picked his friends (usually the pastors of her colleagues), bawled out people for calling after dark, had no humor, except at cards, and then it was grim, very grim, and she sat hatchet-faced every morning at Mass. But she went to Mass, which was all that kept the church from being empty some mornings. She did annoying things all day long. She said annoying things into the night. She said she had given him the best years of her life. Had she? Perhaps—for the miner had her only a year. It was too bad, sinfully bad, when he thought of it like that. But all talk of best years and life was nonsense. He had to consider the heart of the matter, the essence. The essence was that housekeepers were hard to get, harder to get than ushers, than willing workers, than organists, than secretaries—yes, harder to get than assistants or vocations.

And she was a *saver*—saved money, saved electricity, saved string, bags, sugar, saved—him. That's what she did. That's what she said she did, and she was right, in a way. In a way, she was usually right. In fact, she was always right—in a way. And you could never get a Filipino to come way out here and live. Not a young one anyway, and he had never seen an old one. Not a Filipino. They liked to dress up and live.

Should he let it drop about Fish having one, just to throw a scare into her, let her know he was doing some thinking? No. It would be a perfect cue for the one about a man needing a woman to look after him. He was not up to that again, not tonight.

397

Now she was doing what she liked most of all. She was making a grand slam, playing it out card for card, though it was in the bag, prolonging what would have been cut short out of mercy in gentle company. Father Firman knew the agony of losing.

She slashed down the last card, a miserable deuce trump, and did in the hapless king of hearts he had been saving.

"Skunked you!"

She was awful in victory. Here was the bitter end of their long day together, the final murderous hour in which all they wanted to say—all he wouldn't and all she couldn't—came out in the cards. Whoever won at honeymoon won the day, slept on the other's scalp, and God alone had to help the loser.

"We've been at it long enough, Mrs. Stoner," he said, seeing her assembling the cards for another round.

"Had enough, huh!"

Father Firman grumbled something.

"No?"

"Yes."

She pulled the table away and left it against the wall for the next time. She went out of the study carrying the socks, content and clucking. He closed his eyes after her and began to get under way in the rocking chair, the nightly trip to nowhere. He could hear her brewing a cup of tea in the kitchen and conversing with the cat. She made her way up the stairs, carrying the tea, followed by the cat, purring.

He waited, rocking out to sea, until she would be sure to be through in the bathroom. Then he got up and locked the front door (she looked after the back door) and loosened his collar going upstairs.

In the bathroom he mixed a glass of antiseptic, always afraid of pyorrhea, and gargled to ward off pharyngitis.

When he turned on the light in his room, the moths and beetles began to batter against the screens, the light insects humming. . . .

Yes, and she had the guest room. How did she come to get that? Why wasn't she in the back room, in her proper place? He knew, if he cared to remember. The screen in the back room—it let in mosquitoes, and if it didn't do that she'd love to sleep back there, Father, looking out at the steeple and the blessed cross on top, Father, if it just weren't for the screen, Father. Very well, Mrs. Stoner, I'll get it fixed or fix it myself.

Oh, could you now, Father? I could, Mrs. Stoner, and I will. In the meantime you take the guest room. Yes, Father, and thank you, Father, the house ringing with amenities then. Years ago, all that. She was a pie-faced girl then, not really a girl perhaps, but not too old to marry again. But she never had. In fact, he could not remember that she had even tried for a husband since coming to the rectory, but, of course, he could be wrong, not knowing how they went about it. God! God save us! Had she got her wires crossed and mistaken him all these years for *that?* *That!* Him! Suffering God! No. That was going too far. That was getting morbid. No. He must not think of that again, ever. No.

But just the same she had got the guest room and she had it yet. Well, did it matter? Nobody ever came to see him any more, nobody to stay overnight anyway, nobody to stay very long . . . not any more. He knew how they laughed at him. He had heard Frank humming all right —before he saw how serious and sad the situation was and took pity— humming, "Wedding Bells Are Breaking Up That Old Gang of Mine." But then they'd always laughed at him for something—for not being an athlete, for wearing glasses, for having kidney trouble . . . and mail coming addressed to Rev. and Mrs. Stoner.

Removing his shirt, he bent over the table to read the volume left open from last night. He read, translating easily, "Eisdem licet cum illis . . . Clerics are allowed to reside only with women about whom there can be no suspicion, either because of a natural bond (as mother, sister, aunt) or of advanced age, combined in both cases with good repute."

Last night he had read it, and many nights before, each time as though this time to find what was missing, to find what obviously was not in the paragraph, his problem considered, a way out. She was not mother, not sister, not aunt, and *advanced age* was a relative term (why, she was younger than he was) and so, eureka, she did not meet the letter of the law—but, alas, how she fulfilled the spirit! And besides it would be a slimy way of handling it after all her years of service. He could not afford to pension her off, either.

He slammed the book shut. He slapped himself fiercely on the back, missing the wily mosquito, and whirled to find it. He took a magazine and folded it into a swatter. Then he saw it—oh, the preternatural cunning of it!—poised in the beard of St. Joseph on the bookcase. He could not hit it there. He teased it away, wanting it to light on the wall, but it knew his thoughts and flew high away. He swung wildly, hoping to stun it, missed, swung back, catching St. Joseph across the neck. The statue fell to the floor and broke.

Mrs. Stoner was panting in the hall outside his door.

"What is it!"

"Mosquitoes!"

"What is it, Father? Are you hurt?"

"Mosquitoes—damn it! And only the female bites!"

Mrs. Stoner, after a moment, said, "Shame on you, Father. She needs the blood for her eggs."

He dropped the magazine and lunged at the mosquito with his bare hand.

She went back to her room, saying, "Pshaw, I thought it was burglars murdering you in your bed."

He lunged again.

Ira Wallach
THE KEEPER OF THE
GELDED UNICORN

*One of the premier parodists of our time, Ira Wallach here
sallies forth against the clichés of the historical romance.*

*An historical romance which breathes life into a little-known episode in
English history.*

*For readers who are interested in comparing money values, one shekel is
roughly equivalent to $2.98.*

"A hogshead of fine wine!"

The barmaid, her eyes wide with admiration, looked at the man who
had shouted his order with such an air of confident gaiety. He was tall,
lean, with broad shoulders, slender hips, eyes that blazed like live coals,
dark unruly hair, and a twinkle in the corner of a mouth which could,
at times, be stern enough to strike terror into the hearts of the greatest
swordsmen on the Continent and in very England itself.

"Come, maid, God wot, 'sblood, marry!" he called. "Did you not
hear me, maid? A hogshead of fine wine!" He pinched her lightly and
took her to bed, after which she brought the wine, her eyes tender and
moist with devotion.

Two public letter writers whispered in a corner. Outside, the cry of
the fishwives could be heard over the shouts of the children laughing
and clapping as the dancing bear performed in the streets thick with
cutpurses.

The barmaid slipped into the kitchen where her father awaited.
"Who is that young gentleman of noble mien, father?" she asked.

Old Robin, keeper of the inn, took one look and gasped. "The Keeper
of the Gelded Unicorn!" he whispered. "The finest sword in England!

'Tis said he was born a foundling and raised in the court of the Duc D'Ambert who lacked a son. The streets of London are paved with the hearts he has broken, cemented by the blood he has spilled. But he is ever a friend to the poor, and a sworn enemy to Guise, the Earl of Essence!"

The barmaid's eyes filled with limpid tears. "Then he is not for me, father!"

Old Robin shook his head sadly. "God wot, no, daughter," he said. "Good Brogo, the blacksmith's half-witted son, will make you a fine husband."

At that moment Guise, the Earl of Essence, successor to many proud titles, strode into the inn, followed by his retinue. Guise might have been called handsome had not cruelty, avarice, and dissipation left their telltale marks on his countenance.

The barmaid hastened to serve him. Guise narrowed his eyes. "A fine ankle," he murmured. His courtiers smirked as Guise fondled the barmaid's left rump. In a moment a shining blade lay across the table.

"Aha! Meeting in rump session with your retinue! Wouldst cross blades now, my lord Guise?"

Guise looked up into a pair of burning eyes. Slowly, he removed his hand from the barmaid's rump. "Your time will come, Warren of Hastings," he spat, addressing the Keeper of the Gelded Unicorn by his true name, known only to those few who suspected from his demeanor that in his blood ran the cold skill of the English, the wild ferocity of the Scotch border chiefs, the lilting, carefree spirit of the Irish, and the soft and murmurous tenderness of the Latin.

Abruptly, Guise rose and left with his retinue. The barmaid approached the table and put her hand timidly upon that of Warren of Hastings. "You should not have done it, my lord," she murmured.

He snapped his fingers. "What if I do start the Thirty Years' War!" he exclaimed in his carefree manner.

England, in the Year of Our Lord 1746, was torn by dissension. The Queen's faction, headed by Warren of Hastings with the loyal aid of France's Count D'Même-Chose, was plotting an anti-Spanish alliance with the Holy Roman Empire and the Palatinate. The King's faction, led by Guise, Earl of Essence, sought instead an alliance with the Saracen, and the Earl was ready to go so far as to sign a secret treaty with the Czar. Richelieu, disturbed by the development of events, vacillated between the two, and only the Huguenots, tied as they were by bonds of kinship and blood to Austro-Hungary, and influenced by the sinister figure of Oliver Cromwell, followed an unswerving path. No one knew in which direction the Winter King would turn, and over all loomed the shadow of Napoleon. Into this maelstrom grimly strode Philip IV of Spain. Lenin remained noncommittal. Little wonder that heads rolled in the Tower, and that on the streets of London Warren of Hastings, at the head of his faithful band, often clashed with the hired cutthroats and Pomeranian mercenaries brought to England by Guise, the Earl of Essence.

Through a dark street, disguised only by a cloak over his face, Warren of Hastings sped toward the palace. Two public letter writers whispered in a corner. The cry of the fishwives could be heard over the shouts of the children laughing and clapping as the dancing bear performed in the streets thick with cutpurses. In a few moments, Warren of Hastings was in the Queen's bedchamber where he took the cloak from his face and murmured, "My lady!"

She walked toward him slowly, her dark hair gleaming under a caul of tinsel, her arms outstretched. "Warren of Hastings," she whispered, "swordsman, warrior, balladeer, courtier, pamphleteer, lover, poet, and patriot!"

He seized her roughly, importunately, and drew her to the window where he laid his cheek athwart her heaving bosom. She yielded momentarily, then turned her face to the darkening sky. "Not now," she whispered, "not now." Then, "Marry," she said, "notice yon white clouds."

"Not so white as thy teeth," he replied, "not half so regular."

Again she freed herself from his embrace. "God wot, Warren, even now my Earl of Guise is approaching Duncanfayne with a horde of Pomeranians. 'Tis said they will lay siege to Duncanfayne this night!"

Warren of Hastings leaped back, his hand instinctively clutching his sword's hilt. "Duncanfayne, where my lady has hidden her treasures!"

She nodded quietly and only a tear betrayed her thoughts.

"And my liege, the King?" asked Warren of Hastings.

"Carousing with Gisette of Lyons." She said it without bitterness although a trace of irony hardened her voice. "Little does he know that Gisette of Lyons is in the pay of Richelieu!"

"More fool he!" murmured Warren of Hastings.

"Sir!" cried the Queen, stirred to sudden wrath, "you are speaking of our lord, the King!"

Warren of Hastings dropped to his knees and pressed her hand against his lips. "Forgive me, dear lady," he pleaded. "I forgot myself."

"I forgive you," she said, forcing his head against the pillow.

"Even now Warren of Hastings, the Keeper of the Gelded Unicorn, is closeted in the Queen's chamber while we march on Duncanfayne," spat Guise as he rode his charger through the murky night, followed by a horde of Pomeranians.

Across the channel rose a faint glow from the fire whereon Joan of Arc was burning. Hammel de Vyl, the Earl's companion and master spy, smiled a dry smile. "More fool he," muttered Hammel.

The Earl snarled lightly. "Is all prepared?" he asked.

Again Hammel laughed, but with no trace of humor. "The guards are bribed, the moat is down, the bridge is up, and our agent has sprained all the spears in Duncanfayne. Warren of Hastings wots not of this."

"Well done, Hammel de Vyl," remarked the Earl, tossing him a bag of doubloons.

The four-master leaned to the wind, the night foam spraying her bow.

"Wet the sails, ye slobberers!" shouted the captain, his teeth trembling in the gale. "Jettison the cargo!"

The sailors sprang to, and overboard went casks, barrels of sprawns, cauls of lichen, two farthingales, and a huge tusk of billingsgate. Leaning against the mainmast, his feet on the mizzen, his face turned to the flying spray, was Warren of Hastings. Near him stood the faithful Edward Masterfield, a youth whose courage and sword most closely matched those of Warren himself.

"God wot, Edward," cried Warren, "little does Guise reck that we shall cut him off at Duncanfayne by sea this night!"

"More fool he," said Edward, his mouth making a grim line as his forefinger tested the edge of his sword.

From the crow's nest far aloft came a sudden call, "Land ahoy!" All eyes turned to the starboard where, across the bow, faintly glimmered the lights from the storm-tossed battlements of Duncanfayne.

Within an hour's time the good ship *Aphrodite* had tied up alongside and a group of silent men, their faces in their cloaks, slipped ashore.

In bloodstained Duncanfayne, Guise, the Earl of Essence, and Hammel de Vyl saw victory within their grasp. Then the Queen would sing a different tune indeed! Richelieu and the Winter King would have to retreat, and the counsel of the Earl of Essence would carry new weight in Venice before the whole province went to the Doges! Even the crown—it was not impossible, nay, it was probable—might revert to the Earl himself, once the King had become sufficiently involved in his wild dream of an *entente* with Bruit van Hotten of Holland!

The Earl himself led his men to the gates of the treasury. But suddenly the door swung open, a strong hand reached out and pulled the Earl within. The door immediately slammed shut against his Pomeranian followers.

Bewildered, the Earl looked about. The floors were strewn with the Queen's jewelry. Upon the table four candles gave the vault its only light. Lined against the walls were the followers of the Queen's faction, and there in the center, his merry eyes still twinkling, stood Warren of Hastings, Keeper of the Gelded Unicorn.

" 'Sblood!" cried Guise.

"How now, Guise," answered Warren, brushing back an unruly lock of curly hair.

"God wot!" retorted the Earl.

"Marry!" laughed Warren in rejoinder, "shall we try the temper of our swords?"

Guise blanched. "Your men," he said, indicating the band that stood against the walls.

"My retinue will not interfere, will you, retinue?"

"Nay, God wot!" they cried as one man.

"Then, have to!" shouted Warren, unsheathing his blade.

The Earl leaped back and bared his sword to the candlelight. For a moment they fenced cautiously. Then the swords locked at the hilt and the two faces met and almost touched. "I shall carve thee for a roast," hissed Guise.

"Let us see who does the roasting and who does the eating," rejoined Warren between clenched teeth.

They separated. The blades flashed. The Earl advanced, taking the offensive. Skillfully, Warren parried the quick thrusts as he retreated around the table. At that moment he caught the eye of Edward Masterfield and turned to smile. It was a mistake of overconfidence, for in that very moment of turning, Guise's swift blade thrust in, cut through doublet, lumpkin, ruffle, and wattles, drawing a thin line of blood upon Warren's shoulder.

" 'Sblood!" cried Warren of Hastings. Quickly he turned to the offensive and brought the duel to the Earl, his lightning blade catching the fine glints of the candlelight. Another bold thrust forward, and bright steel cut flesh on Guise's thigh. Guise withdrew, but Warren was relentless. A few sudden parries, a feint, an *entrechat,* and to the hoarse cry of "Long live the Queen!" a slender blade shot forward and pierced the Earl's throat.

Warren sighed. "Now open the doors," he ordered his men. The doors swung wide. The Pomeranians advanced, but catching sight of the Earl, now dead, they fell back with a cry of horror, and crossed the Channel.

"A good night's work," murmured Edward Masterfield weakly, as he drew a Pomeranian arrow, shot by a fleeing malcontent, from his abdomen.

It was a gay and lighthearted Warren of Hastings who brought the jewels to the Queen's chamber. Although she had lost neither whit nor tittle of her regal bearing, her eyes spoke for her as she said, "You may kiss me, Warren of Hastings."

Wilder and wilder grew Warren's passion. He heard her murmurous, "No, no," but he was his heart's puppet, and he could not deny his Irish, English, Scotch, or Latin blood. In the bed he drew her still closer as they lay in murmurous and ecstatic silence.

Outside the palace two public letter writers whispered in a corner. The cry of the fishwives could be heard over the shouts of the children laughing and clapping as the dancing bear performed in the streets thick with cutpurses.

"And now, beloved lady," cried Warren of Hastings, "on to the War of the Roses!"

Her eyes filled with tears. "Honor will always take thee further afoot than love," she sighed.

"God wot," he replied, bowing his head. Through the window the sun rose on the battlements and on the triumphant standards of the Queen.

Warren of Hastings silently arose from bed and removed his hat. England was safe.

Frank Sullivan
THE CLICHÉ EXPERT
TESTIFIES ON THE ATOM

*One of the wittiest ideas among modern satirists is the cre-
ation of Mr. Arbuthnot, the official, resident expert on
clichés in all matters. Ready to formulate the appropriate
cliché for any occasion, Mr. Arbuthnot is questioned here
on a matter, yes, near and dear to the hearts of all of us—
the atomic energy cliché.*

Q—Mr. Arbuthnot, you're the very man I want to see. I've been
longing to examine you on atomic energy.

A—Well, my boy, you've come to the right party. I believe I can
say that I know all the clichés on the subject.

Q—How can you say that?

A—Without fear of successful contradiction.

Q—I'm glad to hear it. I suspected you would be making a study
of the atomic cliché.

A—A study! Why I've been doing nothing since V–J Day but
listen to the experts explain atomic energy and the bomb on the air,
or editorialize about them in the newspapers. Indeed I *am* the cliché
expert of the atom. You realize of course what the dropping of that
test bomb in the stillness of the New Mexico night did.

Q—What did it do?

A—It ushered in the atomic age, that's what it did. You know what
kind of discovery this is?

Q—What kind?

A—A tremendous scientific discovery.

Q—Could the atomic age have arrived by means of any other verb
than "usher"?

A—No. "Usher" has the priority.

Q—Mr. Arbuthnot, what will never be the same?

A—The world.

Q—Are you pleased?

A—I don't know. The splitting of the atom could prove a boon to mankind. It could pave the way for a bright new world. On the other hand it may spell the doom of civilization as we know it.

Q—You mean that it has—

A—Vast possibilities for good or evil.

Q—At any rate, Mr. Arbuthnot, as long as the bomb had to be discovered, I'm glad we got it first.

A—If you don't mind, I will be the one to recite the clichés here. You asked me to, you know.

Q—I'm sorry.

A—Quite all right. I shudder to think.

Q—What?

A—Of what might have happened if Germany or Japan had got the bomb first.

Q—What kind of race was it between the Allied and German scientists?

A—A close race.

Q—What pressed?

A—Time pressed.

Q—With what kind of energy did the scientists work in their race to get the bomb?

A—Feverish energy. Had the war lasted another six months the Germans might have had the bomb. It boggles.

Q—What boggles?

A—This tremendous scientific discovery boggles the imagination. Also stirs same.

Q—Where do we stand, Mr. Arbuthnot?

A—At the threshold of a new era.

Q—And humanity is where?

A—At the crossroads. Will civilization survive? Harness.

Q—Harness, Mr. Arbuthnot? What about it?

A—Harness and unleash. You had better learn to use those two words, my boy, if you expect to talk about the atom, or write about it, either. They are two words very frequently used. With pea, of course.

Q—Why pea?

A—Oh, everything is in terms of the pea. You know how much U-235 it would take to drive a car to the moon and back?

Q—No, sir. How much?

A—A lump the size of a pea. Know how much U-235 it would take to ring your electric doorbell for twenty million years?

Q—How much, God forbid?

A—A lump the size of a pea. Know how much it would take to lift the Empire State Building twelve miles into the air?

Q—I wish you would let the Empire State Building alone, Mr. Arbuthnot. It is all right where it is.

A—Sorry. It must be lifted twelve miles into the air. Otherwise, do you know who would not be able to understand the practical application, or meaning, of atomic energy?

Q—No. Who?

A—The average layman.

Q—I see. Well, in that case, up she goes. I gather that a lump the size of a pea would do it.

A—Exactly.

Q—You wouldn't settle for a lump the size of a radish, or a bean?

A—Sorry. The pea is the accepted vegetable in these explanations. Do you know what the atomic energy in the lobe of your left ear could do?

Q—What?

A—If harnessed, it could propel a B-29 from Tokyo to San Francisco.

Q—It *could!*

A—Do you know that the energy in every breath you take could send the Twentieth Century Limited from New York to Chicago?

Q—Mercy on us, Mr. Arbuthnot!

A—And the atomic energy in your thumbnail could, if unleashed, destroy a city twice the size of three Seattles. Likewise, the energy in your . . .

Q—For God's sake, stop, Mr. Arbuthnot! You make me feel like a menace to world security in dire need of control by international authority in the interests of world peace. Kindly leave off explaining atomic energy to me in terms so simple a layman can understand. Explain it to me in scientific terms, and the more abstruse the better.

A—Well, listen carefully and I'll give you a highly technical explanation. In the first place the existence of the atom was only suspected. Then Einstein . . . equation . . . nucleus . . . electron . . . bombard . . . proton . . . deuteron . . . radioactive . . . neutron . . . atomic weight . . . beta rays . . . matter . . . split . . . chain reaction . . . gamma rays . . . alpha particles . . . Mme. Curie . . . break down . . . energy . . . end products . . . control . . . impact . . . uranium . . . Dr. Niels Bohr . . . barium . . . orbit . . . Dr. Lise Meitner . . . knowledge pooled . . . Dr. Enrico Fermi . . . military possibilities . . . Dr. Vannevar Bush . . . U-235 . . . isotopes . . . U-238 . . . autocatalytic . . . heavy water . . . New Mexico . . . mushroom-shaped cloud . . . awesome sight . . . fission . . . William L. Laurence . . . and there you had a weapon potentially destructive beyond the wildest nightmares of science. Do I make myself clear?

Q—Perfectly. Now, Mr. Arbuthnot, what is nuclear energy the greatest discovery since?

A—It is the greatest discovery since the discovery of fire. You will find that "Promethean" is the correct adjective to use here.

Q—What does this tremendous scientific discovery do to large armies?

A—It spells the doom of large armies. It also spells the doom of large navies. Likewise, it spells the doom of large air forces. Similarly, as I mentioned earlier, it may spell the doom of civilization. I doubt if so many dooms have been spelled by anything since the phrase was first coined.

Q—When was that, sir?

A—I should imagine at the time gunpowder spelled the doom of the bow and arrow.

Q—What is the atomic bomb a menace to?

A—World order, world peace, and world security.

Q—What must be done to it?

A—It must be controlled by an international authority. The San Francisco Charter must be revised to fit the Atomic Age.

Q—What does the bomb make essential?

A—It makes world unity essential. It makes an international league for peace essential if the world is not to be plunged into a third war which will destroy civilization.

Q—In short, its use must be—

A—Banned.

Q—What kind of plaything is the bomb?

A—A dangerous plaything. A dangerous toy.

Q—What kind of boomerang is it?

A—A potential boomerang.

Q—What else is it?

A—It is the greatest challenge mankind has yet faced. It is also the greatest destructive force in history. It has revolutionary possibilities and enormous significance and its discovery caused international repercussions.

Q—What does the splitting of the atom unleash?

A—The hidden forces of the universe. Vast.

Q—Vast?

A—That's another word you'd better keep at hand if you expect to talk or write about this tremendous scientific discovery. Vast energy, you know. Vast possibilities. Vast implications. Vast prospects; it opens them.

Q—I see. What cannot grasp the full significance of the tremendous scientific discovery?

A—The human mind.

Q—Whose stone is it?

A—The philosopher's stone.

Q—Whose dream?

A—The alchemist's dream.

Q—And whose monster?

A—Frankenstein's monster.

Q—What does it transcend?

A—It transcends the wildest imaginings of Jules Verne.

Q—And of whom else?

A—H. G. Wells.

Q—The fantastic prophecies of these gentlemen have become what?

A—Stern reality.

Q—What does it make seem tame?

A—The adventures of Superman and Flash Gordon.

Q—Very good, Mr. Arbuthnot. Now, then, in addition to ushering in the Atomic Age, what else does this T.S.D. do?

A—It brightens the prospect for the abolition of war but increases the possibility of another war. It adds to the store of human knowledge. It unlocks the door to the mysteries of the universe. It makes flights into interstellar space a possibility. It endangers our security and makes future aggression a temptation.

Q—What has it done to warfare?

A—It has revolutionized warfare, and outmoded it, and may outlaw it. It has changed all existing concepts of military power. It has made current weapons of war obsolete.

Q—And what may it do to cities?

A—It may drive cities underground.

Q—Mr. Arbuthnot, in the happy event that atomic energy is not used destructively, what kind of role will it play?

A—A peacetime role.

Q—Meaning?

A—Meaning cheap power, cheap fuel. A lump of U-235—

Q—The size of a pea?

A—No, not this time—the size of forty pounds of coal would run the entire nation's heating plants all winter.

Q—What would that result in?

A—Sweeping changes in our daily life and unemployment on a hitherto unheard-of scale.

Q—Bringing about what kind of revolution?

A—An industrial revolution.

Q—Mr. Arbuthnot, should we share the secret with other nations?

A—Yes and no.

Q—If the latter, why?

A—Because we can be trusted with it.

Q—Why can we be trusted with it?

A—Because we would use it only in self-defense and as a last resort.

Q—Who could not be trusted with it?

A—Some future Hitler. Some gangster nation. Some future aggressor.

Q—If we should share it, why that?

A—As a gesture of confidence in other nations.

Q—And anyhow—

A—Anyhow, every nation will possess the secret within five years.

Q—Now, Mr. Arbuthnot, can you tell us what is ironic?

A—It is ironic that several of the major contributions to the bomb were made by scientists whom Hitler and Mussolini had exiled.

Q—In other words, Hitler cooked—

A—His own goose.

Q—What else is ironic?

A—The spending of two billions on the bomb, in contrast to the amounts spent on education, public health, slum clearance, and research on cancer and other diseases.

Q—What kind of commentary is that?

A—A sad commentary on our so-called, or vaunted, civilization.

Q—Mr. Arbuthnot, how ready is man for the Atomic Age?

A—As ready as a child is to handle dynamite.

Q—What kind of little boys do the atomic scientists remind you of?

A—Of little boys playing with matches.

Q—What is a possibility of the future?

A—Atomic bombs a hundred times more destructive than the one dropped on Nagasaki.

Q—What is such a discovery known as?

A—It is known as man's conquest of natural forces.

Q—What does such a discovery advance?

A—It advances the frontiers of science.

Q—And what does the invention of this key to world suicide constitute?

A—It constitutes scientific progress.

Russell Maloney
INFLEXIBLE LOGIC

In this short story, Russell Maloney specifically satirizes the probability theory—the theory that, although we cannot say with certainty what will happen in any given instance, we can predict what is likely over a long period of time. More important, however, is his larger satire on the rigidity of the kind of mind that refuses to accept a series of actions which, though highly unlikely, are nevertheless distinctly possible.

When the six chimpanzees came into his life, Mr. Bainbridge was thirty-eight years old. He was a bachelor and lived comfortably in a remote part of Connecticut, in a large old house with a carriage drive, a conservatory, a tennis court, and a well-selected library. His income was derived from impeccably situated real estate in New York City, and he spent it soberly, in a manner which could give offence to nobody. Once a year, late in April, his tennis court was resurfaced, and after that anybody in the neighborhood was welcome to use it; his monthly statement from Brentano's seldom ran below seventy-five dollars; every third year, in November, he turned in his old Cadillac coupé for a new one; he ordered his cigars, which were mild and rather moderately priced, in shipments of one thousand from a tobacconist in Havana; because of the international situation, he had cancelled arrangements to travel abroad, and after due thought had decided to spend his travelling allowance on wines, which seemed likely to get scarcer and more expensive if the war lasted. On the whole, Mr. Bain-

From the *New Yorker*, February 3, 1940. Reprinted by permission; Copr. © 1940 The New Yorker Magazine, Inc.

bridge's life was deliberately, and not too unsuccessfully, modelled after that of an English country gentleman of the late eighteenth century, a gentleman interested in the arts and in the expansion of science, and so sure of himself that he didn't care if some people thought him eccentric.

Mr. Bainbridge had many friends in New York, and he spent several days of the month in the city, staying at his club and looking around. Sometimes he called up a girl and took her out to a theatre and a night club. Sometimes he and a couple of classmates got a little tight and went to a prizefight. Mr. Bainbridge also looked in now and then at some of the conservative art galleries, and liked occasionally to go to a concert. And he liked cocktail parties, too, because of the fine footling conversation and the extraordinary number of pretty girls who had nothing else to do with the rest of their evening. It was at a New York cocktail party, however, that Mr. Bainbridge kept his preliminary appointment with doom. At one of the parties given by Hobie Packard, the stockbroker, he learned about the theory of the six chimpanzees.

It was almost six-forty. The people who had intended to have one drink and go had already gone, and the people who intended to stay were fortifying themselves with slightly dried canapés and talking animatedly. A group of stage and radio people had coagulated in one corner, near Packard's Capehart, and were wrangling about various methods of cheating the Collector of Internal Revenue. In another corner was a group of stockbrokers, talking about the greatest stockbroker of them all, Gauguin. Little Marcia Lupton was sitting with a young man, saying earnestly, "Do you really want to know what my greatest ambition is? I want to be myself," and Mr. Bainbridge smiled gently, thinking of the time Marcia had said that to him. Then he heard the voice of Bernard Weiss, the critic, saying, "Of course he wrote one good novel. It's not surprising. After all, we know that if six chimpanzees were set to work pounding six typewriters at random, they would, in a million years, write all the books in the British Museum."

Mr. Bainbridge drifted over to Weiss and was introduced to Weiss's companion, a Mr. Noble. "What's this about a million chimpanzees, Weiss?" he asked.

"Six chimpanzees," Mr. Weiss said. "It's an old cliché of the mathematicians. I thought everybody was told about it in school. Law of averages, you know, or maybe it's permutation and combination. The six chimps, just pounding away at the typewriter keys, would be bound to copy out all the books ever written by man. There are only so many possible combinations of letters and numerals, and they'd produce all of them—see? Of course they'd also turn out a mountain of gibberish, but they'd work the books in, too. All the books in the British Museum."

Mr. Bainbridge was delighted; this was the sort of talk he liked to hear when he came to New York. "Well, but look here," he said, just to keep up his part in the foolish conversation, "what if one of the chimpanzees finally did duplicate a book, right down to the last period, but left that off? Would that count?"

"I suppose not. Probably the chimpanzee would get around to doing the book again, and put the period in."

"What nonsense!" Mr. Noble cried.

"It may be nonsense, but Sir James Jeans believes it," Mr. Weiss said, huffily. "Jeans or Lancelot Hogben. I know I ran across it quite recently."

Mr. Bainbridge was impressed. He read quite a bit of popular science, and both Jeans and Hogben were in his library. "Is that so?" he murmured, no longer feeling frivolous. "Wonder if it has ever actually been tried? I mean, has anybody ever put six chimpanzees in a room with six typewriters and a lot of paper?"

Mr. Weiss glanced at Mr. Bainbridge's empty cocktail glass and said drily, "Probably not."

Nine weeks later, on a winter evening, Mr. Bainbridge was sitting in his study with his friend James Mallard, an assistant professor of mathematics at New Haven. He was plainly nervous as he poured himself a drink and said, "Mallard, I've asked you to come here—Brandy? Cigar?—for a particular reason. You remember that I wrote you some time ago, asking your opinion of . . . of a certain mathematical hypothesis or supposition."

"Yes," Professor Mallard said, briskly. "I remember perfectly. About the six chimpanzees and the British Museum. And I told you it was a perfectly sound popularization of a principle known to every schoolboy who had studied the science of probabilities."

"Precisely," Mr. Bainbridge said. "Well, Mallard, I made up my mind
. . . It was not difficult for me, because I have, in spite of that fellow
in the White House, been able to give something every year to the
Museum of Natural History, and they were naturally glad to oblige me.
. . . And after all, the only contribution a layman can make to the
progress of science is to assist with the drudgery of experiment. . . .
In short, I—"

"I suppose you're trying to tell me that you have procured six chimpanzees and set them to work at typewriters in order to see whether they
will eventually write all the books in the British Museum. Is that it?"

"Yes, that's it," Mr. Bainbridge said. "What a mind you have, Mallard. Six fine young males, in perfect condition. I had a—I suppose
you'd call it a dormitory—built out in back of the stable. The typewriters are in the conservatory. It's light and airy in there, and I moved
most of the plants out. Mr. North, the man who owns the circus, very
obligingly let me engage one of his best animal men. Really, it was no
trouble at all."

Professor Mallard smiled indulgently. "After all, such a thing is not
unheard of," he said. "I seem to remember that a man at some university
put his graduate students to work flipping coins, to see if heads and tails
came up an equal number of times. Of course they did."

Mr. Bainbridge looked at his friend very queerly. "Then you believe
that any such principle of the science of probabilities will stand up
under an actual test?"

"Certainly."

"You had better see for yourself." Mr. Bainbridge led Professor
Mallard downstairs, along a corridor, through a disused music room,
and into a large conservatory. The middle of the floor had been cleared
of plants and was occupied by a row of six typewriter tables, each one
supporting a hooded machine. At the left of each typewriter was a
neat stack of yellow copy paper. Empty wastebaskets were under each
table. The chairs were the unpadded, spring-backed kind favored by
experienced stenographers. A large bunch of ripe bananas was hanging
in one corner, and in another stood a Great Bear water-cooler and a rack
of Lily cups. Six piles of typescript, each about a foot high, were ranged
along the wall on an improvised shelf. Mr. Bainbridge picked up one
of the piles, which he could just conveniently lift, and set it on a table

before Professor Mallard. "The output to date of Chimpanzee A, known as Bill," he said simply.

"'"Oliver Twist," by Charles Dickens,'" Professor Mallard read out. He read the first and second pages of the manuscript, then feverishly leafed through to the end. "You mean to tell me," he said, "that this chimpanzee has written—"

"Word for word and comma for comma," said Mr. Bainbridge. "Young, my butler, and I took turns comparing it with the edition I own. Having finished 'Oliver Twist,' Bill is, as you see, starting the sociological works of Vilfredo Pareto, in Italian. At the rate he has been going, it should keep him busy for the rest of the month."

"And all the chimpanzees"—Professor Mallard was pale, and enunciated with difficulty—"they aren't all—"

"Oh, yes, all writing books which I have every reason to believe are in the British Museum. The prose of John Donne, some Anatole France, Conan Doyle, Galen, the collected plays of Somerset Maugham, Marcel Proust, the memoirs of the late Marie of Rumania, and a monograph by a Dr. Wiley on the marsh grasses of Maine and Massachusetts. I can sum it up for you, Mallard, by telling you that since I started this experiment, four weeks and some days ago, none of the chimpanzees has spoiled a single sheet of paper."

Professor Mallard straightened up, passed his handkerchief across his brow, and took a deep breath. "I apologize for my weakness," he said. "It was simply the sudden shock. No, looking at the thing scientifically—and I hope I am at least as capable of that as the next man—there is nothing marvellous about the situation. These chimpanzees, or a succession of similar teams of chimpanzees, would in a million years write all the books in the British Museum. I told you some time ago that I believed that statement. Why should my belief be altered by the fact that they produced some of the books at the very outset? After all, I should not be very much surprised if I tossed a coin a hundred times and it came up heads every time. I know that if I kept at it long enough, the ratio would reduce itself to an exact fifty per cent. Rest assured, these chimpanzees will begin to compose gibberish quite soon. It is bound to happen. Science tells us so. Meanwhile, I advise you to keep this experiment secret. Uninformed people might create a sensation if they knew."

"I will, indeed," Mr. Bainbridge said. "And I'm very grateful for your rational analysis. It reassures me. And now, before you go, you must hear the new Schnabel records that arrived today."

During the succeeding three months, Professor Mallard got into the habit of telephoning Mr. Bainbridge every Friday afternoon at five-thirty, immediately after leaving his seminar room. The Professor would say, "Well?," and Mr. Bainbridge would reply, "They're still at it, Mallard. Haven't spoiled a sheet of paper yet." If Mr. Bainbridge had to go out on Friday afternoon, he would leave a written message with his butler, who would read it to Professor Mallard: "Mr. Bainbridge says we now have Trevelyan's 'Life of Macaulay,' the Confessions of St. Augustine, 'Vanity Fair,' part of Irving's 'Life of George Washington,' the Book of the Dead, and some speeches delivered in Parliament in opposition to the Corn Laws, sir." Professor Mallard would reply, with a hint of a snarl in his voice, "Tell him to remember what I predicted," and hang up with a clash.

The eleventh Friday that Professor Mallard telephoned, Mr. Bainbridge said, "No change. I have had to store the bulk of the manuscript in the cellar. I would have burned it, except that it probably has some scientific value."

"How dare you talk of scientific value?" The voice from New Haven roared faintly in the receiver. "Scientific value! You—you—chimpanzee!" There were further inarticulate sputterings, and Mr. Bainbridge hung up with a disturbed expression. "I am afraid Mallard is overtaxing himself," he murmured.

Next day, however, he was pleasantly surprised. He was leafing through a manuscript that had been completed the previous day by Chimpanzee D, Corky. It was the complete diary of Samuel Pepys, and Mr. Bainbridge was chuckling over the naughty passages, which were omitted in his own edition, when Professor Mallard was shown into the room. "I have come to apologize for my outrageous conduct on the telephone yesterday," the Professor said.

"Please don't think of it any more. I know you have many things on your mind," Mr. Bainbridge said. "Would you like a drink?"

"A large whiskey, straight, please," Professor Mallard said. "I got rather cold driving down. No change, I presume?"

"No, none. Chimpanzee F, Dinty, is just finishing John Florio's translation of Montaigne's essays, but there is no other news of interest."

Professor Mallard squared his shoulders and tossed off his drink in one astonishing gulp. "I should like to see them at work," he said. "Would I disturb them, do you think?"

"Not at all. As a matter of fact, I usually look in on them around this time of day. Dinty may have finished his Montaigne by now, and it is always interesting to see them start a new work. I would have thought that they would continue on the same sheet of paper, but they don't, you know. Always a fresh sheet, and the title in capitals."

Professor Mallard, without apology, poured another drink and slugged it down. "Lead on," he said.

It was dusk in the conservatory, and the chimpanzees were typing by the light of student lamps clamped to their desks. The keeper lounged in a corner, eating a banana and reading *Billboard*. "You might as well take an hour or so off," Mr. Bainbridge said. The man left.

Professor Mallard, who had not taken off his overcoat, stood with his hands in his pockets, looking at the busy chimpanzees. "I wonder if you know, Bainbridge, that the science of probabilities takes everything into account," he said, in a queer, tight voice. "It is certainly almost beyond the bounds of credibility that these chimpanzees should write books without a single error, but that abnormality may be corrected by—*these!*" He took his hands from his pockets, and each one held a .38 revolver. "Stand back out of harm's way!" he shouted.

"Mallard! Stop it!" The revolvers barked, first the right hand, then the left, then the right. Two chimpanzees fell, and a third reeled into a corner. Mr. Bainbridge seized his friend's arm and wrested one of the weapons from him.

"Now I am armed, too, Mallard, and I advise you to stop!" he cried. Professor Mallard's answer was to draw a bead on Chimpanzee E and shoot him dead. Mr. Bainbridge made a rush, and Professor Mallard fired at him. Mr. Bainbridge, in his quick death agony, tightened his finger on the trigger of his revolver. It went off, and Professor Mallard went down. On his hands and knees he fired at the two chimpanzees which were still unhurt, and then collapsed.

There was nobody to hear his last words. "The human equation . . .
always the enemy of science . . ." he panted. "This time . . . vice versa
. . . I, a mere mortal . . . savior of science . . . deserve a Nobel . . ."

When the old butler came running into the conservatory to investi-
gate the noises, his eyes were met by a truly appalling sight. The student lamps were shattered, but a newly risen moon shone in through
the conservatory windows on the corpses of the two gentlemen, each
clutching a smoking revolver. Five of the chimpanzees were dead. The
sixth was Chimpanzee F. His right arm disabled, obviously bleeding to
death, he was slumped before his typewriter. Painfully, with his left
hand, he took from the machine the completed last page of Florio's
Montaigne. Groping for a fresh sheet, he inserted it, and typed with one
finger, "UNCLE TOM'S CABIN, by Harriet Beecher Stowe. Chapte . . ."
Then he, too, was dead.

J. Robertson and G. Osborne
POSTAL SYSTEM INPUT
BUFFER DEVICE

*One of the banes in the life of the average consumer is the
list of instructions which accompanies most gadgets he is
likely to buy. How scientists and engineers who are intelligent enough to invent such gadgets can also be obtuse
enough to write such cluttered, incoherent instructions mys-
tifies most of us. Here, two scientists writing in a technical
journal poke fun at the whole problem.*

Although no public announcement of the fact has been made, it is
known that the United States Post Office Department for some time has
been installing Postal System Input Buffer Devices as temporary information storage units on pseudo-randomly selected street corners. Several models are in use; some older ones are still to be found painted
a color which may be described as yellow-greenish in hue, low satura-
tion, and low in brilliance, but a significantly large proportion are now
appearing in a red, white, and blue combination which seems to provide
greater user satisfaction, although the associational-algebra value-func-
tions remain obscure. Access to the majority of these devices is from the
sidewalk, although a recent modification (including a 180-degree rota-
tion about a vertical centerline) makes some of them accessible from an
automobile, provided that the vehicle is equipped with either (a) a passenger in normal working condition, mounted upright on the front seat,
or (b) a driver having at least one arm on the right-hand side which is
six feet long and double-jointed at the wrist and elbow. Figure 1 shows
a typical sidewalk-access model Postal System Input Buffer Device.

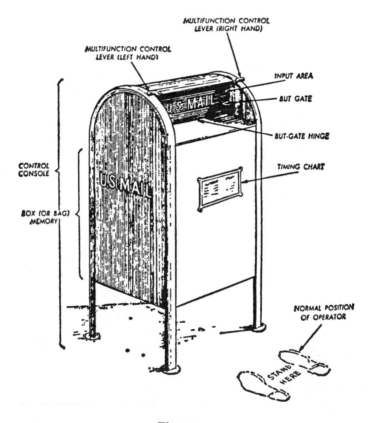

Figure 1.

OPERATION

Most normal adults without previous experience can be readily trained to operate the machine. Children and extremely short adults may find it necessary to obtain assistance from a passerby[1] in order to complete steps 4 (Feed Cycle) and 6 (Verification), or both. The machine is normally operated as described below.

1. *Position of Operator.* Locate the Control Console (see Figure 1). Stand in front of the machine so that the control console is facing you.[2]

2. *Initial Setup.* Grasp the Multi-Function Control Lever (Figure 1). This lever performs several functions, each being uniquely determined by that portion of the Operation Cycle during which it is activated. The lever may be grasped with either hand. With the other hand, position the input in preparation for step 4 (Feed Cycle).

3. *Start Operation.* Pull the Multi-Function Control Lever toward you until it is fully extended. It will travel in a downward arc, as it is attached to a mechanical But-gate hinged at the bottom. (The But-gate, so named because it allows but one operation at a time, is especially designed to make feedback extremely difficult.) Pulling the Multi-Function Control Lever at this time accomplishes an Input Buffer Reset and Drop-Chute Clear. These actions are of interest only to the technician, but are mentioned here in preparation for the following note.

> NOTE. The lever should move freely. If it does not, the memory is full and cannot accept further information until it has been unloaded. The operator may elect to (a) wait for a Postal System Field Engineer (a "mailman") or (b) find another Postal System Input Buffer Device. If choice (b) is elected, refer to description above; also see Figure 1.

Warning. Under no circumstances should the operator attempt to clear the unit; loss of a ring or wristwatch may result. In extreme cases, some individuals have lost 30 years.

4. *Feed Cycle.* Visually check to see that the input area is clear. The input area may be recognized because it is totally dark and makes a

---

[1] In this context, "passerby" may be defined as a member of the set of human beings having a maximized probability of occupying the event space.

[2] The Novice Operator Trainee may prefer to face the console.

425

90-degree downward turn; obstructions are hence not visible under normal circumstances. While holding the Multi-Function Control Lever in the extended position, start the input feed by manually inserting the information package.[3]

> NOTE. One particularly advantageous feature of the Postal Service Input Buffer Device is that, at this stage, the address field may be mixed alpha-numerics (including special characters) and may be presented to the unit in normal format (reading left-to-right and top-to-bottom), backward, or even upside-down.

5. *Transfer Cycle.* Release the Multi-Function Control Lever. The machine will now automatically transfer the input to the delay-box memory (delay-bag in some models). The operator will soon become familiar with the typical "Squeak" and "Clank" signals, provided on all models to indicate satisfactory operation of the But-gate. Actual transfer of the information, however, is not signalled unless the information is very densely packed, in which case a "Thump" signal may occasionally be heard.

> NOTE. A "Boing" signal indicates that the information is unsuited to the Input Buffer Device and that a programming error has therefore occurred.

6. *Verification.* Pull the Multi-Function Control Lever again (see step 3), check to see that the Input Zone (Figure 1) is clear (see step 4), and release the lever. This completes one full Operation Cycle. Additional cycles, when necessitated by large input quantities, may be initiated by returning to step 1 (above).

> NOTE. Step 6 is not actually necessary for machine operation. The Postal Service Input Buffer Device has been designed to permit this step, however, to satisfy the requirements of the overwhelming "Post-Mailing Peek Compulsion" which affects most users of the unit and which has been linked by some writers [4] to the "Unsatisfied Sex-Curiosity" Syndrome.

[3] Perhaps better known to some readers as a "letter" or "postcard."
[4] *Op cit.*

Thomas Meehan
EARLY MORNING OF A
MOTION·PICTURE
EXECUTIVE

*There are at least two satires at work here—the character
satire of the movie executive and the satire on what is
likely to happen to a complex literary classic like Joyce's*
Ulysses *should the Hollywood moguls get their hands on it
and try to turn it into "Box Office." Much of the fun is in
the stream-of-consciousness parody of Joyce, culminating
in that ecstatic flow of* yes's *which echoes the final speech of
Molly Bloom in* Ulysses.

*One of the smallest minorities in Hollywood nowadays is the group that
believes James Joyce's "Ulysses" will be made into a superior movie . . .
behind the entire hoopla is Jerry Wald, the producer . . . he prepared a
memorandum . . . that included the following: "The way I would like to
see this story on the screen is to oversimplify it. It has three levels: Stephen
Dedalus, the intellectual; Leopold Bloom, the passive, ill-informed victim
of habitual feelings, and Mrs. Bloom, sensual, carnal, wholly natural. Thus,
the three leading characters represent Pride, Love, and The Flesh. My feeling
is that this project is really in its purest form: father searching for his son
and son searching for his father. It is a highly controversial book and out
of it could be created a motion picture as exciting as 'Peyton Place' but on
a higher level."—*The Times.

. . . yes a quarter after what an unearthly hour I suppose theyre just
getting out on the lot at Fox now Marilyn Monroe combing out her
hair for the day let me see if I can doze off 1 2 3 4 5 where was it in
Jerrys memorandum yes oversimplify O I love great books Id love to

have the whole of Hollywood filming nothing but great books God in heaven theres nothing like literature pre sold to the public the treatment and the working script by Dalton Trumbo and the finished picture in color and Todd A O as for them saying theres no audience interest in pictures based on great books I wouldnt give a snap of my two fingers for all their motivational research indie exhibs whatever they call themselves why dont they go out and make a picture I ask them and do a socko 21 Gs in Philly and a wow 41 in Chi ah that they cant answer yes in its purest form father searching for his son and son searching for his father chance for myriad boffolas there old man staggers out one door of pub where the beer and the boffola foam while kid goes in other O I love a good laugh Stephen Dedalus the intellectual we might try to get Paul Newman for the part hes a strong BO draw in Exodus certainly hed do very nicely too better soft pedal the egghead bit though make him a newspaper reporter have to shoot a lot of location stuff in Dublin by the waters of the Liffey by the rivering waters of we might fake it on the back lot and bring it in under three million or else knock up the budget and spot celebs the way Columbia did with Pepe it coined a huge forty five thou in its first week on Bway gives the property a touch of class I wonder could we get Bobby Darin on a percentage deal to sing Galway Bay I better have Sammy check in the morning where the hell Galway Bay is its somewhere around Dublin surely long color process shot of the bay at dusk cut to faces of old women in black shawls and the women in the uplands making hay speak a language that the strangers do not know a scene which it will knock them out of the back of the house in Terre Haute

the alarmclock in the maids room clattering the brains out of itself better take another seconal and try to sleep again so as I can get up early Ill call a title conference at ten wait now who was it yes Kirk Douglas already made Ulysses the old story though this ones on three levels we might call it Pride Love and The Flesh that has a nice sound to it Ill have Sammy get ahold of Central Registry and see if the titles reserved Leopold Bloom the passive ill informed victim of habitual feelings problem on the religion bit though dont want Bnai Brith down on our necks well give him an Irish name in any case Leopold Malone and his loving wife Molly sensual carnal wholly natural she wheels her wheelbarrow through streets wide and narrow personally Id like to build the scrip around Molly and get MM for the role so why am I after worrying we cant go wrong with Maureen O Hara flashback to Gibraltar where she was a girl a flower of the mountain yes so are those bimbos all flowers of the mountain lap dissolve he kisses her under the Moorish wall we might send down a second unit to get some outdoor Gibraltar stuff cut in a flamenco dream sequence shoot it there and dub it on the soundtrack later yes chance too for widescreen color background O the sea the sea there crimson sometimes like fire and the glorious sunsets and the figtrees in the Alameda gardens yes well have Louella bawling like a goddam baby baaaawwaaaaaww at the world preem

ah well theres no talking around it were one of the smallest minorities in Hollywood nowadays us thinking that James Joyces Ulysses will be made into a superior movie TJ saying to me Harry youre one hundred per cent crazy him with his two dollar cigars and his Irving Thalberg award chasing those little chits of starlets and he not long married Mouth Almighty I call him and his squinty eyes of all the big stuppoe studio heads I ever met God help the world if everyone out here was like him yes always and ever making the same pictures showdownatshotguncreek whatever he calls the new one ah God send him more sense and me more money O he does look the fool sitting at the head of the conference table as big as you please he can go smother for all the fat lot I care Im unabashedly intellectual and Ill make this movie or Im walking off the lot this day week Ive still got my integrity after all how long is it Ive been out here wait yes since 1923 O I love lying in bed God here we are as bad as ever after yes thirty eight years how many studios have I worked at RKO and Fox and Metro and Paramount where I was a young man and the day I talked to deMille when he was making the original of The Ten Commandments and yes he wouldnt answer at first only looked out over the set and the thousands of extras I was thinking of so many things he didnt know of yes how someday Id have my own swimming pool and go to Vilma Bankys parties and all the long years since Joan Crawford in Our Dancing Daughters and Richard Dix and yes the year Metro missed the boat on Dinner at Eight and Fred Astaire and Ginger Rogers and Asta rrrrrfffff rrrrrfffff and the andyhardy series and The Best Years of Our Lives and O all the Academy Award dinners yes Disney going about smug with his Oscars the Levant what year was it Gert and I took the cruise there I never miss his TV show and Rhonda Fleming with her hair all red and flaming and Sandra Dee and Vista Vision and stereophonic sound cleaning up in the foreign market and Ben Hur and the night TJ asked me what my next project would be when was it yes the night they screened Psycho in Santa Monica eeeeeeeekkk its an Irish story I told him like The Quiet Man or shall we get Rock Hudson I was just thinking of it for the first time yes and I had Sammy give me a five page synopsis and the day in Romanoffs I asked Jerry Wald about it yes Ulysses by James Joyce which it is a highly controversial book and I asked him yes could out of it be created a picture as exciting as Peyton Place and yes he said yes it could yes but on a higher level Yes.

Art Buchwald
TWO COLUMNS

Perhaps the most popular columnist whose stock in trade
is satire is Art Buchwald. He seems to enlist everyone to his
side, to join him in chuckling at the goings-on of the day.
In this technique he is clearly an Horatian satirist, not out
to infuriate and arouse, but to delight and thereby instruct.
He helps us keep our perspective on things, to keep our
judgment balanced. In the first column, he is having fun
with the trivialities that somehow seem to creep into the
supposedly serious presidential press conference. In the
second, he laughs at the clichés of political writing.

A LATE, LATE BRIEFING

PARIS.

The NATO conference now going on in Paris is being covered by 1,793
top-flight, highly paid journalists from every corner of the globe. Every
detail of the conference is being given careful and thorough coverage.
The star of the show is President Eisenhower, and every facet of the
President's stay in Paris is being reported to the public in detail. In order
to keep the press up on the President's activities, briefings are held at
the Hotel Crillon in the morning, at noon and in the early evening, and
there is even a special one held late at night for reporters who can't
sleep.

I happened to attend one of these late-night briefings with several
correspondents of early-morning newspapers. To give you an idea of
what takes place at one of these briefings, I took down a transcript.

The man behind the microphone arrived at 12:30 A.M.

"I'm sorry I'm late, gentlemen, but I thought the show at the Lido

431

would end at 11:30. I have a few things to report. The President went to bed at 11:06 tonight."

Q. Jim, have Premier Gaillard and Prime Minister Macmillan also retired?

A. To my knowledge they have.

Q. Then are we to assume that they will not meet with the President until morning?

A. Yes, you could assume that.

Q. Then does that mean he's going to meet with Adenauer during the night?

A. I didn't say that. As far as I know he'll sleep until morning.

Q. Jim, whose idea was it for the President to go to sleep?

A. It was the President's idea. He was tired and decided to go to sleep.

Q. Did Sherman Adams, or Dr. Snyder, or the President's son suggest he go to sleep?

A. As far as I know, the President suggested the idea himself.

Q. Jim, did the President speak to anyone before retiring?

A. He spoke to the Secretary of State.

Q. What did he say to the Secretary of State, Jim?

A. He said: "Good night, Foster."

Q. And what did the Secretary say to the President?

A. He said: "Good night, Mr. President."

Q. The Secretary didn't say: "Pleasant dreams"?

A. Not to my knowledge. I have nothing on that.

Q. Jim, do you have any idea what the President is dreaming of this very moment?

A. No, the President has never revealed to me any of his dreams.

Q. Are we to assume from that that the President doesn't dream?

A. I'm not saying he does or he doesn't. I just said I don't know.

Q. Jim, how will the President be waked up tomorrow morning? Will it be by alarm clock, or will someone come knock on the door?

A. That hasn't been decided yet. But as soon as it has, I'll let you fellows know.

Q. Do you have any idea who the President will see first tomorrow morning?

A. I imagine he'll see the Secretary of State.

Q. What will he say to him?

A. The President plans to say: "Good morning, Foster."

Q. What will the Secretary reply?

A. "Good morning, Mr. President."

Q. That's all?

A. That's all I can tell you at this moment.

Q. Jim, when the President went to bed last night, how did he feel?

A. He was feeling chipper and in good spirits.

Q. How many blankets were on the bed?

A. I'm not sure. Maybe two or three. But certainly no more than he uses in Washington.

Q. Could we say three?

A. I better check that. I know three blankets were made available but it's possible he didn't use all of them.

Q. One could have been kicked off during the night?

A. Yes, that could be possible, but it's unlikely.

Q. Was there a glass of water by the bed?

A. There was a glass of water and a pitcher.

Q. Jim, could we have another briefing before morning?

A. I don't see what would be accomplished by that.

Q. It might tend to clarify the situation.

A. I think the best thing would be to have the briefing after the President gets up.

Q. What about breakfast, Jim?

A. I think we better have another briefing about breakfast, after it's over.

Q. Thank you, Jim.

A. Okay, see you later.

A TEST FOR GOP SPEECHWRITERS

WASHINGTON.

"So you want to work as a speechwriter for the Republican Party in 1968?"

"Yes, Sir."

"All right. Did you see the television show the other evening when the Republicans answered President Johnson's State of the Union address?"

"Yes, Sir. And it was a brilliant performance by one and all."

"Okay, forget the soft soap. Let's get on with the test."

"I have to take a test?"

"Of course! If you're going to work for the Republican Party, you're going to have to know where it stands on the issues."

"I know where it stands."

"Well, let's just see. First question: what kind of integrity does the Republican Party stand for?"

"The integrity of the American dollar."

"Okay. What has the Johnson Administration failed to do?"

"It has failed to make clear our goals, and it has not been candid with the American people in facing up to the complex and difficult road that lies ahead."

"By heaven, you did watch the show. Now let's go on to the Ship of State. Where is the Ship of State?"

"It is wallowing in a storm-tossed sea, drifting toward the rocks of domestic disaster, beaten by the waves of worldwide fiscal crisis that threaten shipwreck."

"And what can save the Ship of State?"

"A new captain at the helm who will call up full power, break out new charts and hold our course steadfast and inspire the crew to bring us through the storm."

"Good. Now let's go on to cities. What are the cities boiling with at the moment?"

"Frustration and unrest."

"It's 'unrest and frustration,' but we'll accept your answer. And why are they boiling thusly?"

"Because the Administration has been long on promises and short on performance."

"That's well put. Now let me ask you this. What does the Republican Party have abiding faith in?"

"The individual."

"Why did you hesitate?"

"I thought it might be the American free enterprise system."

"We've got abiding faith in that, too. Either answer would have been correct. Let's go on to inflation. What does the President have to do to end it?"

"He's got to cut back on federal spending and impress on the people that we have to live within our means here at home."

"Okay. Now let's go on to Vietnam. What kind of Communist aggression are we trying to stem there?"

"Naked?"

"Fine. You seem to have passed the test. You can start writing speeches in the morning."

"Thank you."

"Thank you, what?"

"Thank you from the bottom of my heart, so help me God."

Jules Feiffer
ON THE ELOQUENCE OF THE PRESIDENTIAL CANDIDATE

Humbert Wolfe
THE GRAY SQUIRREL

Irony is the chief vehicle in this unusual lyric poem. There is also an implied contrast between the squirrel and the keeper like that between the bear and the man in Frost's "The Bear."

Like a small gray
coffee-pot,
sits the squirrel.
He is not

all he should be,
kills by dozens
trees, and eats
his red-brown cousins.

The keeper, on the
other hand
, who shot him, is
a Christian, and

loves his enemies,
which shows
the squirrel was not
one of those.

Thomas Hornsby Ferril

FREUD ON FOOTBALL

In this spoof of social scientific analysis, the author proceeds, like Horace or Addison, gently. The satire accumulates slowly and quietly. Yet the final effect is as powerful as a Juvenalian treatment might be, in that we are likely to view those social scientific analyses we encounter in the future with a certain amount of reservation. That is, the satirist has tried through exaggeration to restore our balance and our critical judgment.

As I look back over the intellectual caprices of the past quarter century, I am amazed that neither the Marxists nor the Freudians ever took out after football. There's not a single book on the subject. It is now too late. In olympian cerebration, Marx and Freud are obsolete; the atom has taken over, and football, for the moment, seems reasonably safe from encroachment, although we may still see a few flurries; cobalt tracers, perhaps for the study of the parabolas of flat passes, but it won't amount to much because the atom is cut out for graver duties.

If the Marxists had been more alert, they could have made something out of football as brutal capitalistic exploitation of the working class. They might have noted a few strikes for higher pay and a court decision entitling a college football player to workman's compensation benefits following injury.

But it was the Freudians who made the colossal blunder. You could argue that they overlooked football on the grounds that it was just too big to be noticed on those Saturday afternoons when the college library was free for their invasion of fiction, drama, poetry, painting, sculpture, music and economics.

Yet why, when the whole town was roaring over their heads, did they pay no attention to the emotional frenzy? Frankly, I think they

437

must have, but the Freudians were notoriously selfish fellows; they wanted everything whole-hog; they were always extremely jealous of anthropologists, and, as you look back on their dilemma as far as football was concerned, their dog-in-the-manger attitude was perhaps justified, for no self-respecting Freudian could ever have done a full-dress job on football without cutting some detested anthropologist in on the gravy.

But had the Freudians been less self-centered and had they welcomed a bit of anthropological assistance, just think of the monumental treatises by which the scientific literature of the period might have been enriched, great books wedding the wisdom of "Gesammelte Schriften" with the profundity of "The Golden Bough."

Let me set down, in nostalgic summary, some of the findings that might have been made, had the Freudians not been sulking in their tents.

Obviously, football is a syndrome of religious rites symbolizing the struggle to preserve the egg of life through the rigors of impending winter. The rites begin at the autumn equinox and culminate on the first day of the New Year with great festivals identified with bowls of plenty; the festivals are associated with flowers such as roses, fruits such as oranges, farm crops such as cotton, and even sun-worship and appeasement of great reptiles such as alligators.

In these rites the egg of life is symbolized by what is called "the oval," an inflated bladder covered with hog skin. The convention of "the oval" is repeated in the architectural oval-shaped design of the vast outdoor churches in which the services are held every sabbath in every town and city, also every Sunday in the greater centers of population where an advanced priesthood performs. These enormous roofless churches dominate every college campus; no other edifice compares in size with them, and they bear witness to the high spiritual development of the culture that produced them.

Literally millions of worshipers attend the sabbath services in these enormous open-air churches. Subconsciously, these hordes of worshipers are seeking an outlet from sex-frustration in anticipation of violent masochism and sadism about to be enacted by a highly trained priesthood of young men. Football obviously arises out of the Oedipus complex. Love of mother dominates the entire ritual. The churches, without exception, are dedicated to Alma Mater, Dear Mother. (Notre Dame and football are synonymous.)

The rites are performed on a rectangular area of green grass oriented to the four directions. The grass, symbolizing summer, is striped with ominous white lines representing the knifing snows of winter. The white stripes are repeated in the ceremonial costumes of the four whistling monitors who control the services through a time period divided into four quarters, symbolizing the four seasons.

The ceremony begins with colorful processions of musicians and semi-nude virgins who move in and out of ritualized patterns. This excites the thousands of worshipers to rise from their seats, shout frenzied poetry in unison and chant ecstatic anthems through which runs the Oedipus theme of willingness to die for love of Mother.

The actual rites, performed by 22 young priests of perfect physique, might appear to the uninitiated as a chaotic conflict concerned only with hurting the oval by kicking it, then endeavoring to rescue and protect the egg.

However, the procedure is highly stylized. On each side there are eleven young men wearing colorful and protective costumes. The group in so-called "possession" of the oval first arrange themselves in an egg-shaped "huddle," as it is called, for a moment of prayerful meditation and whispering of secret numbers to each other.

Then they rearrange themselves with relation to the position of the egg. In a typical "formation" there are seven priests "on the line," seven being a mystical number associated not, as Jung purists might contend, with the "seven last words" but actually, with sublimation of the "seven deadly sins" into "the seven cardinal principles of education."

The central priest crouches over the egg, protecting it with his hands while over his back quarters hovers the "quarterback." The transposition of "back quarters" to "quarter-back" is easily explained by the Adler school. To the layman the curious posture assumed by the "quarterback," as he hovers over the central priest, immediately suggests the Cretan origins of Mycenaean animal art, but this popular view is untenable. Actually, of course, the "quarter-back" symbolizes the libido, combining two instincts, namely (a) Eros, which strives for even closer union and (b) the instinct for destruction of anything which lies in the path of Eros. Moreover, the "pleasure-pain" excitement of the hysterical worshipers focuses entirely on the actions of the libido-quarter-back. Behind him are three priests representing the male triad.

At a given signal, the egg is passed by sleight-of-hand to one of the members of the triad who endeavors to move it by bodily force across the white lines of winter. This procedure, up and down the enclosure, continues through the four quarters of the ritual.

At the end of the second quarter, implying the summer solstice, the processions of musicians and semi-nude virgins are resumed. After forming themselves into pictograms, representing alphabetical and animal fetishes, the virgins perform a most curious rite requiring far more dexterity than the earlier phallic Maypole rituals from which it seems to be derived. Each of the virgins carries a wand of shining metal which she spins on her fingertips, tosses playfully into the air and with which she interweaves her body in most intricate gyrations.

The virgins perform another important function throughout the entire service. This concerns the mystical rite of "conversion" following success of one of the young priests in carrying the oval across the last white line of winter. As the moment of "conversion" approaches, the virgins kneel at the edge of the grass, bury their faces in the earth, then raise their arms to heaven in supplication, praying that "the uprights will be split." "Conversion" is indeed a dedicated ceremony.

Freud and Breuer in 1895 ("Studien über Hysteria") described "conversion" as hysterical symptoms originating through the energy of a mental process being withheld from conscious influence, and this precisely accounts for the behavior of the virgins in the football services.

The foregoing, I confess, scarcely scratches the surface. Space does not permit interpretation of football as related to dreams, or discussion of the great subconscious reservoirs of thwarted American energy that weekly seek expression through vicarious enjoyment of ritualized violence and infliction of pain. To relate football to the Oedipus complex alone would require, as it well deserves, years of patient research by scholarly men such as we find in the Ford Foundation.

I only regret that these studies were not undertaken a quarter century ago, when the Freudians were in full flower. It's just another instance, so characteristic of our culture, of too little and too late.

Jules Feiffer
INTRODUCTION TO
FEIFFER'S ALBUM

A theory of satire is not an easy theory to formulate. Some say satire by its very nature is destructive. Others say it is purely corrective and therefore constructive. Others suggest it must destroy in order to create. In the scene which follows, the famous cartoonist Jules Feiffer lets the satirists speak for themselves. The result, of course, is a satire in which theory is both defended and ridiculed. Even satire is a fit subject for satire.

The scene is the darkened stage of a Broadway playhouse. A spot comes up on the FIRST SATIRIST, *who is seated on a stool reading a newspaper. A second spot comes up on the* SECOND SATIRIST, *who is staring at him.*

SECOND SATIRIST   Are you a satirist?

FIRST SATIRIST   Can't you tell?

SECOND SATIRIST   Well, you *are* sitting on a stool.

FIRST SATIRIST   Want to hear my Kennedy bit?

SECOND SATIRIST   (*Winces*)   I must have the wrong place. I heard there were going to be some satirists here.

FIRST SATIRIST (*Offended*)   I *am* a satirist.

(*A spot comes up on the* THIRD SATIRIST)

THIRD SATIRIST   So am I.

SECOND SATIRIST   Where's your stool?

THIRD SATIRIST   I'm a right-wing satirist. Only liberal satirists have stools. We right-wing satirists have to be ready to make a fast start.

FIRST SATIRIST You right-wingers! You always make yourselves sound so oppressed. Now take me! *I'm* not strictly a liberal. Did you ever hear me do Kennedy?

THIRD SATIRIST I've heard everybody do Kennedy.

FIRST SATIRIST Proves my point. I do a very strong Kennedy.

THIRD SATIRIST Ever been invited to the White House?

FIRST SATIRIST Every time I do Kennedy.

SECOND SATIRIST I don't think either one of you knows what satire is—

(*A spot comes up on the* FOURTH SATIRIST)

FOURTH SATIRIST It's Jewish, isn't it? Lots of words like *schtick, l'chaim, bagel.* That's what I use in *my* act.

(*A spot comes up on the* FIFTH SATIRIST—*a Negro*)

FIFTH SATIRIST Jewish is square, man. The roots of modern-day satire rest in the jazz idiom. Satire has crossed the color line.

FOURTH SATIRIST (*Smiles indulgently at the* FIFTH SATIRIST) Oh, don't get me wrong.

THIRD SATIRIST (*Smiles indulgently at the* FIFTH SATIRIST) Don't get me wrong.

FIRST SATIRIST (*Smiles indulgently*) Don't get me wrong, either. I do a great Kennedy on the phone to Martin Luther King.

FIFTH SATIRIST Martin Luther King? Man, as far as *my* audience goes, Martin Luther King is practically *white!*

FIRST SATIRIST (*Nervously to the audience*) We're all just kidding here. Having fun. That's what satire is. Having fun.

SECOND SATIRIST Do you always apologize?

FIRST SATIRIST A satirist can't teach people anything if he offends them.

FOURTH SATIRIST I offend them. They love it. I make fun of their wives. They love it. I tell them I hate them. They love it. I use words like *schmuck.* You should hear them applaud.

THIRD SATIRIST I like to work with my audience. I like to improvise. I ask them to give me a first line and a last line and a theme. And I build a whole fifteen-minute improvisation around it.

FIFTH SATIRIST Is it any good?

THIRD SATIRIST   Never. But they love it. I ingratiate myself.
SECOND SATIRIST   That's not satire. All you want is approval.
THIRD SATIRIST   Yes. And when they withhold it, I attack them.
FOURTH SATIRIST   Me, too. Viciously.
FIFTH SATIRIST   Man, I don't want approval.
THE OTHERS (*Approvingly*)   What do you want?
FIFTH SATIRIST   Yo' sister! (*The others recoil*)   That was satire.
FIRST SATIRIST   Hey, I can do a great Kennedy. (*Thrusts out fore-finger*) Do naht ahsk what you can do fer Caroline—
FOURTH SATIRIST (*Impatient*)   Everyone does Kennedy. That's not satire. Now the kind of satire *I* like to do—
FIRST SATIRIST   Kennedy is so satire. He's the President, isn't he? When you do the President you're making fun of a public figure, aren't you? You're making him look foolish, aren't you? That takes courage, doesn't it? Well, when I do Kennedy that's satire! Unabashed, unafraid satire.
FIFTH SATIRIST   Do J. Edgar Hoover.
FIRST SATIRIST   J. Edgar Hoover?
FIFTH SATIRIST   Do J. Edgar Hoover.
FIRST SATIRIST   You don't want J. Edgar Hoover.
FIFTH SATIRIST   Man, I'm *colored.* It ain't my F.B.I. Do J. Edgar Hoover. (FIRST SATIRIST *backs off*) You said you do public figures.
FIRST SATIRIST   Yeah, but J. Edgar Hoover. I mean—listen, if you come to my house and we close all the windows—
FIFTH SATIRIST   Do it here—now.
FIRST SATIRIST   I do a *great* Kennedy.
FIFTH SATIRIST   J. Edgar Hoover.
FIRST SATIRIST   On a stage? In front of people? It's bad taste! Let me do the President!
(FIFTH SATIRIST *scornfully turns away*)
FOURTH SATIRIST   The kind of satire I prefer to do is the take-off on the little man—
SECOND SATIRIST   Dear God!
FOURTH SATIRIST   His troubles, his pet peeves.
SECOND SATIRIST   Heaven help us!
FOURTH SATIRIST   The little unnoticed bedevilments of life that may not give the audience a belly laugh, mind you, but will give them a

smile of recognition. "Yes—I'm like that," they'll say. "There I am. There you are. There we all are. Little Man. Peering off into the middle distance."

SECOND SATIRIST I'm ill.

FOURTH SATIRIST "There's my wife. There's my next door neighbor—"

SECOND SATIRIST Together?

FOURTH SATIRIST (*Self-righteous*) Smut is *not* satire.

SECOND SATIRIST Smut, dear sir, is our *only* satire.

FOURTH SATIRIST You're one of those people who has to attack everything!

FIFTH SATIRIST (*To* SECOND SATIRIST) You ain't ever attacked *me*, baby.

SECOND SATIRIST Of course not. Now is not the *time* to attack you. When you've gained equal rights—*then* I'll attack you.

FIRST SATIRIST (*Proudly*) I have a point of view. *I* don't attack everything.

FOURTH SATIRIST (*Proudly*) Certainly! One should be *for* something. Then he can attack those things that are against what he is for. That's the *responsible* approach.

FIFTH SATIRIST You for something?

FIRST SATIRIST (*With inspiration*) Everybody's for something.

FIFTH SATIRIST What're you for?

FIRST SATIRIST (*With inspiration*) Compassion!

THIRD SATIRIST (*With inspiration*) Understanding!

FOURTH SATIRIST (*With inspiration*) Love!

(*All three shake hands*)

SECOND SATIRIST (*To* FIFTH SATIRIST) And you—what are you for?

FIFTH SATIRIST Man, I don't stand for nothin'. I'm just a little old plantation hand doing his bit to make the system work. A civil rights therapist to lily-white audiences.

SECOND SATIRIST (*Exultant*) You *shame* them! You *expose* them!

FIFTH SATIRIST I make them laugh. They relax. They feel very liberal. Then they put on their sheets and go home. That's what satire is, man. Communication.

444

FIRST SATIRIST (*Shaking hands with* FIFTH SATIRIST) A very interesting statement. Satire *is* communication.

FOURTH SATIRIST (*Shaking hands with* FIFTH SATIRIST) Communication! Extremely well put.

THIRD SATIRIST (*Shaking hands with* FIFTH SATIRIST) Communication. Well said. Where did you go to school?

SECOND SATIRIST (*Angry*) Satire is *not* concerned with communication! Satire is concerned with *hate!*

FIRST SATIRIST (*Sweetly*) Yes, but hate is the satirist's bridge to communication!

THIRD SATIRIST (*Sweetly*) Satire should *never* be negative. Hate is only a device.

SECOND SATIRIST (*Furious*) Satire outrages! Satire strips bare!

FIRST SATIRIST I outrage.

THIRD SATIRIST I strip bare.

SECOND SATIRIST (*Screams*) Satire exposes our inner corruption! Satire *destroys!*

FOURTH SATIRIST (*Defensively*) Well I'm sure we *all* want to destroy. (*Brightly*) But only in order to build.

FIRST SATIRIST Yes! That's the only reason we'd ever destroy. To build on the ashes.

THIRD SATIRIST *A better society!*

FOURTH SATIRIST *A saner tomorrow!*

FIRST SATIRIST *An improved image of man!*

FIFTH SATIRIST *A happy people—with a natural sense of rhythm!*

FIRST, THIRD and FOURTH SATIRISTS (*Sing*) Hallelujah!

(*All four shake hands*)

THIRD SATIRIST Don't you see? That's the whole *point* in destroying. That's why satire is *not* negative!

FOURTH SATIRIST That's why it's healthy!

SECOND SATIRIST (*Becoming convinced*) I see! Yes!

FOURTH SATIRIST Not really sadistic at all!

SECOND SATIRIST (*With inspiration*) Yes!

FIRST SATIRIST It builds on ashes.

SECOND SATIRIST Yes! Ashes, we need ashes!

445

THIRD SATIRIST   On which to build!
 (*He lights a match*)
ALL   Ashes! (*They each light a match*)   *Ashes!*
 (*They set fire to the curtains. The Theatre begins to burn—scenery, backdrops, etc.*)
FIRST SATIRIST   Very soon now we will start to build.

 (*All shake hands as the theatre goes up in flames*)

John M. Stuart

A MODEST PROPOSAL FOR THE TERMINATION OF THE WAR IN VIETNAM THE REVISION OF THE SELECTIVE SERVICE SYSTEM THE SOLUTION OF THE CIVIL RIGHTS CONTROVERSY THE REDUCTION OF CRIME AND UNEMPLOYMENT THE ACHIEVEMENT OF INTERNATIONAL PEACE AND A SUBSTANTIAL DECREASE IN FEDERAL, STATE AND LOCAL TAXES

In this 1968 essay taken from Satire Newsletter, Stuart *proceeds with the same mask of sincerity, concern, logic and dedication that identifies the speaker in Swift's* A Modest Proposal—*and offers a similarly monstrous solution to the nation's problems. Never confuse the* mask, *the speaker, with the author. The satire by both Swift and Stuart is double edged; the well-intentioned speaker is also the object of satire. The suggestion is things have reached such a state that it would not be surprising for a Representative to rise before the House (or an M.P. in Parliament) and seriously offer such a proposal. The technique is ironic—its goal, to shock and thereby awaken the passive observer of man's continuing inhumanity to man.*

There can be no doubt that our country is currently beset by an imposing cluster of major problems, both at home and abroad—problems which greatly detract from our national serenity and may, in fact, come to threaten our very existence as an independent and productive state. In southeast Asia, hundreds of our young men die daily in pursuit of an elusive enemy, while at home thousands of misguided idealists spread dissent which strikes at the roots of our national policy. Our stature in the eyes of the world diminishes steadily. On the domestic front, we find a cauldron of racial unrest constantly bubbling, stirred by militant advocates of "Black Power." Our cities, which should be the seats of our industrial and cultural strength, are rife with immorality, crime, and unemployment. Our Selective Service System, which defends the security of the free world, is under continual attack from an army of critics. The costs of foreign war and domestic welfare legislation have reached astronomical heights. The burden of taxation on our citizens has become staggering.

Without wishing to belittle the efforts of other deeply concerned observers of our national issues and policies, I must say that I have not yet seen solutions presented which take into account the total social, ideological, and economic situation of our country. It seems that almost invariably an answer proposed for a fragment of our national problem causes new difficulties in other areas. If we withdraw from Vietnam, we jeopardize the remaining shreds of our prestige abroad. If we bomb China, we risk nuclear war. If we hire more police to reduce crime, we must increase taxation. In alleviating poverty and unemployment with federal funds, we may spend tax dollars to perpetuate incompetence and indolence. If we integrate schools we must suffer acts of violence by white radicals. It becomes clear that America requires a unified policy which is capable of meeting our national needs in their totality. As one who has long believed that the responsibility of loyal citizenship entails constant examination of national interests and goals, I wish to offer such a solution; in fact, a solution which might eventually bring harmony to the entire world.

It seems to me that a disproportionate amount of our national unrest is caused by the paradoxical situation of the American Negro. For well over a century, these people were brought against their will to our land of freedom and equality, and enslaved. This unfortunate practice was, of course, terminated by the Civil War, but the outcome of that war by no means reversed the damage that had been done. In a hundred years it has been impossible to incorporate the Negroes into the mainstream of our culture; remembrance of their origin as well as feelings of social —and often legal—inferiority have separated them from our society in a manner that may well prove permanent. As a result, perfectly understandably, they have been in many ways a detriment to the progress of that society. Though they form only about 11% of our population, they are annually convicted of nearly 20% of our crimes; they occupy over 40% of our substandard housing; and they account for almost a third of our nation's illiteracy as well as a quarter of its unemployment. Less than 5% of our college graduates are Negroes, and Negroes produce only 6% of our Gross National Product. Each year they give birth to 18% of America's illegitimate children, and their numbers include 20% of the country's alcoholics and a third of its drug addicts. Almost half of the federal and state funds expended on the War on Poverty and unemployment compensation are spent on this tenth of the populace.

Moreover, it seems that they do not actually desire assimilation into our predominantly Anglo-Saxon culture. Witness their presence in our cities: it seems that whenever they live in a cosmopolitan area they cluster together, forming ghettos which inevitably become hotbeds of violence and vice. Witness the formation of the Black Muslim movement, based not on any claims of equality, but upon assertions of their racial superiority. Witness the ascendance of those among them who preach "Black Power."

I say these things in no spirit of rancor. To my mind, at least, these facts and statistics imply no blame or animosity toward America's Negroes. They are our victims at least as much as, if not more than, we are theirs. I ask only for the objective consideration of the state of black America in the light of certain evident historical truths.

My thesis is that they have every right, as Americans, to their independence, even though attaining this independence may involve their admitting—and our realizing—that they will never be absorbed into our white, Anglo-Saxon, Protestant nation. Neither, however, is it an adequate or fair solution to their problem to send them back to Africa in ships. They are Negroes, true, but Africans no longer. Two hundred years of American history have made them as separate from African life and culture as they are from ours.

I suggest, in short, that these people now require an entirely new environment. America owes them such an opportunity, an opportunity for freedom, a chance for self-determination as Americans. I propose, therefore, that America's entire Negro community be sent to win liberty in a new land, in North Vietnam.

Undoubtedly there are geographers and other members of the intellectual contingent who will be quick to point out that much of this territory is already occupied by North Vietnamese, and to a certain extent, I admit, this is true. In defense of my proposition, however, I am proud to reply that Americans of the Negro race—I refer in particular to the youth in such sectors of New York City as Harlem and Bedford-Stuyvesant—are among the world's most proficient practitioners of guerilla warfare.

The observations of a close friend of mine, recently the resident of an apartment on the edge of Harlem, offer strong support to this allegation. The young men of this area divide themselves annually into various factions which then roam the streets in order to seek out and destroy the members of other groups or "gangs." My friend's apartment was on the outskirts of the territory—"turf"—dominated by a group called the "Caravelle Street Rippers," whose chief rivals named themselves, ironically, the "Deacons." He reports that the Rippers were adept with small arms, being particularly skilled in the use of broken bottles, chains, razors, and home-made pistols. Roving at night in small patrols, much like the American Army's Special Forces, the members of this group would often kill or wound as many as a dozen Deacons in a single evening, and would sometimes injure an additional five or six policemen or other neutral bystanders as well. When one considers that the median age among these groups is fourteen years, and that there are at least a hundred such organizations in the cities of the eastern seaboard alone, the possibilities become staggering. Further—though, unfortunately, full statistics are unavailable—it is well-known that the female counterparts of such groups are extraordinarily prolific, and these factions have countless alumni—many of whom are already dedicated to the service of our country, either in correctional institutions or the Armed Forces.

But I fear I may have allowed myself to stray too far from the mainstream of my argument, and must proceed to the enumeration of the positive advantages of my proposal. These divide themselves naturally into two categories, the benefits to be received by the Negroes themselves, and those advantages to be conferred on the remainder of the American people.

The prospect of resettlement in North Vietnam offers a myriad of new opportunities to America's Negroes, ranging from the most theoretical, philosophical advantages to a host of improvements in the practical routines of daily living. If, as so many of our modern philosophers believe, the essential values and rewards of life are derived from the process of overcoming adversity, from the actual struggle, then America will be offering its Negro citizens an opportunity for fulfillment unmatched in human history. It is characteristically American to give them this sort of chance, the opportunity for self-help, for a life of vigorous struggle, against the odds if need be—in fact, the very acceptance of my proposal would represent a renaissance of the frontier spirit which has animated our nation from the beginning. First we won our liberty from the British, then we wrested our land from the wilderness, now we combat a foreign ideology in defense of our economic system—it is obvious that America's history is the history of courageous struggle. It is no small measure of our esteem for our Negro citizens that we ask them, as Americans, to represent us in spreading this, our national spirit, half-way across the world.

The immediate task at hand is admirably adapted for them. Of paramount importance is the numerical fact that America's Negro population numbers over twenty million, whereas there are currently less than fourteen million North Vietnamese inhabitants of the territory in question. This statistical truth confers upon the Negroes all the moral and ethical advantages—which they have long observed from the other side in this country—of being a majority race. (These advantages are, of course, in addition to—though perhaps dependent upon—the obvious coercive possibilities of greater numbers.) It is reasonable to assume that the fundamental principle of international relations, that might makes right, will apply in this instance as inexorably as it has in all of our foreign policy since World War II. Thus it would seem that the Negroes—particularly since a disproportionate number of them are already in military service in Vietnam, and since these would, with my proposal in effect, have all the advantages to their morale of the presence of their wives and families—would have little difficulty in securing the actual physical control of the country. Once in power, they would be able to formulate laws concerning such matters as schools, housing, and public accommodations entirely in accord with their own wishes. The surviving Vietnamese could then be given the more menial roles in the labor force; if necessary, they could even be treated as a commodity and sold at auction to perform the various lowly agricultural and domestic chores.

Given this power structure, the Negro would be well suited for life in Vietnam. For one thing, he is—despite his period of American residence—racially adapted to life in a jungle climate; it would be far less grueling for him than for a more conventional, racially mixed, occupation force. Further, Vietnam is presently an underdeveloped country. Surely the Negro has proved by his achievements in such nations as Ghana his ability to thrive in the economic context of development. There are years of hard physical labor to be done in Vietnam, work for which the American Negro is perfectly adapted by temperament, experience and education to perform.

Most persuasive of all, perhaps, is an overwhelming spiritual advantage of my proposal: the tremendous feeling of pride which would come to the American Negro in recognizing the myriad of benefits which would accrue to his country through his absence. I shall enumerate them as quickly as possible to avoid trying the patience of my readers.

First, the Caucasian-American soldiers now serving in Vietnam could return home immediately, if possible in the same ships used for transportation of the Negroes.

Second, the Selective Service System, which is currently responsible for nation-wide controversy, could be eliminated.

Third, the Civil Rights movement, for some time a considerable source of domestic dissonance, would virtually disappear.

Fourth, our prodigious annual expenditure on social welfare could be cut almost in half.

Fifth, crime, immorality, slums, and unemployment in our cities would be substantially decreased, as noted earlier.

Sixth, the present over-crowding in our educational facilities would be considerably alleviated.

The cost of transporting all our country's Negroes to Southeast Asia would, of course, be sizeable—yet compared to the twenty-billion-dollar annual cost of the war, let alone the cost of the problems described in my last three paragraphs, it would be negligible. Further, we would soon find in Vietnam a market for our manufactured goods which would more than compensate for the required cutbacks in our war industries. It is my opinion that the acceptance of my proposal would almost immediately bring about drastic improvement in our balance of trade. In addition, the savings in government expenditure that I have suggested would quite likely permit an across-the-board federal tax reduction of forty to fifty *per cent,* not to mention the savings in state and local taxes, particularly in urban and southern areas.

My projection of this proposal as a means for achieving international peace is a bit more tenuous, but I remain convinced that the possibility is there. Moreover, it would be the sort of peace that no American could fail to applaud: peace resulting from a proliferation of the American

JOHN M. STUART

Way across the world, peace on our terms. To be suggested here is no such insidious scheme as the surrender of our sovereignty to an international organization. Rather, I propose that Vietnam, as subdued and civilized by America's Negroes, might well become the base for the spread of international harmony—a process that would simultaneously increase our own domestic tranquility. Given Vietnam, with its many ports and newly-constructed airfields, as a base of operations, could not our remaining American Indians win control of Thailand? Could not our Puerto Ricans find new happiness in Cambodia? Could not Mexican-America be profitably relocated in Laos? Could not Irish-Americans and Italian-Americans settle productively in North and South Korea, respectively? Given these relatively simple amplifications of my original proposal, is there any reason why America, acting through its Jewish representatives, could not colonize China itself? Given Asia, and it is to be understood that Africans will in all likelihood support the activities of their Negro brothers in Vietnam, will any nation on earth dare to live in a manner contrary to the American ideal? I think not.

There may, perhaps, be certain critics among my readers who will choose to regard my plan as "imperialistic" rather than pacifistic. Though my more enthusiastic supporters will argue that I should disregard the dissentient cooing of this small fraction of my audience, I feel particularly sensitive to the opinions of minority groups, and wish to answer them in order to demonstrate that the principles behind my proposal are invulnerable. In doing so, however, I must firmly request that they recognize two basic truths of international relations, one universally applicable to all human history, the other resulting from the particular ideological stance of contemporary America. It is necessary that the weak serve the interests of the strong. The United States of America, the most powerful nation on the globe, holds resolute opposition to the forces of Communism to be the basis of its foreign policy, a policy further resolved to encourage by all expedient means the spread of democratic government as we know it.

Given these premises, and also the existence of various foreign powers whose beliefs are diametrically opposed to our own, let no one bring forward as alternatives to my proposal such patently absurd suggestions as: a withdrawal of our forces from Vietnam based on a

454

new American dedication to the tenets of the United Nations Charter; our acceptance of a peace proposal such as that suggested by U Thant, involving American negotiation with those whom we must exterminate to ensure our own security; revision of our economic goals to provide for world-wide rather than nation-wide prosperity; the admission of Red China into either the General Assembly or the Security Council of the United Nations; the inception of large-scale trade with the Soviet Union and other nations of the Communist bloc; the major expansion of such relatively altruistic American agencies as the Peace Corps; the abandonment of our well-deserved feeling of superiority to other races, nations and religions; expensive and idealistic efforts to make our nation a model for the world by levelling out men's natural inequalities with government money; the abandonment of such attempts to spread our national truth as Radio Free Europe in favor of a promotional campaign for general peace; the subordination of any portion of our military power to an international organization; or any other scheme for disarmament, which would be the emasculation of our country. Such plans, skillfully articulated by various assemblages of Utopian visionaries, may appear admirable—even desirable—on paper; yet it is obvious that none of them shares with my proposal a firm basis in the realistic truths of modern international relations. I must add that my proposal has a further advantage in that it is but a logical extension of current American foreign and domestic policies, whereas each of the others I have cited would in some way represent a departure from our national principles as defined in these policies.

Let no man suggest that I have been motivated by self-interest in stating my proposal to the nation. Rather, it must be seen as a twentieth-century version of the Emancipation Proclamation for America's Negroes; I offer it to them freely, as a glorious opportunity, with no hope of self-aggrandizement. It is thus with the deepest regret that I must announce my inability to participate directly in the actualization of my proposition, as both sides of my family are purely British, and have been so for some dozen generations.

Edwin A. Roberts, Jr.
IF THE SPIRIT OF
REBELLION RUNS ITS
COURSE

This column from The National Observer *employs one of the oldest satiric devices—exaggerating contemporaneous insanities to their illogical limits.*

In an era of student protests around the globe, it was almost bound to happen. But it still took administrators and faculty by surprise when the pupils at Pine Crest Elementary School went on strike. And because we have two daughters in that educational institution, the seriousness of the youthful ferment was brought home to us in no uncertain terms.

I first learned about the uprising when my wife called the office and said: "Come home right away. The third grade at Pine Crest is picketing the principal's office, and even the kindergarten children refuse to cross the picket line."

"Where are Beth and Leslie?" I asked.

"Beth is carrying a sign that says, 'Down with fractions and decimals.' Leslie and the other first graders are throwing lollipops and bubble gum to the demonstrators."

I decided to head directly for the school, the outside of which was plastered with placards that said: "We Demand Longer Recesses," "Homework Is Oppression," "Compulsory Education Violates Our Civil Rights," "Nuts to Show-and-Tell," "End Testing Now," and "Equal Marks for All."

DRAWING THE LINE

It was impossible to get into the school building because the fifth graders had formed a solid line in front of the entrance.

"Can't this be settled by negotiation?" I asked a fifth-grade militant. "Don't answer him," a classmate shouted. "Never trust anybody over 13."

"This is a nonviolent demonstration," a second-grader yelled. "But we won't be responsible for what happens if parents and teachers don't bow to our demands. We're going to occupy the library, the all-purpose room, and the school office until our demands are met."

The first graders wore red armbands, the second graders blue, the third graders yellow, the fourth graders brown, the fifth graders green, and the sixth graders purple. The kindergarteners had planned to wear white armbands, but none of them knew how to tie a knot so they abandoned the idea.

One teacher was in tears. "I think it all started at the Valentine's Day party we had for the first graders. We ran out of ice cream and some of the children threatened to take the matter to the streets."

Another teacher wanted firm action. "If you kids don't end this rebellion immediately the whole fifth grade will be made to stay after school."

"Fascist!" shouted a fifth grader.

A GREAT TRADITION

There was some talk among the faculty that the safety patrol should be brought in to break up the demonstration, but the more liberal teachers opposed this idea. "We have a great tradition of academic freedom here at Pine Crest, and we don't want to throw away all we stand for just because we're confronted with pupil activism. After all, these kids care about the way their school is run, and they deserve to participate in the formulation of rules and regulations."

"That's right," said another progressive teacher. "You call in the safety patrol and there will be trouble. We're desirous that the present civil disturbance be quelled without the use of force. We want no barbarism at Pine Crest."

At that moment the teacher was hit behind the ear by a well-aimed rock. "It's only a small minority that's resorting to violence," he said, rubbing the purple lump on his head. "The important thing is to attack the causes of unrest, not the symptoms."

457

Another rock came flying and this one hit the teacher right between the eyes. "On the other hand," he said, "an educational institution cannot be run as a democracy." Whereupon he lit out after the rock thrower, leaned him against a wall, and administered several educated smacks.

"It's against the law to inflict corporal punishment on children," wailed the lad. "That's teacher brutality."

I asked a boy who appeared to be the leader of the demonstrators to explain his demands.

"There are only three goals of the pupil activitists," he replied. "We want the complete elimination of homework; we want a permanent ban on testing; and we want everyone to get the same high marks. What we're trying to do is stop teacher oppression of those pupils who hate school and don't do any work. Those kids have their rights too. Also, we might demand TV sets in every classroom and special courses in how to watch television."

"But how are you going to learn anything under those conditions?" I asked.

THE NEW EDUCATION

"The demonstration itself is a learning activity. We pupils are involved. We're fighting for social justice for all kids. We refuse to accept the dreary three-R routine that other generations went along with. We want a voice in the hiring and firing of teachers, and we want to sit in on all faculty meetings."

By this time I was anxious to find my own children and try to talk them out of their commitment to the demonstration. I found Beth perched on a window sill. She was telling her classmates that the kids were winning, that the next step was to begin a major protest against parents' power. "I'm sick and tired of going to bed at 8:30," she said, and the other children cheered. "Let's never go to bed again," chimed in another little girl.

Leslie, my first-grade daughter, was listening to an oration by one of her classmates. "The name 'first grade' is a humiliating title for our educational level. It's only a manifestation of the old class system that

458

has no place in a modern society. Let's eliminate all grade numbers in the name of social justice."

Just then I saw a mobile television truck parked nearby and I could hear the TV reporter providing a commentary as his cameraman focused on the troubled scene.

FREEDOM OF EXPRESSION

"The children, as you can see, are very well behaved," he was saying. "Although the school is now on fire, the boys who put the torch to it did not really seem angry. They were just carried away by the excitement. That car you see being overturned belongs to a fourth-grade teacher who is known for her strictness. It's the children's way of seeking redress of grievances. I think we must all agree that this younger generation has definite ideas and isn't afraid to express them."

Hours later, after negotiations between the pupil leaders and the teachers, it was decided that henceforth any teacher who raised his voice would have to stay after school, that any teacher who passed out a bad mark would be brought to the attention of the local civil-liberties league, and that any teacher who gave a test would automatically have his certificate revoked.

When I finally arrived home, I told my wife all that had happened at Pine Crest Elementary School. She could see I was depressed.

"Never mind," she said, "it's at least nice to know that our children are really getting ready for college."

459

Henry N. Beard and
Douglas C. Kenney
from
BORED OF THE RINGS

One of most hallowed works of the 1960's was Tolkien's
Lord of the Rings *trilogy and its predecessor* The Hobbit.
*These works were sort of "in" classics among students and
even had the distinction of serving as college texts in English and philosophy courses. They were interpreted in
numerous ways by a number of scholars and social scientists, despite the author's persistent claim that he had created nothing more than diversionary tales. We have included here the Prologue to a full-length parody of
Tolkien's trilogy, first published by the* Harvard Lampoon
*in 1969. This witty take-off provides a very good test of the
reader's response to satire. The object of the satire is, in its
own way and among certain youthful groups, sacred. So for
some readers this parody may prove more irritating than
entertaining. Others will enjoy it and see it as a corrective
to a faddish, cultish worship of a delightful but hardly
messianic piece of literature.*

Prologue
CONCERNING BOGGIES

This book is predominantly concerned with making money, and from
its pages a reader may learn much about the character and the literary
integrity of the authors. Of boggies, however, he will discover next to
nothing, since anyone in the possession of a mere moiety of his marbles

460

will readily concede that such creatures could exist only in the minds of children of the sort whose childhoods are spent in wicker baskets, and who grow up to be muggers, dog thieves, and insurance salesmen. Nonetheless, judging from the sales of Prof. Tolkien's interesting books, this is a rather sizable group, sporting the kind of scorchmarks on their pockets that only the spontaneous combustion of heavy wads of crumpled money can produce. For such readers we have collected here a few bits of racial slander concerning boggies, culled by placing Prof. Tolkien's books on the floor in a neat pile and going over them countless times in a series of skips and short hops. For them we also include a brief description of the soon-to-be-published-if-this-incredible-dog-sells account of Dildo Bugger's earlier adventures, called by him *Travels with Gollum in Search of Lower Middle Earth,* but wisely renamed by the publisher *Valley of the Trolls.*

Boggies are an unattractive but annoying people whose numbers have decreased rather precipitously since the bottom fell out of the fairy-tale market. Slow and sullen, and yet dull, they prefer to lead simple lives of pastoral squalor. They don't like machines more complicated than a garrote, a blackjack, or a luger, and they have always been shy of the "Big Folk" or "Biggers," as they call us. As a rule they now avoid us, except on rare occasions when a hundred or so will get together to dry-gulch a lone farmer or hunter. They are a little people, smaller than dwarves, who consider them puny, sly, and inscrutable and often refer to them as the "boggie peril." They seldom exceed three feet in height, but are fully capable of overpowering creatures half their size when they get the drop on them. As for the boggies of the Sty, with whom we are chiefly concerned, they are unusually drab, dressing in shiny gray suits with narrow lapels, alpine hats, and string ties. They wear no shoes, and they walk on a pair of hairy blunt instruments which can only be called feet because of the position they occupy at the end of their legs. Their faces have a pimply malevolence that suggests a deep-seated fondness for making obscene telephone calls, and when they smile, there is something in the way they wag their foot-long tongues that makes Komodo dragons gulp with disbelief. They have long, clever fingers of the sort one normally associates with hands that spend a good deal of time around the necks of small, furry animals and in other people's pockets, and they are very skillful at producing intricate and useful things, like loaded dice and booby traps. They love to eat and drink, play mumbledy-peg with dim-witted quadrupeds, and tell off-color dwarf jokes. They give dull parties and cheap presents, and they enjoy the same general regard and esteem as a dead otter.

It is plain that boggies are relatives of ours, standing somewhere along the evolutionary line that leads from rats to wolverines and eventually to Italians, but what our exact relationship is cannot be told. Their beginnings lie far back in the Good Old Days when the planet was populated with the kind of colorful creatures you have to drink a quart of Old Overcoat to see nowadays. The elves alone preserve any records of that time, and most of them are filled with elf-stuff, raunchy pictures of naked trolls and sordid accounts of "ore" orgies. But the boggies had clearly lived in Lower Middle Earth for a long time before the days of Frito and Dildo, when, like a very old salami that suddenly makes its presence known, they came to trouble the councils of the Small and the Silly.

This was all in the Third, or Sheet-Metal Age, of Lower Middle Earth, and the lands of that age have long since dropped into the sea and their inhabitants into bell jars at the Ripley's Believe-It-or-Not Odditorium. Of their original home, the boggies of Frito's time had lost all records, partly because their level of literacy and intellectual development could have been equaled by a young blowfish and partly because their fondness for genealogical studies made them dislike the notion that their elaborately forged family trees had roots about as steady as Birnham Wood. It is nevertheless clear from their heavy accents and their fondness for dishes cooked in Brylcream that somewhere in their past they went west in steerage. Their legends and old songs, which deal mainly with oversexed elves and dragons in heat, make passing mention of the area around the Anacin River, between Plywood and the Papier-Maché Mountains. There are other records in the great libraries of Twodor which lend credence to such a notion, old articles in the *Police Gazette* and the like. Why they decided to undertake the perilous crossing into Oleodor is uncertain, though again their songs tell of a shadow that fell upon the land so that the potatoes grew no more.

Before the crossing of the Papier-Maché Mountains, the boggies had become divided into three distinct breeds: Clubfoots, Stools, and

Naugahydes. The Clubfoots, by far the most numerous, were swarthy, shifty-eyed, and short; their hands and feet were as deft as crowbars. They preferred to live in the hillsides where they could mug rabbits and small goats, and they supported themselves by hiring out as torpedoes for the local dwarf population. The Stools were larger and oilier than the Clubfoots, and they lived in the fetid lands at the mouth and other orifices of the Anacin River, where they raised yaws and goiters for the river trade. They had long, shiny, black hair, and they loved knives. Their closest relations were with men, for whom they handled occasional rubouts. Least numerous were the Naugahydes, who were taller and wispier than the other boggies and who lived in the forests, where they maintained a thriving trade in leather goods, sandals, and handicrafts. They did periodic interior-decorating work for the elves, but spent most of their time singing lurid folk songs and accosting squirrels.

Once across the mountains, the Boggies lost no time establishing themselves. They shortened their names and elbowed their way into all the country clubs, dropping their old language and customs like a live grenade. An unusual easterly migration of men and elves from Oleodor at this same time makes it possible to fix the date the boggies came on the scene with some accuracy. In the same year, the 1,623rd year of the Third Age, the Naugahyde brothers, Brasso and Drano, led a large following of boggies across the Gallowine River disguised as a band of itinerant graverobbers and took control from the high King at Ribroast.[1] In return for the King's grudging acquiescence, they set up toll booths on the roads and bridges, waylaid his messengers, and sent him suggestive and threatening letters. In short, they settled down for a long stay.

Thus began the history of the Sty, and the boggies, with an eye to the statutes of limitations, started a new calendar dating from the crossing of the Gallowine. They were quite happy with their new land, and once again they dropped out of the history of men, an occurrence which was greeted with the same universal sense of regret as the sudden death of a mad dog. The Sty was marked with great red splotches on all the AAA maps, and the only people who ever passed through were either

[1] Either Arglebargle IV or someone else.

hopelessly lost or completely unhinged. Aside from these rare visitors, the boggies were left entirely to themselves until the time of Frito and Dildo. While there was still a King at Ribroast, the boggies remained nominally his subjects, and to the last battle at Ribroast with the Slumlord of Borax, they sent some snipers, though who they sided with is unclear. There the North Kingdom ended, and the boggies returned to their well-ordered, simple lives, eating and drinking, singing and dancing, and passing bad checks.

Nonetheless, the easy life of the Sty had left the boggies unchanged, and they were still as hard to kill as a cockroach and as easy to deal with as a cornered rat. Though likely to attack only in cold blood, and killing only for money, they remained masters of the low blow and the gang-up. They were crack shots and very handy with all sorts of equalizers, and any small, slow, and stupid beast that turned its back on a crowd of boggies was looking for a stomping.

All boggies originally lived in holes, which is after all hardly surprising for creatures on a first-name basis with rats. In Dildo's time, their abodes were for the most part built above ground in the manner of elves and men, but these still retained many of the features of their traditional homes and were indistinguishable from the dwellings of those species whose chief function is to meet their makers, around August, deep in the walls of old houses. As a rule, they were dumpling-shaped, built of mulch, silt, stray divots, and other seasonal deposits, often whitewashed by irregular pigeons. Consequently, most boggie towns looked as though some very large and untidy creature, perhaps a dragon, had quite recently suffered a series of disappointing bowel movements in the vicinity.

In the Sty as a whole there were at least a dozen of these curious settlements, linked by a system of roads, post offices, and a government that would have been considered unusually crude for a colony of cherry-stone clams. The Sty itself was divided into farthings, half-farthings, and Indian-head nickels ruled by a mayor who was elected in a flurry of ballot-box stuffing every Arbor Day. To assist him in his duties there was a rather large police force which did nothing but extract confessions, mostly from squirrels. Beyond these few tokens of regulation, the Sty betrayed no signs of government. The vast majority of the boggies' time was taken up growing food and eating it and making liquor and drinking it. The rest of it was spent throwing up.

464

OF THE FINDING OF THE RING

As is told in the volume previous to this hound, *Valley of the Trolls,* Dildo Bugger set out one day with a band of demented dwarves and a discredited Rosicrucian named Goodgulf to separate a dragon from his hoard of short-term municipals and convertible debentures. The quest was successful, and the dragon, a prewar basilisk who smelled like a bus, was taken from behind while he was clipping coupons. And yet, though many pointless and annoying deeds were done, this adventure would concern us a good deal less than it does, if that is possible, except for a bit of petty larceny Dildo did along the way to keep his hand in. The party was ambushed in the Mealey Mountains by a roving pack of narcs, and in hurrying to the aid of the embattled dwarves, Dildo some-how lost his sense of direction and ended up in a cave a considerable distance away. Finding himself at the mouth of a tunnel which led rather perceptibly down, Dildo suffered a temporary recurrence of an old inner-ear problem and went rushing along it to the rescue, as he thought, of his friends. After running for some time and finding nothing but more tunnel, he was beginning to feel he had taken a wrong turn somewhere when the passage abruptly ended in a large cavern.

When Dildo's eyes became adjusted to the pale light, he found that the grotto was almost filled by a wide, kidney-shaped lake where a nasty-looking clown named Goddam paddled noisily about on an old rubber sea horse. He ate raw fish and occasional side orders to travel from the outside world in the form of lost travelers like Dildo, and he greeted Dildo's unexpected entrance into his underground sauna in much the same way as he would the sudden arrival of a Chicken Delight truck. But like anyone with boggie ancestry, Goddam preferred the subtle approach in assaulting creatures over five inches high and weigh-ing more than ten pounds, and consequently he challenged Dildo to a riddle game to gain time. Dildo, who had a sudden attack of amnesia regarding the fact that the dwarves were being made into chutney out-side the cave, accepted.

They asked each other countless riddles, such as who played the Cisco Kid and what was Krypton. In the end Dildo won the game. Stumped at last for a riddle to ask, he cried out, as his hand fell on his snub-nosed .38, "What have I got in my pocket?" This Goddam failed to answer, and growing impatient, he paddled up to Frito, whining, "Let me see, let me see." Frito obliged by pulling out the pistol and emptying it in Goddam's direction. The dark spoiled his aim, and he managed only to deflate the rubber float, leaving Goddam to flounder. Goddam, who couldn't swim, reached out his hand to Dildo and begged him to pull him out, and as he did, Frito noticed an interesting-looking ring on his finger and pulled it off. He would have finished Goddam off then and there, but pity stayed his hand. *It's a pity I've run out of bullets,* he thought, as he went back up the tunnel, pursued by Goddam's cries of rage.

Now it is a curious fact that Dildo never told this story, explaining that he had gotten the Ring from a pig's nose or a gumball machine— he couldn't remember which. Goodgulf, who was naturally suspicious, finally managed with the aid of one of his secret potions [2] to drag the truth out of the boggie, but it disturbed him considerably that Dildo, who was a perpetual and compulsive liar, would not have concocted a more grandiose tale from the start. It was then, some fifty years before our story begins, that Goodgulf first guessed at the Ring's importance. He was, as usual, dead wrong.

[2] Probably Sodium Pentothal.

Arthur Hoppe
TWO COLUMNS

This dialogue by the much-admired columnist of the San Francisco Chronicle *recalls those of Lucian.*

MAN'S BLACK MAGIC

Scene: The Heavenly Real Estate Office. The Landlord, thoughtfully stroking his long white beard, is listening to the annual year-end report from his collection agent, Mr. Gabriel.

GABRIEL ... and the exploding novae in Sector 4782 now seem under control, but that runaway galaxy in the 534th Quadrant still requires your attention, sir.

THE LANDLORD (wearily) It isn't easy keeping a billion trillion stars in their courses. Is that all, Gabriel?

GABRIEL No, sir. I still have the special report on that tiny planet you love so.

THE LANDLORD (pleased) Ah, yes, Earth, my little blue-green jewel. (frowning) Are the tenants still gouging up my mountain meadows, burning holes in my forested carpets and befouling my blue seas and crystalline air?

GABRIEL Yes, sir. And they're still brawling, fighting and killing each other off. (hopefully raising his trumpet). Shall I sound the eviction notice now, sir?

THE LANDLORD Wait, Gabriel. There is one thing I don't understand. Don't they know they are all children of God?

GABRIEL Yes, sir, they all know that.

THE LANDLORD Then how can a child of God bring himself to maim or kill another child of God?

GABRIEL   Oh, he doesn't sir. First he performs a magic rite changing his enemy into something less than human. Then, when his enemy is no longer a child of God, he maims or kills him in good conscience.

THE LANDLORD   What an awesome power! How do they manage this incredibly complex transformation?

GABRIEL   Very simply. Look down there, sir. Can you see through that blanket of smog? Now take those two fine men in blue . . .

THE LANDLORD   Ah, yes, two stalwart officers of the law sworn to protect their fellow man. But who are those crowding around them?

GABRIEL   Young idealists, sir, dedicated to social justice. Now, listen. Hear what they're shouting? "Pigs! Pigs! Pigs!"

THE LANDLORD   (aghast)   And they're throwing bricks at those two policemen—trying to maim those two children of God!

GABRIEL   Oh, no, sir. Not children of God. Pigs. The demonstrators have transformed them into pigs and can now maim them in good conscience.

THE LANDLORD   I see. And that big soldier over there in Vietnam shooting at a fleeing old woman? Has he changed her into a pig, too?

GABRIEL   No, sir. He changed her into a gook, a dink or a slope. It was easy. She didn't speak his language. Nor was she familiar with his customs. That always makes the magic easier.

THE LANDLORD   (sadly)   Transforming the children of God into pigs and gooks. How tragic!

GABRIEL   Oh, not only pigs and gooks, sir, but nips and wops and krauts and chinks. For example, they never lynch a fellow man until they have turned him into a nigger or a coon.

THE LANDLORD   (shaking his head)   It's blasphemous.

GABRIEL   (gleefully raising his trumpet)   Shall I blow, sir, and wipe these scum from the face of your Earth?

THE LANDLORD   (his brow darkening)   These what, Gabriel?

GABRIEL   (ranting)   Those rats! That trash! These sc. . . . (suddenly lowering his trumpet, crestfallen) Oh, forgive me, sir. I'm no better than they.

THE LANDLORD   (in a voice of thunder)   Never forget, Gabriel, that he who would transform a child of God into something less than human is an accessory to murder!

468

JUBILATION AT A-CBM

Here governmental rhetoric and just perhaps governmental reasoning feel the sting of satire.

Oh, there's jubilation today in The Anti-Chinese Ballistic Missile Works of Sheboygan, N. J. Mr. Nixon has decided to build an Anti-Chinese Ballistic Missile System after all.

"I don't anticipate an attack by Communist China," the President told his latest press conference. But the untested Anti-Chinese Ballistic Missile, he said, "is virtually infallible against that kind of potential attack."

And we'll all certainly sleep better each night, knowing we have a virtually infallible untested defense against the kind of attack we don't anticipate.

Happiest of all is the chairman of the A-CBM Works, Mr. Mordred Kruppe, who gave reporters a tour of his humming plant the other day.

"The A-CBM was invented by Defense Secretary McNamara back in 1967," he explained. "It was just a cheap, shoddy, little $5 billion system suitable only for shooting down cheap, shoddy little Chinese Ballistic Missiles. Here's a photograph of an early model. We called it The Safeguard. But it was never built."

"Why not?" inquired an inquiring reporter.

"Lack of public demand," said Mr. Kruppe, shaking his head sadly. "The public just wouldn't buy the Anti-Chinese Ballistic Missile. It was the Edsel of its day. So we designed a brand new missile for Mr. Nixon. Here's a photograph of it."

"But that's the same photograph," exclaimed a reporter. "It's exactly the same missile."

"Oh, no," said Mr. Kruppe. "This isn't the Safeguard Missile any more. This is the Sentinel Missile. It's not an Anti-Chinese Ballistic Missile any more. It's an Anti-Russian Ballistic Missile. And instead of defending our cities, it'll defend our missile sites—which, after all, are much more modern and up-to-date than our cities."

469

"What's the difference between these two missile systems?" asked a reporter, examining the photograph carefully.

"About $5 billion," said Mr. Kruppe cheerfully. "But you can always sell the public anything anti-Russian. So we're busy re-tooling. Among the many major design changes, we plan to paint the nose cones red rather than yellow. But this all-new Anti-Chinese Ballistic Missile is going to be a real challenge."

"Do you have a photograph of this all-new missile?" the same reporter asked.

"You're holding it in your hand," said Mr. Kruppe. "And if you're going to ask me again, 'What's the difference?' This time it's about $40 billion."

"Now, just a minute," said a young reporter angrily. "Do you mean to say you're going to try to sell the public the same old missile over and over again?"

"Of course not," said Mr. Kruppe with a frown. "We're going to give it an all-new name. And we'll paint the nose-cones yellow, rather than red. And, as the President explained, it will guard our cities rather than our missile sites and . . . ."

"But that's nothing more than the original Anti-Chinese Ballistic Missile System," cried the reporter. "You're going to sell the public the same missile they rejected in 1967 and charge them ten times the original price."

"It just shows you," said Mr. Kruppe with a complacent smile, "how the threat of an unanticipated attack has grown in the past three years."

SÁTIRE
Some Definitions

BEAST EPIC. A favorite medieval literary form consisting of a series of linked stories grouped about animal characters and often presenting satirical comment on contemporary life of church or court by means of human qualities attributed to beast characters. Some critics hold that the stories developed from popular tradition and were later given literary form by monastic scholars and trouvères, who molded the material at hand. Others find the origin in the writing of Latin scholastics. The oldest example seems to be that of Paulus Diaconus, a cleric at the court of Charlemagne, who wrote about 782–786. Whether the form first developed in Germany or France is still question for scholarly combat, though there is no doubt that in the twelfth and thirteenth centuries the *beast epics* were very popular in North France, West Germany, and Flanders. Some of the animals common to the form are Reynard the Fox, the lion, the wolf, the cock (Chanticler), the cat, the hare, the camel, the ant, the bear, the badger, and the stag. The best known of the *beast epics* are the *Roman de Renard,* a poem of 30,000 lines comprising twenty-seven sets or "branches" of stories growing up in France between 1130 and 1250; the German *Reinhart Fuchs,* the work of Heinrich der Glichezare about 1180, a poem of 2,266 lines; and the Flemish form, *Van den vos Reinaerde,* the work of two men, Arnout and Willem, a poem of 3,476 lines. This last version, which contained rather more than the usual amount of satire, was published in English translation by Caxton in 1481. For evidences of the influence in English literature, see Spenser's *Mother Hubberds Tale* and Chaucer's *Nun's Priest's Tale.*

BEAST FABLE. A short tale in which the principal actors are animals.

BURLESQUE. A form of comic art characterized by ridiculous exaggeration. This distortion is secured in a variety of ways: the sublime may be made absurd; honest emotions may be turned to sentimentality; a serious subject may be treated frivolously or a frivolous subject seriously. Perhaps the

* Abridged from *A Handbook to Literature* by William Flint Thrall, Addison Hibbard, and C. Hugh Holman (New York: The Odyssey Press, 1960). Used with the kind permission of The Odyssey Press.

essential quality which makes for *burlesque* is the discrepancy between subject-matter and style. That is, a style ordinarily dignified may be used for nonsensical matter, or a style very nonsensical may be used to ridicule a weighty subject. *Burlesque* has an ancient lineage in world literature beginning with the *Battle of the Frogs and Mice,* a travesty of Homer. Chaucer in *Sir Thopas* burlesqued medieval romance as did Cervantes in *Don Quixote.* One of the best known uses of *burlesque* in drama is Gay's *The Beggar's Opera.* In recent use the term—already broad—has been broadened to include musical plays light in nature though not essentially *burlesque* in tone or manner. A distinction between *burlesque* and parody is commonly made, in which *burlesque* is a travesty of a literary form and parody a travesty of a particular work.

CARICATURE. Exaggeration or distortion of certain individual characteristics to produce a comic, grotesque, or ridiculous effect. More frequently associated with drawing than with writing, *caricature,* unlike the highest satire, is likely to treat *personal* qualities, though like satire, it also lends itself to the ridicule of political, religious, and social foibles.

CHARACTER. A literary form which flourished in England and France in the seventeenth and eighteenth centuries. It is a brief descriptive sketch of a personage who typifies some definite quality. The person is described not as an individualized personality but as an example of some vice or virtue or type, such as a busybody, a superstitious fellow, a fop, a country bumpkin, a garrulous old man, or a happy milkmaid. Similar treatments of institutions and inanimate things, such as "the character of a coffee house," also employed the term, and late in the seventeenth century, by a natural extension of the tradition, *character* was applied to longer compositions, sometimes historical, as Viscount Halifax's *Character of Charles II.* The vogue of *character*-writing followed the publication in 1592 of a Latin translation of Theophrastus, an ancient Greek writer of similar sketches.

COMEDY. As compared with tragedy, *comedy* is a lighter form of drama which aims primarily to amuse and which ends happily. It differs from farce and burlesque by having a more sustained plot, more weighty and subtle dialogue, more natural characters, and less boisterous behavior. The border-line, however, between *comedy* and other dramatic forms cannot be sharply defined, as there is much overlapping of technique, and different "kinds" are frequently combined. Psychologists have shown the close relation between laughter and tears, and *comedy* and tragedy alike sprang, both in ancient Greece and in medieval Europe, from diverging treatment of ceremonial performances.

Since *comedy* strives to provoke smiles and laughter, it uses both wit and humor. In general the comic effect arises from a recognition of an incongruity of speech, action, or character revelation. The incongruity may be merely verbal (as in the case of a play on words), or physical (as when stilts are used to make a man's legs seem disproportionately long), or satirical (as when the effect depends upon the beholder's ability to perceive the incongruity between fact and pretense exhibited by a braggart). *Comedy,* where it becomes judicial, is like satire; where it becomes sympathetic, it is like pathos and tragedy.

DIATRIBE. Writing or discourse characterized by bitter invective, abusive argument. A harangue. Originally it was a treatment in dialogue of a limited philosophical proposition in a simple, lively, conversational tone. Popular with the Stoic and Cynic philosophers, it became noted for the abusiveness of the speakers, a fact which led to its present-day meaning.

DRAMATIC IRONY. The words or acts of a character in a play may carry a meaning unperceived by himself but understood by the audience. Usually the character's own interests are involved in a way he cannot understand. The irony resides in the contrast between the meaning intended by the speaker and the added significance seen by others. The term is occasionally applied also to nondramatic narrative, and is sometimes extended to include any situation (such as mistaken identity) in which some of the actors on the stage or some of the characters in a story are "blind" to facts known to the spectator or reader. So understood, *dramatic irony* is responsible for much of the interest in fiction and drama, because the reader or spectator enjoys being in on the secret.

DROLL. A short dramatic piece (also known as "drollery" or "droll humor") cultivated on the Commonwealth stage in England as a substitute for full-length or serious plays not permitted by the government. A *droll* was likely to be a "short, racy, comic" scene selected from some popular play (as a Launcelot Gobbo scene from *The Merchant of Venice*) and completed by dancing somewhat in the manner of the earlier jig.

EPIGRAM. A pointed saying; hence an epigrammatic style is concise, pointed, often antithetical, as "Man proposes but God disposes." This rhetorical use of the word is derived from certain qualities of a type of poem known as an *epigram*. Originally (in ancient Greece) an *epigram* meant an inscription, especially an epitaph. Then it came to mean "a very short poem summing up as though in a memorial inscription what it is desired to make permanently memorable in a single action or situation" (Mackail). Hence the *epigram* was characterized by compression, pointedness, clarity, balance, and polish.

FABLE. A brief tale, either in prose or verse, told to point a moral. The characters are most frequently animals, but they need not be so restricted since people and inanimate objects as well are sometimes the central figures. The subject matter of *fables* has to do with supernatural and unusual incidents and often draws its origin from folklore sources. By far the most famous *fables* are those accredited to Aesop, a Greek slave living about 600 B.C.; but almost equally popular are those of La Fontaine, a Frenchman writing in the seventeenth century, because of their distinctive humor and wit, their wisdom and sprightly satire. A *fable* in which the characters are animals is called a "beast fable," a form that has been popular in almost every period of literary history, usually as a satiric device to point out the follies of mankind.

FABLIAU. A humorous tale popular in medieval French literature. The conventional form was eight-syllable verse. These *fabliaux* consisted of stories of various types, but one point was uppermost—their humorous, sly satire of human beings. Themes frequently used in these stories, which were often bawdy, dealt familiarly with the clergy, ridiculed womanhood, and were pitched in a key which made them readily and boisterously understandable to the uneducated. The form was also present in English literature of the Middle English Period, Chaucer especially leaving us examples of *fabliaux*, in tales of the Miller, Reeve, Friar, Summoner, Merchant, Shipman, and Manciple. Although *fabliaux* often had ostensible "morals" appended to them, they lack the serious intention of the fable, and they differ from the fable too in always having human beings as characters and in always maintaining a realistic tone and manner.

FARCE. The word developed from Late Latin *farsus*, connected with a verb meaning "to stuff." Thus an expansion or amplification in the church liturgy was called a *farse*. Later, in France, *farce* meant any sort of extemporaneous addition in a play, especially comic jokes or "gags," the clownish actors speaking "more than was set down" for them. In the late seventeenth century *farce* was used in England to mean any short humor-

474

ous play, as distinguished from regular five-act comedy. The development in these plays of certain elements of low comedy is responsible for the usual modern meaning of *farce:* a dramatic piece intended to excite laughter and depending less on plot and character than on exaggerated, improbable situations, the humor arising from gross incongruities, coarse wit, or horseplay.

GOLIARDIC VERSE. Lilting Latin verse, usually satiric, composed by university students and wandering scholars in Germany, France, and England in the twelfth and thirteenth centuries. *Goliardic verse* celebrated wine, women, and song, was often licentious, and was marked by irreverent attacks on church and clergy. Its dominant theme was "carpe diem." Its name comes from a legendary bishop and "archpoet" Golias.

HIGH COMEDY. Pure or serious comedy, as contrasted with low comedy. *High comedy* rests upon an appeal to the intellect and arouses "thoughtful" laughter by exhibiting the inconsistencies and incongruities of human nature and by displaying the follies of social manners. The purpose is not consciously didactic or ethical, though serious purpose is often implicit in the satire which is not infrequently present in *high comedy.* Thoughtful amusement is aimed at. Emotion, especially sentimentality, is avoided. If a man makes himself ridiculous by his vanity or ineffective by his stupid conduct or blind adherence to tradition, *high comedy* laughs at him. Some ability to perceive promptly the incongruity exhibited is demanded of the audience, so that *high comedy* has been said to be written for the few. As George Meredith suggests in his essay on *The Idea of Comedy* (a classic pronouncement on the nature of *high comedy*), care must be taken that the laughter provoked be not derisive, but intellectual. Laughing at an exhibition of poverty, for example, since it ridicules our unfortunate nature instead of our conventional life, is not truly comic. Although *high comedy* actually offers plenty of superficial laughs which the average playgoer or reader can perceive, its higher enjoyment demands a certain intellectual acumen and poise and philosophic detachment. "Life is a comedy to him who thinks."

HUMOR. A term used in English since the early eighteenth century to denote one of the two major types of writing (*humor* and wit) whose purpose is the evoking of some kind of laughter. It is derived from the physiological theory of humors, and it was used to designate a person with a peculiar disposition which led to his readily perceiving the ridiculous, the ludicrous, and the comical and effectively giving expression to this perception. In the eighteenth century it was used to name a comical mode that was sympathetic, tolerant, and warmly aware of the depths of human nature, as opposed to the intellectual, satiric, intolerant quality associated with wit. In this sense, one may speak of Chaucer's humor but Pope's wit. See WIT AND HUMOR.

HYPERBOLE. An exaggeration or extravagant remark or metaphor, like "You look a thousand years old."

INNUENDO. An insinuation or indirect suggestion, often with harmful or sinister connotation.

IRONY. A figure of speech in which the actual intent is expressed in words which carry an opposite meaning. Irony is likely to be confused with sarcasm, but it differs from sarcasm in that it is usually lighter, less harsh in its wording though in effect probably more cutting because of its indirectness. It bears, too, a close relationship to innuendo. The ability to recognize irony is one of the surest tests of intelligence and sophistication. Its presence is marked by a sort of grim humor, an "unemotional detachment" on the part of the writer, a coolness in expression at a time when the writer's emotions are really heated. Characteristically it speaks words of praise to imply blame and words of blame to imply praise, though its inherent critical quality makes the first type much more common than the second. The great effectiveness of irony as a literary device is the impression it gives of great restraint. The writer of irony has his tongue in his cheek; for this reason irony is more easily detected in speech than in writing since the voice can, through its intonation, so easily warn the listener of a double significance. One of the most famous ironic remarks in literature is Job's "No doubt but ye are the people, and wisdom shall die with you." Antony's insistence, in his oration over the dead Caesar, that "Brutus is an honorable man" bears the same ironic imprint. Goldsmith, Jane Austen, Thackeray—these authors have in one novel or another made frequent use of this form. Jonathan Swift is an arch-ironist; his "Modest Proposal" for saving a starving Ireland, by suggesting that the Irish sell their babies to the English landlords, is perhaps the most savagely sustained ironic writing in our literature. The novels of Thomas Hardy and Henry James are elaborate artistic expressions of the ironic spirit, for irony applies not only to statement but also to event, situation, and structure. In drama, irony has a special meaning, referring to knowledge held by the audience but hidden from the relevant actors. In contemporary criticism, *irony* is used to describe a poet's "recognition of incongruities" and his controlled acceptance of them. Among the devices by which *irony* is achieved are hyperbole, understatement, and sarcasm.

INVECTIVE. Harsh, abusive language directed against a person or cause. Vituperative writing. A long invective is probably a diatribe.

LAMPOON. Writing which ridicules and satirizes the character or personal appearance of a person in a bitter, scurrilous manner. Lampoons were written in either verse or prose. Lampooning became a dangerous sport and fell into disuse with the development of libel laws.

(like Burlesque)

LOW COMEDY. The opposite of "high comedy," *low comedy* has been called "elemental comedy," in that it is lacking in seriousness of purpose or subtlety of manner, having little intellectual appeal. Some typical features of *low comedy* are quarreling, fighting, noisy singing, boisterous conduct in general, boasting, burlesque, trickery, buffoonery, clownishness, drunkenness, coarse jesting, servants' chatter (when unrelated to the serious action), scolding, and shrewishness. In English dramatic history *low comedy* appears first as an incidental expansion of the action, often originated by the actors themselves, who speak "more than is set down for them." Thus in medieval religious drama Noah's wife exhibits stubbornness and has to be taken into the ark by force and under loud protest, or Pilate or Herod engage in uncalled-for ranting. In the morality plays the elements of *low comedy* became much more pronounced, and the antics of the Vice and other boisterous horse-play were introduced to lend life to the plays. In Elizabethan drama such elements persisted, in spite of their violation of the law of decorum, because they were demanded by the public; but playwrights like Shakespeare frequently made them serve serious dramatic purposes (such as relief, marking passage of time, or echoing main action). A few of the many examples of low comedy in Shakespeare are: the porter scene in *Macbeth*, Launcelot Gobbo and old Gobbo in *The Merchant of Venice*, the Audrey-William love-making scene in *As You Like It*, and the Trinculo-Stephano-Caliban scene in *The Tempest*. The famous Falstaff scenes in *King Henry the Fourth* are examples of how Shakespeare could lift *low comedy* into pure comedy by stressing the human and character elements and by infusing an intellectual content into what might otherwise be mere buffoonery. *Low comedy* is not a recognized special type of play, as is the comedy of humors, for example, but may be found either alone or combined with various sorts of both comedy and tragedy.

MOCK EPIC or MOCK HEROIC. Terms frequently used interchangeably to designate a literary form which burlesques epic poetry by treating a trivial subject in the "grand style," or which uses the epic formulas to make ridiculous a trivial subject by ludicrously overstating it. Usually the characteristics of the classical epic are employed, particularly the invocation to a deity, the formal statement of theme, the division into books and cantos, the grandiose speeches (challenges, defiances, boastings) of the heroes, descriptions of warriors (especially their dress and equipment), battles and games, the use of epic or Homeric simile, and the employment of supernatural machinery (gods directing or participating in the action). When the mock poem is much shorter than true epic, some prefer to call it *mock heroic*, a term also applied to poems which mock romances rather than epics. Chaucer's *Nun's Priest's Tale* is partly *mock heroic* in character as is Spenser's finely wrought *Muiopotmos,* "The Fate of the Butterfly," which imitates the opening of the *Aeneid* and employs elevated style for trivial subject-matter. Swift's *Battle of the Books* is an example of a cuttingly satirical *mock epic* in prose. Pope's *The Rape of the Lock* is perhaps the finest *mock heroic* poem in English, satirizing in polished verse the trivialities of polite society in the eighteenth century.

PARODY. A composition burlesquing or imitating another, usually serious, piece of work. It is designed to ridicule in nonsensical fashion, or to criticize by brilliant treatment, an original piece of work or the author of one. When the *parody* is directed against an author or his style, it is likely to fall simply into barbed witticisms, often venting personal antagonisms of the parodist against the one parodied. When the subject matter of the original composition is parodied, however, it may prove to be a valuable indirect criticism, or it may even imply a flattering tribute to the original writer. Often a *parody* is more powerful in its influence on affairs of current importance—politics, for instance—than an original composition. The *parody* is in literature what the caricature and the cartoon are in art.

PUN. A play on words based on the similarity of sound between two words with different meanings. An example is Thomas Hood's: "They went and told the sexton and the sexton tolled the bell."

REDUCTIO AD ABSURDUM. A "reducing to absurdity" to show the falsity of an argument or position. As a method of argument or persuasion, this is a process which carries to its extreme, but logical, conclusion some general statement. One might say, for instance, that the more sleep one takes the more healthy one is, and then, by the logical *reductio ad absurdum* process someone would be sure to point out that, on such a premise, he who has a sleeping sickness and sleeps for months on end is really in the best of health.

REPARTEE. A quick, ingenious response or rejoinder; a retort aptly twisted; conversation made up of brilliant witticisms, or, more loosely, any clever reply; also anyone's facility and aptness in such ready wit. The term is borrowed from fencing terminology. An instance of *repartee* may be cited from an Oxford account of the meeting of "Beau" Nash and John Wesley. According to this tradition the two met on a narrow pavement. Nash was brusque. "I never make way for a fool," he said insolently. "Don't you? I always do," responded Wesley, stepping to one side.

SARCASM. A form of verbal irony in which, under the guise of praise, a caustic and bitter expression of strong and personal disapproval is given. *Sarcasm* is personal, jeering, intended to hurt, and is intended as a sneering taunt.

SATIRE. A literary manner which blends a critical attitude with humor and wit to the end that human institutions or humanity may be improved. The true satirist is conscious of the frailty of institutions of man's devising and attempts through laughter not so much to tear them down as to inspire a remodeling. If the critic simply abuses, he is writing invective; if he is personal and splenetic, he is writing sarcasm; if he is sad and morose over the state of society, he is writing irony or mere gloom. As a rule, modern satire spares the individual and follows Addison's self-imposed rule: to "pass over a single foe to charge whole armies."

TRAVESTY. Writing which by its incongruity of style or treatment ridicules a subject inherently noble or dignified. The derivation of the word, from *trans* (over or across) and *vestire* (to clothe or dress) clearly suggests the meaning of presenting a subject in a dress intended for another type of subject. *Travesty* may be thought of as the opposite of the mock epic since the latter treats a frivolous subject seriously and the *travesty* usually presents a serious subject frivolously. *Don Quixote* is, in a very real sense, a *travesty* on the medieval romance.

UNDERSTATEMENT. Deliberate lack of emphasis, as in "He was not unmindful" for "He gave careful attention."

WIT AND HUMOR. Although neither of these words originally was concerned with the laughable, both now find their chief uses in this connection. At present the distinction between the two terms, though generally recognized to exist, is difficult to draw, although there have been numerous attempts at definition. One great "wit" in fact made a witticism out of his observation that any person who attempted to distinguish between *wit* and *humor* thereby demonstrated that he himself possessed neither *wit* (in the sense of superior mental powers) nor *humor* (which implies a sense of proportion and self-evaluation that would show him the difficulty of attempting a cold analysis of so fugitive a thing as *humor*).

Humor is the American spelling of *humour*, originally a physiological term, which because of its psychological implications came to carry the meaning of "eccentric"; from this meaning developed the modern implications of the term. *Wit*, meaning originally "knowledge," came in the late Middle Ages to signify "intellect," "the seat of consciousness," the "inner" senses as contrasted with the five "outer" senses. In Renaissance times, though used in various senses, *wit* usually meant "wisdom" or "mental activity." An important critical use developed in the seventeenth century when the term, as applied for example to the metaphysical poets, meant "fancy," in the sense of inspiration, originality, or creative imagination—this being the literary virtue particularly prized at the time. With the coming of neo-classicism, however, the term took on new meanings to reflect new critical attitudes, and for a hundred years many philosophers (including Hobbes, Locke, and Hume) and critics (including Dryden, Addison, Pope, and Johnson) wrestled with efforts to define *wit*. Hobbes asserted that fancy without judgment or reason could not constitute *wit*, though judgment without fancy could. Pope used the word in both of the contrasting senses of fancy and judgment. Dryden had called *wit* "propriety of thought and words," and Locke thought of it as an agreeable and prompt assemblage of ideas, ability to see comparisons. Hume stressed the idea that *wit* is that which pleases ("good taste" being the criterion). Amid the confusing variety of eighteenth-century uses of the word, this notion of *wit* as a social grace which gave pleasure led to its comparison with *humor*, and before 1800 both words came to be associated with the laughable, though the older, serious meaning of *wit* did not die out, as the earlier meanings of *humor* (both the medical meaning of one of the four liquids of the human body and the derived meaning of "individual disposition" or "eccentricity") had done. Modern definitions of wit reflect both the original and the late eighteenth-century conceptions: "that quality of speech or writing which consists in the apt association of thought and expression, calculated to surprise and delight by its unexpectedness; later always with reference to the utterance of brilliant or sparkling things in an amusing way" (OED). It is for the most part agreed that *wit* is primarily intellectual, the perception of similarities in seemingly dissimilar things—the "swift play and flash of mind"—and is expressed in skillful phraseology, plays upon words, surprising contrasts, paradoxes, epigrams, comparisons, etc., while *humor* implies a sympathetic recognition of human values and deals with the foibles and incongruities of human nature, good-naturedly exhibited. A few quotations from writers who have made serious attempts to distinguish between the two terms may help further to clarify the conceptions. *Humor* "deals with incongruities of character and circumstance, as *Wit* does on those of arbitrary ideas" (Hunt). "*Wit* is intensive or incisive, while *humor* is expansive. *Wit* is rapid, *humor* is slow. *Wit* is sharp, *humor* is gentle. . . . *Wit* is subjective while *humor* is objective. . . . *Wit* is art, *humor* is nature" (Wells). "*Wit* apart from *Humor*, generally speaking, is but an element for professors to sport with. In combination with *Humor* it runs into the richest utility, and helps to humanize the world" (Hunt). "*Humor* always laughs, however earnestly it feels, and sometimes chuckles; but it never sniggers" (Saintsbury).

Falstaff in Shakespeare's *Henry IV, Part I*, is an example of a subtle interweaving of *wit* and *humor*. The verbal fencing, the punning, and particularly the sophistical maneuvering whereby Falstaff invariably extricates himself from difficult situations with an apparent saving of his face, rest upon his *wit*. On the other hand, the easy recognition on the part of the reader not only that Falstaff is bluffing and is cutting a highly ludicrous figure but also that the old rascal is inwardly laughing at himself, that he sees clearly the incongruities of his situation and behavior and realizes that his lies will be recognized as such by the Prince, is an element of *humor*.

A BIBLIOGRAPHIC NOTE

There is really no wholly satisfactory history of satire nor any really definitive theoretical study. Considering the nature of satire, it should be no surprise that the academic and scholarly aspects of the discipline are not well organized, let alone pinned, wriggling, to the wall. But in the past thirty years there have been some very important analyses of the art, and there now exists a continuing scholarly and bibliographic gathering of material related to satire.

For example, one should read David Worcester's *The Art of Satire;* Robert C. Elliott's *The Power of Satire;* Northrup Frye's "The Nature of Satire" (which appeared originally in the *University of Toronto Quarterly,* 1944, 75–89, and has been reprinted and revised in Frye's *Anatomy of Criticism*); Alvin Kernan's *The Cankered Muse* (especially the first chapter) and *The Plot of Satire;* James Sutherland's *English Satire;* Gilbert Highet's "Satire" in *The Classical Tradition* (tracing satire from its Greek sources through the eighteenth century); Maynard Mack's "The Muse of Satire," in *The Yale Review,* 1951, 80–92; Ian Jack's *Augustan Satire;* Wyndham Lewis' *Men Without Art;* Philip Pinkus' "Satire and St. George," in *Queen's Quarterly,* 1963, 30–49; Ronald Paulson's *The Fictions of Satire;* Robert C. Elliott's "The Satirist and Society," in *ELH,* September 1954; the Preface and critical introductions in John Russell and Ashley Brown's *Satire: A Critical Anthology;* and Matthew Hodgart's *Satire.* These works form a basic bibliography of modern studies of satire.

Among older works, one might enjoy John Dryden's "A Discourse Concerning the Original and Progress of Satire," often reprinted; James Russell Lowell's "Humor, Wit, and Satire," in *The Century Magazine,* November 1893; James L. Ford's "The Guns of Satire," in *The Bookman,* June 1927; J. A. K. Thompson's *Irony;* Hugh Walker's *English Satire and Satirists;* Humbert Wolfe's *Notes on English Verse Satire;* George Kitchin's *A Survey of Burlesque and Parody in English;* R. P. Bond's *English Burlesque Poetry 1700–1750;* Germaine Dempster's *Dramatic Irony in Chaucer;* and Francis Turner's *The Element of Irony in English Literature.*

The whole problem of criticism of satire is explored by John R. Clark's "Formal Straining: Recent Criticism of Satire," in *College English*, January 1971, 498–505.

Finally, anyone who loves satire should become familiar with the "official" journal of the art, *Satire Newsletter*. Since its first issue in the Fall of 1963, this journal has provided a forum for discussions of satire, reviews of new publications in the field, and both a running annual bibliography and periodic special issues devoted to such topics as moral norms in satire and the mask or *persona* used by the satirist.